Hoddle's England: The Road to France has been written by award-winning journalist Harry Harris as a fly-on-the-wall account of the England team's qualification for the 1998 World Cup Finals. As such it has not been prepared, authorised, licensed or endorsed by Glenn Hoddle or any other person connected with the England Football Squad.

HODDLE'S ENGLAND
THE ROAD TO FRANCE

Written By
HARRY HARRIS

CollinsWillow
An Imprint of HarperCollins*Publishers*

First published in 1998
by CollinsWillow
an imprint of HarperCollins*Publishers*
London

© Harry Harris 1998

1 3 5 7 9 8 6 4 2

A CIP catalogue record for this book is
available from the British Library

ISBN 0 00 218837 6

Photographs supplied courtesy of
Mirror Syndication and Popperfoto

Printed in Great Britain by The Bath Press, Bath

Contents

Dedicated to Jordanna

Acknowledgements

My deepest appreciation goes to Anne Vink and Neil Thorns in the Christian Aid press office for the photographs and background to Glenn Hoddle's and the England team's involvement with the orphans in Georgia.

Special thanks to Glenn himself and his representative, FIFA-licensed agent Dennis Roach of PRO International; and to Michael Doggart and Tom Whiting at publishers HarperCollins for their encouragement and support.

Finally, my gratitude for the use of exceptional photographs to the *Mirror* Syndication Department, where Phil Le Blanc and Greg Bennett have provided expert selections over the past two years, and for the co-operation from *Mirror* picture editor, Ron Morgans.

Introduction:
England, My England

Remember 1966? Well, come on, who could forget? Thoughts of *The Boys of 1966 And All That* dance in the memory, provoking the wild thought that one day England will do it again. Maybe, just maybe, Glenn Hoddle will be the manager who brings the World Cup back home for the first time away from Wembley.

Dream on. Look, a hardened soccer writer of nearly 30 years' service doesn't dream. He deals in reality. Can England win the World Cup in France? An outside chance, maybe. When the rose-tinted glasses worn since Euro 96 are removed, the England team appear far from world beaters. It would be a long road to Paris, and the England team would have to evolve under Hoddle quite dramatically.

Mexico 86 was my first World Cup as chief football correspondent of the *Daily Mirror*. That was a fair old England side with Hoddle in his prime as a player. There was a great performance against the Poles when it counted and a smashing win against Paraguay before the team faded in the shadow of Maradona. Italia 90 began with a farcical game against the Republic of Ireland and then a poor performance against Egypt. A commendable draw with Holland and wins over Belgium and Cameroon put England in the semi-finals. A great team effort saw the country move within a penalty kick of the Final. Bloody Germans again! USA 94 cost Graham Taylor his job. It nearly cost him his sanity too. Do we all not like that?

No negative thoughts, please. Remember Moore, Hurst and Peters? Remember buying a 'season ticket' for all the Wembley games including the Final, and one match at the now demolished White City; the rows with the teachers because I wanted time off to watch one of the games and ended up in big trouble at school ... my passion for the game is still there. Before I retire, I would love to cover England's conquest of the world. Having watched them from the Wembley stands as an 14-year-old, that would be the pinnacle of my career. It is possible, so dream on.

I have followed Glenn Hoddle and his England team from the moment he was appointed as national coach in succession to Terry Venables. I have meticulously scrutinized the fortunes of the youngest ever incumbent to the role dubbed by Graham Taylor 'The Impossible Job', plotting the path of the top players in the country, those who have fallen by the wayside and those who have emerged as key personalities inside the dressing room, on the training pitch and in matches.

Why on earth would anyone devote almost two years of their life plotting the nuances of a football team, its management, and backroom staff? The reason is that this is no ordinary team. It is a team I have always believed that, with the guidance of Hoddle, can win the World Cup for the first time on foreign soil.

At a time when the English Premiership has been infiltrated by foreign players, the World Cup will determine whether there is still sufficient home-grown talent for England to make a global impact. Dread the thought that finally the truth will dawn that the power and influence of the Premiership lies in its exotic imports.

My role as the chief football writer on the *Daily Mirror* affords the privilege of being on the inside track with 'Team England'. This involves travel with the England squad, access to the training ground, and endless interviews with all the England players, at ease and ready to provide an insight into their lives and careers.

I have been a close observer of the England football team for more than twelve years on a professional basis, and a fan since the 1966 World Cup. I have seen at first hand the methods of Bobby Robson, Graham Taylor, Terry Venables and now Glenn Hoddle. Over the years, I've seen the game explode in terms of appeal, finance and the import of foreign players to become mass market entertainment. Trend setting started with George Best and the King's Road set of the 1970s, but it was minuscule compared to the Spice Boys and the Gullit–Vialli Revolution at the Bridge. The players are now bigger than pop and film stars.

Star celebrity recognition is the upside of a job in football, not that Hoddle courts such notoriety. The downside is the constant pressure induced by the media. The England manager is either national hero or villain. Failure to qualify for France would have precipitated an outcry for his head. Defeat by Italy at Wembley instantly persuaded his critics to sharpen their knives until a wave of renewed optimism followed wonderful results in Poland and The Tournoi de France, and ultimate success in Rome.

Hoddle demonstrated with remarkable dexterity the ability to adapt quickly to his new enviroment both on and off the pitch. He was tougher, more resilient and more single-minded than most of his critics imagined. The least experienced England manager of all time, Hoddle had enjoyed his best years as a player with Tottenham Hotspur. He joined the North London club as an apprentice at the age of 17 and spent 13 seasons at White Hart Lane before moving to Monaco. He made his Tottenham debut at the age of 17 – thanks to me! 'Glenn Hoddle. That's the boy to watch ...' I was sitting in the old-fashioned panelled wall office of the then Spurs manager Terry Neill discussing the week in my capacity as the local journalist on the North London Weekly Herald. As I probed Neill about the week's events inside the club, the conversation progressed to the budding talent in the Spurs reserve side. The reports on the 17-year-old Hoddle were becoming exceptional. 'Is this boy Glenn Hoddle close to a first-team game?' I asked Neill.

He thought about it and the next week he told me: 'I've watched him and he will be playing very soon.' A week later Glenn commemorated his full debut with a goal against Stoke. An exciting and controversial career was underway. It gave me great satisfaction to think I might have played a tiny part in helping to kickstart Hoddle's Spurs career.

Described as the 'White Pele' of English football, Hoddle was soccer's greatest enigma for more than a decade. The Pele tag seems a touch extravagant, as Hoddle never quite reached the Brazilian's level of world class. But he came close, and might have attained a much higher international status if he had been trusted sooner by England managers. Hoddle suffered constant debate about his talent, either praised as 'genius' or condemned as 'gutless'. There seemed precious little in between. Sound familiar? Well, Matt Le Tissier will know precisely what he went through.

Hoddle's career was haunted ever since he scored that wonder-goal for England, when he conjured an unorthodox side-foot drive from outside the box to score on his international debut against Bulgaria at Wembley at the age of 22. His reward? The axe from manager Ron Greenwood for the next game. In fact, he hardly played two successive internationals until Bobby Robson had more faith in him and England reached the 1986 World Cup quarter-finals in Mexico.

He first proved his managerial ability with Swindon Town, whom he took into the Premier League before leaving for Chelsea in 1993. The following year he guided the London team to the FA Cup Final where they lost to Manchester United, and his tactical acumen was marked by the recruitment of Ruud Gullit from Sampdoria, a startling 'free' transfer coup.

Few believed that Hoddle the player would ever become Hoddle the manager. Hoddle spent his first year in management dispelling the notion that he had a soft centre, a suspicion that hung over his playing days. But not everyone thought that. Brian Clough tried to sign Hoddle for Nottingham Forest. Cloughie said: 'You don't have to bare your false teeth to prove you're a real he-man in football. Some people are morally brave and Hoddle is one of them. I've heard him criticized for non-involvement, but I'm not sure what that means. If you can compensate with more skill in one foot than most players have in their whole body, then that is compensation enough.'

Hoddle accepted the England post even though he knew the threat of media intrusion to his wife, Anne, and three children could, in Hoddle's words only two months before he signed up, 'rip you apart'.

Those who knew him best believed he could cope with the pressure. On the day Hoddle was appointed England boss, his former Spurs and England team-mate Chris Waddle said: 'I'm sure he is big enough to take the criticism that comes with the job. If not, he will have to learn because there is so much attention on the England manager.'

Peter Shreeves, his coach at Chelsea and his manager at Spurs, concurred. 'Despite the fact that they used to call him "Glenda" as a player, he's got a very tough persona. He's mentally strong and because of that I always saw him as management material. When we had the inquests about the last defeat he was always a strong voice.'

Hoddle discovered just what it all meant after England lost to Italy at Wembley in February 1997. The newspaper verdicts were damning. Hoddle was overnight transformed into the new Turnip! It was a relentless four-day assault, starting with the morning papers with their punishing headlines. Then the columnists weighed in on Saturday and Sunday, with television intensifying the debate.

The *Mirror* front page the morning after the match screamed: 'HODDLE THINKS IT'S ALL ZOLA … IT IS, CIAO!' The back page boomed: 'YOU MADE A RIGHT … BOLOGNESE OF IT, GLENN'. On the inside pages, it was just as savage: 'ONE FOOT IN THE G-RAVIOLI'. The *Sun* read: 'HODDLE'S A MUG PUNTER … Glenn gamble fails to pay out' *The Star* echoed: 'WHAT THE HOD WENT WRONG?' The *Mirror*'s back page article was the hardest: 'England were mugged last night … by their own manager. A series of blunders by Glenn Hoddle handed World Cup victory to Italy at Wembley and left England hoping for a miracle to qualify for the finals in France. Hoddle gave out-of-form Southampton star Matthew Le Tissier the job of inspiring his country to victory … then had to admit defeat by bringing him off in the second half after a miserable performance.' The front page of the *Express* posed the question alongside a distraught picture of Hoddle trooping off the Wembley pitch after the game: 'Is HODDLE OUR NEW TURNIP?' Inside the sports sections the vegetable analogies were blooming – chief sports writer James Lawton's analysis was headlined: 'HODDLE LEADS ENGLAND BACK TO TAYLOR DAYS.'

Hoddle remained serene, unmoved and in control despite the first signs of disenchantment with his reign as England coach. Were the fans becoming negative towards Hoddle, or was it just the media stoking the fires of discontent? Hoddle said: 'The only reason they are negative is because they listen to the perception of what the press tell them. I understand the press have got a job to do and I appreciate that. They write it the way they want. They write it and see it sometimes even before the result, one way or the other.'

There was a sting in the tail of that comment; a suggestion, maybe no more than a hint, that some of those lining up to bring him down had preconceived ideas even before his England side kicked a ball.

Hoddle had his own message to the fans. 'I say to the public we still have good players and the most important thing about this result is how we bounce back from it. We've still got a good side, one to be proud of, one that can qualify for the World Cup. And for those that don't agree with that, we'll have to wait and see.'

A love-hate relationship between the England boss and the tabloid press has existed for nearly 30 years. Even Sir Alf Ramsey, after winning the World Cup, wasn't immune to it. Back in those days the concentration of media was far less, but just as sharp and cutting. Sir Alf once said: 'It seems to me that I'm accused of being rude, but in truth I'm the one that's being treated with rudeness. They [the press] stick their faces in front of me, they stick these things [microphones] in front of me. But there's not a word invented that describes the mannerisms of some of the people I'm confronted with. Yet I'm rude.'

Graham Taylor's family background was steeped in journalism. But he was one of the victims of the media. First it was the headline 'SWEDES 2 TURNIPS 1' and from then onwards it was for ever Turnip Taylor. Taylor says: 'I didn't see that headline but I heard about it. I thought it was a very good headline! My father spent all his life in the newspaper industry so it is not as if I'm not aware of certain sections of the press and what they're looking for. I've no arguments with that whatsoever. What people don't have a real understanding about is how they can really hurt people, and not the people they think they're hurting, but those who surround that person. That's when you draw a line and enough is enough. I know newspaper people say that you shouldn't get into the public domain if you don't want it to affect your family, but I don't know how some of this stuff couldn't affect your family. I have parents in their late seventies and early eighties and I happen to be their only son and I'm sure my parents have been hurt. But let's look at the facts. We've won the World Cup once and got to the semi-finals once. We're not very good. They are the facts. We will look back to before then and talk about the personalities of the seventies, and we did have personalities then. Yet, we didn't qualify in 1974 and 1978 and of course neither did we qualify in 1994 when I was in charge. Our record at international level is nothing to shout about and never has been.'

Bobby Robson was the first to be tormented with a front page headline, imploring him 'IN THE NAME OF GOD, GO'. His neck was often in a noose, his failures in the European Championship sparking an unrelenting campaign for his head. Yet the Football Association kept their nerve, and Robson went on to reach the World Cup semi-finals in Italia 90. He blamed the uncompromising circulation war.

'We are so insulated in this country in the way we think we can win every game when we can't. We think we have the best football team in the world and we have not. Don't we think they're good in Spain, aren't they good in Germany, aren't they good in Italy, don't they have good players in Romania and Russia? There are no easy matches any more, and we don't dominate world football. We went to Saudia Arabia, and in that heat, in those conditions we came away with a 1–1 draw. I came back as a plonker. "In the Name of Allah, Go" ... these were the sort of headlines. It's being pilloried. There was one reporter who openly admitted on camera that he was here to "fry" Bobby Robson. When I saw that on film – an Englishman on the England plane with the England team hoping we would lose so he could guillotine me – that's beyond common decency.

'Everybody has their honeymoon, I had two years and Graham Taylor had two years. They give you a chance, they wait and see what you do, and they are ready to pounce if it doesn't go right.' Hoddle had just four games!

Little wonder that Kevin Keegan, Gerry Francis, and Bryan Robson thought more than twice about taking the England job. But Bobby Robson says: 'I never regret taking the England job and I would still recommend someone to take it if they were right for it, and ready for it. It can be very demanding for an inexperienced manager. But if it goes wrong, it won't kill you – but it will partially destroy you. If you are too young, too inexperienced, you wouldn't want the media abuse and you can't blame them, nobody wants a hole in their head!'

When the FA announced Hoddle as their new coach, the first question at the press conference attended by Hoddle and Venables was: 'In 1994 you said that the one thing that worried you was the media and the effect on your family. One, have you changed your mind? And two, are you still worried?' Hoddle replied: 'If I worried about it, I would not have taken the job. It is a difficult task and I'm sure Terry will give me a few pointers. With his vast experience, he can help me out. But at the end of the day that would not be a reason for turning this job down.'

You never know for sure how you and your family will react until the headlines appear at the breakfast table. Hoddle insisted he didn't read the papers in the days preceding and after each game. But the headlines and comments do filter back to him eventually.

Hoddle, though, discovered new depths of resolve within himself. It goes with the terrority of England boss to develop a skin of a rhinoceros. Taylor was left permanently scarred. 'I haven't been to Wembley to see England since I left as manager. One day I will. But not yet.' Taylor didn't hide the fact that he was nervous about the past. 'I stopped going to the door some time ago. I never answer it myself. It was all the attention, the aggravation, the camera lenses that greeted me – freelance operators looking for something to sell.' Taylor hired a personal public relations adviser, Venables preferred personal wining and dining of the media. In complete contrast, Hoddle changed his telephone numbers when he took charge and was completely uncontactable, even by those closest to him in the media.

Hoddle took over the England reins after the hysteria of Euro 96. Venables was a national hero, the Messiah of English football's renaissance, but he hardly seemed accommodating to the new man. He declared on Hoddle's appointment that he was not welcome at England's Euro 96 preparations as his presence might affect the players. He eventually relented to allow Hoddle limited access and discussions with the players, but the point was made. Many thought Hoddle should have been more closely involved in order to gain vital experience for the World Cup campaign. Hoddle hid any animosity, smiled diplomatically and said: 'I've always said the game is all about opinions and Terry is very welcome to his own opinions.'

Hoddle was a tougher cookie than anyone imagined. New FA chairman Keith Wiseman admitted he was impressed. 'I'm sure he's going to cope with it all very well ... I don't think he's going to have any problems. He is a very strong character and he's going to make a first-class coach for the team.'

CHAPTER ONE
Who Dares Wins
Hoddle's appointment by England, May 1996

Glenn Hoddle played with style and grace; his mere presence embellished the theatre of football. I was lucky enough to see him play when he was in his prime. A star with Spurs, Monaco and England, a manager with limited experience at Swindon and Chelsea, he was now the youngest ever England boss. A man to be admired and respected.

Whether or not my confidence in Hoddle is shared by the majority of my colleagues probably matters little to the man himself. He possesses unquestionable faith in his own ability and in the talents of the players he selects. He is a complex character with unusual convictions and beliefs; he places immense faith in the powers of healing and has a remarkable friendship with Eileen Drewery, a faith healer in his home town of Harlow. Glenn is no Bible basher; he doesn't ram religion down anybody's throat, but he takes his religious convictions seriously. After a visit to Bethlehem while on tour with England, he visited the birthplace of Jesus; the growing realization within him that there was perhaps something more to life deepened and cemented there. I sat with Hoddle for many hours as he revealed his innermost thoughts on this subject for his autobiography. He told me: 'There was this spiritual feeling inside me. It was exhilarating. I had never felt it before. When I came home, I read the Bible and other books and realized I had a strong belief. I believe God gives us advice.' He felt guided to take the England job. 'Don't ask me whether we will be successful or not, I just don't know. But I felt it was right.'

His unflinching faith first manifested itself when he realized the power of faith healing. 'I had a hamstring injury at Spurs and was due to be out for six weeks. The mother of a girl I knew asked if I wanted some healing. I agreed to have a session that day. The next morning I woke up and the injury had gone. I played two days later. I went back to Spurs and they thought I had been conning them.' Glenn has used the same faith healer many times. He has told the England players that faith healing is available to them if they want it.

Hoddle is the perfect modern international coach. Clean cut, immaculately dressed, youthful and with an international pedigree respected by the players, he doesn't possess a full FA coaching badge, but he still catches the eye during

England's training sessions at Bisham Abbey and abroad. In his time as manager, Terry Venables directed operations like a squat, tubby general from the middle of the field. Hoddle, in contrast, juggles the ball and runs with it like a man who still treats it as a best friend. He joins in the practice matches and looks as though he should still be in an England shirt at Wembley. He's still one of the best at head tennis. I've observed the players keenly watching him out of the corner of their eyes. If Hoddle cannot get his message across with instructions alone, he can provide a practical demonstration.

Some suggest it has gone from Club 18–30 under Tel to Cell Block H in the Hoddle regime: from Venables' more liberal approach as 'one of the lads' to Hoddle's sterner, stiffer regime of fewer breaks during international duty and confinement to barracks with orders to moderate any drinking. The reality is somewhere in between. Hoddle has always got a smile on his face, happiest on the training field with his players, and just as much one of the lads as Venables. True, Hoddle has reinforced the disciplinary code, with full approval from his employees who were acutely embarrassed by the Hong Kong Jump Club escapades in the dentist's chair during the England tour to China before Euro 96.

By an odd coincidence I spoke to Hoddle a year before he was offered the England job. The fifteen minute appointment with the then Chelsea boss turned into an hour-long discussion about my feeling that he would sooner, rather than later, be offered the post of England coach. He related his fears about such a position, but left me in no doubt that he would accept the position if asked. I recall that he knew that there would have to be sacrifices. 'That's how it must be. If anything, I'm determined and strong-willed about things I want.' He naturally expects others around him to be that way too. If there was a motto to describe himself, he says it would be 'who dares wins', because he's not afraid to experiment. He adds: 'My strengths as a manager are that I know how I want my teams to play.' Flaws? 'Many, but I don't need to publicize them.'

As Hoddle was still a player as recently as 1994, he is able to relate well to the modern-day footballer. He still enjoys a laugh with the players, but he's become more distant – he doesn't want to be perceived as jack the lad but as their friendly manager. He believes football is a serious business and is suspicious of those who clown around too much.

His beliefs enable him to channel bad days into learning experiences. He can always find something positive from the most disappointing occasions. He has often told me: 'Nothing really makes me depressed. Even when things go against me. They are the times when I've learnt most.' So far his most unnerving experience has been nothing to do with winning or losing a football match. 'It was,' he says with typical nonchalance, 'sitting on Nemesis at Alton Towers during a day out with my family.'

Whatever his current achievements, they are insignificant compared with what he has to do with England. Hoddle was a monumental success as a player with Spurs, but managing England is really in the big league. The nation wouldn't accept anything less than World Cup qualification. Hoddle knew full well the price of failure. We discussed the implications. He insisted that his back was broad enough to take the anticipated criticism but planned to avoid it by achieving success. And Hoddle has faith in his own ability to succeed.

Ken Bates knew Hoddle would walk out on Stamford Bridge, once summoned by England. The Chelsea chairman, no stranger to controversy, was sceptical that Hoddle would ever have renewed his contract at the Bridge while there was a possibility that he would coach the England team. Bates was often scathing in his condemnation of the way he believed the FA handled the Hoddle approach, and the 'diplomatic' way Hoddle responded.

Hoddle told a vastly different version of his departure from Chelsea. He suggested that he was motivated by doubts over funding for new players, distress over the boardroom bickering that jeopardized his long-term plans for the team and even the private hope that Matthew Harding would win the battle for control of the Bridge. At first Hoddle said of the England job: 'I honestly think it's got now to the stage where people are put off by everything that surrounds it.' Hoddle insisted when first asked by the media that Terry Venables was still the right man to continue.

From my discussions with him, there was no doubt in my mind that he would take the job once it became officially offered. But there was a long drawn-out process before that day eventually arrived. Naturally enough, the FA would not want their eventual appointment to feel he was not first choice. But the way the FA reached their final decision emphasised the difficulties in appointing a new England coach. It's easier to nominate the Pope. Little wonder the FA are reluctant to sack an existing England boss when the process of finding a successor is so complex.

Before any white smoke would be filtering through the doors of Lancaster Gate, there began a fascinating selection process, conducted behind closed doors. Often it left the outsider, a euphemism for the fan, convinced the FA had little to no idea what they were doing. In reality, the FA decided to come down from their ivory tower, as Graham Kelly put it, and seek the guidance and advice of the professionals, who were sounded out by a specially appointed 'agent', Jimmy Armfield. The FA again adopted the procedure it felt had been successful in reaching the decision to appoint Venables. But this time there would be a significant difference. They would be appointing a 'coach', not a 'manager' in the old tradition.

Kevin Keegan was instantly installed as red-hot favourite. The then Newcastle boss was quoted at even money by bookies William Hill with Bryan Robson 9–4, Howard Wilkinson 8–1, Gerry Francis 10–1, Hoddle 12–1 and Jack Charlton and Joe Royle 16–1. Francis and Keegan were, at the time, spearheading two of the brightest and best teams in the Premiership. Venables recommended his Euro 96 coach Bryan Robson to succeed him and the FA Chief Executive made public pronouncements giving that credence by stressing that 'continuity will be a major factor – we have seen it work on the continent.' But Robson opted to stay at Boro. Meanwhile, Newcastle chairman Sir John Hall wasn't prepared to let Keegan go. He was tied up on a ten-year contract and wouldn't be allowed to leave the North East. How ironic! Joe Royle didn't want to leave Goodison – he had turned down an interview for England several years previously because he was not prepared to give up the day-to-day involvement at Everton. Ray Wilkins at QPR declared himself too inexperienced. Where are they all now?

Alex Ferguson also figured in discussions. The most successful British manager of his generation was considered, but it would have meant such a big shift from tradition, appointing a foreign coach – let alone a Scotsman – that I would have thought the whole possibility remote, if not totally out of the question. At the end of Hoddle's first season in charge, Ferguson decided to let it slip that he was in the frame because he was engaged in the business of selling one of his many books! He said he turned the job down in favour of staying with United at a time when he was having trouble re-negotiating his club contract. The FA were forced to categorically deny he was ever offered the post. An FA insider made it clear that Ferguson did not receive any formal offer and was only ever sounded out. Ferguson's indelicate remark underlined the fact that there was a lengthy procedure before the FA eventually opted for Hoddle, a man who had once remarked that managing England had become a 'horrible job', with the potential to destroy family life.

The hunt for a new manager was in confusion from the outset with so many candidates announcing themselves out of the running. Reality or posturing? A difficult one. Some managers would want it to be known they were in the running for an alternative job in order to improve their conditions and salary at their existing club. Equally, it is true that certain managers either had grave reservations – for instance, Gerry Francis, who turned it down four times before Venables was given the job – or contracts that prohibited an FA move.

Even Hoddle was publicly dismissive at first. Diplomatic again, or just shrewd? Hoddle had begun to learn techniques to avoid giving answers guaranteed to make back page headlines. Maybe he was putting the pundits off the scent by suggesting that the FA wanted continuity. I'm sure that Hoddle believes in continuity, but he wasn't going to fall into the trap of discussing his personal views about his possible candidacy for the England job.

Just three months later, the media had turned full circle: 'GLENN HODDLE EMERGES AS FAVOURITE TO BE THE NEW ENGLAND MANAGER.' Hoddle's cover was blown, he had been 'informally' interviewed by Armfield. The media were now fully aware that he could be lured by the FA because of his increasing disillusionment at the instability inside Stamford Bridge. Hoddle's remarks made that clear. 'No-one has told me what money might be available, and I need to know exactly how the club will be run. I've made my feelings known to the board.'

Armfield, the FA's head-hunter, had a thankless task, working relentlessly behind the scenes, sounding out candidates on the phone and meeting them face to face. He revealed: 'Some quality candidates won't want the sort of pressure they have seen Venables take. A lot of people would have folded long before Terry did. It is difficult because England is everybody's team.'

For an insight into the truth of Hoddle's appointment, I visited the new FA Chairman, Keith Wiseman, at his offices at Lancaster Gate. He felt that with Hoddle, he had an England coach with the correct pedigree. He was in expansive mood, in itself unusual for an FA Chairman, and at ease within his new surroundings. I asked him about the process that led Hoddle to an office not far from his. He told me: 'We found ourselves in an unexpected position. No-one at the FA really thought that Venables would not continue until the World Cup at least. I was actually on the sub-committee to re-negotiate Terry's contract, set up in December, but as Terry took a view that he wasn't going to stay on, that committee never met for that purpose. By the time it did meet we were looking for a new man. We had our first meeting in January for a preliminary discussion. Glenn Hoddle was our only candidate. Of course, we were aware that one or two people had indicated that they were not available for whatever reason. Even if they had been available, it doesn't necessarily follow they would have been our choice!'

The FA had to take their own soundings. 'It is hard to say who really wanted it and who didn't by speculation in the press,' suggested Wiseman. 'We only had three meetings before Glenn emerged as first choice and was offered the job. Clearly, if we had before us four people whom we wanted and who were available then we would have had a choice. There was no such choice. There was no question of anybody else being offered the job. We formally offered the post to only one man.'

Without really knowing Hoddle, how did he come to the conclusion he had hit upon the best choice for the job? 'I felt he had the right football experience. The right breadth of experience having played abroad and managed in this country, and he had the right qualities as far as his personality. He was also very high profile, and we felt that was also right. International football is so different from the club scene when a manager works on a day-to-day basis with his players. I just felt Glenn would be suited to the international game, having had vast experience of it himself.'

Frank Clark and Howard Wilkinson were in the frame if anything went wrong with the moves to lure Hoddle to Lancaster Gate, but this contingency plan was never put to the test. Ironically, Clark and Wilkinson both parted company with their clubs, Notttingham Forest and Leeds, after runs of poor form in the 1996/97 season.

On 25 April 1996 , the FA's international selection committee met at 3 pm the day after England's goalless draw with Croatia. The five-man committee unanimously voted for Hoddle. The next day it was an open secret that Hoddle had been offered the England job. Of course, there was speculation that the FA wanted Ruud Gullit as well. This suggestion was subsequently flattened by Bates who told me that if Ruud had any spare time he could coach Chelsea. As it turned out, he would coach Chelsea full-time, before being replaced by Gianluca Vialli.

On 29 April at 7.00 pm, Armfield made the first formal approach in a phone call to Hoddle's Ascot home. On offer was a four-year deal worth around £1.2 million. The next day at 9.00 am FA officials contacted Bates for official permission to talk to Hoddle. Bates reluctantly agreed. Half an hour later Hoddle called Harding to inform him of the FA's offer, promising not to make a decision before further discussions with Chelsea's board. At noon Hoddle told his players at the club's training ground that he would give his answer within 24 hours.

On 1 May, it was public knowledge that Hoddle had been offered the position of England coach. Yet, at 7.30 am on the same day Harding publicly stated that he still hoped to persuade Hoddle to stay. The news that Hoddle was the FA's choice sent the media scurrying to his family home and gave him the first taste of the scrutiny he would be under once he took the job. A policeman stood guard outside the house and Hoddle only agreed to talk to reporters on the understanding that his wife and children were left alone. Hoddle's statement was brief. 'I have been offered the job. I have been given 48 hours to think about it. There are a lot of thoughts in my mind but the decision hasn't been made yet.'

At 9.30 am Hoddle left home in his N-reg BMW for further discussions with Harding at a 'secret' location. Harding underlined his offer of major finance for further team strengthening in the summer. Chelsea repeated their £7,000-a-week contract offer, worth £1.4 million over four years. At 2.15 pm Harding admitted he still didn't know what Hoddle was going to do.

Hoddle spent four hours listening to Chelsea's attempt to persuade him not to take the England job. It would have been a tense experience for Harding. He had prided himself on their personal relationship; if anyone could talk Hoddle round to staying, it would be him. In reality, it boiled down to a last ditch effort that turned out to be little more than window dressing. Maybe it was no more than begging Hoddle to stay. But Bates had told me of a private meeting between Hoddle, Harding and himself at a much less tense stage when the Chelsea manager was told the realities of Harding's proposed new investment in players. Bates challenged Harding to tell Hoddle how the money would be repaid, and it turned out to be no more than further Harding loans that Bates felt put the club in a weaker financial position.

Bates considered Harding's efforts little more than a media circus, pointing out that his boardroom rival had taken his favourite journalists with him, and made sure that others knew the 'secret' location. Bates also criticized the FA over their approach after an early-morning meeting with Hoddle's agent Dennis Roach. 'I'm very disappointed with the FA. If they had Glenn on their shortlist, they should have approached him a month or so ago so the matter could have been resolved. It's very bad behaviour on their part to leave it so late.' He continued: 'I understand they [the FA] approached him yesterday before they approached the club so they are probably technically in breach of some of their own rules. But anarchy rules these days.'

When Bates was first resigned to losing Hoddle, he told me: 'If he does decide to go for the England job, I wish him all the luck in the world because, frankly, he is going to need it.' Nobody had ever turned down the England job once it had been officially offered. Chelsea offered Hoddle a fortune to stay but the financial incentive was a non-starter. It was not the biggest motivating factor. Hoddle understood that there could be no greater honour than leading England into the World Cup.

After Hoddle had got his feet under the FA desk, Bates explained to me some of the problems he would have: 'Before Glenn can launch his revolution with the England team, he needs a backstage revolution. And that will never happen unless the people at the FA want to sacrifice their selfish interests for the good of the game. As it stands, the Premier League chairmen see the FA as a lost cause. Look, the FA are quite happy to take our players away from our clubs for five days at a time. Top Premiership clubs pay their players an average of £400,000 a year, that's £8,000 a week. The FA should pick up the wages when those players are out there for England – but they don't. The players get £750 appearance money and we get £750. When they buy from us our players at a fair price, maybe then they will get better co-operation. This is the same organization that makes millions from selling the matches to television. Under the previous agreement, the FA and the Football League had an arrangement whereby the League got 25 per cent of the international profits. In the hurry to form the Premier League, this was overlooked. Football associations survive financially by playing international matches and using the club players without paying for them. That is the real reason why UEFA are planning to increase the Champions' League, thus buying off the biggest and most rebellious clubs. For anyone who believes that players turn out for England for the honour of it I would say, if the honour is enough for them why do they want a players' pool or any fee at all? But the root of the problem is that Glenn will not get professional backup from the FA because it doesn't exist.'

The first practical problem for Hoddle and the FA was that Venables was reluctant to have his successor involved in the European Championship for fear his presence could be a distraction to England's efforts. Yet Venables gave Hoddle his backing. 'I think he is a good choice, exceptional. He has the quality he needs, there's no doubt about it. He is the man for the job. He has had that time abroad which will make things better for him.'

Perhaps the biggest drawback for the new coach was that while Venables had two years of friendlies to prepare for his first competitive game, against Switzerland in Euro 96, Hoddle would be thrown in at the deep end. The first England team he selected would play in Moldova in a World Cup qualifier with just five days' preparation at Bisham Abbey, interrupted by players reporting with injuries. Four months after his appointment, his first match would be a vital World Cup tie – without the benefit of a get together, let alone a friendly.

The depth of Hoddle's experience would undoubtedly be questioned. He had not been a favourite with the media during his three years at Chelsea. He was mistrusted by a number of journalists. There was still a lingering feeling of regret over the unsavoury circumstances surrounding Venables' departure.

On the plus side, Hoddle enjoys the challenge of pitting his wits against the best coaches and players in the world. In the 1995 Cup-Winners' Cup, he took an ordinary Chelsea side to the semi-finals. Like Venables, he commands huge respect across Europe. As a gifted midfield player for club and country, he knew what was needed at the highest level and appreciated how difficult it was for individuals with flair to break into the international set-up.

It was ironic that England never really rated Hoddle as a player. Ron Greenwood and Bobby Robson never fully recognized his unique talent. To be appreciated, he had to go to Monaco in the south of France, where he found a mentor in Arsene Wenger. Hoddle and the Monaco coach hit it off and the two are constantly in touch. Hoddle said: 'Arsene told me to love the ball and hurt the opposition with it. He did not want me in our own box. It was music to my ears.' It was Hoddle's reputation that lured Ruud Gullit to English football, his stature such that the Dutchman said: 'When you are asked to come to play in England, you consider many things. But when Glenn Hoddle asks, you are flattered – and you come.'

Hoddle was not satisfied merely to have landed the prestigious post. From what I know of him, his ambition was to be the most successful manager in English football. His philosophy was to change the basic English pattern of 4-4-2 to 3-5-2. He reflected: 'From 1966 through the seventies and a major part of the eighties, a lot of teams were playing 4-4-2 and the game became very sterile. Putting three at the back gives an extra man to get you off the hook, so you can pass the ball into the middle of the park rather than welly it up front.' That was the enlightened path at Swindon, and then Chelsea. At Chelsea's Harlington training ground, Hoddle erected two walls for players to develop their touch. Every daily session involved 20–30 minutes working on ball skills, two or three players in a group challenging each other to improve technique as Hoddle so emphatically honed his. 'If you don't master the ball,' runs the Hoddle creed, 'the ball will master you.'

From the players' perspective, Hoddle offered a welcome continuity with the tenure of Venables, despite differences such as Venables' preference for wide midfielders rather than Hoddle's attacking wing-backs, and his use of the three-man defence.

It's always interesting to see how the English game is viewed overseas by the most respected of foreign coaches. Swedish coach Sven-Goran Eriksson is one such authority with his vast experience in Italian football. He reflected on the advancement of English football, both at club and international level, after Gullit's new Chelsea side won 2–1 in Genoa in a pre-season friendly billed as Gianluca Vialli's homecoming. 'Glenn Hoddle and Gullit have changed the way of thinking in England. Chelsea do not play a British style; they like to keep the ball, play it on the ground and build their moves slowly in a European fashion.'

Enough of these words of wisdom from the pundits and the experts. What about those gut feelings. Aren't they just as important? Of course they are. Hoddle was a player with vision, he took those ideals into management at club level, and why not embark on the campaign for the sixteenth World Cup full of optimism?

The first World Cup in Uruguay in 1930 attracted just four European nations. In 1966 there were 70 teams from around the world embarking on the 12-month qualification road to Wembley with just 14 places awaiting those successful nations as both England and holders Brazil automatically qualified. There were 24 teams in the last World Cup in the States. Thirty years on from 1966, 170 nations set out for the 32 places with France, and yet again Brazil, automatically qualified. There would be a total of 639 qualifying games before the World Cup draw in Marseilles. The expansion of the world's greatest sporting event began in earnest in 1974 when the current FIFA President, Joao Havelange, opened the floodgates to an increasing number of nations, some you've probably never even heard of. While such footballing nations as the Kingdom of Saudia Arabia and Japan could wriggle their way through the qualifiers, there was a possibility that either England or Italy might fail to make it.

CHAPTER TWO

The World Cup Adventure Begins

Hoddle's First England Squad, August 1996

The advent of a new manager and a new season meant that there might be changes in the make-up of the England team. Young players and rejects of the Venables and Taylor eras prepared to raise their game and force the new England coach to pay them some attention.

There were joyous celebrations in the Le Tissier household when Hoddle was appointed. Matt Le Tissier had been the archetypal forgotten man of Venables' reign. After 18 months in the wilderness, his hopes were boosted when Hoddle's right-hand man John Gorman watched him in a pre-season friendly against Wycombe. Le Tiss admitted: 'I know I have a fresh chance ... The World Cup qualifiers are my main aim this season provided I can sort out my form in the league. I have to get myself in the right frame of mind. It is down to me to get my form back.' Le Tissier had won just six caps, making only two starts, and had yet to play a full 90 minutes for his country. His last appearance had been against the Republic of Ireland in February 1995, but that match was abandoned after crowd trouble. He never got another chance under Venables.

The Charity Shield on 11 August 1996 was the first chance to assess David Beckham while a week later, on the opening day of the Premiership, Matt Le Tissier and Southampton were taking on the new Chelsea side, now packed with Italian internationals. Not surprisingly, Glenn Hoddle was at both Wembley and the Dell. Hoddle left Wembley, convinced that Beckham was worthy of elevation to the full England squad. He had made a point of watching Beckham in the Under-21 side in the Toulon tournament even before he formally took over from Venables and had been greatly impressed by the United player's mature display in a 1–0 win over Belgium. Beckham already had England aspirations: 'It was a dream for me to play in a Cup Final and help United win the Double, but my big aim is to play for England in the next World Cup.' His outstanding contribution in United's spectacular 4–0 Charity Shield triumph confirmed that the cultured midfielder was ready to step up and join his team-mates, the Neville brothers, in England's future.

Hoddle dispatched his army of scouts to run the rule over almost 50 potential candidates. On the opening day of the season, at Selhurst Park, Beckham underlined his credentials with his wonder goal from the halfway line against Wimbledon. The goal was the talk of soccer. Hoddle made his own high-profile entrance at the Dell as he ran the rule over Le Tissier. The Southampton man had a magic one minute – the first. In all his majestic brilliance, he showed vision and control as he clipped the bar with a tantalizing lob. Apart from that, he proved only that he would have to sweat a lot more under the guidance of new manager Graeme Souness. There was only one assessment possible – little had changed with Matt Le Tissier.

Hoddle succeeded in his first vital mission before the season began when he persuaded Stuart Pearce into a U-turn over his decision to retire from international football after Euro 96. Pearce quickly thought it over, and called the new England coach to say he would be available after all when the World Cup qualifying campaign kicked off in Moldova. Hoddle was thrilled. 'Stuart's contribution to the England team over many years has already been substantial, not least in Euro 96.'

Pearce discussed how Hoddle had changed his mind: 'Glenn took the trouble to drive north and see me personally. He quizzed me over the decision to retire from the international scene, then stressed he wanted me to continue. I had talked things over with my wife Liz and came to the conclusion that after 70 caps it was the perfect time to step down. However, Glenn told me he thought I still had something to offer my country and asked if I'd reconsider. I didn't need him to ask a second time. If it hadn't been for Glenn taking all that trouble to twist my arm, I don't think I would ever have changed my mind. I am certain England have an exciting future under Glenn. He is going to build on what Terry Venables achieved in reaching the European Championship semi-finals, and it's nice to know Glenn believes my experience and stature can be of some benefit. Nobody – and I mean nobody – enjoys representing their country as much as I do, or regards it as such a high honour. It would be great to think I can cling on to my place in the England team for a year or two, and help us qualify for the next World Cup Finals. That would be a tremendous thrill. But I understand there are no guarantees over selection. Glenn has made it perfectly clear that while he would value having me around for a while, every place in the side is up for grabs.'

Having missed *that* penalty in Euro 96, Gareth Southgate began the Hoddle reign intent on ensuring his international career was not over. He sought solace from Hoddle for his nightmare Euro 96 after so much ribbing from the Villa players. He hoped desperately that the new England coach would allow him to 'start putting the world to rights'. Southgate's flexibility put him high on Hoddle's wanted list and he was determined his reluctant celebrity status would not make him lose sight of the application which earned him recognition in the first place.

Tony Adams, skipper during Euro 96, needed a second operation on his long-term knee injury, having played through the pain all the way to the semi-final. He was gradually building up his strength with weight exercises, bike riding and other light workouts. He said: 'I am definitely putting myself first right now. In the summer I did what I had to for England and just did my best. If it hadn't been such an important tournament, I doubt I would have played but I did even though I was in a lot of pain towards the end of matches.'

Many players fancied their chances of catching the new manager's eye. Many would be disappointed. Lee Sharpe was a perfect example of optimism never fulfilled. He eagerly anticipated that his move from Manchester United to Leeds for £4.5 million would revive his flagging England chances. Sharpe had taken encouragement from a conversation between Hoddle and his new boss Howard Wilkinson bemoaning the dearth of top-quality left-wingers. He believed he could make the position his own if his career took off again at Leeds. A combination of injuries and the emergence of a crop of brilliant youngsters had led to Sharpe losing his first-team place at Old Trafford and with it his chances of playing for England. He turned his back on the likelihood of further honours with the Double winners in favour of a chance to force his way back into the international set-up via a move to Elland Road. 'To get into the England side you've got to be playing regularly for your club and I wasn't getting that at Manchester United. Now I'm at Leeds, I've got to play so well that I make it impossible for Glenn Hoddle to overlook me. Glenn's going to take a good look at everyone and it's up to me to impress. There's a World Cup in two years' time and I want to be part of that.' As things turned out, there was no such luck for Sharpe. Long-term injury and radical management changes at the club conspired against him to such a degree that his career went into a downward spiral from then on.

Liverpool's lethal duo of Stan Collymore and Robbie Fowler had scored an incredible 55 goals between them in the season before Euro 96, but neither had made the England team on any sort of permanent basis. Collymore was the then British record £8.5 million signing. 'Stan The Man' was another high on hope and optimism about his England chances as he tried to add to the solitary cap he won in the 2–1 victory over Japan. 'I've always felt I could do well for England. I didn't play too well against Japan, but I think we're too willing to dismiss players after just one game. It's up to Glenn Hoddle to decide who he thinks will fit into his scheme. But I'm sure I can perform against international opposition.' Teaming up with Fowler for England as well as at club level was something Stan was convinced would work. 'Robbie and I have got a good understanding and I think we could take that on to the international stage.' However, Collymore was sold to Aston Villa in the summer of 1997 after a generally disappointing two seasons at Anfield, and his partnership with Fowler, at least at club level, was at an end.

The biggest enigma of them all was, as usual, Paul Gascoigne. There was to be an amazing series of events that would test Hoddle's nerve and moral fibre. Gascoigne's state of health before vital England games was to become a commonplace worry, although no-one could have guessed how badly his off-the-field problems would get. At the outset, the main concern was his level of fitness. Glasgow Rangers' manager Walter Smith delivered good news for Hoddle:

'England can rest assured they'll have him fit and ready for their opening World Cup tie. He won't need a lot of training to get himself back to peak fitness.' Gazza's mental state, as well as his physical condition, were to prove a nightmare for Hoddle. His marital problems and constant accusations over his behaviour pushed the issues far beyond the sphere of football.

I watched Hoddle, immaculate in a Prince of Wales check suit and England–Green Flag matching tie, enter the Park Court Hotel, close to FA headquarters at Lancaster Gate at 2.30 pm on a lovely summer's afternoon on 22 August 1996 to unveil his first England squad, for the World Cup qualifier against Moldova. The party was: Seaman (Arsenal), Walker (Spurs), James (Liverpool), G Neville (Man Utd), Pearce (Nottm Forest), Pallister (Man Utd), Howey (Newcastle), Southgate (Aston Villa), Campbell (Spurs), Gascoigne (Rangers), Ince (Inter Milan), McManaman (Liverpool), Batty (Newcastle), Le Tissier (Southampton), Beckham (Man Utd), Stone (Nottm Forest), Barmby (Middlesbrough), Anderton (Spurs), Sheringham (Spurs), Shearer (Newcastle), Ferdinand (Newcastle), Fowler (Liverpool).

The seemingly endless rounds of interviews took 90 minutes. The major talking point was, inevitably, the inclusion of Matt Le Tissier. Hoddle stressed: 'I need to work with the guy, find out roughly what's going through his mind, and I'm not going to do that if I don't bring him into the squad.' Hoddle needed to unlock the confidence factor to make Le Tissier a success in an England shirt.

The new coach warded off unwelcome questions with a warm smile and polite reply. He would not be drawn, for example, on exactly how he would alter Venables' successful tactics, but he was clearly delighted to, at last, get down to work six months after his appointment. 'Right through the summer I've been playing Fantasy League football, picking different squads from the European Championship. It's nice to get down to picking my own.'

Hoddle wasted little time in putting his own stamp on the national side with the elevation of Beckham and the recall of Le Tissier. Leytonstone-born Beckham had made just 39 Premiership appearances for United but had already marked himself down as perhaps the most complete all-round midfielder in the country. Undoubtedly, Hoddle had high hopes for Beckham. 'I came across David a couple of years ago when I took Chelsea to Old Trafford and he showed so much maturity. I earmarked him down as a great talent even then. He's come on and on in the last few years and fully justifies being called up for the squad. He has got an eye for goal, and for a midfield player that is a wonderful added thing to have to your game. He's shown a lot of maturity for a youngster and he's playing in an excellent side. Alex Ferguson has brought the United youngsters on and David's come to the fore.'

There was an international revival for Gary Pallister and recognition of David James' commanding presence in the Liverpool goal. Injuries denied Hoddle the services of Adams, Platt and Redknapp, but for the rest of the squad – Tim Flowers apart – that reached the Euro 96 semi-final, there was a deserved retention. Hoddle explained: 'It would have been negative to have radically changed the squad because there were a lot of good performances this summer and a lot to build on. My priority is to win this game. But I need to look at people I think will suit my way of play, which will be a little bit different. I would be foolish not to do that.'

Aston Villa's Ugo Ehiogu, who just missed out on the 22-man squad for Euro 96, was not summoned as Hoddle instead turned to the 31-year-old Pallister as a replacement for Adams. The 6ft 4in giant had been plagued by a sciatica problem since the last of his 20 caps against Switzerland in November 1995, but had opened the new season in excellent form. Meanwhile Newcastle's Steve Howey had recovered from the injury which kept him out of Euro 96 and was welcomed back into the fold.

The make-up of the squad was a heartwarming demonstration of Hoddle's commitment to creative football. But there were the first indications of a pragmatist at work; in the absence of the injured Platt, he threw an international lifeline to Newcastle's combative midfielder, David Batty. Batty had been close to a recall by Venables after he successfully bedded down at Newcastle following his move from Blackburn, and Hoddle was impressed. 'In any good side you need good balance and with the players I've brought in, I think you can see the balance there. He [Batty] has better qualities of passing the ball than people give him credit, added to the bite he's got in his game, and for me he's a very good player – one that's playing well at the moment.' Batty's inclusion was another blow for Villa's Mark Draper, who had been widely tipped to earn a long-awaited promotion.

Flowers was the first victim of Hoddle's gradual shake-up. Hoddle spoke personally to the Blackburn keeper and reassured him that he would be brought back 'somewhere down the line' but felt that James – long over the wobbles which followed his move from Watford to Liverpool in 1993 – 'gave me the impression it was time for him to be looked at'. Flowers had lost out on the back of the decline of former champions Blackburn and played only once for England in their last dozen games, the 3–0 win in China in May. James, meanwhile, had kept 25 clean sheets for the Anfield outfit in the 1995/96 season.

Peter Taylor, in charge of the Under-21s, included Michael Duberry and Jody Morris, two of Hoddle's favourite youngsters from Chelsea, as well as Leicester's Emile Heskey, Wimbledon's Ben Thatcher, Manchester United's Nicky Butt and Lee Bowyer of Leeds. It was Hoddle's edict that the Under-21s, as with all England sides, would play the same system as the senior team.

Hoddle quickly cut ties with the Venables set-up. Venables' chief scout, Ted Buxton, was offered only a part-time post. Buxton, who compiled dossiers on England's opponents, met with Hoddle, but was told his services would be required on only a match-to-match basis. Don Howe was discounted, just as he was when Hoddle took over at Chelsea. However, he remained with the FA as technical adviser.

There were raised eyebrows over Hoddle's choice of backroom staff: John Gorman, Peter Taylor, Ray Clemence, Roy McFarland and Glenn Roeder. He was leaning heavily on his old Tottenham connections, but their management track record was hardly compulsive reading. The biggest shock was the appointment of Scot John Gorman as assistant coach. The FA would have preferred Hoddle to work with Bryan Robson, whom Venables had hoped would be groomed as his successor, with Ray Wilkins staying with the Under-21s. But Hoddle had his own ideas and the licence to implement them.

I've known John Gorman since the first time he played for Spurs in the same side as Hoddle. They became close friends and teamed up again in management at Swindon. It was no surprise to me that Hoddle chose Gorman above other close associates such as Peter Shreeves. There was a unity between the two former teammates that Hoddle felt was as important as Gorman's abilities. But it was a controversial decision to select a Scot who had never played international football and whose experience as a manager amounted to a 17-month stint that embraced relegation and, ultimately, dismissal. Hoddle's first move, as Venables planned his European Championship swansong, was deemed rather peculiar.

Not to Gorman, though. Though circumstances dictated he could find no better employment than assistant manager at Bristol City, in the second division, he still anticipated the call. Gorman told me: 'Funnily enough, I did expect it. I thought that all the stuff about me being Scottish and the fact I hadn't played for Scotland might count against me, but that doesn't really matter if you're a team. Glenn and I have always got on well together, we're a good partnership and he recognizes that. At the end of the day, he is the boss. I'm his choice and everybody should respect that. He has done it for the right reasons and not without thought or just because I'm a pal. He feels I'm the right man and he needs people he can trust. It doesn't always follow that the best managers have been the best players. Look at Roy Hodgson. He was once at Bristol City and is now in charge at Inter Milan [he's now at Blackburn]. Is it a big jump for me? No, I don't think so; not really. I've played at a good level, with some of the top players, and I've been coached by some of the top coaches.'

Born in Winchburgh, West Lothian, Gorman left school at 14, without any educational qualifications, to sign for the great Jock Stein's Celtic, winners of the 1967 European Cup – and joined the ranks of McGrain, Dalglish, Macari, Hay, Johnstone and McNeill. Though an emerging, adventurous left-back, he made only one first-team appearance in five years. Stein sold him on to Carlisle United – 'I think Bob Stokoe, the Carlisle manager, felt Jock owed him a favour. I was that favour,' said Gorman. He then spent spent six seasons at Brunton Park in the company of Bowles, Hatton and Balderstone. 'It was a pretty good team, too. We went up to the first division, as Manchester United came down, and I almost got picked by Scotland. They watched me, but unfortunately I had an off day and I missed getting selected. Maybe if I had played for a more fashionable club I'd have got the nod.'

Keith Burkinshaw paid £80,000 to take him to Tottenham, where he teamed up with John Duncan, Pat Jennings, Steve Perryman, Ossie Ardiles, Ricky Villa … and Hoddle. 'Glenn and I got on almost instantly,' he said. Gorman's 19-year-old son, Nick, still has one of Hoddle's first England caps on show in his bedroom.

A knee injury prematurely ended Gorman's stay at White Hart Lane and, after turning down a youth coaching job at the club, he concluded his playing days in the United States with Tampa Bay Rowdies and Phoenix Inferno. On his return to England, he took in Gillingham and Orient, listening and learning in the wings, before Hoddle enticed him to Swindon as his No 2. However, having clinched a place in the FA Carling Premiership via the 1993 play-offs, Hoddle departed for Chelsea. 'I was going with him,' Gorman said. 'I'd packed my stuff, I was walking out the door and shaking hands with people, but I changed my mind.' Swindon's swift relegation from the Premiership, despite a buccaneering approach, proved inevitable. Six months later, he was dismissed. Sixteen months on from that, he got the call from England. But his appointment not only came as a surprise, it gave the anti-Hoddle lobby plenty of ammunition.

Hoddle also wanted Arsene Wenger as part of his coaching staff as FA Technical Director. Hoddle phoned his old Monaco boss, who was managing in Japan at that time. Wenger, a mentor to Hoddle since the two met up at Monte Carlo, was coaching Gary Lineker's old club Grampus Eight. Although he was eventually lured to English football by Arsenal, Wenger stalled on the Hoddle offer because he was contracted to his Japanese club until November. Wenger's main objection to the post was that he still liked to work with players on a day-to-day basis.

Hoddle often spoke of his gratitude to Wenger for showing him the coaching light. Wenger meanwhile was delighted Hoddle had been appointed England coach. 'I am so happy for Glenn because I always thought, even when he was a player, that he could be a top manager. At first I tried to encourage him to work his way up as a manager and he has made it very quickly from the boss of a club to such a big responsibility as England manager. He was always a good reader of the game and a good support at half-time. He always saw what happened on the field. He's also honest and that's important. And he's a passionate guy even though he doesn't always show it.'

Wenger's decision to succeed Bruce Rioch at Highbury was a disappointment for Hoddle but he paid tribute to Wenger's influence on him: 'Arsene opened my eyes to a new chapter in my life. He is a wonderful coach. I would not be where I am today if it were not for Arsene. Working with him at Monaco stimulated me to go into management. Wherever he's gone, he's been a major success.'

Finally, early in January 1997, Howard Wilkinson was appointed the FA's new Technical Director of Coaching. Hoddle made it clear where the division of responsibility would lie. 'Who plays for England and the way we play will be my decision and I am the only person who will be responsible for results. I will be at the cutting edge, as Howard has been for the last 16 years in a result-orientated job. Now he will be responsible for producing a better coaching structure. The production of quality coaches is very important. I would not send my child to a school which did not have qualified teachers.'

Part of Wilkinson's brief was to join Hoddle's network of scouts, working both in parallel and in tandem with the national coach. Hoddle explained: 'Howard's role is important in both the long and short term, but more so in the long term, from the grassroots up to the senior side. He must produce a better structure to make us a force in world football again. The senior side is my responsibility, although I will discuss things with him. But I must be results orientated.'

Alex Ferguson, Gordon Taylor, Graham Kelly and Hoddle were present to endorse Wilkinson as the country's first Technical Director. Wilkinson, 53, was given a four-year contract and a reputed £200,000 annual salary, to carry out a wide-ranging brief to shake up the grassroots of the English game.

The blueprint included a recommendation for the appointment of a national youth coach to work with England's junior teams and alongside Hoddle, eventually taking over from him as senior England coach – a policy already in place in Germany where Bertie Vogts succeeded Franz Beckenbauer after an apprenticeship as international No 1, and in France where Aime Jacquet had replaced Gerard Houllier as national team chief after learning his trade in youth football.

For his part, Wilkinson wanted to see the building of a National Football Centre for coaching and sports medicine, to provide a home base for England's national squads at all age levels, including Hoddle's senior side.

Hoddle backed Wilkinson's plan to build an England dynasty, but he insisted he did not intend to hand over his job in a hurry. 'The principle of that is correct. It's happened in other countries like Germany. The more I find out about this job, the more I realize that club management is just no apprenticeship for it. It's a one-off job. I spoke to Graham Kelly about this when I took the job on, before a technical director had been appointed. The spanner that's thrown in there is that I'm a bit younger than most and hope to be around a bit longer. Perhaps they'll have to look for a good 12-year-old coach!'

Hoddle envisaged someone being brought in to work at Under-18 level and then gradually introduced at Under-21 and then senior level to get the feel of the job. 'He would be groomed, he wouldn't be brought in straight at the top. That's got to be a longer-term situation. The next step of who he is is a lot further down the line. We haven't discussed that yet. It's going to be very difficult to find the right person. Who would want to do that, to go straight in at that level and be groomed? And it's not to say that person would be right just because he's chosen. We could get four years down the line and change our mind. There's nothing cast in stone.'

Hoddle replaced goalkeeping coach Mike Kelly with Ray Clemence, who won 61 England caps, many of them as an international colleague of Hoddle. Clemence doubles as a coach for the national side and a specialist training

England's up-and-coming keepers. He is a close friend of Hoddle's from their days together at Spurs. Clemence cut his teeth in management at Barnet but the opportunity with England was too good to refuse. 'It's a major coup to have somebody of his coaching and management experience joining my set-up.' said Hoddle. 'Ray is somebody who I've both played with and have known for many years.' Clemence's pedigree could hardly be better. At Liverpool, he was in a team which won five Division One Championships, one FA Cup, one League Cup, three European Cups and two UEFA Cups. He kept 27 clean sheets in his 61 appearances for England during an 11-year international career.

Hoddle contacted Chelsea coach Graham Rix, whom he wanted on a part-time basis but Ruud Gullit denied the former Arsenal player the chance. Rix said, 'Glenn wanted me to work with the players when there was an international. Like me, the club saw the advantage of the offer but Ruud refused to let me go. I fought my corner and said to him that Chelsea had so many international players there was very little for me to do when the World Cup matches came around – I would end up just refereeing meaningless practice matches. But Ruud said no, and I had to accept it. He said I had a job to do at Chelsea. I was bitterly disappointed … and it still hurts.'

Hoddle sought extra help on the training pitch. He was not only on the phone to Alex Ferguson about United's players, but also to enquire about the availability of his assistant manager Brian Kidd. Hoddle wanted to use Kidd in much the same way as Robson worked alongside Venables, but two approaches to the Old Trafford boss received little encouragement – Ferguson wanted all the energy of his assistant channelled into the greater glory of United. Hoddle also approached Wimbledon to release coach Terry Burton. Although Burton was keen to accept, Dons' owner Sam Hammam, in consultation with Joe Kinnear, blocked the move, fearing extra commitments for Burton could have an adverse affect. There had been a similar outcome when Hoddle tried to recruit Doug Livermore from Liverpool. Eventually, Hoddle turned to former Watford manager Glenn Roeder, who worked as a scout and adviser to him during the season.

Between the intensity of the weeks before major internationals, Gorman and Hoddle organize the wide network of scouts. Gorman explained: 'We have kept a close eye on all our group rivals and travelled to every international possible, including games with the French and Dutch. It is also important to touch base with the players between games. Both those in the squad and the unfortunate ones on the sidelines, the likes of Andy Hinchcliffe and Steven Stone, haven't been forgotten. Keeping in touch with the players is an important part of my job.' Gorman delegates the scouting of matches with the main assignments going to Clemence, Taylor, Roeder and Dave Sexton.

The age-old problem is the limited time with the players. 'The players feel like our own for the limited period we have with them. The frustrating thing for both Glenn and I has been the fact that once the match is finished, they jump in their cars and go home.'

There were one or two teething problems for the new staff. Julian Dicks accused John Gorman of telling him that he would never get into the England squad unless he grew his hair – an accusation Gorman strongly denied. Dicks described a meeting he had had with the assistant coach in Tenerife. 'He told me I was just the kind of player Glenn was looking for. He then told me to grow my hair long and I would get in the side. I ask you, what kind of s--- is that.? I wasn't having that. It shouldn't matter what you look like, just how good you are on the pitch. I've seen players picked for England by Graham Taylor and Terry Venables who don't even deserve to be in their club sides. I am better than Stuart Pearce, Graeme Le Saux, Phillip Neville and Alan Wright ... Two or three years ago I would have loved to have played for England. Now I've had enough of the whole scene.' Gorman considered the whole episode 'laughable' and denied he had made the comment. Hoddle stressed that it was a farce to suggest that anyone would be excluded because of their hairstyle.

Meanwhile, Clemence had a run-in with David James. The Liverpool keeper stormed: 'It's disappointing that someone who could help get me to the World Cup isn't pushing my case.' James' remarks followed criticism by Clemence of a gaffe in Gothenburg which cost the Mersey club a 1–0 defeat in their opening pre-season friendly. It was to be hoped that the campaign for France 98 wouldn't descend into such in-fighting.

The business of qualifying was now about to start. The backbone of England's entire World Cup campaign was on board Britannia Flight 740A bound for Kishinev: David Seaman, Paul Gascoigne, David Beckham, David Batty, Paul Ince and new captain Alan Shearer. Also on board was the cream of England's young hopefuls, under the guidance of new Under-21 coach Peter Taylor. The development of the Under-21 side was vital to Hoddle. There would surely be heartbreak and glory among the boys aiming for perhaps one or two places in Hoddle's final World Cup squad.

Here I was, on the start of England's World Cup adventure, knowing as well as Hoddle and any of his players that the country's fate wouldn't be settled, in all probability, until the final game in Rome in ten months' time. It was going to be a long haul, with ups and downs and no doubt total condemnation if Hoddle faltered anywhere along the line. Hoddle needed a good start in Moldova. He dare not mess up at the very first attempt – if he did, it would be the shortest honeymoon in English football history.

CHAPTER THREE

The Shearer Factor

England have a new captain, August 1996

Before we all boarded the flight to Moldova, the new England coach announced the new national skipper – Alan Shearer. Shearer is the perfect example of a working class boy from the North-East becoming sophisticated in the world of commerce, marketing, multi-million pound endorsements and a world record transfer fee of £15 million. But shin pads are the same for every player, and irrespective of whether Shearer earns £3 million or £4 million a year, he puts his career and earnings capacity on the line every time he is on the pitch.

Shearer gave his first press conference as England captain in a tiny room at the airport. No-one present was the least bit surprised by his Gary Lineker-style greeting of each question with a warm smile – his straight bat was as deliberate and as functional as Geoff Boycott's when opening an innings for England.

On becoming England's 100th captain, Shearer said: 'I was surprised when Glenn told me. I didn't expect it at all. In fact, the thought of captaining England had never entered my head. Now that I am, I have to say, even when I look at everything else that has happened to me in football, that this has to be the very best moment in my career. Not much can beat becoming the captain of your country.' On the change of managers, he commented: 'Nobody wanted to see Terry go. We all genuinely got on well with him, and we never quite got to the whole truth behind why he had to go. We lost a great manager, but we gained another one. Both Terry and Glenn are winners, that much is obvious. Both like to not only win, but to win in style, and apart from a few minor tweaks, there has been little difference playing under the new manager. Besides, if it's not broken, you don't need to fix it, do you?'

He was no different at club level when Keegan left and Dalglish arrived; he respected Keegan and he respects Dalglish. He is never fazed, not even by his world record transfer fee. 'I actually enjoy being the world's most expensive signing. I really do.'

It was this attitude that impressed Hoddle from the very first minute the players gathered on Sunday evening at Burnham Beeches Hotel on 25 August. Hoddle began the first full day of training at Bisham Abbey with an incredible sense of satisfaction. 'It is a wonderful feeling being able to pick the best players in the country and face the challenge of moulding that talent into a team that can go on and win football matches.'

Hoddle summed up his first day's training. 'It was important to be relaxed, to make them feel at home and unpressurized. And it was a little bit strange this morning. There were players arriving like Andy Hinchcliffe whom I've never met before, and it was strange to feel that for a week they're your players. If somebody said you could have this job for ten years, you would never get used to it unless you experience something like Terry in the summer when you have the players for three or four weeks. After a match, come Monday morning, the players are back with their club, and that is a strange feeling.'

Sorting out a myriad of problems preoccupied Hoddle: a crippling injury list, the search for understudies, the aggravating club-versus-country debate and dealing with the media.

A central issue for the press was Hoddle's decision to summon David Beckham. The previous evening Alex Ferguson had told the reporters that he did not want Beckham to become the latest victim of the 'build-em-up, knock-em-down' syndrome as he felt that he would be left with the task of nursing him back to health. Ferguson also expressed his fears personally to Hoddle. The England coach promised to shield and protect his wonderkid, but he insisted that he would be right to blood the boy in Moldova, despite the worries that too much was happening too soon. Hoddle said: 'No, I don't see it as a major problem. He can become a great player ... and if you've got talent you should be playing with the best in the country.'

Hoddle accepted that the gifted youngster needed protection from media pressure. 'At that tender age I think it's right. Alex knows him much better than I do so I've got to respect that. I agree with him to a certain degree, we have to be sensible with the boy. He did it with Ryan Giggs and it worked out fine with him, and if he feels that's the same with David Beckham that's not a problem with myself – we won't overexpose him.'

Hoddle's problems included Darren Anderton, whose series of injuries after playing through the pain in Euro 96 had earned him the unwanted nickname 'Sicknote'. Of others in the squad, McManaman, Fowler, Batty and Howey were all rated extremely doubtful for the flight to Kishinev. McManaman and Fowler both had back problems, Howey had broken a toe and Batty had sprained an ankle. Fears that Les Ferdinand might also be ruled out were allayed with the diagnosis of the the extent of the £6 million striker's injury ... a corn between two of his toes!

Meanwhile, Graeme Le Saux, out of action since breaking his leg in a freak accident in a game against Middlesbrough, was invited to Bisham by Hoddle and he was able to take part in the light session. It was a neat piece of forward planning by Hoddle, who would call upon Le Saux as soon as he made a full recovery.

However, Hoddle was full of praise for both the new men in the squad, Andy Hinchcliffe and Mark Draper, who had been called up because of the injury problems. 'Andy has started very well for Everton this season and he gives us some nice balance on the left side. I have been impressed with him for a number of years. He has a smashing left foot and has been a major influence on Everton's start. Mark had a good season with Villa last year and handled everything pretty well. I felt that this was the right time to bring him in.'

As Hoddle pieced together his team, the Le Tissier question was a constant. How would Hoddle fit him in? Le Tissier could operate as the slightly withdrawn second striker, although he accepted that even Hoddle – who tried to sign him for Chelsea – could not afford to be too patient. 'Every player would like more than one chance. But if there's going to be just the one I've got to take it. I've got to look at it as the one game when I have to do it. The problem I've always encountered is that people look to me to score goals and create them, and it might have been a lot easier for managers to pick me if I was good at one thing and crap at the other. But now I've got another opportunity. Some people have suggested that it might be a bit of a risk picking me for Moldova, but I've never lost my creative ability. I think I can create chances every game, no matter who we're playing against.'

One of Hoddle's main concerns was the state of the Kishinev pitch. He registered his complaint that the Under-21s had to play on the same ground the day before the World Cup clash, on the same day that England wanted to train on the pitch. Hoddle said: 'It is a major headache. I've challenged it, but there is no way round it. The rules state that we can have access to the match pitch to train a day before the game. That means we shall have to train on it in the morning, then the Under-21s will play on it in the evening, and then we play on it the next day. Heaven knows what state the pitch will be in if we encounter bad weather. The training facilities are not really good. But we shall have to face these problems and get on with them.'

Shearer was ready for the game: 'They'll be a tough side to beat, especially away, and I'm sure they won't make it easy for us, on or off the pitch. It's all part and parcel of going into Europe. It doesn't just happen at international level, it happens at club level too. With Blackburn in the Champions' League I remember, in Moscow I think it was, that they did things like give you flat balls or send you to one training pitch and you then find it's the wrong one. I've read one or two things about the place, the hotels and everything. But we've been reassured that side of things will be fine. And at the end of the day it's a football match that we've got to go there and try to win.' Whatever was to confront Shearer on the long and twisting World Cup road, he was forever optimistic. Even when a crippling leg and ankle break plus ripped ligaments put him out for six months, he was confidently predicting that England would make it through their final two qualifying games for France without him, and that he would be back in time to fulfil his destiny to be World Cup top scorer.

Shearer looked every inch England's leader. He set the tone with his first major interview on duty under Hoddle. The most deadly marksman of Euro 96 was in no doubt about the outcome of a qualifying group that many viewed as potentially hazardous. 'We have proved we can live with the best, now we have to show we can beat the best.' A millionaire at 25, he craved silverware at the highest level to go with his expanding bank balance. 'We have shown we can match the top sides, that was perhaps the most positive thing to come out of the disappointment of losing in the semi-finals of the European Championships. But now we have to win something. As yet we have nothing to show for our improvement. But the build-up to putting that right began on Sunday evening when we all reported to a new manager and a brand new challenge. What happened in the summer made us realize we are good enough. We proved that. Just a missed penalty kick was all that stood between us and glory. Because all of us believed, had we beaten Germany, we would have gone on to win the Championship. Now after that, we definitely feel we can go on from that. It has whetted everybody's appetite. The World Cup is the big one, and we are ready.'

Shearer had plundered ten goals from 28 appearances for England, after going 12 games without one before the goals flowed again in Euro 96. He had yet to score for England away from home; he wanted to rectify that as soon as possible. 'That's not my fault. We haven't played too many games outside of Wembley! But I'm aware of the expectations. It doesn't add to the pressure. I feel just the same way about myself now as I did when I went on the run without scoring. Big money moves and glory headlines don't affect me. If you start believing everything that's said or written about you, you'd end up round the twist. If the goals continue to come along, that's great. If they don't, it certainly won't be for want of trying. And I always give 100 per cent in every match I play. I can say, hand on heart, that my confidence has never changed from the very first match I failed to score in, until the last game, against the Germans.'

Hoddle rated Shearer so highly, acclaiming the England team as the envy of the world for having him in their side. He nominated Shearer second to Brazilian striker Ronaldo and ahead of George Weah in a poll of 120 national coaches voting for FIFA's official World Footballer of the Year. Shearer eventually came third. Hoddle said: 'He is a formidable force. Every manager in Europe, even the world – with the possible exception of the Brazilian coach, because he has quite a few good players himself – would want him. We are the envy of every other country. Alan does not have the same individual ability or score such spectacular goals (as Weah and Ronaldo), but he knows what he's good at and his work for the team is exceptional. He channels so much energy into his effort for the team and offers more than those two when it comes to scoring because he can score from any angle. He will need another two years probably before he reaches his absolute peak and then you are talking about true world class.'

The awards led Hoddle to recall the day he first set eyes on what he thought was a beach bum trying to flog necklaces, garbed in African robes – it turned out to be George Weah. Hoddle was a player with Monaco when Weah arrived as an unknown. Hoddle reminisced: 'Mark Hateley and I arrived at the training ground and there was this huge guy dressed in African robes with a paper bag under his arm. We automatically thought he was someone up from the beaches trying to sell necklaces or bracelets until he walked into the dressing room and took his boots out of the bag. It's always the same when a stranger enters the dressing room, everyone is a bit wary, but you could see from looking at him that he was a magnificent athlete. We did the usual session and then finished with a full-scale match, the first team versus the reserves. George was playing for us. He hadn't shown that much in the session and didn't get a kick for 15 minutes. Then the ball was played up to him, 30 yards out with his back to goal. Suddenly he took your breath away. He turned two defenders, dummied to shoot, put the goalkeeper on the floor and, as calm as you like, rolled the ball in. There was no celebration, just this huge smile lighting up his face. I looked at Mark and knew we were thinking the same: "this is some player". Although he had scored a brilliant goal, he didn't get another touch until just before half-time when he picked up the ball in his own half. I was in space and screaming at him to pass. But he only had one thought in his head; he left two defenders for dead with sheer pace, then from 35 yards out he pulled back his right foot and the ball screamed into the top corner of the net. Unbelievable! I stood there shouting "pass it, pass it … oh, great goal!" There he was, two touches, two goals, and we all knew he was a bit special.'

Hoddle's eulogy on Shearer was sure to answer any doubt about who he sees as England's long-term captain. 'He works so hard, he's not afraid to put himself around physically and won't be intimidated by aggressive tactics. However, he's also a very clever player who is capable of understanding tactical instructions and then carrying them out, even if it means defensive duties. He's not just after the glory of scoring goals. You see him running to the wings, demanding the ball, searching for space, especially down the right where he crosses the ball in as good as any winger in the game. Hoddle added: 'I'd have loved to have played with him. Many people forget he has suffered setbacks and responded. Look at the build up to the European Championships when his place in the team was being questioned because he hadn't scored for some time. His answer was to finish as top scorer. That's mental strength, that's character. Don't forget, he's returned from a serious knee ligament injury and then two hernia operations in the last seven months. It's incredible really because it hasn't affected him and again it shows his mental strength.'

It wasn't long before Shearer was counting the currency value of the captaincy of England. His earning potential soared to a potential career total of £30m. Braun, the shaver company, joined Umbro, Lucozade and Jaguar as his blue-chip sponsors; the combined value of these to Shearer is £5m. Two further sponsors were being sought – only respected major companies need apply. The £15m striker was inundated with offers but he prefers to work with just a select band of sponsors. 'I prefer that to having my name splashed everywhere. I can't do much about people using my picture or my name but I prefer a handful rather than doing something different every week. They're all big companies, Braun, Jaguar and all well-named companies who don't need any introducing.' Braun's deal was part of their £10m sponsorship of the 1998 World Cup. As such, it represented an act of faith in the England team. 'My job is on the line if England don't qualify,' the company's UK brand manager said.

Southgate, Ince, Pearce, and Adams had been the other contenders for the England captaincy. Adams was England captain in Euro 96, and was disappointed not to have heard from Hoddle when it was announced that Shearer was succeeding him. But Adams was out injured and not on the trip to Moldova. Moreover, he had confessed to alcoholism and wasn't the easiest person to reach, as Hoddle explained. It was overcooked in the media as 'an amazing omission' by Hoddle not to keep a check on key players.

Adams was one of England's heroes in the European Championships; a lionheart in defence, braving a knee injury that subsequently needed a further cartilage operation. However, he confessed he went on a drinking spree after England's semi-final defeat by Germany, and had been in rehabilitation ever since.

When Ince was selected for leadership against Mexico because both Shearer and Adams were out injured, he had a private chat with Hoddle. Ince said: 'He told me I was close to being the captain of England but with Alan Shearer being in the country all the time, he thought he'd be best. It was no problem, Alan has the right image, he's a great player and a great advertisement for English football, so I wasn't too disappointed.' Hoddle said of Ince: 'He's shown great leadership qualities in his character, certainly since I've been involved, on the pitch. He's learned quite a lot by going abroad and playing. He's added to his game and he's added to himself as a person as well. That happens when you change your environment. When you're out somewhere on your own for a lot of the time, you learn certain things about yourself. All that comes into being a good captain.'

Hoddle's choice of Shearer as captain enhanced the profile of the most marketable figure in the English game, a clean-living family man without a hint of scandal, a throwback to old-fashioned sporting heroes. From his rise at Southampton, through Blackburn to his goal-scoring triumphs at Euro 96 and his Messianic homecoming to Tyneside to captain of England, his attitude never wavered. 'I'll never change. I might change when I get out on the pitch and that's because I want to be a winner so much. But the Alan Shearer you see off the pitch is what you get. I certainly don't change when I'm with other people, or with my family.'

CHAPTER FOUR

March on Moldova

Moldova v England, Kishinev, 1 September 1996

Well, they said Glenn Hoddle was too 'nice' to be an England coach. Now we would find out. England's last competitive away game – San Marino in Bologna, in November 1993 – had been under Graham Taylor, when a 7–1 scoreline proved irrelevant in their attempt to qualify for the 1994 World Cup after the 2–0 defeat in Holland a month earlier. Taylor's successor, Terry Venables, had taken England teams to Dublin, Norway and the Far East but as he had wanted to familiarize his team with Wembley to maximize home advantage in Euro 96, the players had had little experience of away games in difficult environments. Before the game with Moldova in Kishinev, Hoddle stressed: 'The major thing is that we've played at Wembley every single game and now we face a very difficult place to go and play – just the venue alone. The players have got to perform in front of a crowd that can be quite intimidating, so there is going to be a different mental approach. We have to be more focused in what we do.'

Moldova was a fascinating country, its capital Kishinev prettier than anyone had expected. Poverty and depravation were everywhere. Alan Shearer's estimated £15 million worth on the transfer market accounted for the entire gross national product of a country where the average wage is £26 a week, compared to Shearer's £30,000 a week. Everyone was appalled to learn of the 200 children, aged between three and sixteen, from the Casa de Coppii orphanage who were dying from extreme cold, malnutrition and neglect. An emergency appeal was launched by the European Children's Trust to raise around £40,000 to keep it running. This was backed by Paul Gascoigne, who leant his name to the cause.

Back on the football front, Shearer believed the summer's team spirit would be invaluable. He talked endlessly about the atmosphere in the dressing room after the European Championship games, describing it as 'something I'll never forget'. He explained: 'The laughs, the jokes, how well we all got on … I hope we can carry on that team spirit. You had to be in the camp to fully appreciate it. We all looked out for each other; whoever scored, all of us scored, whoever made a mistake, we all made the mistake. That's the way it's got to be.'

Shearer was on the prowl for his first England goal away from Wembley. Yet he insisted: 'It doesn't matter to me where I score and once you get out onto a football pitch, you rarely feel you're at home or away. There are goalposts at either end and it's green.'

Gascoigne was unable to train at the start of the week after suffering a reaction to the Achilles problem which dogged him in pre-season, but he soon showed he was back to full fitness. Batty, recalled by Hoddle after more than a year in the international wilderness, was making rapid strides in his recovery from injury. At first Hoddle rated him '60–40 in his favour', but the coach relied as heavily on the player's will and commitment as the daily medical bulletins from his staff. Hoddle protected Batty with limited training and Ince and Sheringham were similarly nursed through.

The hand of 'Hod' was wrapped protectively around the shoulders of young David Beckham. The new England coach had sat beside the precocious Manchester United star at Bisham Abbey for his first massive media inquisition. It is always a momentous task for any England debutant, particularly one of such tender years as Beckham. He was made a special case. Hoddle monitored the session but he only had to interrupt once to quietly but firmly remind the country's leading football writers to concentrate on the match in Moldova instead of prying so relentlessly into Beckham's personality. The youngster, though still clearly star-struck by his new environment, came across as level-headed, thoughtful, enthusiastic and ready for the challenge. There was even a touch of humour. When Beckham picked out Hoddle as the player he most admired, the England boss smiled: 'He's learning fast.' Surely, that guaranteed him his debut!

The presence of team-mates Pallister and especially room-mate Gary Neville, who made his own England debut at 20, was a big help to Beckham. 'I've always been good friends with Gary. I was pleased to be able to come down with them because they helped me a lot with my nerves, telling me what was going to happen and what to look forward to.'

When Gascoigne was interviewed, he said that he could see Beckham emerging quickly, but he applauded it, rather than feared it. 'It's a big thrill to see the young lads coming through. I was 18 when I first started playing for the England sides, but I was 21 or 22 before I broke into the full England team. There were senior players like Terry Butcher, Bryan Robson and Chris Waddle to tell you to relax and enjoy it. They were ready to pass on their experience to the young kids.'

Gazza had instantly taken to the new man in charge. 'I nearly had the chance to play with Glenn Hoddle at Spurs. I'm pleased that his ideas on the game are similar to Terry Venables'. I enjoy the way he wants to play football.'

Neville Southall backed England to get it right where Wales had gone so badly wrong. He was in the Welsh team that crashed to a shock 3–2 defeat in Kishinev in October 1994, virtually ending their Euro 96 qualification hopes. While Southall warned England they would not find the drab surrounds of downtown Kishinev a bundle of fun, he was equally convinced that Hoddle's reign as England boss would begin with three points. Wales' nightmare trip saw their bags go missing at the airport and the players staying in a dreadful, cockroach-infested hotel. From then on it all went downhill pretty quickly. Southall felt the miserable conditions had played their part. 'It was a bit unnerving, but you can't expect everywhere to measure up to what you are used to at home or in other places in Europe. I don't think football teams get very affected by things like that. They just want to get on with the game, then get home. Moldova is one of those places you want to be in and out of as quickly as possible, but with all these new countries coming into international football, you just have to learn to adapt. It's not a place I would hurry back to, but they are all part of the world game now and you have to be as professional as possible in all circumstances. I expect England to do that.' Wales' problems were compounded by the off-field troubles; the FA planned not to make the same mistakes. FA press officer Steve Double was part of a fact-finding delegation which flew out at the start of the year to make sure of the best preparation possible. 'Glenn and his players are staying in the best hotel in Kishinev, and the Under-21s are in the next best,' said Double. 'We think most of the food out there should be fine, but we're taking out some fresh vegetables, because they're in short supply, plus things like salad dressing, baked beans and breakfast cereals. I think we've realized the possible pitfalls. We're aware of the difficulties Wales faced and we're determined to avoid them as much as we can.'

It would certainly be a sober experience. Hoddle would not tolerate any repeat of the drinking antics and Mile High Club frolics that blighted England's build-up to Euro 96. He quietly but firmly issued a strict code of conduct. He said: 'It's no different than what I've done at every club I've been with. We've had a light chat about it. In many respects, it's been made a little bit easier for me because it's a lesson learned, isn't it? So that's virtually what we've been saying to the boys.' The FA expected Hoddle to take a hard line if there was any repeat of the high jinks on the flight bringing the squad back from the Far East tour, when the airline claimed £5,000 in damages to their Club Class cabin.

But Hoddle wanted to retain the team spirit of Euro 96. 'It's the start of a new campaign but we would be going down the wrong road if we didn't use what happened in the summer. They should have it in the forefront of their minds, to be nice and positive, confident about going out and winning football matches. It shouldn't be a case of "that was the European Championships and now it's altogether a fresh start".'

Just 24 hours before Hoddle's opening World Cup tie, another of Gascoigne's practical jokes backfired. I was part of the larger than usual media corps that travelled to watch the Under-21s because there was nothing else to do. When it started to rain the England players watched youngsters scamper over a wall for shelter in the only covered area – the press box – before joining them. As Ince scaled the wall, Gazza pulled down his blue shorts to expose a bare bottom. The picture ended up on the back pages of the Sunday tabloids. Hoddle left it until after the World Cup tie before making any comment. While the England coach let off the Rangers star with a warning, he made it clear he would not tolerate such pranks in future. I felt Hoddle was being earnest, even sincere, but in reality it would be virtually impossible to find the right punishment for such a daft prank. Hoddle said: 'It was a joke between players and you get that when you're away. It happened when we were climbing over a wall to get away from the rain. I climbed over – but I suppose no-one was going to pull my trousers down! It's a trivial thing. We'll have a chat about it, but it won't be anything heavier than that.' Graham Kelly made it plain that Hoddle would be left to deal with the situation in his own way.

Gascoigne went some way to redeeming his reputation by scoring England's second goal of the qualifier. Ironically it was Ince who set it up for him, with another example of his determined, aggressive football. The game ended in a highly satisfying 3–0 win.

Beckham produced a professional, sound rather than spectacular, debut but did enough to retain his place; the new captain collected his first England away goal as promised, although he should have scored two; and Nicky Barmby worked hard, making and scoring the other goal. You couldn't have asked for anything more from Sheringham's late replacement. Seaman took one difficult bouncing shot with ease; Gary Neville was a tireless right wing-back; Hinchcliffe gave the team balance; Pearce was reasonably solid on the left side of the three-man central defence; Ince was the mainstay of the midfield; Pallister became stronger as the game progressed; and Southgate needed to concentrate a touch more and was liable to an error or two, but was generally reliable in defence. Of the subs, Le Tissier showed a few neat tricks but in the little time he had, he kept it relatively simple and never wasted his possession, while Batty moved into midfield as if he'd been there throughout the entire game.

It wasn't a scintillating, inspiring performance, but it was a job well done considering how many times England teams in the recent past have fluffed their lines horribly on foreign fields at vital times. For that reason alone there was every reason for all the back slapping and handshakes that greeted the end of Hoddle's first match in charge.

It had been a hesitant start by England, particularly in defence. Moldova illustrated that they were capable of a shock when after 14 minutes Mitereu squandered a good opportunity. Happily, England's nerves were settled by Barmby's goal eight minutes later. Hinchcliffe's cross to the far wing was whipped back by Gary Neville for the ex-Spurs and Middlesbrough striker to score from close range with a simple side-foot. Two minutes later another former Spurs player gave Hoddle a two-goal cushion, Gazza simply looping his header over the keeper after the impressive Ince had stretched to meet Barmby's cross.

England should have had a penalty before half-time but the Finnish referee, Koho, failed to spot Shearer being pulled down by his shirt. The new England captain, still suffering the frustration of that decision, was then guilty of a glaring miss when he scooped his shot over the bar after Ince's square free-kick had been moved on sweetly by Gazza and Barmby. However, he made amends on the hour. After Southgate's frantic clearance was headed on by Neville, defender Secu made a mess of an interception, and Shearer was able to poke the ball over the line.

But then bad memories came flooding back for Pearce when the ball caught his arm and the referee awarded a penalty even though it was an obvious unintentional handball. Justice was done, however. as Testimitanu struck the underside of the bar.

Hoddle's analysis of the game centred on the result rather than the performance. 'Our attitude had to be just right and it was. There were a few banana skins out there we had to avoid. We would have settled for that score before the match because we knew it was potentially going to be a difficult tie. It has put us ahead of the game. Other nations in our group must come here now, and in conditions that won't be so favourable. They'll have to play in the winter when it will be very cold, so of course I'm very pleased that we have got off to this kind of start. It wasn't easy and after an unsteady start we settled down and did well. They're no San Marino, no Faroe Islands. They're better than that and somewhere along the line I feel they might just trip someone up. I hope they do.'

Hoddle gave a broad smile as he suggested that if the grass had been cut, as the Moldovans assured him it was, 'then they must have used scissors'. Hoddle pointed out that with such long grass it was always going to be difficult to pass the ball how he wanted. Hoddle said: 'We had to abandon that to a certain degree. The grass didn't allow us to play at the tempo we wanted. We wanted to get into midfield quickly, but sometimes when people were available the lads had to take an extra touch to get it out from under their feet. By then it had closed up.'

Shearer was equally satisfied: 'We hadn't played together, so this team needed to get used to one another. It took a while, but after that we settled down nicely. Considering it was such a diabolical pitch, we did well. It was very bumpy and the grass was too long and that meant it took two or three touches to control the ball. It was also the reason why we had to play so slowly, we couldn't get our one-touch going. But it was a great feeling for me in my first international as captain to score, and for England to win the match.'

Hoddle felt that the foundations were there to build a far more impressive side. 'There's a lot there to be improved upon. But the big plus for me was that when we got into the penalty area we always looked as if we were going to score; there's a real cutting edge there. That's the exciting thing with Alan Shearer in your side, and we've got plenty more who will get us goals. We had big Les [Ferdinand] on the side; he didn't come on but he's going to shape up at some point, while Teddy [Sheringham] dropped out at the last minute. And from midfield we've got players – Gascoigne and Beckham obviously, Le Tissier who came on, and there's McManaman as well – who are all capable of scoring goals. To have that cutting edge sometimes is the difference between winning and losing at international level.'

Hoddle had immediately shown that he was his own man, redistributing the Venables inheritance far more radically than injuries demanded and further demonstrating with his post-match criticism of the performance that he would not settle for the easy option. Ince rather than Gascoigne was the heartbeat of the side, while Hinchcliffe and Gary Neville were effective as wing-backs. He had been bold to blood Beckham from the start.

'David needed 10 or 15 minutes to settle and then started to influence the game,' said Hoddle. 'He was one who was affected with his passing, but he adapted to that and turned his game round, which is good to see a youngster do. I wanted to give him the 90 minutes, he's going to learn more and more as time goes on. He was always in the forefront of my mind and it was probably best for him to come into this type of game. He will gain a lot of experience from playing away from home under these conditions. He wasn't overawed at all and he's further down the line now. Andy worked extremely hard and we didn't perhaps get enough ball out to him, but when we did get in behind, he put in some lovely quality balls. We're disappointed we didn't pick up a couple of goals from corners because his delivery was special at times.'

Hoddle looked ahead to the Polish game, knowing another win would take command of the group. 'It's all about marrying performances with results. Sometimes you can play well and draw. That would have been a bad result for us. This way we go into the Wembley game with a boost and a positive stride. It's not so long ago I was performing there myself, so it's not so daunting as some might imagine to go back as coach.'

Gareth Southgate accepted that a few wrinkles had to be ironed out. 'The important thing was the win, because it could have been a graveyard for us. Perhaps it was the sort of game that in the past we might have slipped up in. We were conscious of the necessity of coming back with the three points and while the performance wasn't great, we can improve. Everybody would say that we could have played a lot better but the pitch wasn't the greatest and I think the important thing was that we kept a clean sheet – just about – and got the three points. We started a bit slowly. We didn't know quite what to expect and I'm sure the other teams in the group will go out there and have very difficult games. They pushed three players on to Gary Pallister, Stuart Pearce and myself at the back and that didn't allow us to play the ball out as we would have liked. But we realized that, showed we were adaptable and changed to suit the situation.'

Gazza's state of mind as much as his physical state began to worry Hoddle again. The Rangers man revealed that he feared for his life after a maniac had threatened to slit his throat in Glasgow. Gazza had upset Catholics with his flute imitation after scoring his first goal for Protestant club Glasgow Rangers. Gazza had been driving home from training when he stopped at traffic lights. A car pulled up alongside and a man wound down his window. At first he was talking normally, just politely warning Gazza 'You can't do that sort of thing in Glasgow, Gazza.' Gazza replied, 'Yes, I know … I shouldn't have done it.' When Gazza thought the conversation was over, the man leaned menacingly out of the window and said 'If you do it again, I'll find you and cut your f------ throat.' Gazza says he 'shat himself', the threat terrified him.

Hoddle also planned to ring a few managers to politely ask: 'What's going on?'

He returned from Poland after watching his next World Cup opponents lose 2–0 to Germany to find that England crocks were suddenly as fit as fiddles just days later! McManaman and Fowler's back problems were too severe for them even to contemplate flying to Moldova with the rest of the squad, let alone train or play. But three days later, there they were, bounding about at Coventry, helping Liverpool to a 1–0 win. Howey's broken toe had required him to be sent home from England training early, but it was not too bad to keep him out of Newcastle's 2–1 win at Sunderland. And Anderton, withdrawn early from the squad with what some claimed was a season-threatening recurrence of his groin problem, was straight back into Premiership action with Tottenham.

Hoddle kept his thoughts to himself until he had time to clarify the situation, but he felt badly let down in his first trial of strength with the clubs. The FA considered a rule change, preventing a player from playing for his club for up to six or seven days after he had missed an England game through injury. Legislation had been introduced under Graham Taylor requiring a player to report for inspection by the England medical team, rather than the old system of relying on a club doctor's sick-note, but this would be a further step.

Sheringham pulled a thigh muscle during training at Bisham Abbey, while Arsenal lost Seaman to a hamstring injury suffered in the win in Kishinev. Ian Walker damaged his back while warming up with the squad in Moldova. That, argued the clubs, was why some managers were reluctant to take any risks with niggles and strains.

William Hill made England joint sixth favourites with Holland to win the World Cup, at 14–1, with holders Brazil the 5–1 top tip.

Moldova (0) 0 England (2) 3
Seaman, G Neville, Pearce, Ince, Pallister, Southgate, Beckham, Gascoigne, Shearer (capt), Barmby, Hinchcliffe

	P	W	D	L	F	A	Pts
England	1	1	0	0	3	0	3
Georgia	0	0	0	0	0	0	0
Italy	0	0	0	0	0	0	0
Moldova	0	0	0	0	0	0	0
Poland	0	0	0	0	0	0	0

CHAPTER FIVE

Football's Coming Home

England prepare for the visit of Poland, October 1996

One player who missed out on the Moldova match but who was in outstanding league form with Arsenal, was Paul Merson. Hoddle saw him score a brilliant goal in Cologne the night before announcing the squad for the Poland game and, in the absence of the injury-hit Anderton and Stone, found a place for him.

Merson deserved recognition for both his bravery and ability. He had won the last of his 14 caps in Venables' second game against Greece in May 1994, six months before his personal problems became painfully public. In his bleakest hour he had even contemplated suicide. 'My life was such torment that I actually felt like killing myself,' Merson recalled. But after undergoing rehabilitation for his addictions, he returned leaner, meaner and back to his gifted best. The FA felt sympathy, not anger, for the first England international to own up to alcohol and drug addiction. They saw a kid who had gone badly off the rails and who needed help. Had the FA banned him, then I know it would have broken him.

Merson knows that there are many more alcoholics out there playing Premiership football who need to find the courage to confess and change their lives. He fights his addictions every single day, from his first waking minutes. He tells himself over and over again 'I will stay clean of drugs, I will stay clean of drink and I will stay clean of gambling.' It is a constant war within himself. There have been times when he has been close to relapse. Who wouldn't be?

It was in the Warwick Room of the Park Court Hotel, Lancaster Gate that the Arsenal forward had cried as he admitted his destructive addictions to drinking, gambling and cocaine – and pledged to beat them. Twenty-two months later, Hoddle sat in the same room and hailed the 28-year-old's crusade to beat his problems.

Merson had set himself the England target in that emotional press conference in November 1994. Hoddle said: 'People need goals when they're going through a bad time in life, obviously. I'm delighted that he's put it right. It's a great example for people who are maybe not in the public eye but are going through problems similar to what Paul had. It's all credit to the lad and all credit to the people who stood by him and gave him help – people who are not even now at Arsenal Football Club. Bruce [Rioch] and Stewart [Houston] should be applauded for that. I'm not sure if you're ever over something like that but he's certainly dealing with it and he's a great example to others with the same problem. It takes a lot to come out and say these things. Like Tony [Adams] has come out now, afterwards you're not living a lie any more. It was probably the start of his rehabilitation when he did that. He's shown a lot of professionalism, not just on the pitch, but off it.'

Merson had to make another apology to his long-suffering wife Lorraine – but she could not have been more delighted. His England call-up meant the cancellation of a Concorde trip to New York. Merson said: 'She's taken the news well because she knows how brilliant this is for me. We can always go to New York another time, but getting called up for England is something special – something I really didn't expect. I've played for England 14 times before but just being named in the squad now gives me a better feeling even than when I was told I was actually playing in all those other games. I've got my life in perspective now because I've had to win bigger battles than just the ones in a football career. Don't say that this completes my rehabilitation from all those problems, because it doesn't. That will never be complete – it is literally one day at a time for me now because you can slip back at any time. I know the first drink or the first bet that I have will probably finish me now. But I've got a lot of people to thank – Arsenal, my counsellors, the FA and everybody who stood by me. But most of all Lorraine, who has been just a tower of strength.'

He recalled the last time he played for England, just over two years ago. 'I was in a bad way. My head had gone. We beat Greece 5–0 but I wasn't even good enough on the night to have got into their team. It has been a long road back and I've had my ups and downs, which I was told to expect. It was good enough to be playing well again for Arsenal, but this is the real icing on the cake. It's another milestone for me.'

Merson's Arsenal team-mate, Tony Adams, was still struggling for full fitness after a knee injury and that, rather than his self-confessed drink problem, was the explanation for his continued omission from the squad for the Poland game. There was a media fuss that the England coach had not contacted Adams after he admitted his drink problems. In fact, Hoddle spoke to Adams the night before he announced the squad. 'We've chatted about the football front and there's no problem. I just felt he hadn't had enough senior games – he's not played 90 minutes yet. This fixture has come a little too soon for him. I think he's quite pleased that he hasn't been put under more pressure to play a little bit too quickly, and perhaps set himself back. The other thing about his drink problem, that's something you don't speak about over the phone. A lot's been happening at Arsenal and I will be sitting down with him face to face at some stage. A 100 per cent fit Tony Adams is going to be in the forefront of my mind. There are opportunities for others to come in and show me what they can do but Tony, with his experience, will always be in my mind.'

The first youngster to benefit from Adams' absence was 22-year-old Dominic Matteo of Liverpool, brilliantly converted from left-back to sweeper-cumplaymaker by Roy Evans. Hoddle said: 'This kid's been in superb form. I've seen him three times this season, John Gorman's seen him three times. Every scout we've sent to watch him has come back with nothing less than nine out of ten. The lad knows he's got to prove it in more than eight or nine games. But he's 22, and we keep saying, can we find footballers from the back who can defend and also play with the ball as well? This lad can certainly play with the ball.' Matteo thought Evans had been coerced into a practical joke by his Liverpool team-mates when his club boss announced his England call-up. 'I couldn't believe it. I'm made up. It's a big surprise, really. A few of the lads were messing about and joking about it earlier in the week, but it came as a bit of a shock and I suppose now I've got to get on with it.'

Hoddle had very nearly been left short in Kishinev, so he named an intriguing eight-man standby panel including Ian Wright, who had won the last of his 20 caps against Romania at Wembley in October 1994. Hoddle was convinced that he was still among the country's top marksmen. Also on the list were Blackburn's Jason Wilcox and Tim Flowers, Liverpool's Jamie Redknapp, who had yet to start a game at Anfield that season since being injured during Euro 96, Newcastle's Rob Lee and Steve Howey and Villa's Mark Draper and Alan Wright.

Hoddle travelled to Tyneside at the end of September to watch Newcastle's 4–3 win over Villa and see the Ferdinand-Shearer partnership. A deadly first half double from Ferdinand was followed by a third goal from Shearer. The goals from Ferdinand underlined his conviction that he could partner Shearer for England. Shearer was adamant that he and his Newcastle striking partner were the best in the business. Shearer said: 'We have both been playing reasonably well and have both been scoring goals. That's all we can do. You can't ask for any more. The partnership is improving with every game. Les sets me up, I set him up, so it's going all right. Now it's up to the England manager. Only he can decide whether to play us. I remember Matt Le Tissier being on fire during our time at Southampton. Well, Les is certainly on fire now. He is playing really well and is scoring goals. I believe the partnership which a lot of people said wouldn't work is improving after every game together.'

If Hoddle harboured any doubts, a glowing reference to the then standing of the Tyneside duo was proffered by Gareth Southgate, who had suffered at the hands of the Newcastle stars. Southgate was glad he did not have to face the prolific pair every week. 'I know all about Shearer and Ferdinand from the England training sessions. But knowing about them and trying to stop them are two completely different things. They are both very powerful – the best I have faced this season. They have everything and they compare with anything I have experienced as a defender. If it's not Ferdinand coming at you, it's Shearer. Once they have the experience of playing together for a decent period of time and click fully, they will be virtually unstoppable. We had the best defence in the league before the game against Newcastle. Now look at what happened. Les really looks the part. He is outstanding, in fact they both are.'

Hoddle was concerned by Gascoigne's past indiscretions. The afternoon before England's vital World Cup tie with Belgium in 1990, Gazza had been found playing a vigorous game of tennis with a hotel guest. In Norway three years later he made a visit to a sauna on the morning of the match to shed those excess pounds. It made him so weak that he was drained for the big match. Even Venables, a manager for whom Gascoigne would do anything, was forced to pull him out of training for fear of burnout. Hoddle warned him to stop boozing and grow up if he wanted to be remembered as one of England's all-time greats. The advice came on the day his latest drinking exploits were exposed in a television programme. Hoddle said: 'He is a married man now with a baby son. He should look at the little child and realize a baby needs carefully looking after. It's special. When you get to 30, so does your body. You have to take care of it. Do things properly. Don't abuse it. And I include drinking when I say that.'

Hoddle covered a wide range of subjects in his chat with Gazza. 'I have spoken to Paul about a lot of things and get the impression he wants to change his life. I know what has been said about his drinking, but I am not interested in the Paul Gascoigne before me. I'm more concerned about Paul Gascoigne now. I know people have talked about his boozing, but I can only take him on face value.' Hoddle continued: 'There has been a "Grim Reaper" around Paul for too long. Now there is no need for him. Paul can pull the curtains back on a whole new career. When you get to his age, if you have skill, life should get easier, not harder, provided that you look after yourself and stay free from injury. Ask Ray Wilkins and Gordon Strachan. I have told Paul that he has reached an important stage of his career. When you move into the thirties, so much can happen. He is the kind of player who can dominate matches, with knowledge, skill and ability. Gazza should get up every morning and feel ready to take on the world.'

Hoddle faced the awesome task of trying to harness England's greatest talent. 'I have now spoken to Gazza about what he wants. And what I find is a person with wonderful skill, good attitude, and who is also a caring person. Maybe it's taken him this far in his career to realize how good he is. He can play on longer than he thinks he can. Go on until he's 35. This World Cup and even another. In Moldova he was not 100 per cent fit, but he was worth the gamble because of his ability. We got away with it. Now he's leaner, fitter, and producing outstanding football for Rangers. I didn't get the chance to get to know him in Moldova but we've talked this time. And I've had my eyes opened. He wants to succeed and I'm very impressed. He hasn't won anything with England and that hurts him. Just two semi-finals. That's all he has appeared in. But time is not running out for him when you have that kind of ability. But he must look after himself. I believe this World Cup will be great for him. He knows the country is behind him, so am I. Everyone is. However, he must keep himself on an even keel and realize he is a footballer and a family man. I've loved watching Gazza the player. Now I know the man, I like what I see. He has a lot more to offer than just the image that people see. So many have made their own impression. I know what mine is.'

Hoddle did not want England's efforts to be undermined by players picking up needless cautions. He spoke about the need for restraint to Gascoigne and Pearce, who was booked, with Ince, in Moldova. But Hoddle also believed the emphasis on stricter refereeing would allow the flair players to flourish. 'One good thing about the rule changes is that it's taking man-for-man marking out of the game. We won't see players like Claudio Gentile again. You can't get away with some of the things they did in the first ten minutes of the game. So this gives a chance for the technical players, like Gazza and Matt Le Tissier, to benefit. But Paul has got to calm himself down when the opposition have got the ball, so he doesn't get caught up in the wrong scenario.'

Ince had become a fixture in the England side. Glance down at his boots and you see his role summed up in gold lettering. 'The Guvnor' is more than just a nickname; the branding is actually emblazoned in gold on the tongue of his Adidas boots. Ince's name goes on the team sheet as one of the few virtually automatic selections. But Ince already had one caution and faced an automatic ban if he picked up a second. 'If that happens so be it,' he said. 'There's no way I'll change the way I play even if it means another card. It won't even be something I'll be thinking about. Making sure England win is more important. I have learned to control myself, but occasionally things do go on and you react in the heat of the moment. Things are said, aimed at you, there is a fair amount of verbals, not the racial stuff, but industrial language. But I'll still play it my way. I can walk away from most of the aggro now and frankly if you want to be the player people expect you to be, you just have to.' He walks a tightrope, because he is so committed. 'I can't change,' he went on. 'And really I don't want to. But there are always things being shouted at you. Once I would have turned round and wanted to fight. Now I know there is no use behaving like a lunatic. I try not to get wound up. But that doesn't mean to say it prevents me from sticking my foot in. I'm not nasty. But I play a certain way. To win.' In his role in front of the back players, Ince has become England's destroyer – hunting down the ball, winning it, totally involved, creative when he has the chance. He also has the ability to get forward and the skill to be an incisive link man.

Hoddle proudly anticipated his Wembley managerial baptism with a message for every England fan ... back the England boys just like you did in Euro 96. He wasn't worried about his own ovation as the new England boss, he wanted the crowd roaring and singing 'Football's Coming Home'. 'We've got to continue that with the crowd and use that as a major advantage. To win the group we've probably got to take home advantage and the crowd have got to be part of that. I just hope they can recreate the atmosphere of the summer. There's always a good atmosphere in night games anyway, and if we can get the crowd on board they can play a big part in whether we perform well and get the results we need at home. I know there are expectations there. I'm more concerned that they get behind the players than get behind me. But I'm hoping it will be a nice and positive reaction. That's the beauty of coming to Wembley to watch your country play.

They're all kicking the same way. When you go there in a Cup Final, half the stadium wants you to trip over.'

Poland, who had not won for 11 games, were likely to defend and seek a point that would echo their wrecking visit of 1973. Hoddle warned his players to beware of frustration – their own and the crowd's. 'Poland look to hit people on the break. They are a very disciplined, hard side. If we get the early start we're looking for, that might change the shape of the game. But a point will be a good result for them, away from home early in the group, and then they can have a go at making up the lost ground over there. If there's frustration, the players have got to deal with that. You want the supporters with you, but there comes a time in a game when, if it isn't going your way, you've got to be strong enough to switch off [from the crowd]. You almost have to cocoon yourself and keep focused on the things that are going to get yourself the result. That's why you need experienced players. If it happens, we've got to keep our nerve, keep playing and wait for the moment. At international level they don't come along as often as at club level.'

But Hoddle was brimming with confidence. 'The most pleasing thing in Moldova is that although we did not get enough quality time in the final third, and that was due to the pitch, whenever we were in there we looked to have the cutting edge to score goals. At this level that's where maybe the difference is. If you look at Euro 96 and the eight teams that qualified for the quarter-finals that's where maybe the tournament was won or lost. We have excellent players in the last third, not just one. We also have a lot of competition for places and the quality is not going to change whoever plays in the front positions. We have an array of talent who can score from all angles – from midfield as well as the strikers. There will be a side chosen that's going to look as if we're going to attack.'

Hoddle had the squad together for seven days to work on passing, movement and 'recovery' after the negatives of that passable win in Moldova, but he made a remarkable confession about the timescale before his own ideas and plan would really kick in. 'This won't really be a team of mine until six, seven or eight games down the line. It won't be the finished article tomorow night, but as long as I can see an improvement there, then I'll think we're on the right lines.'

Trying to alleviate the pressure on his players, he said: 'We have to be switched on mentally and be very positive in our approach, but we also have to be relaxed. If you're too uptight, you can't perform. The best teams in the world marry those two things together.'

For Hoddle's first game at Wembley as England manager, he would be given moral support from family, friends and Arsene Wenger, who was even staying in the same hotel as the Poles. Hoddle dined with Wenger that week – 'He owed me dinner', said Hoddle. He added with a smile: 'No-one was supposed to know he was staying at their hotel!'

Poland were portrayed as a team in disarray, just waiting to be mauled. Hoddle knew differently. Veteran coach Antoni Piechniczek, who steered the Poles to third place in the 1982 World Cup and also took them to Mexico four years later, had returned to the helm in June. But defeats at the hands of Russia and Germany, and a draw with the less than mighty Cyprus, had extended Poland's winless run to 12 matches. Piechniczek was hoping to guide his side to only their second win over England – the sole victory, in Katowice in 1973, helped cost Sir Alf Ramsey his job. Striker Andrzej Juskowiak, scorer of three UEFA Cup goals against Arsenal for Borussia Moenchengladbach, fellow frontman Wojchiech Kowalczyk of Spanish side Real Betis and Feyenoord midfielder Tomasz Ivan all refused to play again for the coach after rows. Piechniczek refused to back down, and instead opted for youth. He said: 'England are one of the best teams in Europe. They played some great football in the European Championship, especially against Holland, and while Glenn Hoddle is not Terry Venables he has many of the same players. The style of play hasn't changed much and, as far as I'm concerned, the crowd at Wembley will be England's 12th player, like the summer. That will make it difficult for us. But we didn't come here for a holiday, for an excursion around London. We came here to play and fight. We want to present England with a surprise and make life tough for them. We will be like a boxer, defending ourselves with two hands then looking to counter-attack when we get the chance.'

Playmaker Piotr Nowak suggested: 'There have been problems for us and this is a young side, but we must play our football, not just try to stop England. If we just try to defend our 18-yard box we cannot win. We respect England and know they are dangerous. I think all our players are a bit nervous of Wembley but we must also get forward. If we do that, we have a chance. We are worried about Shearer. He's so strong, can shoot from anywhere and we know we must be careful of him.' Piechniczek agreed: 'The England midfield is excellent, but Shearer is the scorer. Wherever he gets the ball, he is dangerous – he can score from any position. Only Spain stopped him from scoring in Euro 96 and any team who play England must fear him and them.'

Warzycha gave England an uncomfortable reminder of the 'headless chickens' night when they were slated by Taylor after a scare in Katowice in 1993. The striker warned: 'Midfield is where this match will be won or lost. Obviously the 'headless chickens' label was a statement by the England manager and I don't agree with it myself – Gascoigne and Ince are both fine players. But as far as we are concerned, they will need to be at their best at Wembley. Some of us watched the documentary about Gazza on TV the other night and there has been a bit of chatter about it among the squad in training. I played in the World Cup qualifier seven years ago which finished 0–0, a result that sent England to the Finals of Italia 90. But we hit the bar in the very last minute and could have qualified ourselves. And since then England have twice drawn 1–1 in Poland, scoring a late equalizer each time – and we are looking for some fortune of our own this time. England have three lions on their shirt – but we have a white eagle, and we take just as much inspiration from that.'

Most of the Polish side had no experience of Wembley. Former goalkeeping star Jan Tomaszewski, who defied England in 1973 and cost them a World Cup Final place said: 'I know that in all my career I never faced anything so terrifying. The noise came at me from all sides. If it is anything like that again, then some of the Polish team will find the occasion too much for them.'

CHAPTER SIX

A Wembley Baptism

England v Poland, Wembley, 9 October 1996

Four days before the England-Poland match, Fabrizio Ravanelli saved Italy as they scrambled a narrow 1-0 victory over England's next opponents, Georgia. The Italians were booed continually in the second half as the Perugia crowd lost patience. They struggled desperately as the second half wore on and were lucky to hold out for their narrow victory. Coach Arrigo Sacchi dismissed immediate calls to quit as outraged fans increased the clamour for his resignation. However, the result meant that England definitely needed to beat Poland to maintain the initiative over the Italians.

The Wembley tie didn't go according to plan. Fortunately, Hoddle was rescued by Alan Shearer, whose two goals, a devastating header and a wicked shot into the top corner, brought his impressive statistics to eight goals in his last seven internationals, adding up to 13 in 30 games for his country. His blistering drive for the second had brought Hoddle off his feet as England finally went ahead, but there was a serious expression on the new England coach's face as he left the scene of his inaugural Wembley game as England's boss.

Hoddle began with a more adventurous team than against Moldova, linking Ferdinand with Shearer. In the past Venables had opted for a split-striker system, the blueprint specifically drawn up to ensure that England were not overrun in midfield. In Hoddle's quest for goals, the England midfield against Poland looked stretched and the defence so shaky that the Poles were able to go into an early lead.

Southgate returned to the scene of his penalty miss against Germany as though the nightmares were still haunting him. He missed a cross from Tomasz Hajto in the sixth minute, inexplicably Gary Neville followed suit and Marek Citko, left unmarked, shot past a stranded Seaman. It could have been even worse when Southgate missed his kick and Pearce was left to edge the ball round the post. The majority of England fans in the 74,663 crowd were stunned into silence as Poland grabbed the initiative. Enter the England captain. First Beckham lofted a cross to test the keeper in the air, which paid dividends as Shearer bravely went in to beat Andrzej Wozniak. The Shearer–Ferdinand partnership then worked when it mattered most. When Shearer's shot was blocked, Ferdinand controlled the rebound with his midriff and laid it off for Shearer to let rip into the top corner.

Southgate settled his early nerves and began to look the influential player of the summer before going off injured five minutes into the second half. Then it was substitute Pallister's turn to have his wobbly moments.

Gascoigne found it tough to cover the wide gaps between defence and attack, particularly when England's attacks broke down. The frustrations were showing as the German referee seemed to have forgotten his yellow card. Finally Gascoigne almost took off his shirt to give it to an opponent who had just tried to rip it off his back. It brought a laugh, and a minute later Hajto finally received a yellow card for a foul on him.

A relieved Hoddle saluted Shearer: 'I said earlier in the week that Alan was the number one striker in Europe over the European Championships in the summer. And I know the goal in his mind is to become possibly the world's best – and he's definitely got the attributes to achieve that. They were two magnificent goals for different reasons. The second goal was something special, hit with terrific power, tremendous – one from the Bobby Charlton scrapbook.'

The unpretentious Shearer warned terrified opponents that he was working overtime to become an even more fearsome proposition. 'It's nice if the manager talks about me becoming the best striker in the business, but I'm only interested in being part of the best team in the world. I'm always learning and improving and I'm looking to get better in every aspect of my game. No-one can say they're the complete footballer and there's nothing I can do perfectly.'

Shearer's fearless attitude brought him his opening goal. 'I saw the keeper coming out of the corner of my eye and thought it was cut head and split eye time. But I wasn't going to pull out of it, and for some reason the keeper stopped and the ball ended up in the net. Scoring the second gave me a great feeling, but I don't rate that goal any higher than all the others. It doesn't matter whether it's from six yards or 30 – they don't count double from outside the box. It wasn't a vintage performance, but the result was all-important. We got off to a sloppy start, but the lads responded well and came back to take a grip. The atmosphere was tremendous and the fans really gave us a lift. As far as my goals are concerned, it is amazing how things go. For a spell at the start of my international career I couldn't put the ball away. Now everything is going really well.' Hoddle mentioned Shearer in the same breath as men who have won the World Cup for their countries – Paolo Rossi, Jurgen Klinsmann and Mario Kempes. Lineker also sprang to mind as the new England coach spelt out the importance of Shearer. Without Shearer, England have much less chance of winning the World Cup. Little wonder Hoddle looked to heavenly assistance and said: 'Alan, if he stays injury free, will always score goals and in many different ways: spectacular, tap-ins, headers. That's a major asset to have in any team, one that's to be respected and will be envied.'

Having observed Shearer and Lineker off the field as well as on it, I felt they shared an ideal temperament; Shearer never lost his self-belief or nerve when the goals dried up, nor does he go overboard when he is back on a roll. 'He has such a great temperament, he's so single-minded when it comes to goal-scoring,' said Hoddle. 'It doesn't matter if you're 5–0 up and coasting, or you're digging a result out from 1–0 down, if a chance comes, in his frame of mind nothing changes.'

Shearer has no weak side, he's strong in the air and on the ground and has pace enough to beat defenders. His off-the-field attributes persuaded Hoddle to make him his captain: 'His work rate is there for everyone to see; I saw him chase two lost causes into the corner. He didn't get the throw-in or corner but he put pressure on people. He does push himself to the limit. He commands instant respect from his own team-mates, his opponents and everyone in football. That makes the right chemistry for a captain. But you can't get any better way of leading on the pitch than by putting the ball in the back of the net. That's why we went for him as captain. There's all types of characters in football. Alan keeps his life on an even keel. He's always done that and I think he'll maintain that. Giving him the captaincy hasn't taken his goal-scoring gift away. Sometimes in cricket the opening batsman's given the captaincy and for some reason the runs stop. But this lad's continuing and it's worked out fine. He has every attribute. He's not even poor down one side like a lot of strikers. He will manufacture goals for himself and if he ever went abroad, I know he would be successful.'

However, Hoddle was furious with the catalogue of errors which presented Poland with the gift opportunity so early on. Hoddle said of the defending: 'For the first 20–25 minutes, we went out there with just an offensive head on. I don't know what the reason for that is and I can't put my finger on it. Possibly it was the euphoria of playing back at Wembley and the expectations – I don't know. But that was not a reflection on our performance and as a complete side we can defend better than that. When you're not defending and can't win the ball back as a team it's going to be unnerving. At times there was too much pressure on our back three. It was a sloppy goal to give away, a dreadful goal. We had some stern words at half-time and spoke about how we first of all had to win the ball back. But I thought very positively throughout, even after we went behind so early, because there was still a long way to go. But I said what I had to say in the dressing room. You keep your cool, that's when you earn your crust. And to give credit where it's due, we came back, turned it round and have got the three points. I always knew this was going to be a tough match. I feel this will be the toughest group to qualify from and I was delighted at overcoming this hurdle.'

Hoddle was convinced the basic strategy was right, though it was easily pulled out of shape with Southgate and Gary Neville having their most traumatic games in the back three. Most worrying was the way Ince was isolated and Gascoigne spent most of the match on the periphery. 'We have to get the shape right and then go hunting the ball as a team. We were hunting as individuals,' said Hoddle.

Ince emphasized that England were in the winning habit, even when not firing on all cylinders – and how crucial it was to take maximum points at all costs from the home games. He said: 'We know we didn't play that well, as was also the case in Moldova, and that when we re-assemble as a squad next month, there will be a lot of things to work on and improve. But we have got the points in the bag after overcoming, despite what some people might have been saying, a good Polish team, and are joint top of the group with everyone's spirits high. I believe we can also beat Italy and Moldova here and then it will be a case of trying to nick something from the away games.'

Ince also believed it was vital for England to keep the wins rolling along to maintain the newly-found esteem in which the side was held after Euro 96. 'Everyone respects us now – and if they don't they are stupid. I have spoken to my team-mates at Milan and one or two have said they couldn't believe how well England played in Euro 96. People are frightened of England now and us keeping on winning will make people continue to keep on looking up to us.'

Southgate insisted Euro 96 had not crossed his mind when he stepped out onto the Wembley pitch for the first time since that heart-breaking occasion in June. 'It was pleasing to go back and play there again but the events of the summer didn't really enter my head. People ask whether I had exorcised a few demons – but Wednesday was a completely different situation.'

Seaman felt that England had acquired an inner belief that they would come out on top. Seaman, whose fingertip save from Polish dangerman Piotr Nowak just before half-time proved to be crucial, said: 'We went a goal down early on but we didn't panic. It was a situation where a lot of sides might have then crumbled. We kept our calm and a few reassuring things were said. We showed a lot of character which is as important as the good football we are capable of.'

However, an overall poor performance had been masked by the Shearer factor. Gary Pallister said: 'Alan got us out of a bit of trouble with two great goals but then we know he is the best striker – certainly in Europe – if not the world. We didn't start too well and were never in full control of the game. We had good possession in dangerous areas but never really made it tell. But there is that confidence in the squad from Euro 96 which everyone is trying to carry on into the World Cup games, and maybe the Poland match is one in the past that might have slipped away.'

Shearer praised Ferdinand. 'One of the reasons I went to Newcastle was to play with Les. Although things didn't go great from the start we both believed the partnership would work and the signs are encouraging at club and international level. If you work hard enough then things will happen and I thought Les' overall play against Poland was tremendous. I wish he could have got a goal at the end to cap things off but he worked so hard all game and was even popping up at left-back defending on occasions.'

But Ferdinand was fearful he would be jettisoned. 'Only Glenn Hoddle knows whether I will be judged on the 90 minutes against Poland. I hope he doesn't, but he will do what he feels is right for the side. I've always been in and out of the team and it's been frustrating. It's difficult when you are in for one game and out for the next three or four. You always feel under pressure to prove yourself and a striker needs a run in the side to do that.'

BBC television's Jimmy Hill headed the critics insisting that Sheringham had a better understanding with Shearer. Ferdinand hit back: 'Jimmy Hill is entitled to his opinion and it doesn't upset me. Teddy and I play different roles. I'm similar to Alan, but I'm starting to understand the runs he makes. International football is different to playing in the Premier League because of the man to man marking. But our partnership is improving with every game. We will get better. We wouldn't have played together for England if it wasn't for our partnership at Newcastle. I suppose Alan's the man who got me into the team. He's making goals for me and I'm making them for him.'

Hoddle's England were dismissed as a one-man team. Polish skipper Piotr Nowak said: 'When we watched England at Euro 96, we thought they were very strong. But now we know better. We found a lot of faults in England's defence and were surprised at how many chances we had. We got through to goal very easily and were very unlucky not to win. Without Shearer, they wouldn't have beaten us. He was the only England player who really troubled us. He is such a good player and a great striker. He only had two chances and scored two goals, which is the mark of a world-class marksman. But England will have to improve a lot on that performance if they are going to qualify from this group and go through to the Finals. Everyone is talking about England and Italy coming top, but we're happy with that. This was our first qualifying game, and if we play as well in our next game against Moldova we will have no problems.' Nowak added: 'We will be waiting for England when they come to Poland next year. And we will beat them.'

The big concern for Hoddle, and indeed England, was the health of Alan Shearer. Two days after the Poland game he visited a specialist in London, fuelling speculation that he might need another operation on his groin. Initially, Shearer dismissed these fears, saying, 'There's nothing to worry about.' But later that month he underwent surgery in a London clinic which meant he would almost certainly miss England's next game against Georgia. The England coach had, in fact, spoken to Shearer a few days before the operation. 'He told me then that there was every chance he'd need an operation,' said Hoddle. 'Both Alan and I hope his recovery will be as speedy as it was pre-Euro 96.'

An England star supposedly on the mend was Darren Anderton, who had missed virtually all of the 1995/96 season after hernia and groin operations before coming back in time for Euro 96. He had then undergone more hernia surgery in September. The injury had so far forced the 24-year-old out of Hoddle's thinking.

It had been an odd Wembley baptism for Hoddle. He said: 'I didn't feel any emotion whatsoever right through the day, even when I came out of the tunnel. You have to cut yourself off, almost cocoon yourself, as a coach. You have to keep your cool. I'm pleased the way we turned it round. It's been a strange day. I didn't expect it to be like that.'

England (2) 2 Poland (1) 1

Seaman, G Neville, Pearce, Ince, Southgate, Beckham, Gascoigne, Ferdinand,
Shearer (capt), McManaman, Hinchcliffe

	P	W	D	L	F	A	Pts
England	2	2	0	0	5	1	6
Italy	2	2	0	0	4	1	6
Poland	1	0	0	1	1	2	0
Georgia	1	0	0	1	0	1	0
Moldova	2	0	0	2	1	6	0

CHAPTER SEVEN

Trouble with Gazza

Rangers star faces public outcry over wife beating,
October–November 1996

I've known Paul Gascoigne well since he first arrived at Spurs from Newcastle in July 1988 and was dubbed 'the Fat Boy'. I was also at a tournament in Toulon with the England Under-21s when he took his bow on the international scene, scoring against Morroco with the first goal of the competition, a brilliant free-kick. Everyone was predicting a big future for a youngster with enormous talent. There, in the luxurious team hotel in the south of France, the curly-haired kid pitched all sorts of missiles out of his fifth storey window down onto journalists waiting for the daily interview with coach Dave Sexton. Pleased with the antics that amused his young team-mates, Gascoigne came bursting out of the hotel to roll around in the street in the mess he had created. At the age of 20, it was his first real trip abroad. On the field, his talent and personality shone through. After he scored that wonderful goal against Morocco, he ran over to the non-existent stand at one side of the ground to celebrate with a non-existent crowd. In those days we all loved his impishness. It was fun then, but later it just seemed to all get out of hand. Gascoigne could never cope with the Gazza phenomenon.

His future with Glasgow Rangers was hanging by a thread after he was shown the red card for kicking Winston Bogarde as the Scottish champions crashed 4–1 to Ajax in the Champions' League. Gazza was blocked by Bogarde as he went for a cross. As keeper Edwin Van Der Sar cleared the ball, Gazza kicked out.

But there was much worse news for Hoddle to stomach over his cornflakes the next morning ... a disturbing and emotive photograph of a battered Sheryl Gascoigne on the front page of the *Daily Mirror*. The accompanying report read: 'Drunken soccer star Paul Gascoigne savagely beat up new wife Sheryl in a hotel room, the *Mirror* can reveal. Sheryl, 31, was left with a black eye and facial bruises – and every finger but one on her left hand was dislocated in the furious assault.'

There was widespread condemnation as one of Hoddle's key World Cup stars tried to piece his life back together and tears from Gascoigne as he begged his wife to take him back. But all this was hardly a huge surprise. Gascoigne admitted in 1994: 'I beat up Sheryl for two years. I'd end up arguing with her and then I'd fight her and slap her. I'd be violent in a number of ways.' Sheryl agreed to marry him after he vowed never to hurt her again.

Henry Winter in the *Daily Telegraph* was typical of the call for Gazza's international head. 'Hoddle, possessed of a strong faith, does not preach from the pulpit but the intimated message is hard to ignore. Standards count. Those invited to play for their country must be untainted by current problems. That is why Hoddle must consider leaving Gascoigne out of the squad for Georgia, due to be announced in two weeks. Until the allegations are dealt with, it is impossible for England to countenance having Gascoigne in their midst.'

The day after the scandal broke Hoddle contacted Gascoigne to try to ease his personal trauma. Hoddle said: 'I've spoken with Paul on the telephone. As he's already said publicly, he is very upset about the events of the past few days. My first concern is for him and his family. We'll be keeping in regular touch. Any football decisions I will take at the right time when I'm aware of all the circumstances. But, anything I can do that's helpful to Paul and his family at this time, I will seek to do. We'll be speaking again soon.'

Gazza's spirits were lifted by the helping hand of Hoddle, as the clamour to oust him from the England team intensified. Trusted accountant Len Lazarus spoke to Gascoigne after the conversation with Hoddle. Lazarus told me: 'He believes that his only redemption is his football ... He would be absolutely devastated if he was dropped by England. He has spoken to Glenn, and has been encouraged. Glenn knows just how passionate he still is about playing for England. He told me "football is my life, if I've not got my football, I'm finished." He has been told nothing by Glenn to suggest that he will be left out [of the next England game]. He has been desperately upset about what has happened. He feels that he has been crucified about the sending off at Ajax.'

The red card was nothing compared to the wife-beating controversy. But Lazarus added: 'His private life is his private life and he doesn't feel that should influence his ability to play football. He hopes very much that Glenn stands by him and picks him [to play against Georgia] next Thursday. He is mentally right to carry on playing. In fact, that is the only thing keeping him going. He wants to play for his club and desperately wants to play for his country.'

Gascoigne's only fear was that the decision would be taken out of Hoddle's hands. But FA insiders insisted to me at the time that Hoddle would be given a free hand. How could the FA single out Gascoigne for any special ban when other England players with their own private problems were considered for selection? Worse still, the FA would not know who might be next. Alan Shearer? Where would it all end? No other country would handicap themselves in the World Cup by omitting one of their top players on a moral issue. The FA would be setting a dangerous precedent, especially if revelations about other key England stars should emerge. The criteria for the FA and Hoddle would surely be if Gascoigne, or any player, was guilty of a misdemeanour while on England duty.

Gascoigne began his personal rehabilitation by issuing a public apology to his Rangers manager, Walter Smith, his team-mates and supporters for being ordered off in Amsterdam. 'There were stories about me leaving or being sacked by the club. It's easy for me just to pack my bags and walk away from football. I ain't going to do that.' His only reference to the reports of his beating his wife was to say that he took 'a domestic problem' into the match against Ajax. 'First of all, what happened the other night, I'm disgraced in myself for letting down the manager, the chairman, the staff, Archie Knox [Smith's assistant], the players and obviously the supporters. It happened last year and I said to the gaffer it wouldn't happen again. I thought throughout the season I became stronger for that. I have to stand up for myself after what has happened and come back stronger and try and play to the best of my ability for Rangers Football Club. I deeply regret it. I've let down everyone at the club. I'm sure they don't need what I've given them in the last 48 hours. I love the club. The supporters have been great. This time last year when I let them down in a Champions' League game, I came back stronger for it. Hopefully I can do that again.'

For his red card Gascoigne was fined two weeks' wages – £30,000 – by Rangers. He responded by scoring his eighth goal in 12 appearances with a stunning free kick in a 2–2 draw with Aberdeen. Smith told BBC Scotland viewers that the decision to pick Gascoigne, while tough, was one he had to make. 'I just felt it was one of those where I had a decision to make and while it was an awkward one, with a great deal of pressure on it, I felt if he was going to come back and play for Rangers, he was as well facing the music against Aberdeen. He went out and managed to handle that. He had a dodgy first ten minutes or so when I think he showed he was under a little bit of pressure, but he came through that and acquitted himself well for the rest of the game.'

The Professional Footballers' Association chief Gordon Taylor urged clubs to set up a counselling service to try to help players avoid the kind of pitfalls which had befallen Gascoigne and Merson off the pitch. Taylor said clubs should be able to provide the sort of expert guidance that may nip in the bud the personal problems encountered by players. 'We are not particularly trained to deal with these personal problems and to some extent highlighting them is a good thing because it brings into the public eye the fact they are real issues which need to be sorted. It is quite apparent because of the high profile nature of the game and the pressures on players that it is important for football management, football clubs and football as a whole to have counselling programmes. It is important that we look at the lives of players away from football and to try and make sure they do not take on too much and can cope with things. We have a drug problem in society and at times that will show itself in football. We are not divorced from that and at the same time there can be violence in society and problems with relationships. That is why football has got to provide a good counselling service because clearly if the likes of Paul Gascoigne are able to have a much more sombre and careful private life, then it will make him a better footballer.'

Jack Charlton, the former Republic of Ireland boss who took his adopted country to unprecedented World Cup success, believed Gascoigne was still a must for the England team, even though he was shocked by the latest revelations.

Speaking at the launch of his autobiography in London, Big Jack, who first brought Gascoigne into top soccer, said: 'What he did was unforgivable in my eyes. There are some things you don't do in life – and this is one of them. I was really disappointed with the events at Gleneagles last week. Everyone has faults, but attacking a woman is something you don't do. In my eyes there are lines you don't cross as a human being and Paul went over this one. I was very saddened and sorry to read what happened. But if Gascoigne had been a player of mine with the Ireland team I would never have dropped him. As a manager whatever you think of somebody, you don't cut off your nose to spite your face. You've got to remember that Gazza is, from what I know of him, basically a nice lad who is constantly under pressure. He's had to fight back from some terrible injuries and has spent key years of his career in recovery. But he's done that and is still one of the best players around.'

As the debate raged over whether Gazza ought to be censured by the FA and not picked for England, Hoddle met FA Chairman Keith Wiseman. The FA were prepared to wait and see how the situation developed, as Gascoigne turned to counselling to help him save his four-month marriage and control his temper.

It was not only women's groups calling for extreme sanctions, and Wiseman saw this case as the first test of his leadership. He was not helped by his predecessor, Sir Bert Millichip, whipping up the debate. He wanted the player disciplined. 'I don't see why the reasons for possible disciplinary action against any player should be limited. It is not purely a case of what has happened on the pitch. Behaviour off the field is just as important – and that includes wife-beating. A strict moral code relating to England selection was introduced during my time as FA chairman. I sincerely hope that this will be continued now that Keith Wiseman is in charge, and I trust him to do so. Players guilty of poor conduct, which obviously includes being sent off, were dropped for the next match by England. It was not a matter that was left to the manager. The decision was taken at the highest level – by me! England players must always be aware that they have a duty to their country. They are ambassadors for the whole nation, and as such, are expected to set the best possible example for young people to follow.'

This was an incredible piece of double standards. Millichip was the man in charge when the FA hit Gascoigne and the other players with 'massive' fines totalling £5,000 between the entire squad (the cost of the damage itself) for embarrassing the FA before Euro 96! The FA stood aside and allowed Venables to sort it out. Sir Bert abdicated his responsibilities on that occasion, no doubt on the grounds of convenience.

Gazza, anxiously biting his nails, spoke out after helping Rangers reach the Scottish Coca-Cola Cup Final with a 6–1 demolition of Dunfermline. 'It's been a difficult couple of weeks and it's still bad really. I am very nervous and when I feel like that, I know I have got to sort out my problems. But I've just got to try to keep my head up and get on with things. I've got to focus on playing for Rangers.' He admitted he feared the Ibrox fans would turn against him. 'I'm a bit worried about everything at the moment but the fans have been great. All I can do is try to concentrate on and off the field. That's all.'

There was some feeling within the FA that Gascoigne's inclusion against Georgia would be an unwelcome distraction in the build-up to a key World Cup game. An unnamed source was quoted in one paper suggesting that there would be opposition. But Lazarus discounted such claims when he told me: 'From the people I have spoken to at the FA, there has been nothing but support.' The FA released a statement, part of which read: 'Glenn Hoddle's intention is to seek to do what is right for the England team as well as for Paul and his family. He will have further contact over the next few days with Paul as well as with the Rangers manager Walter Smith. As has already been reported, he has also kept the FA chairman, Keith Wiseman, fully informed.'

Rangers Chairman David Murray condemned Gascoigne's behaviour, but said he would stay at Ibrox. Murray said: 'Gascoigne can't go anywhere without people following his car. He's partly brought in on himself, but I wish people would give him a break. Nobody should have to put up with what he puts up with. But he will not be driven out of Scottish football by the pressure. I think he is stronger than that and I think Rangers are strong too. He is a tremendous player – if you ask any fan they would love him to be at their club. There's no pressure on him to go and the supporters appreciate what he does on the park.'

Gascoigne again met Hoddle in private to receive further evidence that the England coach wanted to save his international career. Hoddle went to such monumental trouble because he believed that Gascoigne could still be part of England's midfield in France. Hoddle had the courage to pick him. It would have been hypocritical of the FA to usurp their coach, when they allowed Venables to sort out the mess of the Cathay Pacific flight home from Hong Kong. Lazarus spoke on behalf of Gascoigne and confided to me: 'Gazza wants to be judged by what he does on the football pitch, and he feels sure that what has happened in private doesn't in any way affect his ability at the highest level for England. Paul has the ultimate respect for Glenn, both in his days as a player and as England manager, and it is certain that whatever Glenn decides will be the right decision. Paul is in constant communication with Glenn who has been very understanding and helpful. Paul will obviously accept whatever Glenn decides is best for him.'

Already shorn of Alan Shearer through injury, a self–inflicted ban on Gazza didn't make much footballing sense. Hoddle's view was that Gascoigne must abide by a strict code of conduct while on England duty, and if he stepped out of line there, then it was within his jurisdiction to take disciplinary action.

The FA were acutely aware of the potential backlash of public opinion. Wiseman stressed: 'I view the image of the England team as being very important. A player like Alan Shearer projects the right image, which is one of the reasons Glenn made him captain. When I speak to Glenn, he will go through what he has learned from speaking to various people, including the player himself. There will be three points to address:

1. Is he suitable for selection on the basis of current footballing ability?
2. Whether, even in the abstract, there is evidence that the player's state of mind could override point 1.
3. The overall background and situation which has surrounded Gascoigne in the past few weeks.'

The 'abstract' Wiseman was no doubt talking about was allegations of wife-beating. He added, a little less abstractly: 'Gascoigne has been playing for England for six or seven years now and I think any new coach would like to feel he has been given a proper chance to deal with such a situation at least once in his own way. I do think that a new coach should be able to come on board with a clean sheet and decide himself what he feels is the right way forward. I am sure Glenn will do the right thing.'

Gascoigne told Hoddle that he wanted to play and assured the England coach that he was in the right frame of mind to silence his critics, and he said that missing the crucial World Cup clash with the Georgians would devastate him.

I couldn't support the outcry to kick Gazza out of the England team. The task of picking an England team has to rest with the manager; he stands or falls by his selections. If such decisions are taken out of the manager's control, then there has to be a clear cut criteria for representing your country, so everyone knows precisely where they stand. In Bobby Robson's time, the FA decided that any player under club suspension couldn't play for their country. Then they discovered that key players like Bryan Robson might have to sit out a vital World Cup qualifying tie. Suddenly the 'rule' changed so that players under club suspension couldn't play in friendly matches, but would be free to play in competitive games. And as time went by the 'rule' was completely forgotten. The reason? World football considered it a huge joke that the FA would tie one hand behind its back with self-inflicted punishments. The FA realized that if any player steps out of line in the context of football then FIFA and UEFA have a universal disciplinary code. No-one would axe a player for anything that happened in their private life.

The sin bin would be so full that the latest England coach with his Christian beliefs would be forced to watch the Monastic League before he named his squad. The old school tie rulers of the FA had hardly set any moral standards. If they had had done so, then it would be different now. Gascoigne would have known the score.

Hoddle's decision to stand by Gascoigne received the full backing of the FA, in an unprecedented joint statement issued by Wiseman and Kelly, and a second from Hoddle. The written statements by the England coach and the FA were distributed before the press conference on the day the England squad was announced – with Gascoigne selected. Kelly's statement pointed out that Hoddle had consulted with him and the FA chairman, and that the decision was 'totally endorsed by us'. Kelly's statement added: 'Glenn has rejected the easy option. He personally believes he can guide, and – with counselling – help Paul Gascoigne and his family with their current deep-rooted problems. Crucially, he believes he must waste no time in doing so. The Football Association, as is our responsibility, has considered the interests of the game as a whole. We have some knowledge of private and very personal matters that relate to the situation of Paul Gascoigne and his family. Clearly we cannot discuss them. But again, we too have chosen not to take the easy option. The chairman and the chief executive have been convinced that Glenn's judgement is absolutely the right one given the facts he has been made aware of. We don't condone unacceptable personal behaviour. We condemn it. We expect high standards. We also have to accept that people are human, and that when problems arise, each must be assessed on its merits. We are fortunate to have at the top of our game many excellent role models. Their standards are those we expect all our players to aspire to.'

Hoddle's statement disclosed that he had attended counselling with Gascoigne. It revealed: 'I was with him on one occasion. Sometimes the meetings lasted as long as five hours. Paul and I have also spent long periods talking on the phone. I believe I now have a clear understanding of the problems he and his family are experiencing, and that he has sometimes taken with him on to the pitch. Much of what I have learnt has to remain private. I am aware of much that is not – and should not – be public knowledge ... I have been deeply impressed by his determination to address his problems and the progress that he has already made. I believe that with my help and that of counselling, we can guide and help both him and his family to go further. I will certainly do everything I can for them. My assessment is that Paul should be in my squad for the Georgia game on merit. At no time have I – or would I – condone what Paul has done. I expect high standards. I also accept that people are human. When they have a problem, each case has to be assessed on its merits. In this case Paul and his family need immediate help and support. Paul knows he has to change in the long term. My aim is to do nothing in the short term that might turn out to be unhelpful in the future.' Hoddle stressed that Gascoigne's selection had been his decision.

I thought it was amusing when Hoddle was asked whether his job was even harder than the Archbishop of Canterbury. Hoddle replied: 'One of the prime things Jesus spoke about was forgiveness. I don't condone what Paul has done but I want to help him change. People can change – Saul was one.' Hoddle had heard the confessional of Gascoigne in hours of therapy meetings with an expert counsellor. Hoddle had offered Gazza the chance to become St Paul on the Road to Tbilisi. His Christian heart overruled his head – and the hostile objections.

However, Hoddle's patience was not inexhaustible. 'He knows he's got to change. He's not happy with the way things have gone for him and that's the first point of recovery in many ways. I want to give him that opportunity to learn from his mistakes. If you want to call it a last chance – I'm not calling it a last chance – but the ball's in his court.'

Like Merson and Adams, ironically recalled to the squad also, a recovery programme of counselling offered salvation. Hoddle refused to go into details of what therapy Gazza had undertaken, or the minutiae of events in the player's private life that had persuaded his selection. 'He needs to be looked after, guided and helped long after Georgia. This is something I've felt that perhaps he's needed for a long time. I always felt there was something there I needed to talk to him about and this has maybe brought the situation round. If I had bought him for Chelsea two years ago, I might have been able to put things to Paul then and discussed them. Other people have made mistakes. Paul Merson has made mistakes. You have to have a chance to learn from those mistakes. The facts are that if Joe Public had done exactly the same thing and there had been no police involvement, that man wouldn't have got the sack from his job or his capacity to earn wouldn't have been taken away from him. They [footballers] are no different from anyone else, they're human beings, they go through problems. They have added pressures, more than a lot of people. The pressures have multiplied because of money and the media; football's become so big. There are people out there going through problems, why should footballers be any different? In fact, the percentage of footballers with problems is pretty small.'

Hoddle promised his special charge would be given equal treatment with everyone else. 'I wouldn't have brought him into the squad if he hadn't been in contention. This has taken a lot of energy and time but I still have enough to focus on the team. We've got enough time to get over this. It's obviously been the focal point – no-one's asked me about Alan Shearer yet. It's up to all of us to make sure the main issue is football once we get over to Georgia.'

If anyone emerged from this affair with credit, it was Hoddle, who had removed any lingering doubts that he was strong enough to carry off this job. 'It's easy to judge and I was not going to keep everyone happy, whatever decision I made on this issue. In the end the decision had to come from myself, honestly, knowing every single detail. It would be done for any other player ... not just Paul Gascoigne.'

Hoddle was accused of putting soccer before the safety of women. Campaigners against domestic abuse had hoped that Hoddle would jettison the star and send a message of support for abused women across the country. Julie Bindel, spokeswoman for an international conference on violence and abuse of women, said: 'Hoddle has clearly shown that football and winning a match is more important than the safety of women.' It was 'an outrage' that Gascoigne 'is to be made a national hero in this way, and that he will be even more of a role model for many boys and young men'.

Amid all the controversy there was still the small matter of a football game to be played. The squad for the Georgia game was announced. It was: Seaman (Arsenal), Walker (Spurs), James (Liverpool), G Neville (Man Utd), Pearce (Nottm Forest), Hinchcliffe (Everton), Southgate (Aston Villa), Adams (Arsenal), Campbell (Spurs), Matteo (Liverpool), Ince (Inter Milan), Gascoigne (Rangers), Beckham (Man Utd), McManaman (Liverpool), Platt (Arsenal), Batty (Newcastle), Le Tissier (Southampton), Barmby (Everton), Ferdinand (Newcastle), Sheringham (Spurs), Fowler (Liverpool), I Wright (Arsenal), Merson (Arsenal).

The England coach discussed the inclusion of Ian Wright. On any other day the recall for the Arsenal veteran, more than two years after the last of his 20 caps against Romania would have caused a sensation. Hoddle enthused over the striker he pursued assiduously during his Chelsea tenure. With Shearer out, Wright was back on the strength of 12 goals in 12 club games. 'He's back to his very best,' said Hoddle, who had watched Wright carefully since his early-season recovery from injury. '17 or 32, it doesn't matter. I tried to buy him for Chelsea, as everyone knows. To lose Alan Shearer and to be able to bring Ian Wright in, that's a fantastic substitute. And this isn't just about Georgia. Okay, we have to win this game and pick the right team for that. But if he remains in that sort of form he can still be there or thereabouts come the World Cup if we qualify.' Wright admitted: 'I could not have asked for a better present. Things have been going very well for me and the team so I was hopeful of getting in the England squad although I didn't hear from Glenn before today's announcement. My goals have obviously helped but I am enjoying it more than ever and I am trying to work harder at keeping the ball and finishing when I can. I thought it was all gone for me. All I've tried to do is score goals and it seems to be rewarded now, I'm really pleased. I had a feeling with Terry Venables the door closed on me after the Romania game. I wouldn't say it's because I didn't take my chance, but for whatever reason, it didn't happen for me in his squad. All I try and do is score goals at the highest level, and now it's been rewarded with the call-up. How do I feel? I'm on top of everything. I feel really good, my family will be really pleased. All the people who came up to me on the street all the time and said "Get back in the England squad", I have to say thanks to them for their encouragement. Fans from all over, they've kept me going. I'm coming up to 33 now, and I don't know what the secret is. I'm just enjoying it more than anything, and I'm trying this season to work harder on keeping the ball. And I'm trying to finish when I can, and it's been going pretty well.'

A favourite of Graham Taylor, Wright had scored in just two of his 20 international appearances, including four in his mentor's farewell against San Marino in Bologna, and was discarded swiftly by Venables as an international misfit, cast aside for not having the right touch, let alone the right temperament. Hoddle explained: 'I can't comment on the way he was handled or what managerial schemes were there at the time. All I know is that if you can tell me a better Premiership striker to bring back into the squad, then have a chat with me!' However, Liverpool's fit-again Robbie Fowler – seven goals in his last five outings – was also back in the frame. In reality, were they really just fighting over a place on the subs' bench?

Adams returned for Pallister, and in Shearer's absence, was in contention for the captaincy. Adams said: 'That is up to the manager. I am just delighted to be back in the squad and we will take it from there. The way things are going at Arsenal have helped. We are enjoying it a great deal under the new manager Arsene Wenger. The new boss has some interesting ideas.' The Highbury boss returned the compliment by recommending Adams for the captaincy. 'To me,

Tony is a natural leader,' said Wenger. 'I did not hesitate to keep him as captain when I came to Arsenal. He has all the right qualities and is undervalued by many people outside the game. His technical ability is much higher than many people think and I am not at all surprised Glenn has recalled him to the squad after what happened in the Wembley match against Poland.'

Georgi Kinkladze, starring for Manchester City, would be the big threat to England. Steve Coppell, then Manchester City manager, joked that he would go to great lengths to stop 'Kinky' in his golden tracks. 'I'll kick him after our game at Swindon to stop him joining up with Georgia.' Coppell also placed a bet on England. 'I only wanted to bet Gio £20 but he was adamant that it should be £25. It's hard to get a conversation going with him but he was able to understand that.'

Compatriots Mikhail Kavelashvili and new City signing Kakhaber Tskhadadze were also in English football, but Coppell warned that Kinkladze was a real danger. 'Georgi can definitely be a match winner for his country. That's for definite. If you have seen him often enough, you know that when he gets the ball in certain situations, he will take some stopping. Glenn is aware of what he can and can't do. And I am sure he will be making plans to deal with him. Georgi hasn't said anything about playing against England other than that he's looking forward to it. And it's a game they need to win to be realistic contenders in the group. Georgi's skill and class can be awesome. It's been well documented on TV what he's capable of. And seeing him in the flesh, he's lived up to all the billing. He has a huge potential to score goals. He's scored three in five games for us and that's what he needs to do. As a special player, he has to accept the responsibility of performing week in and week out. He's not talkative, even in his own language. He's a quiet lad and never says a word in the dressing room. But he's mischievous and I like that in the lad. He enjoys training, well, certain aspects of it anyway, and we seem to make him smile.'

Georgia's coach, former Soviet captain Alexander Chivadze heaped praise on England but made it clear he was hoping to beat them with a touch of magic from Kinkladze. Chevadze claimed England's team under Hoddle – whom he once played against for the USSR – was stronger even than the 1966 World Cup winning team. But he was quietly confident of an upset in the frenzied atmosphere of Tbilisi's huge Paichadze Stadium in the biggest home game since Georgia's independence from Moscow in 1991. 'I attended the European Championships in England and have studied the Moldova and Poland games on video. Besides that, we get Premiership games on TV here including Manchester United and Liverpool, so I see a lot of the way the English play. It's also useful having Georgian players who play in England – they help me.'

Chivadze recalled that after playing against Hoddle for the USSR in 1986, the pair had attended the same coaching course in Denmark. 'He was a great player with a vision beyond the British style of play and a very strong personality. I respect him very much.' He added: 'In my opinion, your current team is the best in England's history.'

Hoddle's stiffest task in the three days before the squad flew out to the Black Sea state was to prevent the Gascoigne circus from distracting the Rangers man and the rest of the party. Gascoigne joined his manager and the FA's Head of Media Affairs, David Davies, for a 'one-hit' press conference at the Bisham Abbey training ground headquarters. Gascoigne asked Hoddle to allow him to brave the fierce scrutiny of the footballing press as he explained why he had pledged to become a new man. Gascoigne was visibly nervous, but he soon relaxed and even showed a few sparks of wit as he talked about his rage, regret and his planned reformation. It was a fascinating 15 minutes, from which I have selected some of the more interesting questions and answers.

'Can you describe this rage inside?'
'I can't really describe the rage inside us. I am getting counselling off two separate people. One is personal, and one is with my wife. I can't actually go into great detail. Obviously what happened with my wife I deeply regret, and that will live with me for ever. I don't blame the likes of the women's rights, I don't blame anybody for wanting me kicked out of the squad. They have their right to say something and I have to live with that as well. Like I say, I deeply regret what happened.'

'In a recent documentary you talked about not liking to be on your own because you don't like to think too deeply. Counselling involves a lot of critical self-analysis. How difficult is that for you?'
'It was hard, to meet up with a stranger and actually give him your problems. But I've come out of it and already I feel a better a person for it. You can tell, I'm talking to you guys! The counselling's helping us, it's making me relaxed on the pitch already with opponents and with referees. I feel a better person generally all round.'

'Is this something you would have benefited from doing a lot earlier in your career?'
'Maybe, yes. But the thing that happened with Sheryl, I really regret that ... I'm under pressure, a lot more than other players, and I have been for five or six years. I've just let everything bottle up inside us, instead of just coming out with things. Obviously the thing with my wife was the last straw and now I've started to sort it out, and I'm really pleased.'

'Are you intending to talk to Tony Adams and Paul Merson, bearing in mind they have also had personal problems and needed counselling?'
'They are different types of problems. The people I'm seeing ... they see people for what they've got wrong with them and I'm seeing people for what I've got wrong with me. And the people I'm seeing is working.'

'Glenn says he has already seen the change in you. Do you accept that this might be your last chance?'
'Yeah. Without a doubt. And I don't mind that. It's up to me. I've been given this chance again and I just want to come and prove that I can still do the business for England … I've scored one in two games for Glenn and I've scored 11 goals for Rangers. I've just got to try and keep that going. And obviously sort out my personal problems as well.'

'Paul, there will be people that say you have said sorry about other things before and have been full of regret. Do you feel different as a person now?'
'Definitely. Since I've been getting the counselling I feel a completely different person. Players at the club have noticed it, the players here have noticed it. In time – because I'm with them a lot and you're not with us – you'll obviously see it as well.'

'How do you feel different, more relaxed?'
'I feel more relaxed than I did five minutes ago! I'm not being funny but it takes some bottle to do what I'm actually doing, sitting here facing you, knowing everybody wants my head, the women's rights. And I don't blame any of you whatsoever. I'm just pleased I've been given the chance. I could have been kicked out on my backside. I just want to put everything behind us now and get on with it.'

'Were you genuinely scared that your career might be over with England?'
'I love playing for England, everybody does. If I wasn't in the squad this time I'd have had to think hard. With the counselling I'd be getting hopefully Glenn would have seen the change in me. There's other players who have been out of the squad for a few years and then come back in. I think that's what would have happened with me. I would think "I ain't in the squad, right, I'm going to knuckle down, I'm going to carry on with the counselling, I want to sort everything out". It was one of them "I'll show 'em".'

Hoddle: 'That was an option I had thought about. But I felt the way Paul had reacted, his willingness to put it right, I felt it would be detrimental to the football side of this issue not to bring him in now.'

'Have you read any pieces written about you recently?'
'I'm not getting the papers this morning, which has obviously been the same for the last two weeks. But when I go into the dressing room there's seven or eight guys with different papers, so you can't actually hide from it.'

'*How do you feel about it all?*'
'It's frightening. It's one thing I want never to happen again. I just hope from now on for the rest of my career I'll hopefully try and get good things written about me.'

Hoddle: 'That's the point, though, Paul. We've chatted about this. He's not hiding from it any more. That's why he's here.'

Gascoigne: 'This is one of the things if you speak with the likes of Tony (Adams) and Paul (Merson), it helps you, coming out and talking, saying things, instead of building them up inside you. It makes you a better person.'

'*How do you assess your form and what might we see in Georgia this week?*'
'I'm pleased with my form. The game in Moldova, I wasn't really fit and I still scored. The second game I worked really hard, I did my midfield duties where I was supposed to. For Rangers, I'm pleased with it. Eleven goals is not bad for a midfield player. In Georgia I don't pick the team. I've just got to prove to Glenn in the next week or so when we're together that my mind is on the game. Then the selection is up to the manager.'

'*You will be more in the spotlight. Won't that affect you?*'
'I am anyway and I know that. It won't affect us. I've just got to go out and concentrate on the football. That's it. When that's finished, concentrate on the counselling and the football as well.'

Hoddle: 'If he's chosen to play next Saturday, it's part of my job and the management team to make sure he feels part of the team. He can't go out there and play on his own.'

'*What made you seek counselling?*'
'I reached the decision because what I did, I couldn't believe that was me the following morning. I thought I've definitely got to get that sorted out.'

'*You're being very honest, but how long do you think it will take for people to accept you as Paul Gascoigne the footballer?*'
'I want to be accepted as Paul Gascoigne the footballer and Paul Gascoigne the person. More than Paul Gascoigne the footballer because football has a short period, I maybe have five years left and then you've got to look at Paul Gascoigne the person. So hopefully people will see the best of both.'

'You've been in a few situations like this where you've been put under pressure. In a lot of them you regarded yourself as a victim. Have you addressed that and said "I'm not a victim any more"?'

'Obviously I've done things out of, whatever you call it, I've just done it, you know. Heat of the moment or whatever. And then the next day I've regretted it. Then I've tried to hide it by joking and that and pretending I didn't regret, which I have done. Before I do things now obviously I have to think about doing it before I do it. Then I won't be in as much trouble as I have been in the past.'

'Have you fallen as far as you can fall, is this the bottom for you?'

'Hopefully. In all aspects, with my wife and with my football.'

'Are you trying to channel the aggression in the right direction now?'

'The only aggression I want to show now is on the field. I'm aware of the aggression. In the past I seemed to hate everybody for no apparent reason. No doubt yourselves, whatever. That's one thing I'm getting rid of and I just feel a better person, that when I go on the pitch it's controlled aggression.'

'Glenn said before the Poland game that if you looked after yourself properly, you could play up to this World Cup and beyond. Do you feel that way?'

'When I was young, I used to binge and do daft things. Now I'm on a more controlled sort of thing now. I like to think I eat the right sort of things. I look after my body more, I'm doing more in the gym. When you get to my age you sometimes have to do two sessions a day, work in the morning, have a break and then sometimes again in the afternoon. It's things like that which I've been doing and I feel physically good.'

'Do you realize how much young kids in this country look up to you?'

'Yes, I do. And like I said, I deeply regret what's happened and I have to try and get those young kids back on my side.'

'What part did alcohol play in your problems?'

'You go on about it. People went on about it in Italy. I think I've been nightclubbing about four times in six years. They lasted three months at a time! It's controlled and that's the way I like to keep it. Any time I go out it's to a restaurant. With the counselling I've been getting, the situation what happened, I would like to think that will never happen again.'

'Are you concerned about leaving the counselling behind while you go to Georgia?'

'Well, I had one [session] yesterday. When I get back, there will be another one and I'll continue like that. I'm OK. With the other lads' help, I'll be alright through the next few days.'

Gazza departed with a 'Thanks lads, take care.' There was a ripple of applause. Someone suggested it was like a Mexican wave at Rosemary West's trial.

Hoddle remained in the Elizabethan Room at Bisham Abbey to talk further about his options. Asked whether normalizing Gascoigne as a person would normalize him as a footballer, he responded: 'I don't know. Paul has been given a gift from an early age.'

Hoddle had no regrets selecting him, but he stressed: 'I didn't send out the message that I am backing wife beating, I didn't send out the message that I condone everything that he did. I'm trying hard for the long-term solution. Everybody has to be patient, women's rights or whatever. If he does it again next week … that's a different story.'

CHAPTER EIGHT

Georgia on my Mind

Georgia v England, Tbilisi, 9 November 1996

The players reported at 6 pm on Sunday evening at the Burnham Beeches hotel and Hoddle breathed a sigh of relief as his squad came through the weekend's action unscathed. Forced to plan without the injured Shearer, Pallister and Anderton, the last thing he wanted was a flurry of withdrawals, the curse of every international manager. Fowler, McManaman, Matteo, James, Ferdinand and Batty checked in later after their respective matches that afternoon.

Hoddle felt Gascoigne deserved another chance. Now it came down to a footballing decision – to pick him for the team or leave him on the bench. Hoddle confessed that he had yet to make up his mind, and wouldn't do so until he assessed him in training and in more talks. The big decision was whether to start with him or bring him on for the second half to conserve his energy. Hoddle stressed that Gazza would be able to cope with omission from the side but, again, that it would be a footballing decision. 'He can deal with it if he is left out, he can cope with it. But it would be a slight test, maybe the test he might need. He might not want it, but he might need it. If we do pick him we must sit down and make sure he is part of the team. Sometimes you can try too hard. It is something I will have to assess later in the week, but it will be a footballing issue whether he plays or not.'

Sandra Horley, chief executive of the women's group Refuge, welcomed Gascoigne's remorse, but said: 'A public apology is one thing but this still doesn't excuse his violence. He must accept there is no excuse for beating your wife ie: drinking, football, stress or provocation. Recognizing that women abuse is wrong is the first stage towards rehabilitation for any man who beats his partner. Gazza needs professional help to overcome his violent behaviour. Receiving treatment for alcohol abuse is not enough.'

Hoddle's decision to keep Gascoigne in the England fold was 'fully supported' by the managers' union. Howard Wilkinson, the chairman of The League Managers' Association at that time, said: 'He is much closer to the situation than almost anyone else and is in the best possible position to make such a decision. Many of us have faced similar problems at club level. We have to remember we are human beings first; soccer people second. If the game can be a means of rehabilitation, then it has a duty to be so. Critics say Paul has a poor track record and they may be correct. But, quite rightly, he starts with a clean sheet as far as Glenn is concerned and, hopefully, with Glenn's support, Paul will honour the England shirt both as a player and as a person. The game has seen more than one high profile example in recent times of the beneficial effect of lending a helping hand when most needed. Of course, as I am sure Glenn accepts, the situation is very different if the offer of help is spurned.'

David Seaman has spent hours with Gazza fishing; he knows the player's character better than most. Seaman sat relaxed in the interview room, with hardly anyone taking much notice with so many more pressing issues to be aired. He told me: 'Yes, I believe he can change. He will be alright, but he needs a lot of people behind him, people who will give him encouragement. He's under a lot of pressure but we all are getting together behind him.' Gazza is only really at peace with the world when he's fishing. The Arsenal keeper said: 'Whenever we join up with England we go fishing. We go to get away from everything, but it's serious stuff when we're fishing. We won't give each other's secrets away such as the kind of flies we're using! I'm sure people will be surprised just how seriously he takes his fishing. He is totally into it straight away.'

Les Ferdinand said: 'We all want him in the team – we believe England are a better side when he's playing. He's still the best at opening up defences. The boss has handled the situation just right. He has not judged Paul on anything to do with his personal life, and has been absolutely fair to him. All I know is that I want to play to make a point and I certainly want Gazza behind me if I'm picked. It's a very difficult situation, but the main thing is, Paul has been accepted back by the boys in the team. I hope he plays. It would be just the boost he needs after the week he has had. We know the situation is delicate, but Gazza has been accepted back. There is no change and the spirit is great.'

There was a warning from Rangers' Trevor Steven: 'There are certain things which need to be taken straight out of his character but I don't know how you do that without affecting the rest of him. The problem with Gazza is that he gets so frustrated when he's not playing well. That's when you've got to be careful with him. It's then that he gets annoyed with referees and opponents. Now he's trying to cope with it, to be calm and settle down. And he's got to do that for his own benefit. Certain matches get him really excited. He'll work frantically in the gym prior to a big game. He pumps himself up with weights and the amount of energy he seems to release is very unusual. He's trying to focus on the game but it becomes so overpowering that we have to tell him to calm down. I still feel he has all the ability in the world and despite all that's happened, he's still streets ahead of most players I've seen.'

Ian Wright believed Hoddle had got it right with his relaxed and sympathetic management style although the coach had been criticized for his kid-glove treatment of problem players. But Wright felt that it was better than the old-fashioned, regimental sergeant-major approach of Bruce Rioch which drove the veteran Arsenal striker to the brink. He was prospering again under Hoddle's friend, Arsene Wenger, and his goals had put him back in England contention. Wright was impressed by both Hoddle and Wenger: 'That old school method, how it was before, the fear factor and frightening kids into playing, that's the past. The game's gone on since then. This way, like the boss here and Arsene Wenger, is the new way forward. They treat people like adults and get the best out of them on the pitch. You only have to explain things to people – everyone wants to do well, no-one wants to be in the first team and not do well, to lounge about and not train properly. When I was really down [at Highbury] and eventually put in a transfer request, I didn't even want to go into training sometimes. That's never happened to me, but I didn't want all the pettiness that was going on. But I just got on with it and now I'm out of the tunnel, there's pure light there.'

Wright could see Wenger's influence on Hoddle. 'Arsene's a very laid-back sort of guy and there's the same kind of relaxed manner with them both. It's not uptight, they come over and talk. They both treat it like they love it and they want you to do it right because it's the right thing to do. It doesn't need to be with a whip and a chair. They're very composed and calm and relaxed about it all.'

Meanwhile, Dominic Matteo was sent home suffering from a knee injury. He felt his England career was jinxed; called up for the first time for Poland he had withdrawn through a recurrence of an old injury. Hoddle sent him back to Merseyside with reassurances that he would still get his chance.

The England boss was worried about Paul Merson's chances because of a groin injury; it later became clear he was not going to make the flight. This was not just a bitter blow for Merson, but also a setback for Adams, who, as a recovering alcoholic, was relying on Merson for moral support. England were down to 18 outfield players. Hoddle, however, decided against replacements because he felt 'there are areas of the team where we are strong in depth'.

Gareth Southgate was touted as an outsider for the captaincy, but he was honest enough to concede he would be fortunate to keep his place in the team after the flawed victory over Poland. 'I was conscious that Glenn Hoddle had given me that responsibility and I didn't want to let him down. Playing in the middle of that defence is a job I can do. But I'm still learning as a defender, never mind an international footballer.'

Nick Barmby was in the England squad for the first time as an Everton player, having switched from Middlesbrough for £5 million. He believed partnering Duncan Ferguson would keep him in the international picture. 'Playing with him week in, week out can only help me because I benefit feeding off a big striker. Hopefully he'll be able to boost my chances of playing for England and help Everton climb the table. Joe Royle is building a good squad here and it's going to be an exciting time for everyone connected with the club and I'm just glad to be a part of it.'

Outside of the immediate World Cup assignment, Gary Pallister was on the way back less than a week after having a cartilage removed from his left knee.

After being sent off, Draper was unable to get back into the Villa team; his lack of first-team football was putting his international prospects in jeopardy.

Hoddle wanted to call a halt to the endless debate about Gascoigne; he wanted a line drawn, and that line was the moment he stepped onto Britannia Airways Charter Flight BY801A to Georgia. 'I see the plane journey as a significant cutting off. The counselling is no longer an issue with Paul Gascoigne. It's football now. I want to think about football. I wouldn't be doing my job right if we were focusing on anything else but Paul Gascoigne the footballer.'

Hoddle believed that any tough decisions he had to take over Gascoigne and Adams hardly compared with his troubles at Swindon in his first weeks as player-manager, when he had to inform three distraught YTS boys they would not make the grade. 'Everything after that is simple and easy,' he said. 'Every decision I make takes me back to something I had to do in my first three weeks at Swindon. I had to take three YTS boys into my office and tell them they weren't good enough. When you've got three lads who have done nothing wrong except involve themselves in an industry where they were not going to reach the top, and they are so distraught in your office ... and you've only been in the job three weeks yourself ... it is very tough. It is the hardest thing I've ever done and will ever do. It was very unfortunate for them, but in its own way it was good for me because everything after that was easy. I had to tell them to find another niche in life, while at the same time knowing I had burst all their dreams. It was very hard to be that person and I now know some managers might have left it to somebody else, but I was too naive at the time. Anyway, I always try to do as much of that kind of thing as I can. They were 17-year-olds, it is a unique situation and it didn't compare to dealing with the issues surrounding Paul Gascoigne and Tony Adams or anybody else, or even deciding on Alan Shearer and the captaincy. In many ways, going in to the job at Swindon and taking on the task with England was very similar. There were tough decisions that needed to be made quickly.'

The recalled Adams was the obvious candidate to take over from Shearer as captain, though Hoddle signalled that he wanted a less macho style of leader and the Arsenal defender was coping with his own personal problems. Hoddle said: 'There are a few candidates for the captaincy. You need leaders like this and we have them. I have spoken to Tony and he is in good spirits,' Hoddle said, before quickly correcting himself. 'Better make that in good health!'

The flight carrying England's players to their next World Cup destination in Tbilisi landed as dusk was falling on the Georgian capital. Greeting the England party was a committee of press and photographers, police, military and secret service officials. The team were accommodated in the Metechi Palace Hotel, Tbilisi's only 'luxury' hotel, the FA having commandeered three floors, with security officers on regular patrol along the corridors.

Word filtered back from the 'closed' training session that Hoddle was far from satisfied with the state of an uneven pitch. The players eased through a 45-minute 'stretching' session as Hoddle put it, 'to iron out the numbness and back aches of sitting in the plane for so long.' He added: 'We didn't get the balls out!' Well, that said it all.

The following morning, amidst the grumbles about power cuts and expensive telephone links, Glenn Hoddle entered the grand Salkhino Suite for his first press conference on Georgian soil. He described Georgia as 'a very technical side, strong in midfield. I would think of Portugal, perhaps not the same experience.' He was then asked: 'If you were playing Portugal, what would your tactics be?' His reply? 'It's a secret.' With a mixture of wise diplomacy and caution, Hoddle praised Georgia for the way they frightened Italy. 'They played very well, in the last 20 minutes of the game Italy were quite fortunate not to finish up 1–1. Georgia grew in confidence, and made it a difficult game for Italy. We will face a passionate crowd, it will be a difficult game for us.'

With the English press he elaborated on the problem with the playing surface. 'The pitch is worse than Moldova. To be fair, it won't suit them. It has deteriorated in the ten years since I played here. It's disappointing. There are patches all over the place, some bare, some brown, some green. The main problem is the divots.'

Hoddle indicated his belief in the front players: 'We have such a depth of striking talent that we can afford a couple of injuries and still go out there with a cutting edge. We could lose two more despite Shearer, and come kick-off time we would still be capable of scoring. That is a great feeling for a coach, the terrible feeling would be "Where's the next goal coming from?" As for Wright's chances of an England comeback, Hoddle evaded the question and said: 'I'd hate to have seen him when he was 23 or 24, because at the age of 33 he's as sharp as a razor, he really is. He's good to have around the place, so infectious, a good trainer, he's kept his body extremely fit. You look at his sharpness and it's quite remarkable the way he's kept that. He has a great awareness to make that run off the ball and he's still got that killer instinct. We have six strikers that any country would respect. Robbie Fowler is coming back into it, there is Les Ferdinand and Teddy Sheringham. Alan Shearer has got that all-round ability, he's got everything. But the good part for me is that we have other strikers in this squad. And competition is fierce, we have such healthy competition that even though we have lost Alan Shearer we've still got some terrific players up front. Lots of countries are striving to have that and we have that array of talent, and a cutting edge with it.'

But Hoddle was happy he had not given too much away as he strolled out of the hotel into the warm afternoon sunshine to meet five orphan boys. A delegation from Christian Aid brought the delighted group of youngsters, orphaned by war, to meet Hoddle. The England coach signed autographs and handed out souvenirs as he posed for pictures. This might have looked like nothing more than a photo opportunity, but Hoddle did appear genuinely sincere in his concern.

Back home, the man who would have been captain wanted his England team-mates to be on their guard. Shearer said: 'It will be very tricky. I saw Georgia on the television against Italy and they are a good side. They will give a few people watching a shock.'

The England team went through their training paces at the Lokomotiv Stadium, a short coach journey from their hotel past delapidated buildings scarred by civil war. The stadium itself was a wreck of crumbling concrete, the few hundred Georgians fans present scrambling for pictures of the England team which were being handed out by David Davies.

The Georgian players were showing their guests an equal amount of respect. Kinkladze warned that Gascoigne carried the biggest threat to Georgia's qualification hopes. 'Gascoigne may have problems at home, but he won't on the pitch. He is still a very good player and our biggest danger,' added the 23-year-old who joined Manchester City in a £2 million deal from Dynamo Tbilisi. Kinkladze also singled out McManaman (Hoddle's deliberate policy of keeping his team selection strictly confidential clearly gave him an edge as Georgia felt the Liverpool ace would be a prime danger man). Kinkladze relished the opportunity to face England. 'It would be the biggest thing in my career if we won. Now that I actually play in England is a big gain for me personally. We have the ability to beat England, but I would say our chances are 50–50. England are one of the toughest, most well-known teams in world football and any side would enjoy it if they beat them.' Georgia had lost their last four games, and had not played at home for more than a year. Kinkladze was one of ten players selected against England who earned their living in other countries – a fact coach Chivadze believed could be crucial.

Hoddle talked to a number of players individually. Adams was singled out for a one-to-one to discuss his particular problems. The day before the game there was another press conference. Hoddle began with regrets as 'a few people had picked up slight injuries', but he would 'rather not' name names (in other words, Southgate and Pearce).

Adams was asked about his private problems. 'I'm managing very well and delighted to be back in the team.' Then came an amusing little question from the locals about England's training. 'Kicking at goal, do you always miss? Do you do that all the time?' 'I'm waiting for the game' replied the England skipper. Adams was highly impressive. He appreciated that Hoddle had been brave enough to reinstate him as captain. 'It's fantastic to be back as captain and I'm very grateful to the manager. I'm delighted because he has shown great faith in me and I will do my best to repay him. I'm doing the best I can to become a better person. You are not going to get the highs in life if you don't experience the lows, too. Out of the lows I think I've grown.'

The new look Adams should not be confused with the old one with attitude. The Tony Adams in Tbilisi spoke softly and at great length, of his gratitude at being restored to a sanity in his life. There was a strange humility that recovery from the alcoholism inspires. 'I have been this person who has had this mask on for all these years. I have had a good look at myself, warts and all, and I think I am changing in lots of ways.' He looked lean. 'Well, I'm not drinking Guinness.' When did he know he would be captain? 'I had an idea when Glenn started calling me 'Skip',' he said.

I realized that Adams was a far cry from the figure who took the intercom on the plane trip home from a successful raid on Auxerre with Arsenal and sarcastically thanked the press for winding up the team by writing them off. 'I think Glenn knows I have changed,' he went on. 'In footballing terms, I have tried to lead by example. I'm doing it more for myself now. If I get myself performing to the best of what Tony Adams can do, then I am going to help everyone else. I said to the players at Arsenal: "Look, you might not get the verbals or a kick up the backside like you used to, but have a look at me. I can assure you I will be giving 100 per cent, my best for the team. I am running and heading and kicking for me and for you." If I see someone not pulling their weight or not doing something, then I am only human. I will talk to them. But there are certain ways of putting things over. There is a thin line and you can go over the top a bit. I have seen certain players go over the line. If it's all verbal, it goes in one ear and out of another. If you are constructive with it, it works.'

Under the tutelage of Wenger at Highbury, he has been given greater freedom. 'It opened up new fields for me. With George Graham, for eight years I was suppressed in the way I was playing. He wanted a particular style of playing, a back four, and we all want to please our boss. Besides, he got success with it. Going into a different system when he left, I have been able to express myself a bit more and I think a few people have been surprised that maybe I can play a bit. But I do think it is important in that position to be able to defend. Some people have talked about a Glenn Hoddle-type player in there, but sooner or later you have to head and kick the ball. At some stage, the other team is going to attack and I would rather have a defender in there. I can bring the ball out a little bit, but then I give it to Gazza or whoever.'

He talked constantly to 'the right people'. At £7.50 a minute to telephone England, it was a costly business. 'That's for the FA,' he said with a smile. With the average wage of a Georgian worker £3.50 a week, Adams' bill would keep a Tbilisi family in food for a year. 'The phone is a good tool – I'm not sure what I would have done without it. I made several calls back home to those who understand my situation, including Paul Merson. It was disappointing for me he couldn't make the trip in the end because he's been so supportive, but at least I've been able to keep in contact. No longer do I wake up wondering where I am but rather what is ahead of me for the coming day. I can't even think about tomorrow. It's a cliche but I have to live for today – and I feel a lot better for it.'

Hoddle gave his assessment of Adams: 'The best teams always have several captains in their side. We have another in Paul Ince, whom I considered to take over the job. But Tony did so well in the European Championships in that role, and having overcome injury and his personal problems, he's returned to the Arsenal side in excellent form. I felt he was the right choice to lead for this game.

The main thing has been his form after his knee operation. He has probably come back leaner after his injury than he has ever looked in the last three or four years. That's probably significant in the fact that he is addressing his other problem, the fact that he is trying to put things right, that might be a good example not just for the players, but for everyone. I think that's the point we are trying to make this week. He's a super example in many ways of how people can turn their lives around and he's getting his just reward for it.'

The coach did reveal he would be retaining the 3–5–2 shape of the team, with the composition of the midfield crucial, as this was Georgia's strongest department. He needed to install an extra ball winner in midfield, David Batty, to protect Gazza and eschew the flair of Le Tissier and McManaman further forward, relying instead on Sheringham and Beckham. The back three had to be more recognizable as central defenders, rather than full-backs. 'The vital period for us is the first 25 minutes,' Hoddle said. 'We have to make sure they don't get on top, because if they do, they have players who can respond.'

The Georgians were a talented collection of individuals, for whom consistency was the problem. 'I have seen them lose 0–5 and win 5–0,' Hoddle said. 'They are a side with individuals who respond to good support and we have to make sure we don't give anything away early doors. It wouldn't be a disaster if we drew, but we will be trying to win this game. It is significant that the Italians don't play competitively this week and if we get the three points against Georgia, then going into the Wembley game, it will be an edge to us psychologically.'

Hoddle had to ensure total concentration on the task ahead. The performance against Poland revealed certain areas of vulnerability. The priority for Hoddle was to ensure a good result … and England had never lost a match when Ince and Gascoigne were together in midfield. The pressure was on to win, qualify and, somewhere along the way, develop a settled team. For the moment, results were more important than any grandiose long-term plans. 'For now, my job is to pick the right team for the right occasion. I want to pick a balanced side that can win the game for us. I've watched Georgia and I know that we cannot afford to underestimate them. Although they lost in Italy, I thought they played exceptionally well. The Italians were hanging on for the last 20 minutes.' Yet, a win was expected back home.

Hoddle sought his own counsel with Gascoigne, who jogged in stocking feet on to the coach for England's secret final training session at the Boris Paichaidze Stadium. At the two-hour workout, he was 'bouncing off the walls', as one player described his mood. He was in, although no-one was saying for certain.

On the morning of the main event, there is usually an international press match. I've played off and on in these games for more than 20 years. Trevor Brooking is a veteran of these games, taken seriously by the press corps, even though few are still fit enough to take part. The England press team consisted of photographers, sponsors, FA staff, ex-England stars with jobs on radio or TV, and the occasional football writer. The idea that Gentleman Trevor would be involved in a scrap is quite preposterous, but it happened. A Georgian journalist floored him with a right hook. Brooking scored in the 1–1 draw but, having been fouled repeatedly during the game, he turned on his marker to protest and was promptly punched on the brow by another opponent. By his own high standards, he positively exploded with rage! 'There was what you might call a verbal exchange,' he said. 'Apparently, while this was going on,' he continued, 'another fellow ran 20 yards. I just saw him at the last minute from the side and he thumped me with a real right hook. He must have caught me with a ring or something because he cut me wide open just above the right eye.' He needed four stitches from the England team doctor. 'I only ever had three bookings in my career and I have never been involved in anything like this. Then again, I always had Billy Bonds to look after me. Who is there to help me this time? Ray Wilkins!'

For the real international, James, Barmby and Fowler were the odd ones out, not even among the subs. They wandered around the periphery of the pitch until they found seats at the end of the dugout.

When Hoddle took over, the nation thought it would get the beautiful game: Le Tissier, McManaman, sweet passing, balletic movement. Instead it was more the fixed-bayonets, battling face of football: Adams, Ince and now that grizzled campaigner Batty. But as Hoddle significantly observed: 'If I picked a team in my own image, we would never win the ball off anyone!'

England marked their 100th World Cup match with discipline rather than quality; an appropriately professional job which drew the sting from potentially dangerous opponents in difficult circumstances. This was a most formidable, composed and calculated England away win. Hoddle's game-plan worked to perfection. His team selection took most by surprise, but there was sound logic to it. With Georgia's strength in midfield Hoddle countered with the tigerish Batty playing alongside Ince. Batty was an inspired choice and was quite outstanding while the three central defenders, splendidly organized by Adams, formed a formidable grey wall. Hoddle gambled more with Campbell's full debut than by sticking with Gascoigne in a sounder midfield formation. The result was that England kept up their 100 per cent record in the group.

Gascoigne did not exactly turn from wife-beater to world-beater but he produced a disciplined, controlled performance, clearly enjoying being pushed further forward. All eyes were on him, and while it was not a vintage virtuoso performance, he justified Hoddle's backing. In the fifteenth minute his first-time flick found Ferdinand. The ball was then moved on for Sheringham to score. After 37 minutes Gascoigne ran 30 yards before slipping it to Sheringham who passed for Ferdinand to shoot home. Afterwards, he emerged from the dressing room to thank Hoddle for keeping faith with him, and vowed to sort out his domestic problems. 'In the last month I have let down my wife Sheryl and Glasgow Rangers, and I just could not afford to let down England. The Football Association stuck by me and Glenn Hoddle was under a lot of pressure because he would have had a lot of flak if it had all gone wrong. I like to think that I have repaid him.' He also thanked his team-mates for their support. 'The lads have been brilliant with me and I really appreciate that because they could have gone the other way. I see this as the first small step towards getting back on the right road. I have got to sort out my football and my family and I will work hard at doing both.'

Hoddle was pleased with Gascoigne: 'I have seen improvement in him already. I'm not saying he is the finished article, but he's shown people he is trying to change. But he is doing it without it affecting him as a footballer. The first ten minutes was a difficult time for Paul but he overcame that.'

The England coach went on to discuss the whole team: 'Above all, England have proved they most certainly are not a one-man team. Shearer is a world-class striker, but to lose him and still have these sort of players to come in is a credit to the football in our country. We have produced a lot of good strikers who can give us that cutting edge. All in all, it was a good performance from the youngsters, the new faces and the experienced players as well. I have seen them [the Georgian team] tear sides apart here.'

The opinion on Gascoigne's performance was divided. Counsel for the prosecution argued Gascoigne showed little flamboyance, the old magic was missing and the darting penetrative bursts were no longer there. Counsel for the defence stressed he had a hand in both goals, plundered expertly by Ferdinand and Sheringham.

Hoddle wanted Gascoigne as a potent force. The only counsel that counted was that of the England coach. Hoddle said: 'There are two separate issues, one is a football match and then there is the other side. Paul needs the back-up and help and hopefully in 18 months' time we can look back and see that this was the turning point. At his age he can evaluate games in different ways. What he might lose on one hand he can definitely gain on the other. Maybe those moments of magic will be there but not as many times. Another set of curtains can open for him.' In reality it could have been curtains. If Gazza hadn't played to Hoddle's specific orders, there might not have been another chance.

The mean streak as a manager had shown when Hoddle demanded that his players hunted in pairs as a unit against the Poles at Wembley, but instead found yawning gaps in midfield and at the back. 'This was only our third get-together and the penny's dropped. I could be a bit sterner with my words, to say "there's no option really, this is what I want, get on board or you could find yourself outside the squad." We've got talent outside the squad that I haven't brought in yet. But they listened and they've gained the fruits, they've worked hard and made a team that can be formidable look average.'

Hoddle knew his England stars were living on a high from Euro 96 and the hype sent them into waves of attacks against Poland which wrecked the shape of the side. That was amended as Hoddle ordered his players to be more compact. Batty joined Ince in order to give Gascoigne a midfield shield, while McManaman was dropped. But Gascoigne played to orders. Hoddle said: 'What we asked him to do was spot-on.' Everything Hoddle plotted was exactly right: the full debut of Campbell, the recall of Sheringham, the return of Adams in defence and as captain and best of all, the selection of Batty, who quietly and efficiently went about his duties.

Batty was Hoddle's man of the match. 'He did all I asked of him and more. 'I said to Paul Ince and David Batty they had to stand up. The last thing you want to do is make a tackle on players like Kinkladze. By standing up you can be just as effective and they took that on board. It forced them to go into areas where we had plenty of bodies. If we'd have tried to win it off them, those boys would have got right behind our midfield. They did that on two or three occasions and looked very dangerous. But it would have happened on six, seven or even eight or nine occasions and then we'd have been in real trouble. David Batty did exactly the job and more. I've always felt, even in his Leeds days, that he is a smashing passer of the ball and doesn't quite get the credit he deserves. Every team needs that type of player. He and Paul [Ince] are very similar in their approach; they can both use the ball, but they are not scared of hard work when the other team have got the ball. If you play the right people around them, then you've got a good chance of getting the balance right throughout the team. We needed that in this game.'

Batty was unmoved by all the praise and adulation. 'Playing for England has never been uppermost in my list of priorities. I've a family now. I enjoy being at home. Right or wrong, I prefer that kind of life to traipsing around the world. I've got a job at [Newcastle] United now staying in their team. So although playing for England is a big honour, I've always looked on it as a bonus. I've always had on too much at club level to be worried about England squads. To be honest I didn't even know when Glenn Hoddle's first one was announced. But that was definitely my best performance for my country. It was a big game for us, because unless we denied them time and space, they could have caused us a lot of problems.' It was his first start for 16 months when he began the game against Brazil at Wembley and England were beaten 3–1. He gave the first goal away, and was after that overlooked by Venables. 'When I first came into the England squad under Graham Taylor's management for the World Cup qualifiers, I got injured. That taught me to take things as they come. It's a long time before the next qualifying match against Italy in February, so I won't worry about staying in the side until then.' Hoddle had a midfield player who knew his own strengths. 'I enjoyed the way we snuffed out Georgia. It was my kind of match. My kind of situation,' said Batty.

Hoddle would think long and hard about whether to keep the Batty–Ince combination in the formidable contest against Italy. 'I don't know. I have a few months to think about that when I will be focusing on Italy.'

The England boss was delighted with the quality possession of his team. It had been a long time since England were able to completely control a game, particularly in the second half, with the kind of techniques more associated with superior continental players. 'The possession we had, that pleased me,' said

Hoddle. 'It is important when you're working so hard to win the ball back and if you can keep it even at the tenth or eleventh pass something might open up. Even if you keep simple possession or move it backwards, if you keep that ball after you've won it, it's amazing how openings can appear. Even their crowd enjoyed our performance.'

Ferdinand and Sheringham worked well as a partnership. 'I decided to play that pairing, if fit, within two days of Alan getting injured,' explained Hoddle, even though he spent much of the build-up talking up Wright. 'Well, he was on ten minutes and nearly scored,' he countered. 'But Teddy hadn't started a game under my management and I felt the things he had done in the summer and remembering what they did against Bulgaria, those little balances persuade you sometimes. And Robbie Fowler wasn't even on the bench – it's frightening.'

Not even his savagely taken goal guaranteed Ferdinand his place against Italy; he accepted that when Shearer was fit, he might be back on the sidelines again. 'I went to Tbilisi not expecting to play. So I have to believe that when Alan is fit again, it could be me who goes out'. Ferdinand's fifth goal for his country kept him marginally ahead of the cluster of front men in competition for the place alongside Shearer. 'I can only keep on playing well for my club, hope I can maintain my form for Newcastle. But I know I'm more relaxed with England now. I no longer go into games thinking I must do well to stake my claim. And I like to think I'm a better front player now I've paired up with Shearer.'

Sheringham also felt he had a point to prove. Getting England's first goal, and setting up the second, went a long way to making it. 'You always want to do that. So I am relieved that I did get a goal. I have played better, but it was a very satisfying team performance.' Sheringham always believed he should be an automatic choice for his country, even at a time when, with Spurs not playing well, his own form had dipped. He has his critics, but Hoddle admires his intelligent play. He's able to fit into any system and can produce the kind of quality finish that makes it hard for Hoddle to leave him out. 'I want to be in the team for the next game,' said Sheringham, who missed the Group Two opener against Moldova through injury and had to settle for a place on the substitute's bench against Poland. 'I just want to be playing for England. But it's not for me to say if I should be Alan's partner when he's back. There is a lot of competition among the strikers. For the five of us who were in Georgia, there were another ten at home. It was good to get the opening goal,' added Sheringham of his first for England since the double against Holland in Euro 96. 'It gave us the start we wanted.' Sheringham impressed with his all-round play, confirming he was the best foil for Shearer and would have figured in Hoddle's plans beforehand but for the early-season thigh problem. The 30-year-old believed England's unbeaten start to the group had put them in control, though a few more goals would have heaped even more pressure on their group rivals. 'Everybody said it was going to be a very difficult game, but we got our tactics spot-on. We approached it in the right way. It was a very professional performance. It would have been good to have got a couple of more goals. At 2–0, if Georgia had got a goal back, it might have made the last 20 minutes very difficult. We were able to control the game after scoring the two in the first-half. But if we'd got a couple more goals, it would have put a lot more pressure on other teams who have to go there.'

The Italians wrote off Gazza as a damp squib. Sacchi's two Italian spies, who hitched a ride back on the England team plane, weren't impressed by Gazza – it was Andy Hinchcliffe they were raving about! Sacchi's No 2, Pietro Carmignani, suggested either Gascoigne or David Beckham would have to go when England were confronted with the mighty Italians at Wembley. Carmignani just shrugged his shoulders when asked about Gazza's merits in the England side. But he said: 'Batty and Ince allowed Beckham and Gascoigne to attack. I've never seen an England side that had such an organization that allowed for more than one player to go forward and express themselves. Overall, technically that was as tight an England team as I've ever seen, but against Italy I don't think England will be able to play Beckham and Gascoigne in the same side. We will have to remember that this is an England team with the ability of the forwards to score at any time. But you should not underestimate the value to this team of Hinchcliffe. I read in the English press that you don't think much of his skill, but he is as important as any other player when the England team are in possession of the ball because he holds the shape to the team. Crucially on that left side, he allows the team to function. It comes from Hinchcliffe.' Hoddle's tactical expertise in shoring up the midfield, the Georgian's strongest department, in selecting Batty alongside Ince, was a master stroke that shocked the Italians. It was not a typical English formation, but with Gascoigne in a calculated role, playing for the team rather than as a maverick. The Italians would surely now give Hoddle and his side extra respect.

Hoddle said his farewells to his England players at Luton Airport as the flight from Georgia touched down an hour before midnight. He wouldn't be seeing them again as a group until the clash with Italy in February. Whatever his frustrations about fixtures, Hoddle was coping well, sitting on a World Cup cushion of nine points from his first three games, which put him two ahead of schedule. Having got the best of the autumn weather in Moldova and Georgia, and having taken Poland while fresh, England had two home games to consolidate their position. 'We can enjoy our Christmas and look forward to Italy next February, knowing that they and Poland still have to go to Georgia. They will not find that easy.'

Georgia (0) 0 England (2) 2

Seaman, Campbell, Hinchcliffe, Southgate, Adams (capt), Batty, Ince, Gascoigne, Ferdinand, Sheringham, Beckham

	P	W	D	L	F	A	Pts
England	3	3	0	0	7	1	9
Italy	2	2	0	0	4	1	6
Poland	2	1	0	1	3	3	3
Georgia	2	0	0	2	0	3	0
Moldova	3	0	0	3	2	8	0

CHAPTER NINE

Mid-term Report:
So Far, So Good

Hoddle assesses the year ahead, January 1997

Nineteen ninety-seven dawned brightly for England as they found themselves placed 12th in FIFA's world rankings, a climb of nine places in 12 months. The improvement was based on their semi-final place in Euro 96 and the unblemished start to the World Cup campaign. Inevitably, Brazil were still No 1, followed by Germany and France.

Arrigo Sacchi had resigned as Italy's manager, just two months before the Wembley game. His replacement was Cesare Maldini, an assistant to head coach Enzo Bearzot when Italy won the 1982 World Cup. He had also led the country to the 1992, 1994 and 1996 Under-21 European Championships. As a player, he had been a star defender with AC Milan for 12 seasons, helping the club win four league titles in the 1950s and 1960s, and was capped 14 times. A player for the Azzurri in the 1960s, his son Paolo is the current Italy captain. Maldini Snr agreed a two-year contract worth £260,000. His deputy was Marco Tardelli, one of the heroes of Italian soccer after his goal in the 1982 World Cup Final against favourites West Germany.

Talking live on BBC's *Breakfast with Frost* on 12 January, Hoddle claimed that England's emerging crop of exciting youngsters would put themselves on the brink of ultimate World Cup glory once they had completed the mission of qualifying. He commented: 'We've got to qualify first and we're in a hard group. We're on course at the moment, but for me to sit here and say we're going to win the competition would be a foolish thing. In international football, the standard of teams is so close now. But I would say that with the talent we've got in the squad and in the country – the youth and the experience – we are good enough to win the World Cup.'

England's future was in the hands of youngsters like David Beckham. Sir Bobby Charlton said: 'The crowds love him and his shooting. So do I. He scores the spectacular sort of goals and blasts the kind of shots that lift the fans out of their seats. I do see parallels between his long range shooting and mine. I remember when I used to hit them like that, from way outside the box, everybody enjoyed it. And it's a great feeling. Beckham is such a natural footballer, he will go from strength to strength. He is potentially a truly great player. He is gutsy, he has enormous skill and he is not afraid to shoot from way out … he just loves doing it. And he is a good passer of the ball as well. He practises all the time. David has wanted to be a footballer since he was a little lad.' Beckham is the Hoddle ideal, the sort of player the England coach wants the FA technical director, Howard Wilkinson, to produce.

Alan Shearer had made an astonishingly rapid return to first team action for Newcastle against Chelsea at Stamford Bridge, exactly one month after his latest groin operation – but just how fit would he be for the Italy game? Strike partner Les Ferdinand was definitely still several weeks away from a return to action after suffering a depressed cheekbone in Newcastle's home draw with West Ham.

Gascoigne emerged from his troubled period to take part in Rangers' thrilling 4–3 triumph against Hearts at Celtic Park in the Scottish Coca-Cola Cup Final. He scored twice in two second-half minutes to finally extinguish Hearts' hopes of ending a 34-year wait for silverware. Gascoigne then announced that he felt ready to hit top form after weeks of worry: 'I've been nervous in the last few weeks. I've not been myself and you know the reasons why. I am starting to come to terms with what happened. It's not too bad. Now I am starting to concentrate on my football and hopefully this is the start of good things to come again.' Gazza played down a first-half flashpoint with Ally McCoist which almost resulted in an exchange of blows, arguing that having rows keeps Rangers on top. 'There wasn't much to it. I said something and Ally obviously wasn't happy. At half-time everything was sorted out, it wasn't a problem.' Walter Smith said: 'Gazza has been under a bit of pressure in the last few weeks but he is always liable to do something like that. They were two terrific goals. His ratio of goals from midfield is very high this season and when we needed them, he came up with them. We had the best of the first half-hour, but Hearts had by far the better of the next half-hour. It was Gascoigne's goals which effectively won it for us.'

Bobby Robson turned Gazza into a World Cup superstar in 1990. The Nou Camp boss put Gascoigne's decline as a force into brutal perspective. 'Paul's still a very good player – there's no doubt about that. But he's not the same player he was. In my opinion, he was the best young player at the 1990 World Cup Finals by far. He was brilliant and had the world at his feet – he was good enough to be based in Italian football and for Lazio to offer all that money for him. But it all went wrong for him a year or so later. Circumstances changed and left him in a situation where he wasn't quite the same player.'

The 'change of circumstances' to which Robson referred was Gascoigne's recklessness in the 1991 FA Cup Final. He got away with a wild lunge at Nottingham Forest's Garry Parker, but a dreadful tackle on Gary Charles minutes later rearranged Gazza's knee ligaments. Then, with his recovery progressing well, he fractured his kneecap in a mysterious tumble down the stairs of a Newcastle nightclub. Robson compared Gazza with Ronaldo, the Brazilian magician then playing for Barcelona: 'Ronaldo is a phenomenon,' purred Robson. 'He's the best player I'm aware of in the world today. But I can see similarities between him and Gazza even now. When I left Paul after the West Germany game in 1990, he was just like Ronaldo is now – the best young player of the lot and incredibly cocky about his talent. Already he could stride the same stage as the Gullits and the Van Bastens. All I wanted for people to do was to give him the ball, because his game had everything. I really grew to like the lad very much, even if I had to tick him off once for poking his tongue out during "God Save the Queen". But my worry, even then, was whether he had the capacity for self-control, to reflect what was right and what was wrong. You wondered if he knew who he should put his trust in, who to turn to when in doubt. Poor lad, I feel very sorry for him right now. His potential has been unfulfilled, he's been unhappy and it's all down to himself. I can say that because there are lots of people who have tried to help him and who had his best interests at heart. Right from the moment he committed that horrendous, stupid tackle in the Cup Final, he hasn't been able to think clearly at the critical time. I really don't know how he would cope without football when the time comes to call it a day. If he has to go out and earn a living nine-to-five, I just can't think what he can do.'

In the tranquility of Keith Wiseman's Lancaster Gate offices, the chairman of the FA discussed with me his blueprint for stability for the national team. After just three months in the England coaching position, Hoddle's appointment was Wiseman's best decision in many years. 'From the FA's point of view, stability is as beneficial as it would be in a club situation, perhaps more so,' said Wiseman. 'I'm not sure how long an individual would want to do something as high profile as the England manager's job. Twelve years might prove a long time ... but eight is more realistic.' Wiseman had been deeply impressed by Hoddle's strength of character in dealing with the Gascoigen crisis so early in his reign. 'It always amuses me how it was all built up in the media when Glenn was meeting me over the question of whether to select the player [Gazza] or not. Quite simply, Glenn came here to my office to discuss the matter immediately after the story broke in the *Mirror*. There are three issues to consider in this situation. Firstly, if it is a question of a player's form, then it is clearly a case for Glenn. Secondly, if it's a question of assessing a player's emotional well-being, again it is the domain of the England coach. Thirdly, if it is a background situation of such significance that it would affect other players chosen, or have wider implications of some sort, then both Glenn and the FA, or myself representing the FA, if you like, would need to discuss the matter. Clearly, this case called for consultation. Glenn needed to find out the facts for himself ... he told me how he wanted to deal with it. He indicated to me that he wished to pick him [Gazza] in the squad.'

But Wiseman made it clear that there would be no further reprieve for the wayward Gazza. 'Glenn would have told him exactly what would be expected of him in the future. I have a good working relationship with Glenn ... I would expect our views to coincide. If Glenn didn't get the response he was looking for from Gascoigne, then I'm sure he would take a view himself before coming to see me about it. I would be very surprised if he didn't.'

Hoddle delivered a stark warning to his England stars as they looked forward to their next World Cup qualifier, the showdown against Italy in February: do it my way, or you're fired. He demanded that there be no repeat of the shambles against Poland when the team hadn't played to their instructions. Hoddle pointed out: 'That enables us to say: "Look, this is the way it's going to be played for this certain game, get on board or you might find yourself out of the squad." I love my teams to express themselves at the right time and in the right areas. I love the passing game, and we'll always have that. But every side now in international football needs discipline and needs a tactic. Players need to know what's going on in the team shape and they didn't do it against Poland.' He added: 'I wasn't satisfied with Poland, but, in many ways, looking back, Poland's performance did everyone a favour. Because we won the game, and normally at international level, if you play poorly, you get punished. So it's encouraging that we won the game not playing so well.'

Italy were still formidable foes. Talking to Gary Lineker on BBC1's *Sportsnight* the England boss said: 'It's false to think because they [Italy] got eliminated early in the European Championships, they're a poor side. I saw them in those games and they were very unfortunate. I feel that if they'd got through that phase, they'd have probably gone onto the latter stages, if not the Final, and maybe would have won it. They've got good individuals, they're always going to be solid and they have this patience about them. And they'll have this patience at Wembley and I feel we have to be patient as well. Those are the sort of things you work on this week. As open as we were against Poland, we were very tight against Georgia. But we shouldn't be fearing anybody at the moment, especially when we're playing at Wembley.'

The long gap to the next game was a chance for detailed scouting. David James was hoping his reward for helping Liverpool go into 1997 as clear title favourites would be that first elusive England cap. Hoddle saw him star as the Merseysiders beat Southampton 1–0 at The Dell. Seaman hadn't played for a month because of broken ribs while his England No 2, Ian Walker, had conceded six in a Coca-Cola Cup tie at Bolton and seven in the Premiership at Newcastle. Flowers had also suffered a loss of form at Blackburn as the Lancashire club struggled – which left James as a shining candidate. Liverpool boss Roy Evans was in no doubt about his man's qualities: 'He keeps getting a mention when he makes the occasional mistake, but he is a very positive goalkeeper. He'll come off his line, catch balls and has made some fantastic saves. Over the period of a season his benefit to us is unbelievable. I'm not picking Glenn's team, it's bad enough picking my own. You can throw all the names in, but I think David is ready for England and I think it would stimulate him even more. I can say it and we have been saying it for a couple of years now. We think he's fantastic. Talent-wise, physically-wise and on the mental front, he's come on a ton. And that mental thing was a little bit of a doubt for him in the early days. Yes, we've felt he's been the best for a while but it's nice when someone else says it, because then I think people take more notice.

Glenn Hoddle: Dawn of a new era

Above: Glenn Hoddle's first press conference as England Coach. Terry Venables listens intently, knowing his decision to quit after Euro 96 paved the way for the early appointment of his successor.

Right: Well, if Ian Wright can make the England team then, no, of course you're not too old! Glenn poses with the Shredded Wheat girls for publicity shots for his television commercial – which was ditched after his marriage break-up.

Glenn Hoddle would lend his name to a variety of charitable causes. Here he pins a rose to his tracksuit to attract publicity for the British Heart Foundation.

Right: Glenn made five Georgian orphans ecstatically happy on 8 November 1996, taking time out of his busy schedule to meet the children from the Monastery of the Transfiguration, near Tbilisi.

Below: Glenn is touched by the Georgian orphans' drawings of him. These were hung in the FA's library at Lancaster Gate.

Left: Hoddle loves teaching the kids. Here he launches a back-to-the-future project for schoolchildren before an England training session.

Below: Alan Shearer's absence from the final matches of the campaign could have been catastrophic but England proved they were not a one-man team.

'Look, Alex, I know I've got seven of your team here, but I'm sure you wouldn't mind if I called up Brian Kidd as well...' Amazingly, Glenn needs to use a phone even with his connections!

Above: Remember, Le Tissier and Shearer used to play for Southampton together. But Hoddle's decision to pick Le Tiss for the Wembley crunch with Italy backfired and led to intense criticism of the defeat – unjustly according to the England coach.

Left: My Spice Boy! Hoddle called up David Beckham in the days before the United youngster became engaged to Posh Spice, and he's been part of England's World Cup plans throughout the qualifiers.

Above: Hoddle's backroom team stand to attention for the one-minute silence in honour of Princess Diana before the World Cup tie with Moldova. From left to right: John Gorman, Hoddle's closest confidante; the England coach; physio Gary Lewin; and Dr John Crane (far right with moustache).

Right: Part of the Tottenham connection ... former England and Spurs keeper Ray Clemence, now the goalkeeping coach and a member of Hoddle's scouting 'team'.

They might even call him the Cliff Richard of football! But G!enn enjoys a game of tennis, like most of the England squad ... as well as a chance to wear his personal sponsored Mitre shirt instead of the Football Association's Green Flag and Umbro gear.

The kind of recognition he has received from Glenn can only serve to stimulate him more.'

But then James' form took a tumble and Nigel Martyn's name was touted. He kept Leeds in the FA Cup with a last-gasp penalty save at his old club Crystal Palace, with Graham tipping him for a call-up against Italy. Martyn said: 'I've been playing as well as I have ever done. All I've got to do is play as well as I can and keep my fingers crossed. But it was one of the reasons behind my move to Leeds last summer. The Premiership is a much bigger stage than Division One, it's the place you've got to be.' George Graham commented: 'He's a very good player and he should be in the England team. I didn't realize that until I worked with him. He's exceptional.'

Meanwhile, Gareth Southgate had suffered further ligament damage in the ankle he first hurt against Poland. There was a big question mark over his fitness for Italy. He pledged not to make the same mistake twice and rush back, even though it could cost him his England place. 'I tried to play for Villa against Sunderland only two-and-a-half weeks after injuring the ankle on the first occasion against Poland, and in hindsight I realize that it was too early. This second setback is annoying and I will be out of the picture for at least a month unless I can make some sort of miracle recovery. But this time I have got to rest and make sure I don't try and come back too early. However much you want to play, you will not be doing anybody any favours if you cannot do yourself justice.'

Alex Ferguson feared that Gary Pallister might be set for another unhappy spell on the sidelines after a recurrence of the back injury. Despite being plagued by the injury for more than a year, Ferguson continued to rule out surgery. The United manager explained: 'I'm not considering surgery, that would keep him out for a long time, so we are trying to find a way round that. Treatment and rest will help and hopefully he will be back quickly.'

Hoddle was at White Hart Lane to watch Steve McManaman return to form, and score one of the freakiest goals of the season, the ball hitting a divot and bouncing over Ian Walker. Evans believed the elusive McManaman would be one of the best players in the world if he could find a killer instinct in front of goal. The Liverpool boss said: 'Steve would admit himself he needs a better percentage of end product from the positions he gets in. I don't think he's far off world class now, but if he got a few more goals, he would be right up there. He's a different player from Ronaldo, but he's just as valuable to us as the Brazilian is to Barcelona. And he's beyond offer.' We shall see ...

Norwich winger Darren Eadie was one of the players Hoddle wanted scouted. And Ugo Ehiogu wanted Hoddle to sit up and take notice, but the 24-year-old Aston Villa defender had been overhauled in the international stakes by Sol Campbell. But he vowed: 'My England ambitions are stronger than ever. Good luck to Sol, who seems to have got ahead of me in the queue by seizing his big chance with both hands. I was struggling for my best form with Villa at the beginning of the season, which probably affected Glenn Hoddle's thinking. That is all behind me, though, and I will be pushing to persuade him that I am worth considering when the squad is named for the clash with Italy.'

Stuart Pearce wanted to make sure his England place would not be in danger because he had become Forest's manager. 'Make no mistake, the England situation is of uppermost importance to me. I have made that quite clear. Don't pay any attention to the fact that I retired for a week or so late summer. It is extremely important to me and I'm not jeopardizing my England place or being involved in the England squad for anything. But I am hoping that Glenn Hoddle is flexible – and I am sure that is the case. He's only concerned about how a player performs on a football pitch. But if he felt that me being the manager of Nottingham Forest – and it's a full-time commitment -might cause a problem, then it is something that I would have to address.' John Gorman spoke briefly to Pearce before giving his vote of confidence. 'Stuart has taken a hell of a lot on his shoulders but it doesn't appear to bother him. It is Glenn's decision, but I will certainly make my feelings clear on the subject. We all know how much England means to Stuart, and the benefits he brings to the whole squad.'

The fiercely ambitious John Scales switched from Liverpool to Spurs for £2.5 million in search of an England comeback. Scales rejected Leeds, insisting that Gerry Francis and the England internationals at Spurs swung it for him. 'I have won three England caps. I'm 30 now, but it's not too late to work my way into the World Cup squad. I can achieve that. I have great faith in my ability.'

There was no sign of a return for Forest's Steve Stone, while Andy Hinchcliffe would be out until the next season with serious knee damage. The Everton defender injured his cruciate ligament during a goalless draw with Leeds. His then boss, Joe Royle, said: 'You can only feel for the lad. It's taken him a comparatively long time to reach the top of his profession, and to suffer a setback so soon is sickening for him. It's terrible news for him and ourselves.'

Hoddle watched Graeme Le Saux's progress with Blackburn at Selhurst Park against Wimbledon. Fast and attack-minded, Le Saux was the ideal wing-back for England. The 28-year-old Channel Islander had recovered from the fractured ankle that sidelined him for ten months and saw him miss the European Championship. He was still recovering full match fitness and was not back to his absolute best, but Ewood Park caretaker-manager Tony Parkes believed he deserved his international recall. Parkes said: 'Graeme came back into the Blackburn side ahead of schedule and I now feel he's ready to be called into the England squad. He can only go from strength to strength now. He doesn't train every day at present and he's still not 100 per cent right but his quality on the ball makes up for that. Because of that we had no hesitation about bringing him back at West Ham a few weeks ago, even though it was a bit too soon for him.'

Apart from Pearce, there was only real competition from Phil Neville, but the talented Manchester United defender was ruled out by glandular fever. He had been dogged by injuries, which had kept him out of all three of Hoddle's opening World Cup ties.

Cesare Maldini's first task as Italy's coach was to organize a friendly to help prepare for England. He said: 'Clearly we can't go to Wembley with a whole new group, but there will be some changes. We have a lot of work to do but the conditions are there for success. No coach is a saviour, though. The players are the protagonists.' Two days before Christmas, a fixture was confirmed after days of haggling over the match fee! Northern Ireland accepted the offer of a lucrative friendly in Palermo. The game came three days before the next round of FA Cup ties and the release of top players, even for such a prestige game, gave the then Northern Ireland manager, Bryan Hamilton, a headache.

The end of the year saw recognition for David Seaman's heroics in Euro 96 with the award of an MBE in the Queen's Honours List. 'It's a great end to a brilliant year for me,' said an ecstatic Seaman. Official confirmation of the award marked a day of double delight for the Arsenal keeper, who came through his first training session after having been out of action for six weeks with cracked ribs.

Meanwhile, Hoddle travelled to France early in the New Year to study the set-up for the summer tournament, the Tournoi de France. 'I'm not here in advance of the World Cup, we still haven't qualified for that yet. I've come to look at things before this summer's tournament, and England against Italy in June will be a really big match.' A couple of weeks later, he again took the short flight to Paris to be in place for the launch of the French tournament.

Hoddle was at the luxurious and mightily impressive Hotel de Ville in the centre of Paris for the official launch of the competition which carried a prize of around £625,000 for the winners. He believed the tournament would be of great merit ahead of the World Cup. 'We are looking forward to the challenge. It will be a good experience for the players and for me to find out a bit more about ourselves in a tournament. I've only been in the job for six months, and while of course qualifying for the World Cup is the important thing, I'm looking upon this summer as a dress rehearsal for 1998. We will be coming to France to win next summer because it is prestigious, but the main objective is to gain some extra experience as a team ahead of the real test which we hope to have next year.'

The fact that England would be playing Italy in a friendly between two World Cup qualifiers aroused some concern, although Hoddle did not seem overly worried. 'As far as we are concerned, it isn't a problem. We have to play Italy in the qualifiers but this will be totally different. When you're playing a World Cup game, the result is all important, the only thing you can think about. But in a friendly, even in a tournament, it gives you the chance to experiment, to look and see what you have, what options are available.' Maldini displayed a similar lack of concern about the prospects of a 'shadow-boxing' clash. 'For us, like England, qualification is the prime objective and we know how big a game it will be at Wembley. We don't have to be told that England are a strong team. You only have to look at the likes of Shearer, Ferdinand and Beckham to see that. There are other players as well, but perhaps we are helped a little bit because now we have players like Zola and Ravanelli who are playing in England.'

CHAPTER TEN

Zola and the *Azzurri*

The Italians arrive in London, February 1997

By 2 January, the last 10,000 seats for England v Italy at Wembley had been snapped up. The tickets, the first to go on open sale to the public, were available from the Wembley box office at 9 am and had all been sold by 12.45 pm, making it a 76,000 sell-out.

Gianfranco Zola was making a big impact for Chelsea in the Premiership. A few days before the qualifier he said: 'Whoever wins will take a big step towards the Finals. It's going to be a hard game, a very tactical battle and we will be as afraid of England as they will be afraid of us. Gazza is an excellent player – I came up against him in Italy and he's a very influential man when he's fit and in form. Glenn Hoddle has a lot of midfield players to choose from and a lot of possible permutations. When you look through the England team there are several players who could be protagonists, like Gascoigne, Shearer and McManaman. They are all potential match winners and we will give them every respect.'

Zola admitted that the man-marking in the Premiership had given him problems, but he would not mind if England put a man on him. 'It is something I am used to,' he said. 'I expect man-marking every game.' Dean Austin, who had man-marked him for Spurs, observed: 'There were times when I had to go into tackles against other players and I was left desperately looking for him. It was very hard because I wasn't in the game. Chaperoning such a player, you only have to leave him for a split second and you're dead. Suddenly the ball is in the net. Either he has put it there or laid it on for someone else. His movement off the ball is superb and his runs are devastating.'

Roberto Di Matteo watched Gascoigne play the joker for three years at Lazio – but now he feared he would be England's Wembley trump card. Gascoigne's was the first name the Italians looked for on Hoddle's team sheet. Di Matteo said: 'If a player of Gazza's ability doesn't play at Wembley, maybe our job will be a bit easier. He's still a great player and he can make all the difference to his team in one moment.' Di Matteo took a sympathetic view of his miserable attendance record at Lazio. 'If we didn't often see Gazza at his best in Italian football, that's probably because he was a bit unlucky with injuries.'

Matt Le Tissier was experiencing extremes of form and fortune. His then boss, Graeme Souness, hinted that he couldn't be guaranteed a place in the Southampton team but he hit form just as Hoddle brooded over his Italian selection. But if Hoddle kept faith with the new generation, notably Beckham, then Le Tissier understood. 'If that happened, I would be able to handle the situation better than I did when Terry Venables dumped me. That experience upset me so much at the time, but it has made me mentally tougher. It has also made me more determined to stay in the England squad.'

Hoddle flew to Palermo to watch Italy's only warm-up game, against Northern Ireland. Maldini changed to a sweeper system, in preparation for stopping Shearer. The watching Hoddle also discovered that Zola was in as devastating form for country as he had been for Chelsea.

The smoke had hardly cleared over the La Favorita Stadium after the firework display greeting a new Italian era when Zola opened the scoring with one of his specialist strikes. 'I've always thought that technically Zola is up there with the best in Europe,' said Hoddle, 'but I also think he's very clever, very astute. We all know about international defenders who can read the game when the other side have the ball. Zola is an attacker who reads the game extremely well when his own team have the ball. If you give him space, he'll use it. I've always admired him, which is why I tried to buy him for Chelsea. He's a lovely footballer.'

Perhaps most interesting for Hoddle was the return of the sweeper, the role handed to the experienced Juventus defender Ciro Ferrara. Even a wickedly depleted Northern Ireland side, with only a couple of Premiership players, showed the watching England coach that there might be the odd chance for Shearer. Naturally, Hoddle also appreciated the variety of long-range passes from playmaker Demetrio Albertini.

The debate centred around Zola, Del Piero, Albertini and Italy's return to type and the sweeper system. But Hoddle, if he was to fulfil his aspirations, had to concentrate on the emerging talents of Beckham, the conviction that Shearer could become the world's number one striker, that Gascoigne could truly change his ways and that Seaman was the world's top goalkeeper.

The biggest threat to that dream was Italy. Hoddle was keeping his thoughts privy only to his trusted aide Gorman. He let his armour slip momentarily when he said: 'The Italians have very good players if you give them time and space, if you allow them to use the ball. But we have got individual players with possibly more flair, if you talk about Alan Shearer, Teddy Sheringham, Matt Le Tissier, David Beckham and Paul Gascoigne, all scorers of free-kicks just as well. Maybe we have more individual flair through the squad. Whether we have more in the team, let's wait and see.'

Hoddle went on: 'They've got great individuals who can turn a game. I watched them closely in Euro 96 – the personnel hasn't changed, but the way they play has. They're a lot different to Italy under Arrigo Sacchi. They went with three at the back. They were nowhere near as rigid in their shape or structure, and that means we will be given more time on the ball. There's great experience in their side and you could see that they weren't worried about Ireland putting so many players behind the ball. They just waited to pick them off when the time was right, but it will be much different at Wembley. Under Maldini they don't go man for man at the back; they are content to play a zonal marking game which is a major difference, and one I wasn't expecting. When they made changes in the second half it was like for like, so that leads me to believe they will pretty much be the same team and formation when they come to Wembley.'

Hoddle came away with a notebook containing the details of how an attack led by Shearer could pierce the Italian defence; equally, he wasn't underestimating the talents of Zola and Del Piero. 'Whether they think they can play both of them at Wembley, I don't know, they're obviously rivals for the same place. You look at Zola and see the way he played for the first 15 minutes or so and you can see why he's regarded so highly in Italy. He was at his best, and so were Italy for that period. Zola and Del Piero caused problems when they're given time and space and we will have to work hard to deny them that at Wembley. We'll also have to be alert to stop them getting the ball in forward areas where they can destroy any team in the world. But I want them to be worried about us. We won't be anywhere near as defensive as Ireland and will have players going forward to trouble Italy – hopefully, not the other way round! To that end I saw areas that they can be punished in. It was difficult to call them vulnerable because they weren't put under the same amount of pressure as we will put them under. It was invaluable for me to see it. I learned a lot and I saw a lot that I can work on in the build-up to Wembley. I'm not going to say that I feel what their weaknesses are. But let's say I feel encouragement. And, there are definitely areas that are great food for thought.'

Zola picked out McManaman as the danger to Italy. Yet, McManaman was not even sure he would be picked! He was turning into just as big an enigma as Matt Le Tissier. Brilliant on the ball, a wonderful dribbler, virtually unstoppable, but, perhaps unlike Le Tissier, a woeful finisher. Yet Zola said: 'McManaman is excellent, he can turn a game round when it's "stalled".' Zola's English was rapidly improving, but he meant 'deadlocked'.

Gazza feared he would be out of the Italy game after a moment of madness had left him crocked. He limped away from Glasgow Rangers' Euro six-a-side tournament in Amsterdam with a seriously injured ankle following a crazy tackle. Hoddle spoke with Gazza and Walter Smith. He planned to contact them both again for an update on the situation. A spokesman for the FA said: 'It looks as if Gazza is very doubtful. We cannot write him off at this stage, but the chances of him being fit are not very good.' In the end Gazza was to be included in Hoddle's squad, despite having his left ankle in plaster.

In the absence of Hinchcliffe, there was to be a key role for Le Saux. Hoddle said: 'It is a position that there aren't many players who can play it naturally. Graeme is one, Andy Hinchliffe is another and he did a terrific job for the three games. You feel when Graeme is playing left-back, he wants to get forward more than he is allowed in a back four and that is what you're looking for in players in that position.' His crossing power, allied to that of Beckham from the other flank, would be vital against a side which had suggested an aerial vulnerability in Sicily. Le Saux said: 'I still feel a little hesitant, but I've had a few tackles recently and everything feels fine. I'd like the opportunity to play against Italy but that's up to the powers-that-be. I guess getting in is not an ultimatum for me. I've come a hell of a long way in a short space of time. Just to hear others say I should be in is flattering. Right now, I've had 13 games. I didn't even think I'd play reserve team football until December.'

Team-mate Chris Sutton, who himself was out for eight months with ankle problems, said: 'Graeme isn't only an excellent player, he's also a very good organizer on the pitch. I think the statistics since he came back speak for themselves. I would say he has to be back in the England squad.' Sutton, too, was tipped for a surprise call-up, with Blackburn's caretaker boss Tony Parkes reminding Hoddle of the deadly partnership he formed with Shearer in their first season together. Parkes added: 'It's strange but when people look at the top strikers behind Shearer you hear the names of Les Ferdinand, Robbie Fowler and Ian Wright. Nobody ever seems to pick up on Sutton. Yet Chris has been a key figure in our revival. OK, I would be surprised if he came into the squad virtually from nowhere. But when you remember how well he played with Shearer in our championship season, it might be a good thing to put them together again.'

Teddy Sheringham was certain to be out after damaging his ankle in a freak training ground collision with Spurs' reserve keeper Espen Baardsen at the start of the month. At Manchester United, Beckham had to fight off an ankle injury and Pallister's old back problem was still plaguing him.

The England squad eventually named for the game against Italy was: Seaman (Arsenal), Walker (Spurs), James (Liverpool), Flowers (Blackburn), Southgate (Aston Villa), Matteo (Liverpool), Pearce (Nottm Forest), Le Saux (Blackburn), G Neville (Man Utd), Adams (Arsenal), Campbell (Spurs), Ince (Inter Milan), Gascoigne (Rangers), Beckham (Man Utd), McManaman (Liverpool), Batty (Newcastle), Lee (Newcastle), Merson (Arsenal), Barmby (Everton), Wright (Arsenal), Ferdinand (Newcastle), Le Tissier (Southampton), Shearer (Newcastle), Fowler (Liverpool).

Tim Flowers and Robert Lee were back. Both might have been forgiven for thinking their England careers were over after the harshest of setbacks in the space of three months in the summer of 1996. Lee had suffered the unkindest cut of all when he was among the six men omitted from Venables' Euro 96 squad after the Far East tour to Hong Kong and China. His form had subsequently suffered, as he admitted, although he had since returned to near his best. He was recalled in place of Platt. Hoddle commented: 'Rob's in good form. He gives us a bit of a threat from midfield and he can play in other positions as well.' With Gascoigne's left ankle in plaster, it was a wise precaution to include the versatile Newcastle man. Flowers had paid the price for Blackburn's problems and his own loss of form when he found himself relegated behind James in the goalkeeping pecking order when Hoddle named his first squad of the year. But he was selected as one of a quartet of keepers, along with Seaman, Ian Walker and David James.

The only other change was the return of Shearer for the injured Sheringham. Shearer was a certain starter but, unexpectedly, Hoddle was non-commital on the return of the captain's armband. Instead, Hoddle wanted to talk to both Shearer and Adams before making any public pronouncement: 'I said from the outset that Alan would be given three games and I would assess it after that. Obviously I didn't know he was going to be injured for the Georgia trip. I think I said Alan would probably return as captain, but to be honest, I prefer to talk to the lads when we meet up next week and discuss that. There won't be any 100 per cent decision made at this time.' Euro 96 inspiration Adams took over in Tbilisi and led England to a fine 2–0 victory, but there was no doubt that Shearer was more his kind of man than the fire-breathing Arsenal defender. 'Abroad they looked to Platini, to Maradona, that sort of player. Not necessarily the best captain for 90 minutes but someone who commands respect from everyone in the world, including referees, which is a big advantage,' said Hoddle. There was no doubt that Shearer fell into that class, only Ronaldo and Weah matching his current standing among the best in the world. He was to be named captain.

After a moderate performance in Tbilisi, the debate over whether England could afford to do without Gascoigne had become less pressing. Gascoigne's status had diminished while that of others had grown. England had strong alternatives and Gascoigne's ankle injury could have proved convenient for Hoddle. However, Gascoigne, at his best, remained irreplaceable. He announced he was sure to be fit. 'I've spoken to Glenn and told him I will be ready for the England match – there's no doubt about it. Monday is vital for me, as I'll see if I'm training Tuesday or Wednesday. Hopefully next Wednesday I'll be kicking a ball. Obviously I've got to stay fit for the England game and hopefully I'll get called into the squad. I'm also looking forward to the Italy game. It's nice playing big games and this is one of the biggest since the European Championships. Italy have a fantastic squad and it will be a packed house at Wembley.'

There was a familiar pragmatism to Hoddle when he said that though it was a 'crunch' game in the qualifying group, he felt no more excited than he had for Moldova and Georgia. You don't get an extra point for beating Italy, he pointed out.

When the England squad gathered at Bisham Abbey, Hoddle began the job of urging patience from players and public alike and reminded his men how they had rectified the mistakes of a scrambled victory over Poland by winning in Georgia. He reiterated the importance of showing respect for, but not fear of, Italy.

Parma striker Enrico Chiesa was recalled by Italy. Maldini made three other changes to strengthen his defence. In came defenders Antonio Benarrivo and Real Madrid's Christian Panucci, while out went injured AC Milan midfielder Stefano Eranio. Otherwise, Maldini stuck to the midfield which had so impressed Hoddle in the Northern Ireland match. 'What's important is being able to change things during the match, which means I need all-round players. I'll also be counting a lot on those with international experience,' said Maldini.

Pierluigi Casiraghi, the £5 million-rated Lazio frontman vowed to make the most powerful 'come and get me' message possible at Wembley. 'Liverpool are my favourite English team, but I'd love to play in England, especially in London. I think I'm an English-type player, so it will be a big test for me at Wembley to see what I can do against English defenders. Nobody from England has actually been in touch with me or my agent yet, but I know that my name has been mentioned and that there is some interest. The only problem will be that there are quite a lot of centre-forwards of that type in England, and I'm one of the few over here. But I'd love the chance to see what I can do.'

Tino Asprilla backed Newcastle team-mates Shearer and Ferdinand to get among the goals. The Colombian striker, who played for Parma before his £7 million move to Tyneside, insisted: 'There's no reason why Shearer and Ferdinand won't score on the night. Without a doubt they have the capability – they are two of the best players in the world at the moment. But the game won't simply be about those two. It really depends on how the rest of the team performs from front to back.' Asprilla warned England to watch out for his former Parma partner, Zola. 'England must try to keep his vision in check. Zola has an extraordinary imagination and an excellent football brain. It's going to be a tough, testing game for England ... and I have no idea what the result will be!'

Paolo Maldini took his first look at Wembley in seven years as the Italians trained there in the morning on the damp turf the day before the big game. He said: 'There is no point in coming here to look for a draw. That would be playing into England's hands. We must look to impose ourselves on England, make them play to our rhythm. Our aim from the start is to win the game, to take all three points back home with us, and so we will be willing to attack England. Of course, we won't go for it totally, because it would not be right to attack too much and it is a game we cannot afford to lose if we want to win the group. But we must look to impose ourselves on England, make them play to our rhythm. It's crucial that we do that, that we try to win the game.' Maldini, now a 75-cap veteran, was only at the start of his international career when he played in the goalless draw against Robson's side in 1990, a game in which his opposite left-back, Pearce, was the only England survivor. Seven years on, there was a hint of apprehension as he weighed up the prospect of playing the new-look England, the success of Euro 96 still propelling them onwards. 'I have fond memories of the game here in 1990, but we know it will be very different this time. This time I feel a little nervous, nervous for me and not my father. Of course, that's normal, but this is such an important match for us, as it is for England.' Uppermost in Italian thoughts was the England skipper, Alan Shearer. Maldini observed: 'We know Shearer is the best striker in England, and everybody remembers what he did in Euro 96. Since then, he's gone on to prove himself one of the best strikers in the world. He won't do anything to surprise me, because at home we can watch the Premiership on television and can watch every match. We're not worried about him, or Beckham, but we have respect for what he can do. We know he is world class.' Maldini felt he had something to show people, after his reputation had been called into question when he was caught out by Karel Poborsky during Euro 96. Maldini promised: 'We are a better team than we looked in Euro 96. This is our chance to prove it.'

Cesare Maldini was hoping to kickstart a bright new future. He said: 'The days of defensive football in Italy are now a thing of the past. We have not come to Wembley to defend against England. We know we must try to win. England are the home team, and of course the favourites, but our hope is to stop their attacks and then sting them with our counterplay.' Inevitably he was besieged by an army of Italian media and a strong contingent of eager British press, almost wrestling one another to hear his words. Would it be a disaster if Italy lost to England? He insisted not. 'Certainly it is an important game for both teams but there will be no tragedy if Italy lose. This game has come too early in the qualifying group and I admit I would have preferred a little more time, but that has been long accepted because there is nothing we can do about it. What happens will be all about the football on the night. There are so many great players on both sides and there is a growing respect for English football, not only in Italy, but everywhere. I have inherited some excellent players from Sacchi, however, and they are my players now. I am sure they will play well and I believe England will play well also. Finally it could all be decided by a single mistake.'

The newly-acquired English knowhow of Zola and Di Matteo could give Italy an edge, but Maldini said: 'There are so many videos around today, you can see every player in every country and know everything about the way he performs. The English know both Zola and Di Matteo and what they can do, but they must still decide how to stop them doing it. It is similar with the excellent English players. We are hearing now that Paul Gascoigne is fit and will play, but we are not afraid of him. We respect him but only just as much as all the others.'

When Adams and Seaman reported for World Cup duty, they went straight to physiotherapist Gary Lewin's treatment room. Seaman had played through Arsenal's FA Cup defeat by Leeds with an injury, wearing tracksuit bottoms to protect a heavily bandaged knee, while Adams had twisted an ankle.

Hoddle fretted over Gascoigne's fitness but vehemently denied stories coming out of Scotland that Gascoigne had pulled out of the match. 'I believe there have been some reports coming through, but put it this way, I've not spoken to Walter Smith about it. Our medical staff have spoken to the Rangers medical people. He is still a doubt for the game, for sure, he's only just come out of plaster at the weekend. We shall have to see whether we have a fit Paul Gascoigne, but there is no communication problem with Glasgow Rangers, and Walter has given his blessing for him to come down here. Certainly, Paul's muscles need strengthening, when you've been in plaster for two or three days there can be some muscle wastage, not just the ankle but the calf. If he does come back, we don't want him pulling a calf muscle. I have six influential players who won't train for two or three days. I've waited three months for my next game and I've ended up with that scenario. I can't tell you how frustrating it is.'

Maldini was already sure that Gascoigne wouldn't be playing. He scoffed at Hoddle's complaints about his injured sextet, Gascoigne, Adams, Ince, Shearer, Seaman and Lee. 'Hoddle is talking about injuries, but I have my doubts about how many will be out. The thing I am certain of is that Gascoigne won't play a part, but I'm sure the others will be available.'

If key players were ruled out, would England have difficulty filling in the gaps? Stuart Pearce answered: 'I think this is the strongest group there has ever been. A few years ago, if an England team had been threatened with the loss of Gary Lineker, we might have wondered where the goals were going to come from. Now, as much as we need Alan Shearer, there would be someone as capable to step in. That applies through the team. There is a strength in depth through the squad. We have good, versatile players in all positions.'

With Gascoigne struggling, McManaman was favourite to replace him. The Liverpool man commented: 'It is a role I play, but Paul Merson can play there too and he has been in excellent form. I was very disappointed not to play in Georgia, but I accepted it because the decision to change the structure was right.' His quest for self-improvement concentrated on his finishing. 'I've got eight this year, but I'd like to think I could score 25 in a season. I get a lot of chances. Sometimes I'm a bit unselfish and I pass, but people tell me to be more greedy, to shoot in the box. Maybe that ruthlessness is the difference between being a midfielder and a centre-forward. A centre-forward's first thought when he receives the ball is to look for goal, maybe I am looking for the pass to put Robbie through or whatnot. It frustrates me. I've hit the woodwork many times this year, so it is a fine line. I regularly do shooting practice with Robbie – I am better, but on the pitch he has that killer instinct. Goalscoring is a major thing missing from my game, but there are other parts I have to improve on –

defending, heading. Even the good things can be improved. I see people dribbling and I feel I can learn off them.'

Hoddle wanted McManaman to concentrate on his all-round game, not just his shooting and goalscoring. 'He needs to improve in the last third, and his finishing could be better, but he is a provider. Maybe he needs to go back to just being a provider. He makes space with his runs by drawing defenders towards him and maybe he needs to put the creator's hat on again more than the goalscorers. He will probably pop up and score then. His best position is the one he plays at Liverpool, but within a team shape you have to ask if you can afford a floating player. There is discipline when the other side have the ball – he only floats when Liverpool have it.'

Jamie Redknapp's call-up was something of a surprise as he had been in the international wilderness since Euro 96. His last appearance for England – against Scotland in June 96 – had ended with him being stretchered off with damaged ankle ligaments. Redknapp said: 'I can't honestly say that I deserve to be in the squad after the way I've been playing. But I hope no-one begrudges me the call. Playing for England has cost me dearly on two occasions, so I'm going to take this chance with both hands. It is a tremendous compliment to be picked by Glenn Hoddle, especially when I haven't been doing quite as well as I would have liked. It is a huge psychological boost to be selected for your country and hopefully it will be the thing to spark my season.'

Meanwhile, Hoddle took the unusual step of issuing a statement, prompted by unconfirmed reports that Gascoigne had left the hotel without permission just a few hours after the squad met up and that he was planning to divorce his wife. The England camp were tipped off that a tabloid would be running the story on their front page the next morning. 'Both stories are untrue,' Hoddle said. 'I have spoken to Paul personally in the past few minutes in the hotel. He has assured me that he is working to make his marriage work. That is one of the aims of the counselling he continues to have. He spent last weekend with his wife and children. I am disgusted to hear that Mrs Gascoigne has been besieged at her home in Hertfordshire. I suspect this is only happening because we are in the build-up to an England game.'

David Batty rekindled an association with Graeme Le Saux which a year earlier had ended in an incredible on-pitch fight. The two had scrapped during a Blackburn Champions' League tie. Two weeks later Le Saux so badly damaged an ankle that he was out for ten months, while Batty was transferred to Newcastle. Batty said: 'There are no problems now, but at the time it was very embarrassing for both of us. We had lots of regrets about what happened. It's finished now.'

Inter Milan's Paul Ince was Hoddle's spy in the camp. 'Being in Italy shows me how far I have come in my career. We've got a lot of great players in England and it's a shame there aren't more of them out there with me, we've certainly got the talent. It's not as physical as English football, and that makes me all the more pleased with how I have adapted because last year a lot of people were saying I would never make it in Italy, that I should come back to England. And here I am now doing well for Milan. That's a big thing for me personally.' Ince warned that the demise of Sacchi and rise of Maldini had perked up the Italians. 'Everyone's a lot happier now they have changed manager, but I don't understand why because, under Sacchi, if Zola hadn't missed a penalty, they would have been in the Euro semi-finals, and they won his last two games. Living out there I could see people did not like him. Now, under Cesare Maldini, people are smiling again. It's a big game for both of us. We have the utmost respect for the Italians. I'm sure they have the same for us.'

Maldini is famed for his traditionally defensive brand of football, but he admitted the *Azzurri* would have to adapt. 'The English game has changed compared to the stereotypes of the past – they no longer play with just long passes. Their teams have a more organic game now, based more and more on physical performance. Chelsea, Newcastle and Liverpool have a more complete game and the fact that the English have not won internationally for a while doesn't mean a thing; there's always a first time. If we take the pitch at Wembley thinking we can simply "contain" the English, they will crush us and slam us into our own goal. So we'll need to play with caution, but we cannot give up [attacking] – we'll have to play the kind of game that Italy knows how to play in these circumstances.' Maldini was from Italy's old school of football that preached *il catenaccio*, or 'the bolt': defending in numbers and attacking on the break. While not immune to changing tactics, he prefers a traditional libero and two marking defenders. 'That's why I called up Chiesa. I remembered that he played winger for Cremonese and could offer us an alternative on the right side of midfield to Di Livio.'

Shearer's goal prowess worried the Italians. Casiraghi, top scorer in the Italian squad with 11 goals from 38 appearances, said: 'Shearer is a complete striker. It will be good for me to be able to compare myself with him as well. He's so good in the air and he has the ability to strike and score from all sorts of angles and positions.'

Ravanelli spoke to Italian journalists in Florence about the strengths and weaknesses of the England team. He had given Maldini a rundown on the England players and named Shearer and McManaman as the men to watch. 'McManaman is the central hinge of the team, the man around whom England's whole game turns. He can get past defenders very easily and would be a plus for many Italian teams. He's England's most in-form player. But we all know Shearer. He's got an innate sense for scoring goals, with a strong game in the air and a better right foot than left. But he sometimes has problems with aggressive defending.'

Ravanelli saluted Seaman as one of the best goalkeepers in the game. 'I know him well because he has caused me all kinds of problems. He managed somehow to block two of my shots which were virtually already goals.' He added that Adams 'appears slow, but is no snail. We've got to watch out for his headers from corners.'

Zola raised the temperature by accusing English defenders of becoming hatchet men when confronted by skilful players. His experience in the Premiership had convinced him that the influx of continental players had exposed many defenders as being too slow and clumsy to deal with opponents of genuine flair. 'Players like myself are different from typical English strikers. The marking in England does not trouble me and their defenders are uneasy facing me, in comparison with big, lumbering forwards. It is an advantage for me, but also a hazard – they bring me down when they challenge me. England have been insisting that they will play a tactical game but I don't believe them. Their temperament is completely different from ours. When an Englishman sees a brick wall he will charge at it and try to knock it down instead of going around it.'

Zola and his Italian team-mates had a great deal more respect for English attackers. Zola's warning that 'Shearer's shooting is equally deadly from any position' was reinforced by Ravanelli. 'England's star players are in peak form and Shearer is scoring some sensational goals. It will be a tough game for us.' Chelsea's other Italian, Di Matteo, passed on the message that England had added some subtlety to their traditionally robust approach. 'England can make us suffer by their use of the high ball. It is their main style of play, but fortunately we have got enough big men at the back. Unluckily for us, however, players like Steve McManaman and Paul Gascoigne are able to combine skill and strength.'

Defender Alessandro Costacurta said: 'Shearer reminds me of [the Brazilian striker] Careca, who had great instinct for goals and could score with his head and both feet. He was the only centre-forward who ever made me lose sleep on the eve of a game. This is another big challenge for me.'

If Hoddle was faking his concerns about injuries, it was an act that deserved an Oscar. He was anxious about the 'spine' of his team, Seaman in goal, Adams at centre-half, Gascoigne and Ince in midfield and Shearer up front. 'In an ideal world I'd like to know the situation by Sunday night, but I can't see that happening. It's not what I wanted but I'm going to have to adjust and allow that to happen right up to Tuesday. Players would have to be shuttled around if two or three certain players didn't make it. It would be bad to lose those five because they are all key players and any coach would be worried about that situation.'

Hoddle needed a full strength team to take on the Azzurri, who had only lost four World Cup qualifiers in the last 38 years. 'I've got to plan for three or four different scenarios of my team. The injuries are not ready to be tested yet so that forces my hand. If we were confident about bringing them into the group and letting them have their first day's real training, we would have done that. I'm not going to gain at all by holding them back longer than they really need, because both Pauls [Ince and Gascoigne] got their injuries nine or ten days ago, and Paul Ince has been out suspended. So they will need some training. But Tuesday must be the cut-off point. I would be foolish to risk them in such a big game if they are only 80 per cent fit – both for club and country.'

Hoddle failed in his quest to get closer to his players by bringing the England dugout nearer to the touchline. Instead of the promised co-operation, Wembley officials told him he would be obstructing paying spectators' views if he moved forward from the present position 20 yards away from the touchline. He had first asked for five seats by the advertising boards. No. He asked for just three. No. Hoddle joked: 'I'm too tall. Perhaps I'll end up getting the sack for being 6ft 1in!' He refused to give up. He believed it was important to get over his message to the players. 'The situation with spectators viewing from behind is the major problem if I bring the seats up to the boards. Wembley dictate the seating arrangements and when we revamp the stadium it's something we must seriously think about. The distance at the moment is too far to communicate with players. You just want to be sitting nearer the pitch so you can get something across when it's needed. Other countries seem to do it and it doesn't seem to be too much of a problem. We will continue to work on it.' Hoddle was asked if he could not move just himself: 'I'd look pretty silly sitting out there on my own!' he laughed. 'We asked for five seats up against the boards and then we knocked it down to three. The subs and physios would stay where they are now. But in the end it was still a problem. I can understand the reasons why and we're working to overcome them.'

Although it was getting closer to his biggest test, there was no sign of nerves. Hoddle was in great form. Asked his opinion of Paolo Maldini, he replied: 'His major strength at the moment, he's the son of the coach.'

'There's not a lot between the two sides,' was Hoddle's assessment. 'They are an excellent side and we believe we can be an excellent side. If we make the players perform as well as they can within the team framework, then we will win. It's who is going to play in a relaxed manner with the right frame of mind. We have to be excited but not too tense. We need steel and a positive frame of mind without going over that line where you freeze and there is too much fear. We need to use the support rather than let it overwhelm us. Sometimes the opposition can get too tense. It is hard, though, to see the Italians being overwhelmed; the best players should be inspired in such an environment. I think it's going to be a patient game at times, with their philosophy, but I don't think they will be ultra-defensive. They will press and try to score goals. Sometimes it's easier to get three points away from home. But I thought the crowd were patient with England in the summer. I enjoyed being there and seeing that.'

On the Monday morning Hoddle proclaimed Gascoigne fit. Was the England coach playing a devious game of double bluff with the Italians? Hoddle was convinced Gazza was making an effort to reform. 'In between the last get together he has worked extremely hard at the problems he had, as well as his football. His form has been good – we've watched him very closely. He hasn't been in trouble with referees as much as before, he's definitely trying hard on and off the pitch to change a little. He will always be the cheeky chappie, you won't change that and I think it's right he stays that way. He's very humorous and good to have around the camp. The main thing for me is his performances, and when he gets out on the training pitch he's professional, trains extremely hard and pushes himself. Sometimes he pushes himself too far and we were a bit worried about that with him just having come out of plaster, but his attitude has been spot-on.' Hoddle revealed that Gascoigne had come through a fitness test, but as he discussed the player's improvement, there was still a lingering suspicion as to whether he would play.

But Hoddle's further comments suggested that Gascoigne, Seaman and Shearer would all make it! 'The positive sign is Alan, Paul and David came through in good shape. All the players had tests today and we've had different degrees of improvement. I'm very positive about those three and I hope they'll be available. I'm a little worried Alan may wake up in the morning with a reaction in his back. He hasn't trained for three or four days and it was a fairly stringent test today, but at present I think he'll be okay. David's knee was fine and Paul also came through and I'm very optimistic for the three of them. '

Propaganda from the Italian camp suggested Ravanelli and Del Piero would not start. Hoddle said: 'That just means Pierluigi Casiraghi and Zola will come in. They're all good players and the standard wouldn't drop, nor would the system change much. We're very well-matched. They have quite a few players you would love in your team, as I'm sure Alan Shearer would be first on the team sheet for the Italian coach. You would love to have Zola, while Del Piero is a young player similar to David Beckham, someone with a bright future for the next ten years. You could easily swap. I am sure they will play it tight but I'm equally convinced they will come to attack us at the right time. I always have one eye on the opposition but my main concern is how I want to play. Georgia had five skilful players in midfield and we nullified them. But that didn't dictate how I picked my team. I know how I want my team to play first. We know Zola will play, and the decision on whether to use man-to-man marking will be made when I know their team.'

Hoddle argued that it would be important, not decisive, with both countries still to go to Poland before the group climaxed with England's visit to Italy. But England had won three from three against Italy's two from two, and Hoddle said: 'We're not in a comfortable position, we're in a position we've earned and one we would like to maintain. If we get three points, qualification will not be there. We will still have a lot of work to do. If we draw the game or lose we will have even more work to do. But if we win, we will be in a positive position, and psychologically that will then put the pressure on the Italians. I could talk for another three hours about it but Wednesday is the moment of truth.'

Paul Merson drew a line under every aspect of his past. Two championships,

FA Cup, League Cup and Cup Winners' Cup medals and 14 England caps ... but for Merson, those were all collected in the dim and distant days, during the time when he was somebody else. Asked about Zola, whom Merson faced when Arsenal won the Cup Winners Cup in 1994, he said: 'I can't remember him playing. It's like the match never existed. If I do play on Wednesday, it will be a second debut, 100 per cent. It's just nice for me to be thought of as possibly playing for England again. I don't want to talk about it as sealing my comeback, though, because it's just another football game, and the other things will continue. It won't suddenly all be rosy for me just because I've played for England at Wembley. It would be a great thing, though.'

As football's most eligible bachelor, Beckham found even his love life under close scrutiny: 'If you're in the public eye it's something you must put up with. If you go out for a quiet meal in the afternoon and get photographed, it's one of those things. It is on the increase. I've been photographed four or five times in the last two weeks just walking around in Manchester. Most of the time it's fine by me. Sometimes I think it's unfair on the person you're with, but they also expect it.'

If he got the chance, he would show the Italians why Hoddle believes he will one day be England's greatest inspiration. 'I've always been able to score goals, from Sunday League through youth level and the reserves, and now I'm getting my chance in the first team. The Wimbledon goal is my favourite as it was different to all the rest and the one I enjoyed most. That gave me a taste for long shots and now every one I hit seems to go in. My dad has told me to shoot on sight, from anywhere, it doesn't matter what happens. I would love to do it at Wembley, and if it's on again, I'll try it. I won't be scared to have a go.'

He added: 'For someone like Ravanelli and other players who have said things about me in the papers, it's brilliant to be recognized by people like that.' The biggest compliment to how he is handling his success came from Hoddle. The first time he introduced Beckham to the media, he sat alongside the youngster in order to protect him. Now Hoddle believes he can handle it alone. 'He is very level-headed and has a massive future if he maintains that. He must look at the way Alan Shearer deals with things. If he stays along those lines he'll be a massive bonus for English football. He's become an international player and had a lot of publicity with obviously things off the pitch like promotional work, but he's taken it all in his stride.'

Seaman came through his first real training session in a week unscathed, but he was aware that he would have to be 100 per cent in mind and body if the Italians got a set-piece chance. Seaman – red-faced after admitting his injury was sustained watching television on the floor at home – had no doubts of the dangers. 'They seem to have a real range of free-kicks, and we know they can bend the ball around a lot. Whether they can do it on a wet Wednesday at Wembley is another matter. It's warmer there, and the ball moves differently. But I know I've got to be aware of them. It's not as if they've only got one special free-kick and can only put it in one corner, because they can all mix it up and you know they can have a go from any angle.' Not that England were without one or two specialists of their own, as Seaman agreed. 'When you see we've got Matt Le Tissier and Alan Shearer to take them, you know we've got two as good as anybody they have. Alan doesn't just bend it, because he can give it a real whack as well, but the Italians can really disguise where they're putting them. If there's just power, you can see it all the way – although it doesn't make a lot of difference if it's in the top corner. But Zola and Del Piero don't just hit it true and straight, but can make it go left and right. You have to be prepared for that.' No one suspected that Seaman might be missing with the spotlight fixed constantly on Gazza's state of health.

Hoddle remembered the striker who put fear into the hearts of every England player when they saw his name on an Italian team-sheet: Paolo Rossi. It was England's turn to have a name that conjured dread into the Italians: Alan Shearer. Rossi won the World Cup for Italy. Shearer might do it for England. Hoddle said: 'Years ago, when Paolo Rossi was playing, he had the psychological edge over us and many other teams. When you have a natural goalscorer, that's a great advantage. They'll certainly be aware of him and he'll be marked very, very tightly. But he's had that before and still been able to score goals. But we don't just have one out-and-out goalscorer, we have players who can score from all positions. That's an added bonus for us and to Alan as well. It's about taking chances. And there's no-one better at the moment than Alan. It could be such a tight game that it might need the door being unlocked, or it might come down to a lack of concentration defensively. They have players who can pick the lock and so have we, while as a coach you're always hoping someone doesn't make a stupid mistake. That might be all there is in it.'

Shearer was ready for the captaincy role against Italy. 'I'm delighted that Glenn Hoddle has put his faith in me to captain England ...My back's fine now, as far as I'm concerned I'm 100% and I'll be as fit as I can be.'

Rekindling the hype of Euro 96 was a double-edged sword, something that Hoddle appreciated. His players had failed to heed his warnings and flirted with disaster in the first Wembley game after the Championships. 'Poland punished us, they went 1–0 up and made us show that we have a side that can turn a game round and never knows when it's beaten. We learned the lessons of that game, going into Georgia. But I did feel a tendency that it was always going to be a problem going back to Wembley for the first time after last summer. We didn't give Poland the respect they deserved and I think that was a carry-over from the summer. John Gorman and I sensed that in the dressing room a bit, right up to the kick-off. Then you have to hand the reins over to the players and they didn't really switch into what we had been working at that week, and they forgot their responsibilities a little bit. It was too much off the cuff. And, if it's too much off the cuff then you leave yourself wide open. But that has enabled us to really pin that down.'

Hoddle had never experienced such intensity of interest in the build-up to a match. 'There is excitement around the country in the last few days, and media attention here, but within the camp there has been a good spirit. The only problem has been the injuries and not being able to name a team early has been the only real blemish. Personally, it doesn't matter to me if there are 17 cameras or one camera. I still have to talk into a camera, it is the same in every game. Moldova was a big game for me as an individual coach, my first game in charge was a pressure game. Of course there is no bigger game than Italy, and we shall respect a very good side.'

Hoddle's message to the players was that it was a game won by the head. 'It's going to be a patient game. Italy have always played their football that way and it will be no different this time. In the summer the crowd were very patient at times and that was good to see. They are being educated domestically, with the foreigners coming into our game. There has been an excitement around the country for a few days now. In the camp, the only problem has been the injuries and not being able to name the team earlier, to get down to some decent work. The spirit is good and the lads are looking forward to the game for sure.'

With both sides defending 100 per cent records, England after three games, Italy from two, did a draw look the most likely? 'I wouldn't be content with it but if it came along it wouldn't be a disaster,' said Hoddle.

In a pre-match press conference, Italian journalist Giancarlo Galavotti launched straight into Hoddle, convinced the vast number of injuries being cited by the England coach were a cover-up. 'If it has not been a smokescreen, then why have they made miraculous recoveries,' quizzed Galavotti. 'Have you used a faith healer?' Hoddle calmly refused to rise to the bait. 'Who said everyone is fit? Adams and Ince are still doubts ... and Paul [Gascoigne] is still feeling his thigh injury.'

Although Seaman might have been publicly passed fit for a number of days, he was still struggling with his knee injury – a closely guarded secret within the camp. He needed a test just before kick-off and, with Walker also an injury concern, Flowers or James might even have to deputize. Adams wasn't going to make it either, so Campbell stood by.

Hoddle made a promise to the nation: his England would perform with pride and passion, without an ounce of fear. Respect, yes; fear, no. Hoddle said: 'We shall have confidence, but not flippant confidence. I just want us to go out and win the game, without fearing them. We are going to give them respect they warrant, that's all. I have been talking to them throughout the week. I want the team believing they can win the game.'

CHAPTER ELEVEN

Italian Heartbreak for England

England v Italy, Wembley, 12 February 1997

Late on Tuesday evening, Italian captain Paolo Maldini was told that Hoddle had picked Matt Le Tissier. As the news spread in the Danesfield House Hotel in Marlow-on-Thames, Luciano Nizzola, president of the Italian FA, gave instructions for twelve bottles of Pommery champagne to be chilled slowly. Italian confidence, encouraged by England's pre-match injury concerns, grew further with the knowledge that Gazza was out. Hoddle's careful attempt to keep his England line-up a secret had seriously backfired.

Paolo Maldini believed that his criticism of England's lack of technique and flair, repeated on arrival in London, had provoked Hoddle into trying to show the world that England possessed a player as gifted as any in Italy. 'I don't think what I said about England was all that negative,' he said. 'But it seems to me that Hoddle decided Le Tissier would have what it takes to trouble us since perhaps he is not typically English.' It was an illusion of grandeur. Hoddle simply felt Le Tissier was the right man for this match once Gazza had been ruled out

Hoddle did not intend to shock Italy. But he wanted to surprise them with his formation and tactics. That idea was scuppered when the England team was leaked to *The Times* and its sister paper, the *Sun*. There were plenty of theories as to the source of the leak. One was that Steve McManaman, a *Times* columnist, had been indiscreet. The brother of Le Tissier compounded the damage by talking openly of the strategy behind the selection on national radio. Hoddle might as well have given his team talk in the Italian dressing room! Maldini decided not to change his line-up – with the aerial threat to his defence of Ferdinand and Adams removed, he was even more sure he had made the right choice.

The *Mirror* disclosed that Seaman might not make it, which was a real shock. While Hoddle insists to this very day that the savage criticism of Le Tissier's selection was overcooked, there can be no doubt that the absence of the goalkeeping hero of Euro 96 was perhaps the most devastating blow for England and the greatest confidence builder for the Italians. They must have felt they had a good chance of beating Walker, especially as Di Matteo had already done so in the Premiership from distance, whereas Seaman's goal had looked impenetrable in Euro 96 – even from the penalty spot.

Seaman's absence proved crucial, but there was a preoccupation about the Le Tissier Mystery, which began to take on proportions of an Agatha Christie whodunnit! It was certainly the worst kind of news to greet Hoddle's biggest day in management. But he was determined to concentrate on the task ahead, rather than open an immediate inquest.

If Hoddle could cope, Le Tissier was certainly in a tis. He found himself accused of damaging Hoddle's plans by telling close friends, including brother Karl, that he was in the team. Karl then went on Radio Guernsey and announced how England would play – and who would be playing. One FA official was quoted as calling Le Tissier 'an idiot'! But he wasn't the only one suspected of breaking ranks. Theories that Hoddle was so incensed that he was tempted to drop the Southampton star were nonsense. But he was clearly not best pleased.

Karl told BBC Radio Guernsey: 'He was very surprised. We were very surprised too, because he has played a lot better than he is at the moment and never got on. He has a very close relationship with Glenn Hoddle – they are both on the same footballing wavelength and talk to each other a lot.' Then Karl really let the cat out of the bag by adding: 'He's got a free role just behind Shearer. Matt and McManaman both have the freedom to roam around. He is so delighted. He's a bit nervous at the moment, but he has waited so long for this opportunity and I am sure he will do himself proud.'

Only after the match did Hoddle address the issue publicly, promising to take action against the mole. But he refused to make this an excuse, insisting it probably made no difference to the result: 'At the end of the day, it's 11 against 11.' Beset by injuries, he had hoped to compensate with the element of surprise. 'It's disappointing but someone, somewhere is doing their job,' he said. 'On the day it was the least of my problems, especially after the news that David Seaman was out. It will be dealt with but I'm not going to make a big issue of it.'

The injury situation forced Hoddle to play an experimental team. Still, no-one really cared as they made their way in droves to the Twin Towers. The atmosphere was electric. West End star Michael Ball belted out 'God Save the Queen' in near-soprano tones. Hoddle, on the bench, followed suit and all the players sang their hearts out. They were up for the occasion, there was no doubt about that.

Ninety minutes later, Hoddle made a lonely and desolate walk from the bench to the dressing room, a walk where many of his predecessors had experienced the lonely realization of England's shortcomings. A slow ballad replaced the rip-roaring 'Football's Coming Home'; it was a lament for England's first World Cup defeat at Wembley as Zola, one of the tiniest men in world football, virtually clinched Italy's place in the World Cup Finals and left England's passage hanging by a precarious thread.

There had been no Gazza, no Adams, no Sheringham and, most importantly of all, no Seaman. While Italy's efficient defence strangled the Shearer menace, Seaman was not there to stop the red hot goalscoring form of Zola. England have suffered World Cup nightmares in the past when one keeper was so dominant that others had very limited experience. Gordon Banks had failed a late fitness test in the World Cup in 1970 in Mexico and his replacement, Peter Bonetti, was blamed for the defeat against the Germans. Would Seaman have saved the Zola strike that beat Walker at his near post?

In the 18th minute, a clearance from Costacurta was perfectly controlled by Zola on the edge of the penalty area after the ball had cleared the head of Pearce. Campbell, deputizing for the injured Adams, tried to get across but failed to block with a desperate lunge as Zola's shot whipped past Walker at the near post with the merest of deflections off Campbell's studs.

Five minutes later, Walker two-fisted away another Zola shot; a second goal then would have wiped out any chance of an England comeback. On the hour Hoddle jettisoned Le Tissier for Ferdinand's aerial strength. Ironically, the best header of the night had come from Le Tissier four minutes before the interval when he beat Angelo Peruzzi to a Batty cross but was just two yards the wrong side of a post.

Le Tissier looked sharp right from the start with a clever piece of trickery on the touchline but might have done much better with a 16th minute chance. Pearce rampaged down the left flank, his cross deflected to Le Tissier who was just inside the box, but his touch to control the ball was one too many. By the time he struck his volley, both Maldini and Ferrara had executed the perfect double block. An England lead then might have given a vastly different complexion to the tie.

England had their chances: a Le Saux free-kick was touched over, and in a frantic final eight minutes, McManaman's substitute, Paul Merson, cracked a shot across the face of the goal but Ince was prevented from touching it home by Costacurta. Then, from a corner, Campbell's backheel was just too far ahead of an England player.

It was a painful first defeat for Hoddle. The atmosphere was perfect and the crowd had been right behind the team, but the Italians had banished any lingering misconceptions that England had a squad of immense depth to cover for the loss of key players.

'A setback, but not a disaster', was the Hoddle verdict. He commented: 'I said before this game that win, lose or draw, the winners of this group won't be decided until later on. There's a lot more football to be played although we are all very disappointed. Italy have got some tough games coming up, but this makes our match in Poland a very important one. It's a big, big disappointment but it's one I feel we have got to bounce back from. There's a long way to go in this group and I am sure we can perform better than that at home in the future. The players gave every effort and if the ball had broken a bit more in our favour, then it could have been different. They had one chance and scored, and the game was so tight. But in my mind there is no way now we are out of this World Cup campaign.'

Hoddle defended his selection of Le Tissier. He said it was not an adventurous decision at all: 'It didn't pan out that way but if he had put us ahead with the two chances he had, you would be asking me different questions. That is how close it is sometimes. I picked him and I also had the option of changing it, that's why we can use three substitutes. It was a game that was going to be so tight, with so few chances and a player like Matt can just turn a match in one moment. Ironically the two chances fell to him, a header and a shot just over in the first half, and he couldn't turn it on on this occasion.'

The England coach refused to blame Walker: 'It was unfortunate, but I've seen the goal on a replay and Zola's shot just took a slight defection off Sol Campbell. And that may have been the difference between Ian getting it and not getting it, and on the night that has also gone against us.'

Goalkeepers usually have to hang their heads in shame when beaten on their near post, but Walker, making his first start in his third appearance, insisted that he had had no chance. 'It was brilliant work by Zola but I had his shot covered until it took a deflection off Sol Campbell's studs. I honestly believe I couldn't do a thing about it and I won't let it completely ruin what was a proud experience for me. It was fantastic going out there for my first full England game at Wembley and in such a huge match as well. Obviously the result sours it more than a little, but I don't think I have anything to be ashamed of. We will take a lot out of the fact that we proved we are in the same class as the Italians in the second half. After the goal I had only one more serious save to make from Zola again and it was just frustrating watching the lads banging away for the equalizer without getting the break we needed. But we are still not out of it. We are quite upbeat and we certainly don't think the Italians are a lot better than us.'

Walker continued: 'If you are to be beaten by a single goal and you've had saves to make, it always feels slightly better. Nobody's happy with losing to the Italians at Wembley, but I'll never forget the experience of my full England debut. I certainly wasn't going to swap that No. 1 jersey with anybody. I knew I would be playing on Tuesday night when David Seaman had a setback with his knee injury. I've been injured myself and had to have a scan on a shoulder before I joined up with the squad. But I was prepared for it and I think we all were. Okay, we had to change some of the personnel through injuries, but we all knew what our shape would be. I couldn't believe the way it felt when I walked out there, though. I've been on for England for two 25 minute spells as a substitute before, including Hungary at Wembley last year. But actually starting and standing there with the rest of the lads for the national anthem is such a proud moment.'

Campbell admitted responsibility but did not blame himself for the deflection: 'These things can happen and if you don't stick out a leg, people ask why you didn't try to stop it. But I know I should have covered Zola's run in the first place. He came from deep and went past Stuart Pearce and perhaps I was a bit flat. I should have covered it slightly better. Nobody has said anything to me in the England camp but I've got to be self-critical. If you are aiming for perfection, which is what you need in an England shirt, you can't hide from things. You just have to take it and not make excuses.' Campbell, who collected only his second England cap, added: 'Other than the goal, it went quite well for me. It was a big responsibility playing in the centre without Tony Adams, and I was very pleased to play that role. But if you want to get on at this level, you have to own up and admit to any mistakes you make. I blame myself and it's no good thinking otherwise.' Technically, Italy's winner was Campbell's second own goal in successive matches as two weeks earlier he had gifted Zola's Chelsea a first-half lead in their 2–1 win at White Hart Lane.

Walker had been drafted in at 24 hours' notice. He had also been carrying an injury, was unable to train fully, and needed an injection to get him through the match. Spurs physio Tony Lenaghan revealed: 'Ian has a problem with his left shoulder. He has had inflammation for some time and it has restricted his movement. He kept it to himself for a while but we noticed he was going for shots on his left side with his right arm, such as when Di Matteo scored against us from long-range in the Chelsea game … A painkilling injection eased it and it was decided to give him a hydrocortisone injection last Saturday. That requires three or four days' rest, so he was unable to train most of the time. But the specialist said he could only play on Wednesday if he was able to train without pain on the Tuesday, which he did. It is not a severe problem and he can probably play out the rest of the season with it, but if it got any worse, we would need to have it seen to.'

Hoddle was oblivious on the night of the match to the growing criticism over Walker's injuries. Two days later Hoddle formally responded with a statement through the FA's press office. He retorted: 'There are no circumstances in which I would play anybody in an England team against medical advice.'

The vanquished England stars were unanimously upbeat and optimistic about eventual qualification before they left Wembley that night. Shearer led the backs-to-the-wall, we'll-show-you brigade as he said: 'We can still qualify. Both teams still have to go to Poland and I've got a sneaky feeling they could take something off Italy. Obviously they've got the edge as they've a game in hand and could go three points clear, but it's far from over. We gave it everything but there were times when the ball simply did not run for us. But we still have to play them away. Of course it is a disappointment. There is no point in saying anything else.' Shearer, superbly shackled by Cannavaro, added: 'We were restricted to just one or two half chances. We've held them at bay and in the second half we were camped around their box without creating a decent, clear-cut opportunity. Of course you are going to miss players like David Seaman, Tony Adams and Paul Gascoigne because they are world-class performers. We've gone down tonight, but it wasn't for the want of trying.'

Pearce was another senior player standing firm behind the manager: 'We are all very disappointed but there's still a lot left in the group. It was a game when we didn't expect a lot of chances and they took their opportunity very well. There are still a lot of points to play for and I believe we've got a lot of capability in our squad. We will come out kicking and fighting like England teams in the past have always done.'

Young David Beckham was grim-faced: 'I never got the ball enough to be able to run at Paolo Maldini as much as I wanted. We made a good start but seemed to ease off for a period in the first half, although it was much better in the second and I thought we deserved something. We needed to get behind them and we couldn't do that. They are not bad at defending but it's all part of the learning process for people like me.'

David Batty commented: 'We gave it a good crack in the second half. It wasn't enough in the end, but we all believe we are on the same level as Italy and there's more games to come in this group yet. We didn't do ourselves justice on the night but I believe that we've confirmed we can still compete on level terms with the Italians. They are a very good side who know how to defend an early lead, but the result and the disappointment doesn't make us feel inferior to them. It seems pretty obvious to me now that we've got to go out there in October and get something from the last qualifying match. You can never tell what will happen in football, but I don't think we can rely on the Italians slipping up against the other teams in the group. And we know we are capable of beating those other teams, too. It will probably go right to the last game and the match out there in Italy will likely be built up even bigger than the Wembley game. The result went against us this time and you know people are going to feel disappointed. But I think it's a mistake if they see it as proving Italy are superior to us. In the second half we had them on the back foot most of the time and I thought we deserved to get something … When we play the Italians again out there, we are certainly not going to go into it thinking they are so much better than us. We feel we can give them problems and that it will be a different sort of game.'

Les Ferdinand also pledged his backing for Hoddle. His reward for scoring against Georgia, in arguably his best England performance, had been to find himself on the Wembley bench again. Hoddle eventually held up his hands by sending Ferdinand on for the final 30 minutes, providing Shearer with much-needed support and causing the well-marshalled Italians more concern. Ferdinand said: 'I was disappointed when Glenn told me I wasn't in the team, especially after scoring in Georgia, but then again you always feel like that when you're not in, and you should do as well. You know with this manager that he is always willing to change things to suit the game. He felt that Matt and Macca in behind Alan would offer something a bit different, something they might not be able to cope with. The thing is that the manager picks his side and picks the players he wants to do a particular job. You've got to accept that decision, even if you're the one to miss out.' Ferdinand suggested his more muscular and direct threat had worked to undermine some of the Italians' defensive confidence. 'The Italians are past masters at going a goal up and then sitting back and holding on to what they've got,' he said. They're just so very good at it, the best in the world, and they proved it again. When I went on, it maybe gave them a bit more to worry about because it meant we had two up there with me and Alan. In the beginning he was on his own which was very difficult. Once I went on, it was always going to mean they had a few more problems. It didn't quite work out. I've said before that I'd like the chance to play three games in succession, which I still haven't done, and you always want to play. But I certainly feel I've still got a big part to play for England and it's not over by any means yet, despite what happened.'

Zola disclosed that the Italian camp had been surprised by Ferdinand's absence. 'We were a little surprised when we saw the England team. We expected to see Ferdinand in the side and thought that he would play, and then there was also some news that it might have been Paul Merson. It isn't for me to say if England put out their best team or not because it is Mr Hoddle's job to decide things like that. But we knew that Ferdinand could have given us problems and trouble because he is so strong and so good with high balls into the area. We had prepared ourselves to find a way to control him and it's easy to say that players should have played in hindsight. Looking back, I would have to say, yes, it was an advantage for us that he did not play, but nobody can say that beforehand and I know that Mr Hoddle is an intelligent person and had an idea in his mind which he thought was right. In football now there are no secrets. He could have played any of four people with Shearer. We know all of them, we would have been prepared and we would not have been surprised.'

There was sheer delight in the Italian camp. Cesare Maldini said: 'It was a great game and a great result for us. We beat a very good team who have a great tradition on a pitch where it is not usual to win. I know England had some players absent but I wasn't surprised by Le Tissier playing – we had arrangements for all their players. And we knew all about Shearer as well. Zola scored the goal but that's his job. He's an important player but so are the other ten players. Who will qualify? At this time we just want to enjoy our success, we're very happy with the three points but the goal difference is the same. Everything went exactly according to our plans. I'm so happy and I've hardly got any voice left. It was a great game for us, a great result against a team with such great traditions.'

Before jetting back to Pisa, the exultant coach – whose previous visit to Wembley was as the winning AC Milan skipper in the 1963 European Cup Final – predicted the Italians were ready to reclaim their place at the top of the footballing mountain: 'You cannot have any illusions about football, and the truth is that good play only serves you to a certain point. You need to win games. But I thought we were fantastic in the first half, and while England created a few problems after that, it was foreseeable.

'I was really satisfied with the way the players listened to me and understood the arguments I put to them during the week. They were totally receptive. In my heart, that win over Benfica 34 years ago means more to me at the moment. But if you look in the annals of footballing history, two nations stand apart from the rest, Brazil and Italy. In the future I can see other horizons for this team, great victories and much more.'

Maldini, not surprisingly, was particularly pleased by the display of Cannavaro, who previously had only played 18 minutes of international football, as a late substitute against a defensively-minded Northern Ireland in Sicily. Along with Ferrara and surprise sweeper Costacurta, he had managed to nullify the menace of Shearer, Le Tissier and McManaman. Maldini said: 'It wasn't a surprise for me, because I know him so well. I've worked with Fabio for four years with the Under-21 side. I know what he can do, what could happen with him, but he responded so well to everything I said to him.'

Defeat would have had the ever-critical *tifosi* screaming for Maldini's blood, and the wily coach took the opportunity to get one back at the Italian pundits who had questioned his appointment. 'When I took the job, there were some people who talked about me as being a bread and salami manager, a very basic coach,' he said. 'But now I ask them just what kind of bread and salami they saw at Wembley on Wednesday night?'

Zola was ecstatic. 'I just hope the Chelsea fans will understand. They have given me such a warm welcome in England and I hope they will not put this goal against me. Surely they know I had to do this important thing for my country. It was my dream from a small boy to score a goal such as this, especially against England at Wembley. The control of the ball, the first touch, was everything for me. It gave me the position to make a shot and I knew I would score.' Zola added that England's footballing stock had not plummeted as a result of the defeat. 'It would be wrong to think that England are not at the same level of teams like Italy or Germany just because of one defeat. You cannot make judgements like that after just one match. The level of English football is growing all the time and I am sure the English team will be able to demonstrate it is a very good team. It is harder for them now to reach the World Cup Finals because only one country goes through automatically. They have to win every game now because a bad result could mean their exclusion, but we have to as well.'

Hoddle cleared up the mystery of Gascoigne's absence. Gazza had walked silently away from the dressing room area after the match, refusing to discuss his situation, fuelling questions over why he had not featured. 'Paul came through the session on Monday but then had a reaction the next day,' said Hoddle, who added that he would return to Glasgow for a scan on the ankle. 'I can assure you that if he'd been fit he would've shaped up; even if he'd only been half fit, we'd have had him on the bench. At the end of the day the ankle was still sore. We had to test him but the response was poor. I'd have had to consider his match fitness even then, but I would at least have wanted him on the bench.'

Astonishingly, England had lost only two of the 35 matches Gazza started since his debut in 1990, but without him they had won only three competitive games in that time. Hoddle lost Gazza after a frantic behind-the-scenes battle by the medical team. Gazza went through a relentless and exhaustive three-times-a-day schedule which had progressed so well that two days before the match he thought he would make it. Later, Gazza explained: 'That's what made it so frustrating. One minute it was good, then not so good. Then I had to face the fact I was out. Glenn Hoddle talked to me about the situation: it was Italy, they'd be super-fit, so he'd name me as a substitute. There was no argument about that as far as I was concerned. I went through a fitness test, a mild one, no problem. There was a reaction later, then it was a bit sore on the Tuesday and I told Glenn I didn't want to chance even being on the bench.'

Gazza returned to Rangers for treatment and a new plaster on the injury. 'It's nothing much,' he said. 'There is no question of me not being ready for World Cup action against Georgia in April or the Mexico friendly next month. I can't wait to play again. It was very frustrating having to watch us at Wembley. England mean so much to me, seeing them lose was a bad experience, very disappointing – but it would be crazy for anyone to consider we're out of contention after one defeat. I felt for the lads because the training had been especially good. I've been around England squads for a long time, but there was a real buzz in the build-up. I thought it was right, that we would be okay. You expect the Italians to play quick balls and move, yet when their goal came it was a long pass and a deflection that did for us. We were all down, those who played and those who didn't. But by the time we get together again, we'll be up and ready. We'll listen to what the boss has to stay and get on with it.

'Having so many experienced players out made it difficult and I know there has been talk about it not exactly being a coincidence the injured have been involved with hardly a break since the Umbro Cup two summers ago and through Euro 96 last summer. It may be the case for some of them but not for me. I have had to sit around too often and for too long through injury in recent years. I'm fit and I feel fresh. My ankle knock has nothing to do with pressure of matches. I can understand there is a feeling of gloom about after our defeat, but there is no reason to lose faith. The players won't and neither should the fans … We'll qualify for the finals, I'm certain of it. And we'll qualify, even if we have to win our last match in Italy to do it. We were unlucky in all sorts of ways against Italy – injuries, the way we lost the goal. But the Italians could be cursing their misfortune the next time they play. Who knows?'

Ince reflected on the damage Zola had done to England's World Cup dream. He felt that Gascoigne's absence had been the killer blow. 'When Zola scored we were in a bit of a state of shock for 15 minutes, but then we upped the tempo again at the end of the first half and did it even more in the second. It was just like the Germany game in Euro 96. We had the chances and just didn't get the breaks. But that's where you're going to miss a class player like Gazza. When you're playing against an Italian defence, you know how important it would've been to have somebody like him. People were saying that perhaps it wasn't the right game for him, but you can't ever say that because he's such a great player. In the second half, when we tried to unlock them, was where we missed him. We couldn't quite manage it and that's where a little bit of magic from Gazza, even if he wasn't 100 per cent, could've made the difference and got us through.'

While the despair of defeat was clear, Ince remained defiant and denied that English footballing pride, restored so vibrantly in the summer, had taken a battering. 'We didn't get the result we deserved. We were all over them in the second half, they didn't have a shot, and that makes it even more frustrating. What we must do is take encouragement from the way we played in the second half. We know that we're up there with the best in the world. We beat the Dutch in the summer and should've beaten the Germans and we should never have lost to Italy. They're the three big teams in Europe. I'm not saying the best three because we're up there with them, but they are the ones people keep talking about and we've proved we're more than a match for all of them. We can certainly still qualify. As far as I'm concerned there's going to be twists and turns all the way through the qualification and there's no reason why we can't go to Italy and get a result there. We've proved we can match them. We're still confident in what we set out to achieve and we believe we can do that. It's not gloom and doom at all. To be absolutely honest, we knew after the Poland game that we'd been lucky, because they murdered us, and in the same way we know that we deserved better from the Italy game.'

Ince flew back to Milan, pleased to have buried some personal ghosts by his own performance. 'It was important for me to play well, because I was really disappointed with myself in Georgia. That was probably the worst game I've had for England and it was eating away inside me all through the week, telling me that I had to play well against Italy. I didn't want to have two disappointing games on the trot. Sure, there will be a bit of stick for me when I go back, but I can go back with my head up high. I'm not ashamed to go back to Italy. We played well and I'll be all right, no problems. I suppose I'll get a few slaps from the lads, but that's the way it is, what you have to put up with.'

Ince pleaded with England fans not to turn their backs on the side after one defeat, especially with crucial games against Georgia and Poland coming up. 'It's a big defeat psychologically, but we've got to hold our heads up high. We can't afford to let it get us down. We've got to tell ourselves that this is the last and only defeat we'll have. We must kick on from here. But we want everyone to be with us. We don't want people to say "that's it now, it's over, our chances have gone". People saying we're out of it is the last thing we need. We want them to stick by us and help us go on from here. We need everybody to be with us.'

Ian Wright felt elated, despite his blink-and-you-miss-it performance for England. He had been sent on as an 88th minute substitute for Batty in a vain bid to cancel out Zola's goal. 'People say it was only two minutes, but I was very pleased just to be involved with England again. I'm not looking at it in a negative way. I'm happy Glenn Hoddle wanted to throw me on for the last few minutes and had enough faith in me to score a goal in that time."

Gareth Southgate vowed to prove that Hoddle had been wrong to drop him. Armed with a new £2.5 million contract from Villa, he said: 'I want my England place back. I was very disappointed to be left out against the Italians and, if the truth be known, a little bit surprised as well. My task now is to produce the kind of form in Villa's shirt which will make it hugely difficult for Glenn Hoddle to ignore me next time. England play Georgia at Wembley on 30 April, and I intend to be there. Any player in my situation would say the same.' Villa boss Brian Little revealed: 'Gareth is absolutely intent on being picked for England's next game. A lot of people can't understand why he was left out in the first place, because his ability to sense danger is second to none. It is not as if England had been losing matches or letting in goals with Gareth at the back. In my opinion, Gareth and Ugo Ehiogu are as good as any pair of centre-halves in the country. Now I want them to prove it. Gareth has again been exceptional for Villa this season despite a couple of injury problems. He, more than anyone, is responsible for Villa still being in touch with the leading group of clubs at this stage.'

Hoddle had spent the first half frantically scribbling notes and the second bawling from his distant touchline seat. When he talked to the press after the game, his mood had barely mellowed. A deeply sombre Hoddle failed to smile once as he admitted: 'Hard lessons have to be learned from this defeat. We can still gain even though we lost.'

Having gained an early lead, Italy's coach had been able to drop midfielder Dino Baggio onto McManaman to complement the admirable man-marking which gave Shearer his most frustrating international. Le Tissier, however, was the inevitable scapegoat, but when Hoddle re-examined his football philosophy, would he compromise his beliefs? No. Instead, he aimed to repair the damage and hoped for a favour or two from the other teams in the group.

Injuries had forced Hoddle's hand. He explained: 'It wasn't helpful going into the game not knowing my team until so late, even down to David Seaman on the morning of the match.' Gascoigne also suffered a reaction to his ankle injury on Tuesday and that forced him out, along with Adams who was always struggling with a similar problem.'

Hoddle had a friendly against Mexico to repair the damage but by the time England returned to World Cup action against Georgia, it was possible that Italy would be six points ahead (after their games against Moldova and Poland). But if the Poles could pull off a shock, the group would swing open again. 'It's a long way for me to think ahead to the last game against Italy,' said Hoddle. 'There's a lot of football to be played between now and then. It's put the Italians on the front foot, without a doubt. We've got to make sure we get a win under our belt against Georgia. Italy are delighted and we are disappointed. But they've got to go to Poland and Georgia and those games are not going to be easy. If they get tripped up there, we have to make sure that between now and the Rome game we get our results right. It's going to need a massive performance over there, but I can't look that far ahead.'

Hoddle was asked why he had not used Beckham in his club role in central midfield where he might have been more effective than out wide on the right flank. Hoddle explained: 'In the second half David came inside more. He popped in because I thought they were nullifying him out wide. Sometimes it's a case of trying to get the space, sometimes it's best to be out and come in. There were times when he came inside and used the ball very well, and that's something we had a chance to work on.' Hoddle was reluctant to give him too much responsibility, too early. 'At this level the boy still needs to find his feet. He's not ready to pull the strings at international level. He's still got lots to learn. He has the ability to put in wonder crosses.'

Le Tissier faced the World Cup axe, as did Pearce and Walker. Hoddle discussed with Le Tissier the reasons for his substitution. 'What was said is between me and Matt', said Hoddle, cutting the subject short, when asked about the Wembley conversation. 'We had a quick chat and I told him the reasons why I had taken him off. He said "fine", he could see the reasons why.' Hoddle defended Le Tissier sternly in public, but clearly the manager's precise opinion of his performance was to be kept private.

While Le Tissier was the focus of attention, there were more alarming areas, such as who was the best cover for Seaman? Martyn, not even in the squad, became a strong candidate. And as for defence, it was clear that Pearce couldn't last forever. England needed a more orthodox central defender, and the country was hoping that Gary Pallister's back complaint would not prove to be a permanent disability.

Italy's success in reducing Shearer's effectiveness had been almost entirely due to the leech-like qualities of the two men who took it in turns to mark him – the young and inexperienced Cannavaro, and the more rugged Ferrara. The two-man operation, a variation on the man-to-man marking system particularly impressed that doyen of coaches and professor of Italian football, Don Howe. 'It was flexible man-marking,' he said. 'Cannavaro rarely pulled away from the left, and Ferrara rarely from the right, but they were intelligent enough to let each other pick up Shearer as and when. Or one take Shearer and the other take Le Tissier without it mattering which defender it was. But as the ball arrived, one of them arrived too, and if they could get in front they got in front. I would have liked to see Shearer rotate with Le Tissier a bit more. That might have made it a bit more difficult for Italy.'

Cannavaro, Shearer's principle marker, felt he had had a comfortable evening. 'I expected much more from him, but then he was not used to having so little space. As an experience, this was not as striking as my two European titles with Italy's Under-21s.' Costacurta was still trying to figure Hoddle out. 'I think Ian Wright would have given us a really hard time. But Wright seems to be at the bottom of Hoddle's list.'

Paolo Maldini continued to provoke. 'In England, you play with great energy and pace. But in the rest of Europe, they play with energy, pace *and* technique.'

England (0) 0 Italy (1) 1

Walker, G. Neville, Pearce, Ince, Campbell, Le Saux, Beckham, Batty, Le Tissier, Shearer (capt), McManaman

	P	W	D	L	F	A	Pts
England	4	3	0	1	7	2	9
Italy	3	3	0	0	5	1	9
Poland	2	1	0	1	3	3	3
Georgia	2	0	0	2	0	3	0
Moldova	3	0	0	3	2	8	0

CHAPTER TWELVE

A Slap in the Face for Hoddle

Gazza makes a public apology, March 1997

When Hoddle announced his squad for the friendly against Mexico, Paul Gascoigne's latest unsavoury off-the-field antics took precedence over his injury and absence from the match. Hoddle planned to speak to him after his latest brush with controversy. Gazza was in New York, three thousand miles away from the aftermath of an alleged assault on a woman who had tried to talk to his showbiz pal Chris Evans.

Hoddle was reluctant to comment directly on the latest allegations, but he was clearly concerned. 'I last spoke directly to Paul nine days ago and that was about his ankle injury. But I will be speaking with him about the leg again – and other matters might come up,' he said. 'I've been away watching games all week. I don't know the facts of what happened with Paul and I am not going to comment until I know them. Walter Smith at Rangers will know the facts. I haven't spoken to him, although I will do when things calm down, but while they are still up in the air I am not prepared to comment.' However, he confirmed that Gascoigne's absence from the squad was the result of the ankle injury, not the controversy. Pressed on his reaction to the fact that Gascoigne was recuperating on the other side of the Atlantic – his wife Sheryl had said that she had not seen her husband for a month – Hoddle was evasive. 'That's a matter for the club, not for me,' he replied. 'He's not fit and available for the international football game I have coming up. But if he is out of the country, that's something for him and his club.'

A Canadian woman, Diannah Dean, complained to police that Gazza had struck her across the face as she approached a limousine in London. She reported the alleged incident, saying: 'I was shocked, angry and humiliated – what he did was wrong and he should realize it.' The young tour guide said she was with two friends when they spotted a white stretch car cruising down London's Regent Street. 'You don't see this sort of thing very often back in Canada, and this is what drew our attention to the car. Then a head popped out and I saw it was Chris Evans. I went across to tell him how much I enjoyed his radio show. He thanked me and we shook hands – he was very pleasant. Then suddenly Gazza appeared through the sunroof and, without speaking, slapped my face. I realized I was not dealing with your average Joe from a bar, but someone who has a reputation for hitting women. He needed to know what he did was wrong and that he has no right to go around hitting people.'

Mel Stein refuted the charge. Stein also denied reports that Rangers wanted to drop the controversial star. 'Quite the opposite. They want to renew his contract. He is still the best footballer in Europe. Any suggestion that he has run away is complete fabrication.'

The troubled player flew back from New York to Glasgow, heading straight to Ibrox the next morning for a carpeting by Smith. Gascoigne and Stein wanted to hold a press conference immediately, but Smith vetoed it, and Gazza was left in no doubt that Rangers were running out of patience with his antics. In his eventual 732-word statement, he apologized six times, four times to Rangers, once to his family, and once to Ms Dean. It was another desperate bid to save his career following his boozy week in London and his disappearing act to America. He said: 'If I've let the club or the fans down in any way by the publicity they and I have received, then I apologize. If anybody in Glasgow, either at the club or on the terraces, thinks I've let them down, then I apologize. I fully understand that the club, the fans and the media have been upset with me and that is the last thing I want. I have 15 months left on my contract and it is the intention on both sides I will see that contract out.'

That public apology saved him again, in the short term at least, from the boot Rangers were sorely tempted to give him. Smith was privately livid at Gascoigne's latest drunken oafishness, but refused to discuss his views in public. However, he did let slip one grim aside. Smith said simply: 'Actions speak louder than words.' But along with his £30,000 fine, the maximum allowed under Scottish rules, came a warning that no more stupidity would be tolerated.

Gascoigne's marathon session had begun on 8 March. Rangers were not playing, so he flew to London to meet Chris Evans and Danny Baker. Over the next few days they lurched around the city, drinking. This spree culminated in the alleged assault by Gazza in Regent Street on 12 March. Two days later, Gazza headed for New York, where he booked into the £400-a-night Peninsula Hotel. But by then Ms Dean had reported the incident to Scotland Yard and police had begun their inquiries. Gascoigne stayed in New York over St Patrick's Day, before leaving for London. He insisted: 'I was given a fortnight off by the club. I was grateful to them at the time and I'm grateful now. I accept that as a Rangers and England player, I should not be giving papers the chance to write anything about me other than in respect of my performances on the pitch. I realize that as Paul Gascoigne, I have an added responsibility and I promise I will try my hardest. I have been injured for some time and that has been frustrating. It's never easy sitting and watching from the sidelines, and it's harder for me than most because I live football and I live and breathe Rangers.'

Gazza was embarrassed by the candid words of his club boss. Walter Smith had said: 'His actions have tarnished the club's image and my own a great deal. I was the person responsible for bringing him here, and it's been a very unpleasant side for me to have to handle. It's easy for people to look at the daft lad image, but there's a deeper and darker side to him.' Smith was especially repulsed by revelations of Gascoigne's wife-beating. 'Paul Gascoigne knows that Rangers Football Club were totally unhappy, from all levels at the club, at what happened there. On a personal level, he is also fully aware of how I feel about it. Every time something happens with him, I feel it myself. Believe me, there have been many times when I've sat down and thought I'd made a mistake. When I signed him, I was 100 per cent clear about my judgement, but the percentage drops with every incident that happens – and so does the level of backing at this club. Off-pitch incidents can only happen so many times to one person, whether it's with me or his previous managers. For all his daftness, he could portray a far better image of himself than he does right now. And the dreadful pity of it all is that he possesses so much talent as a footballer, yet he may well be remembered for his off-the-field exploits. The on-field part has been a pleasing aspect of him coming to Rangers and he's been successful, to a reasonable degree. His relationship with the supporters has been good, too, but the other parts, away from the pitch, have made me seriously question my own decision to bring him here. They have undoubtedly damaged him, and damaged people's perception of him. He says he won't do it again ... but he does.'

Hoddle told me of his reaction to the situation, with regard to Gascoigne's position in the England squad. He said: 'I've kept him very much in my mind. It seems that 50 per cent of people believe he is out of it while the other half think I'm going to keep him in. It's very simple. He's like Alan Shearer – there's no difference – he's out through injury and so too are other players like Les Ferdinand.' When I asked Hoddle if there was any blackballing of Gazza, he said emphatically: 'Of course not.' He added: 'The main thing for Paul is to get himself fit, and if he is playing well, he will be very much in my mind. He's got to get over the injury first and that's the main thing for him and his club – and it's the same thing for Alan.'

In the build-up to the Georgia tie, Hoddle had made it plain that he wanted Gazza to sort out his life. The England coach had explained: 'He is an excellent footballer and an immense talent. He still has time to get back to his very best. Anyone in this country would want Paul Gascoigne, in two years' time, playing like he was six years ago. The whole country would want that. But a lot depends on his club form, regaining his fitness and there has to be a balance on the mental side of things as well. You can't do certain things when you're 30 that you could get away with when you were 21. There are a lot of things to put right. People in football, for some reason, consider 30 years of age time to get things right. Paul has got to think to himself, "If I can keep myself in good nick, I can play until I'm 35 or 36". I'm not bending over backwards for Paul Gascoigne. But I know the amount of pressure that's put on him and the things that surround him, but I look at him and other coaches would as well, in football terms. Of course, there are many other issues for the media and public. But I must ask "what has he got to offer as a footballer?" That's why we're talking about him now. I've spoken to him and to Walter Smith at great length. He has not gone a season without a long-term injury to worry about. His first port of call is to sort that out. It's difficult when you're an England coach and you're not with him day to day. But if we're going to see Paul return after this injury and back to his best, he has to do a lot of thinking and there has to be a lot of prevention work so he doesn't pick up these injuries. We've tried to help him; the counselling has helped to a certain degree. He's started to respond to that. But certain things have to change in his life. He's got to overcome this injury and get back to form. He needs a year free of injury. He's had injuries for the last four years that have dragged him back.'

When pressed about his 'mental' side Hoddle elaborated: 'He's picked up strange things [injuries] on the training ground, that's what I mean by a mental thing. He's got to understand that it's a training ground situation and although I want to see players apply themselves, there's a line to be drawn.' One can only imagine that Gazza takes the training as seriously as he does a World Cup Final!

Hoddle put himself forward to help Gazza as much as he could at a time when the Rangers man needed it most, when his future at Rangers was wide open to speculation and none of the major Premiership clubs were showing the slightest sign of interest in the wayward genius. Hoddle emphasized that, while he would help as much as possible, only Gascoigne could rectify his decline. 'He is the only one who can change things, there's got to be maturity there as he approaches 30. If he gets his form back, and this applies to any player and not just Paul, he has a future with England. And, in Paul's case, he's a talented player. But I can't answer the questions. It is up to Paul … it's a question of keeping control and then you can have a future to the age of 34 or 35. Paul is no different. I was out for two years as a player, and I came back and played on until I was 38. In many ways two years out is a negative, but it actually had a positive effect on me as I was able to recharge my batteries.'

Hoddle kept faith with Gazza despite his off-the-field problems. 'He has allegedly got himself into trouble, but I've had to look into situations that were not really there. I deal with facts, not fiction, and 75 per cent has been fiction. Yeah, there's been a guilty side and there are facts there to be dealt with. But after he played in Georgia, where's he gone from there? He's been injured since then and he's had a few nights out since then, but I can't control that. It's difficult from the outside, I'm not in control. I haven't got the reins on the player. But I've given him his chance and he needs to change, and he's working on that. And he's had a nasty injury as well. There's going to come a time when it either happens or it won't. At the moment he's in mid-area, but a decision is going to come more from Paul Gascoigne, not from me, on how he overcomes his injury and what goes on from here.'

Asked what his instincts told him would be the outcome, Hoddle admitted: 'I don't know. I can't give you that answer, but at this moment a lot of people are still prepared to get the best out of him. It's the instinct within Paul that counts.

He has got to settle himself down with his club and the answer will come from Paul and what he does with his football.'

Graham Taylor was convinced Gazza had gone too far downhill. 'I think there is a distinct possibility that his England career is now over. Three or four years ago, I was heavily criticized because I could only refer to it as that he had a refuelling problem. Everybody knew what I was talking about, but they weren't prepared to go along with it. That problem is now surfacing because that's been a problem for Paul for a number of years. You have got to look after yourself and you can't continually abuse your body and expect to stay at the very highest level of international sport. That problem has been there for a number of years.'

There was also some surprisingly harsh criticism from Brian Laudrup, Gazza's team-mate and Rangers' player of the year. Laudrup said: 'It's a shame Gascoigne has ruined everything for himself. I believe he is one of the biggest talents the English game has ever produced. Yet what he has done is not healthy for him and not healthy for the club. I just hope he opens his eyes and sees what he's about to destroy. The players love him here. He can be a fantastic person when he isn't drunk. But if you do the things he has done throughout the season, he hasn't been much help in a lot of the games. I think he has let a lot of people down. He is 29 now and, perhaps with the lifestyle he has been living for many years, it's getting more and more difficult for him to get rid of injuries and get back to the right fitness again. Gazza's reached the age where he – and other people – cannot make excuses for his behaviour any more. He is a grown-up man now. He is married and has a baby son – it's not like saying he is young. Maybe five years ago, you could have said he was young, that he would mature, but you cannot say that any more. Gascoigne has to show whether he's a grown-up or whether he would like to continue to live the way he's been living. If he wants that, then it would be difficult for Hoddle to pick him. To be honest, it will be difficult for him to change. If he hasn't changed now, I can't see him changing a lot.'

Laudrup added: 'In his first year, Gascoigne was magnificent and, though there were some off-the-field problems, he was concentrating on his football. But now the way he lives is not healthy. There have been a number of very serious problems with him, and people always link Paul Gascoigne with Rangers. Walter [Smith] said the other week that perhaps he made a mistake when he signed Gascoigne, and I think that's a shame. It shouldn't be a mistake when you sign a player like Gascoigne – it should be a fantastic gift for a club. But I think the club have been very tolerant with him – and I believe that point has passed now. I have never heard Walter make remarks about a player the way he has about Gascoigne. Walter has always protected his players. Gazza has won a couple of championships here, but in a career of more than 12 years that is all he has won. He won an FA Cup medal when he got injured, but he never played the full game. If you look at the clubs he's been playing for at the highest level, he hasn't won anything, and that is a shame. A player like Gazza – with his talent – should be playing in the best teams in Europe and at the best of his ability.'

Sports Minister Tony Banks, then an opposition backbencher, said: 'I don't want to be rude about Gascoigne but I think that when God gave him this enormous football talent, he took his brain out at the same time to sort of equalize it up a bit.' Asked if Gazza should be excluded from the England team because of his wife-beating, Banks said: 'That's not much of a role model, is it? How many times has Paul Gascoigne burst into tears and said he is never going to do it again? That he's going to turn over a new leaf? I think people in the end just lose patience with that. It seems to be happening at Rangers at the moment. And it's a shame because the guy really has sublime talent. I just think he has thrown it all away because he is not a boy any more.'

Gascoigne responded to the critics again writing off his international career by aiming for a comeback in the away tie in Poland. 'These people have never played football in their life. My message to them is that I've had it before, I've had it for ten years – it doesn't bother me one bit. I've spoken to Glenn Hoddle, no problem, I agree with everything he's said. I've only played for 20 minutes and I just need a couple of games. I played in Steve Walsh's Leicester testimonial the other night and I just need to get a few games under my belt before 20 May. Hopefully, with five to six games behind me, I'll be fit for selection for the Poland game.'

Terry Venables was alarmed by the calls to end Gascoigne's international career. He warned it was 'time to look at himself again,' but insisted: 'Gazza's still got a lot to offer and I wouldn't write him off yet. I would take him back tomorrow. Although he's had more injury problems this year, he's still a special player. He has a lot of desire – a lot of people lose that enthusiasm and energy, but he hasn't. The one thing he still wants to do above all else is play football and compete against the best. In Euro 96 he did very well, much better than people gave him credit for. How can you underestimate his goal against Scotland? That was the mark of a really special player. If a Brazilian had done that, we would still have been doing cartwheels about it. Gazza still wants to be the best, but now he's got to prepare himself for later years. Maybe it's time for him to have a look at himself again and see where he goes from here.'

But it was John Gorman who took the most practical view: 'There comes a time when you've got to toe the line and Paul knows that. But he's a flamboyant character, and you either love him or you hate him – but you can never afford to lose patience with someone of his ability.'

CHAPTER THIRTEEN

The Trouble with Friendlies

Injuries disrupt Hoddle's plans, March 1997

The friendlies with Mexico and South Africa, followed by a three-match summer tour with a World Cup tie in Poland in between, brought a storm of protest from the Premiership clubs as the oldest row in town, club versus country, flared up again. Were the friendlies irrelevant, a rude interruption to the business of championship and relegation, or a vital chance for Hoddle to experiment?

England's summer plans, which Hoddle had inherited, ran into opposition from Alex Ferguson, Roy Evans and Kenny Dalglish although Arsene Wenger gave his backing. Ferguson said: 'I think these games are unfair. I said to Terry Venables at the start of his England management that I wouldn't play friendlies because you're going to get players withdrawing and you aren't going to play your best team. I don't think there's any advancement in these games. There will be 112 teams in the UEFA Cup next year, the Champions' League is being expanded and the international focus is growing. We have so many League and Cup games to fit in and there has to be an effect – it's only natural. Over the last few years, we've played an average of 50 games, and this season will be no different. Then there are internationals and friendly internationals. It's such a strain and, with young players, it can't be done. This summer will be a rest for the Manchester United players, it has to be. Some of them will be playing in World Cup qualifiers on 8 June – we can't do anything about that – but we can about the others. We could play our last game as late as 28 May, and then we start back in training on 4 July. How can we rest the players unless we take those five weeks?'

Evans objected to the summer tour. He was convinced that McManaman and Fowler had felt the effects when they were kept on the go in Euro 96. 'This season has not been Robbie's best in many ways because he has struggled with injury. After the European Championship we gave him and Steve a bit of a rest because I don't think you can play continuous football. They both have great temperaments, they take things in their stride, but there is pressure on them day in, day out.'

Dalglish believed there should have been consultation with club managers. Hoddle stressed that the tournament had been organized before he had taken over, and that had he begun with a blank piece of paper, he would have thought twice about it.

Since Euro 96, a large percentage of England's squad – Shearer, Seaman, Platt, Gascoigne, Anderton and Sheringham among them – had suffered long-term injuries. Hoddle's argument was that he could name twice as many Premiership stars who had not figured in Euro 96, but had also suffered serious injuries.

Was there an element of hypocrisy? Some clubs that complain about too many games are not averse to arranging lucrative overseas tours of their own, either at the end of the season or in pre-season. Manchester United were to tour the Far East in July, yet England's summer tour of five matches in 18 days was unacceptable to Ferguson. United's Oriental excursion involved fixtures in Bangkok on 17 July, in Hong Kong on 20 July and in Tokyo two days later, not to mention two changes of time zone and inter-connecting flights. Perhaps the riddle had a simple explanation, not unconnected with the contract United have with Umbro, who paid a sum that could rise to £60m for the reproduction rights to United's playing strip. Umbro saw the Far East as a market with huge potential and used United's visit as a sales platform, not only for United shirts but a range of other products. 'It is an area with considerable potential because of the massive interest in soccer there,' explained Peter Draper, Umbro's UK marketing director.

Ironically, it took a foreigner to appreciate the benefit of the international team. Wenger solidly backed Hoddle by promising him the Arsenal players and criticizing clubs like Manchester United. Wenger believed it would damage the domestic game if top stars missed the tournament in France. 'If you pull your players out of the English national team, it is destroying English football. If England go and field their third team, it devalues the exercise, there is no meaning. If they can't take their best players, they should stay at home. If I get a request to let my players go, then I will do so. I would give them extra recovery time and they will start pre-season training later. I understand Alex Ferguson's point, but in France you don't have a choice. If the players don't go, they are suspended. England are the only country where managers have the choice to keep their players or not. I can't understand it.'

Gerry Francis joined forces with Wenger. The then Spurs manager said: 'Having been an international player and captain, I don't think you can stop players from wanting to represent their country. I don't think as a manager I could do that, but I do feel, with the seasons getting longer and more demands being placed on international players, that we have to look at giving these players a rest somewhere along the line. I remember with myself, back in the 1975/76 season, when I had my back problem, that it was brought on by playing too many games. That year I captained QPR to second in the League behind Liverpool, then we had the home internationals, which was three games in a week. That was followed by a trip to America for the Bicentennial tournament against Brazil, Italy and an American side. Then we flew to Helsinki for a World Cup game against Finland, towards the end of June. I came back and had about ten days off before pre-season started and I was off to Majorca to play against Barcelona in a friendly. It was at that stage when I started having problems with my back and it cost me two years out of the game. I think we have to be careful and recognize that rest is very important these days. But we also have to understand that an England manager needs his preparation time with players, so it is very difficult to be fair to everybody. But you cannot stop the players from playing because that could lead to problems with them.'

United's threat to withdraw players seemed unnecessary. After all, even if United won the European Cup they would play only 54 matches, including the Charity Shield. No Premiership side would play 60, while Everton would play just 42. When Tottenham won the UEFA Cup in 1972, they played 70. The trump card for Hoddle was to threaten to evoke FIFA rules and call up the Manchester United players for the full five days before the Poland World Cup tie, which would have ruled United's England contingent out of the European Cup Final – had they got there. The Final was due to played in Munich on 28 May – three days before England faced Poland in Chorzow. Hoddle had no intention of depriving English football of a such a prestigious international success, but in return for his co-operation he would expect the same from Ferguson.

Casualties conspired to deprive Hoddle of so many key players that the Mexico game was in danger of becaming a non-event. Operations to Shearer, Seaman, Merson and a setback for Gascoigne combined with long-term worries over Adams, Pallister, Southgate, Ferdinand, Anderton and Sheringham.

Sheringham faced an agonizing wait to see whether he would be fit enough after playing his first game of the year following an ankle injury. Shearer was ruled out for six weeks by yet another groin operation. Seaman had undergone a knee operation to repair an injury picked up at home. Merson was also ruled out by a knee operation. The next piece of bad news was that Gazza feared he would miss the rest of the season, and was therefore clearly a big doubt for the World Cup qualifier against Georgia.

Pallister had missed Euro 96, and even the Italy game when Hoddle was short of central defenders, but was now playing immaculately. However, he had been blighted by 18 months of back trouble. He had to sleep on hard boards on overnight trips and the driving seat in his luxury BMW has been modified to support his spine. 'I know that I could go down with the problem again,' he said. 'But, most important of all, I am now convinced in my own head that I can carry on playing. One thing that has kept me going is the fact that my specialist has never hinted at surgery. I have also learned to take special care. I've got my bed board, and my car seat has been specially strengthened. I am now fully aware of the problem and I have come to terms with it. That simply means that I take all the precautions I can to guard against another attack, and so far this season, I'm happy to say those precautions seem to be working. People who have been suggesting I'm some sort of cripple are way off the mark. I have a weakness in one area of my body, just as other players might have dodgy hamstrings or problems with their ankles.'

The glut of injuries wrecked the Mexico game to such an extent that it turned into little more than a get-together with a practice game at the end of it. But the match still retained importance to those players who were given a chance.

The squad for the Mexico game was: Walker (Spurs), Martyn (Leeds), James (Liverpool), Flowers (Blackburn), Southgate (A Villa), Adams (Arsenal), G Neville (Man Utd), Le Saux (Blackburn), Campbell (Spurs), Pallister (Man Utd), Matteo (Liverpool), Keown (Arsenal), Ince (Inter Milan), Beckham (Man Utd), McManaman (Liverpool), Batty (Newcastle), Redknapp (Liverpool), Lee (Newcastle), Butt (Man Utd), Anderton (Tottenham), Barmby (Everton), Fowler (Liverpool), Le Tissier (Southampton), I Wright (Arsenal), Sheringham (Spurs).

Hoddle was eager to defend yet again the enigmatic Le Tissier's selection after all the flak he had received. 'If it was me who was criticizing him, then possibly he wouldn't be in this squad. The criticism has come from outside the camp and unjustifiably so. I have analysed the [Italy] game and he was as productive as anyone.' Hoddle repeated that if he made a mistake against Italy, it was taking him off too early. 'I should have left him on, not taken him off. At the time I felt we needed a different style so that was the decision I made. But where everyone was saying he played so poorly, I am saying that if anything, I should have left him on for another ten minutes because he was a lot more productive than any others on the night. But that's in the past now.'

Hoddle recalled Arsenal defender Martin Keown and Leeds keeper Nigel Martyn to international colours for the first time in nearly four years, and gave a first call to Manchester United midfielder Nicky Butt.

Martyn celebrated his recall after months of campaigning from George Graham and the Elland Road supporters. Martyn, who cost the Yorkshire club £2.25m, proved one of Leeds' shrewdest additions. Howard Wilkinson's last buy helped establish a much-improved defensive record under Graham. He said: 'I thought there was a possibility while I was at Palace that my chance had gone forever. But it's come quicker than I expected after less than a year back in the Premiership. I got a phone call from the club telling me they had a letter from the FA saying one of their players had been selected. At first I thought it might be someone else. I am excited to be included, a bit nervous, and a bit apprehensive at the thought of going down there and performing in front of everybody. Now I've got to make sure I don't do anything wrong to get pushed out of it again.' The 29-year-old, who won the last of his three full caps against Germany in 1993, paid tribute to Leeds' goalkeeping coach John Burridge for his call-up. 'A good percentage of my form this season has been down to John. I've also had tremendous support from the fans, both home and away, and if I play it will be a big thank you to them.'

Keown gave credit for his recall to Wenger. The Arsenal defender, who had won the last of his 11 caps in a pre-World Cup tournament against Germany in America four years earlier, said: 'He has given me a defined role as centre-back, whereas before he came I was mostly a bits and pieces player. George Graham often used me as a man-marker and, last season, Bruce Rioch played me in midfield in front of the back four. I was happy to do both jobs when needed, but it's a fact that once people see you in a specific role you can progress and get rewards for it. It's good to be able to play in a number of positions but sometimes it can go against you. I was delighted to hear I'd been picked for the England squad again – and a little surprised as well, because other people seemed to have been pushed more than me in the media. But I did have a few whispers that I might be close to getting in the squad again and I'm keeping my fingers crossed now that I actually play against Mexico. It would be great to line up at the back alongside Tony Adams, I think it has only happened once before with England. I'm 30 but there are people older than me in the squad and I've never felt better really. The new manager has come in and given us all a different outlook. His methods work for us on the training ground and he's told us to believe that if we are good enough, we are also young enough.'

'When he first played for England, I didn't think that he used the ball well enough,' said Hoddle. 'Now he's shown that talent has always been there.' Keown agreed: 'I've tried to improve my passing. I've had criticism about that in the past but I've worked on that at Arsenal. Perhaps when I was younger I was only really interested in winning the ball and stopping people from playing, without thinking about finishing it off by passing to one of my team-mates.'

The goalkeeping issue became one of the most heated of all the debates. Martyn instead of Walker ... Pressman instead of Walker and Martyn. Was James ready for a debut? Had Graham pushing Martyn's cause done the trick, or had it put Hoddle off? Graham was convinced Martyn was playing better than Walker. After seeing Martyn deny Everton a point at Elland Road with an outstanding performance, he urged Hoddle to end the goalkeeper's England exile.

Ian Walker will forever be haunted by the Zola goal. Jibes of 'dodgy keeper' have followed him ever since. 'I'll tough it out, but I can't see why in one game I've gone from being the No 2 keeper in England and an international squad player for two years to a load of s--t in some people's eyes. I accept it was a big game and playing for your country is a big responsibility, but I'm not as bad as people say. What hurt most of all was when Sol Campbell offered to take the blame for Italy's goal, someone wrote that he was being honest, whereas I was hiding away. I couldn't believe it. Hiding is the one thing no one can ever throw at me. The lads will tell you I admit my mistakes. Even when Spurs lost 6–1 at Bolton, I never hid. I accept I haven't done as well this season as I have the last two years. We've had results like 7–1 at Newcastle, 6–1 at Bolton and 4–3 at West Ham – it hasn't been my best year. But I wouldn't get in the national team if I hadn't put in two years of playing well for Spurs and England.'

Walker studied Zola's goal to see if he could have done better. 'I've watched it on video. I even slowed it down to individual frames so I could see the direction the ball took. I know in my heart there was nothing I could do about it. I know I'm the scapegoat, but if you look at the goal, it's a shot that deflects off Sol Campbell. People have even had a go at him, which is ridiculous because he was just trying to block the shot. It caught him and beat me at the near post. Some might say "Ah – the near post", but they don't say it was coming straight at me until the deflection. I felt disappointed, too. Disappointed to have let a goal in, disappointed to lose, but I didn't expect all this. I suppose it's the price for playing at the highest level – but it hurts.'

Walker even received hate mail. 'I hardly had any hate mail – but it went up after the England game. I get it vetted now. My wife did do it at one stage but she gets a bit upset about things. So it's best for an individual at the club to do it now. I just palm it off to someone else, I don't even bother reading them. That is apart from the good stuff that comes through – I think that's a good way to handle it. But I don't let the hate mail, or whatever you like to call it, bother me. It comes from people who can't write properly or haven't got anything better to do. I had a bit after the England game but that's the way it goes I suppose – it can't be roses all the time.'

Kevin Pressman, Sheffield Wednesday's in-form 29-year-old was again overlooked. But he remained philosophical. 'It's vital that I make sure my level of consistency at club level doesn't suffer. That's the only chance of eventually forcing my way into the squad – by turning in performances that are good enough to keep me in contention. If I keep plugging away, something might be round the corner for me.' David Pleat even accused Hoddle of caving in to the media over his selection policy, rather than picking players on merit. The then Hillsborough boss, who rarely spoke out on international issues, claimed Pressman was unfairly overlooked because of a media monopoly enjoyed by the nation's biggest clubs. Pleat suspected the call-up of Martyn was influenced by public pressure from Graham. 'I'm surprised that Walker and James have been selected after one or two less than efficient games while Pressman, who has been outstanding all season, hasn't got into the group. It seems to me that the nub of interest has always been areas like London and Manchester. They get a media projection which isn't always merited. For instance, if an Arsenal player does well for a few games, he'll get a massive push. If he plays for Wednesday, he would need to produce 30 good games to get half a shove. The England management should use their own eyes and not be swayed. Martyn has had continual media projection by his manager. The good defensive platform built by George Graham has also helped him, whereas Pressman plays for a team who have gone out to win games. He's been watched by Ray Clemence on several occasions and I feel Kevin's form has spoken for itself.'

David James watched a video nasty of his worst game of the season. The Liverpool keeper forced himself to watch two re-runs of the 4–3 thriller with Newcastle and reckoned he could have saved all three of the Geordie goals. James prayed his dodgy display in front of Hoddle and Gorman wouldn't cost him the chance of a first senior cap. The 6ft 5in giant was favourite to replace Seaman against Mexico, but he confessed: 'I've watched the game twice and I don't need telling I could have done better. The first goal was very sloppy on my part and the other two were saveable. I think the fact we were 3–0 up and I had had nothing to do was a factor. My concentration has improved and I haven't been caught napping like that for a long time. Had it only been 1–0 or 2–0, I would have been more alert. At the moment there's a lot of speculation concerning which goalkeepers are doing well and who warrants England selection. I found out later Glenn Hoddle was there, so you could say it was the worst time to make a mistake like that. If I'm going to get dropped from the squad because of one bad game, then there's nothing I can do about it. But I hope people will look at my form over the last two years when I feel I've been pretty consistent.'

Roy Evans backed his keeper: 'I think it's great when people hold their hands up if they feel they've made a mistake. He's been excellent all season. His consistency has been a big factor for us but there's always going to come a time when a goalkeeper has an indifferent day. Fortunately it didn't cost us. It's not just about the goalkeeper – we didn't defend in front of him as well as we should. As for his England chances, you should never make a judgement on one game. There's not been a goalkeeper born who hasn't had a bad day and let a few goals in, and we've had some of the best keepers here over the years.'

James hit back at the 'dodgy keeper' chants. However, he admitted that he had spent so long playing his computer games that he had wrecked his pre-match preparations in the past. 'I haven't stopped playing my Nintendo but I'm not stuck on it for eight hours a day any more. As a professional athlete I was playing the games at the wrong time. Preparation isn't just going to bed early the night before a game or warming up properly. It's how you prepare in the whole week before.' James admitted he's had to get used to the taunts of opposing fans after Liverpool's 4–3 win against Newcastle. 'I've been fortunate this season because I've played badly on the right days. It happened against Newcastle at Anfield but we still won 4–3. Against Forest in our next game I took more flak for their goal, but again we didn't lose and stayed in the title race. I don't mind taking stick if it's justified and as a goalkeeper that's something you've got to be able to handle. From day one I've been in the position where I can save ten, let one through my legs and I'm a villain. It's a tough position to play. You need a different approach to the outfield players and tremendous self-confidence. I was getting the "dodgy keeper" chants before we even kicked off at Arsenal on Monday. I had the entire stand at Forest singing it so you just try to shut them out and try to make a joke of it.' He was on the bench for the first time against Italy and was keen to take that progression further. 'I'm very keen to play on Saturday. I'd love to play ahead of David Seaman every game, but it doesn't happen that way.'

Robbie Earle was on standby for the injury-hit squad for the Italy tie and his phenomenal scoring record from midfield put him in line for a chance against Mexico. 'Great if it happens,' said the 32-year-old former Port Vale midfielder who had been at Wimbledon for nearly six years. 'It would be a terrific honour and would mean Wembley again. I suppose I must have a chance after being on the standby list last time although, to be fair, quite a few players were injured then.

But if it doesn't come about I'll have the consolation of a few days off and there have not been many of those at Wimbledon this season. I had a taste of international football on the standby side and it only made me want more. I am having the season of my life and desperately want to be involved. I know I'll get the job done.' Earle was not selected and, eventually, he instead chose to help Jamaica into the World Cup Finals.

Hoddle cleared up any misunderstanding that he had a hard and fast 'rule' that players must report for assessment by the English medics. 'It is down to me to decide whether they must team up and be assessed. The reality is, I've been conversing with the managers and there have been no problems. It is not just about turning up to be assessed, other things can take place, players can have scans, visit specialists and copies of those things are sent down to us. It is a question of whether it is right for the players. And for Pallister and Beckham there would have been no positive steps served for me, them or their club if they had travelled all the way down. There are also other aspects why I would want players to join up. Gareth Southgate is coming down, even though he is injured at the moment. But it can be a chance to have a chat with him to discuss a variety of defensive things and at the same time we can assess his injury.'

With 13 players either ruled out or struggling from his original selection, Hoddle drafted in Stan Collymore, Stuart Pearce and Philip Neville, admitting, with the benefit of hindsight, that he was wrong to pin so much hope on an international game at such a critical stage of the domestic season. Although he had attracted a great deal of flak from inside and outside the profession, he insisted that the match still served a valuable purpose. Asked if it would not have been better to have held a training camp rather than a full game, Hoddle said: 'If you could have got your crystal ball out five or six months ago when we had to make a decision to take the friendly and told me [about the injuries], I would have agreed with you. We've just been unfortunate with the injuries we've got. The reasons behind having a friendly at this stage of the season are that my first four games were World Cup qualifiers and the first option on the fixture list was this date. So it was common sense to have a friendly. There are a lot of players who are going to fall by the wayside because of injury. The only way for me to look at that is that there are opportunities there for other people, like Stan Collymore and Nicky Butt. It's probably ahead of their time but if they're in control of the shirt they've got a chance.

'So there's a positive side, as well as a negative. If we get nothing else out of it, the experience these players will get will be a bonus for them. Whether they're ready or not is neither here nor there, they'll learn from training and playing at this level.'

Hoddle had hoped to signal a change in tactics and to get across the lessons from the World Cup failure against Italy, but the absence of so many of his first-choice players short-circuited his plans. 'It's not ideal because I would have loved to have had all my players, I would love to have introduced a certain system that

I wanted to work on. We have to try out things we might want to use further down the line, perhaps when we play against South American teams.'

Collymore had earned the last of his two England caps as a substitute in the 3–1 Umbro Cup defeat by Brazil in June 1995. With Barmby joining the list of definite absentees, there was an outside chance that Collymore would partner Liverpool team-mate Fowler in the starting line-up. Collymore had drifted out of the England reckoning under Venables despite his then-British record £8.5 million move from Forest and Fowler had jumped ahead of him in the queue. 'If I'm just going to be judged on the one game I had, I'll let other people decide if I'm capable,' said Collymore. 'But I've always been confident in my ability.' Some have suggested that the striker was treated harshly by Venables, although Collymore demurred. 'Not at all,' he countered. 'After the Umbro Cup I was called into the squad for the Croatia game last season, but there were a lot of exceptional strikers doing the business. I think that when you move up a level, it takes a bit of time to adjust to new surroundings. The first thing I noticed, even against Japan, was that teams keep possession longer. Perhaps that was missing in my game before but hopefully it's developed now, and I'm trying to enjoy things.' That development came at Anfield, despite Collymore's various public differences with the club. 'I think I can play right up there or further back, depending on the situation. I don't see myself as an out-and-out striker or only as somebody who drops off, although I like to get the ball and run at defenders to give them something to think about. The style we play at Liverpool has helped. We've got a lot of players with a lot of international experience, and it means they play with patience. Some clubs get the ball to the strikers early, whereas while we're always looking to create openings, we're also not scared to go back to come forward again. You can make half-a-dozen runs and not get the pass, but then on the seventh you can get in. It's a bit different to the way we played at Forest when I was there but it's effective and I think there's a similarity when it comes to England.' He hadn't expected the call from Hoddle. 'It's something that's come out of the blue, and I've got no illusions about what it means. My aim is to do well for the rest of the season with Liverpool, because I think I can play a major part in bringing success to the club, and whatever happens with England, I'll take it in my stride. It's not the be-all and end-all, although it's nice to be in Glenn's thoughts. I won't be looking beyond this week. I know that I was a late inclusion and only because a lot of players are out. But I want to enjoy it and we'll see what happens from there.'

Hoddle sensed a new degree of purpose about the player. 'We all know what Stan can do and how he hit the heights, both for Forest and for Liverpool. He has been below par at times this season, but I felt in the European game that his appetite was there. Stan's always had the talent, that's always been there, but I saw that appetite to have the No 8 shirt and keep it.'

Hoddle confirmed that Pearce would start against Mexico, and then smiled as he took a swipe at those suggesting he was experiencing problems with club managers. 'Stuart was delighted when I rang him. He's pleased to be called up and wanted to know when he could get here – and this time I didn't have to go to the manager first!' Hoddle also considered handing Pearce the captain's armband for the tenth time if Adams was ruled out.

Hoddle turned to David May when Pallister dropped out again. Since returning from a much-needed hernia operation earlier in the year, the quiet 26-year-old had been in wonderful form, looking an outstanding centre-half as Man United stormed through to the Champions' League semi-finals. The United fans, who once mocked him, had picked up the tune of 'Jesus Christ Superstar' and sang 'David May, superstar, got more medals than Shear-ra-ra!' After his £1.4m move away from Shearer and Blackburn, his problems had begun when Paul Parker was injured and Ferguson employed him as an emergency full-back. 'I'm much happier in the middle. I've played there all my career. To move to right-back, I was like a fish out of water. It was a learning experience,' he said ruefully. 'It really showed me what type of character I was and it showed me a lot about what type of friends I've got. You know who your real friends are when things are going badly for you. Everyone I knew stood by me, my family and my friends and that was the most important thing. Now I've been called up by England it's great for them too. I was overawed coming from a club like Blackburn. It's not as big as United. But I never regretted the move, I never doubted my ability. I always thought I could do it at United and that's what's happening now.'

When his name was missing from the original 25-man squad, with Keown included, he feared he would inherit Steve Bruce's mantle as the best defender never to be capped by England. 'A lot of people have been saying it's about time I was called up, but really I was concentrating on doing well for United and then I hoped the chance might come. It was just unfortunate what happened to Brucie. When you think what he did for United, it was remarkable he was never called up for England.'

For the first time, he waved goodbye to the odd United first team straggler instead of the other way round, when he would go home and put his feet up and wonder what it must be like to be an international squad member. 'My mum and dad are delighted for me and I'm so pleased for them and all my friends who backed me. It's brilliant.' Superstar? 'Well, it doesn't scan, but it puts a smile on my face.'

Reformed bad boy Lee Bowyer was the latest unexpected call-up. The 21-year-old Leeds midfielder was summoned from the Under-21 squad. A £2.6m signing from Charlton, he has the talent to succeed, but what has always been in doubt is his temperament. He was one of the first players caught by the FA random doping control unit, found to be using cannabis. Having overcome that problem, he landed in court after an affray at a McDonald's restaurant. George Graham rated Bowyer highly, making him an ever-present after he had recovered from a head injury sustained against Manchester United which kept him out for nine games. Hoddle admitted his elevation had perhaps come somewhat ahead of schedule. 'I spoke to George Graham and he agrees with me that Lee probably isn't ready for it yet, but it's a great opportunity for him to come here and join in.'

Rio Ferdinand, just 18, was only just preparing for his Under-21 debut against Switzerland. Hoddle ruled him out from the Wembley bench even if he was down to a bare bone sixteen players but said: 'He impresses me every time I see him. If I get a few injuries, who knows?' Ferdinand had started just seven senior games for West Ham.

Injury forced Le Tissier and Campbell to return to their clubs, bringing the number of withdrawals to ten. Hoddle was left with just four starters from the Italy game: Le Saux, Ince, Batty and Pearce – an indication of how the game was diminishing in World Cup relevance.

The next qualifier, at home to Georgia, was already on the agenda in terms of injuries. Hoddle admitted: 'I've had one eye on Georgia as I assess the injuries this week. I didn't want to make any of them worse. The Georgia game is not a million miles away and we're obviously hoping that some of the players outside my original squad, like Alan Shearer and David Seaman, will be back. Alan's coming on well, he's getting closer but ultimately it will be down to his club.'

After all the bad news, there were some positive developments with Southgate, McManaman and Sheringham all closer to fitness than the manager had hoped. Southgate had been expected to be ruled out with an ankle problem but Hoddle revealed: 'Gareth came through a good running session with Steve today which is excellent news. To be honest, I didn't expect him to respond to his treatment as well as that and it is a bonus. Steve is feeling his thigh a bit, but he came through the running without a problem although for him, Gareth and Teddy, who might train tomorrow, that will be the crucial day.'

Fowler accepted there were still a few players ahead of him, even if they were not all fit to play. 'No one actually knows who is playing or what the team will be, so I just hope I will be selected to play. There is also Ian Wright who has been playing absolutely brilliantly for Arsenal and he is in with a chance of playing. There are a few players who are ahead of me, such as Les Ferdinand and Alan Shearer, who are both top quality players.'

Fowler had been in the news for trying to persuade the referee to not give a penalty in his favour against David Seaman during Liverpool's game at Highbury. He talked about his new image as a thoughtful, conscientious objector to football convention rather than a trouble-prone Scouse scallywag. 'The 'scally' thing has been over-exaggerated,' said the goal ace. 'I've never been a bad lad. It's just that everything you do gets scrutinized. But I've been getting picked on because I've done one or two silly things and people think you're going to carry on like that all the time, which I'm not. I am quite a sensible lad and I hope people will look at me in a different way now. I know some people don't take me seriously. I'll just go about my job, I don't really care what people say about me. If you want to succeed at this level you've got to keep your feet on the ground and that's what my family and friends do.'

Fowler's talent has not yet been fully utilized by England, but Hoddle said: 'Robbie's talent has been there all through this season. He's a scorer, he has wonderful movement, but he's still a young lad and inexperienced at this level. That's the bonus side of playing this type of game. He's earmarked to progress as an international player. There are things he is going to learn at this level that are different. He is finding them out now in Europe with Liverpool and is learning at this level. He's a born scorer. We've seen Alan Shearer and Gary Lineker develop and I think Robbie's another one who could go that way. He's got a lot of hard work ahead of him but he can achieve that by the time he's 26 or 27, that's when he will be in his prime.'

Pearce confessed that he was happily turning his back on the Forest manager's job to play for England, leaving Dave Bassett to run the show on transfer deadline day in a bid to prolong his international career. He insisted: 'I'm the only manager who doesn't fear the sack because I still see myself as a player and that's what I enjoy most. I was disappointed to be left out of the original England squad and I'd prefer to be here than going to the club at 9.30 am and trying to work out a training session to keep the players bright and interested. It's nice just to get on the coach, have a game of cards and go out training with the lads instead of worrying about everyone else's injuries and problems.'

Pearce revealed that he hadn't asked Hoddle to be left out of the original squad. 'Glenn wanted to try one or two different ideas and thought my time would be better spent at the club. I was disappointed but I wasn't going to kick up a fuss because I'm now in the same boat and know what a nuisance it is to have to explain every decision to every player. You prefer them just to accept it and that's what I did. I always want to play for England and take the view that you miss one game and you never get that cap back. That's why I hope to be involved in the summer tournament in France. And I can guarantee that the Forest boss won't try and pull me out! As for the future, that's a bridge we'll cross in the summer, but at the moment I want to play every England game I can. After all, you're a long time retired.'

At the team hotel during the evening meal, Hoddle asked Paul Ince for a quiet word. In the absence of Shearer and Adams, Ince was told the skipper's armband would be his. The 30-year-old Inter Milan midfielder had led his country twice before – on the infamous US Cup tour under Taylor in 1993. It meant even more to him this time round. He had become England's first black captain in the 2–0 defeat by the USA in the Foxboro Stadium in Massachusetts and then led the side in the 1–1 draw with Brazil later that week. 'It's always a great honour to captain your country, but every player's dream is to walk out as skipper at Wembley,' said Ince, who would win his 28th cap. 'I've captained the side twice before, but never in my own country in front of our own fans. Now I've got a chance of doing that and I know it will be a really good day for me.'

England's first black skipper wanted his first Wembley goal to go with the armband. Under Hoddle he felt he had been let off the leash, whereas he had been restrained under Venables. 'The fact that he has brought in David Batty gives me a chance to express myself going forward. I've always wanted to do that. In my early days I used to score quite a few goals for West Ham but somehow I stopped doing it. Even though I enjoyed playing under Terry Venables – he was a great manager – I felt myself limited in what I actually did. I never felt that after 90 minutes that I came off having given my 100 per cent, that I was sweaty and knackered. In the Italy game, I had the chance to express myself. I've always had it in my locker to do those sort of things. It's just that I've had a set job to do and I've done it. But everyone enjoys scoring goals. Everyone has always said I don't score enough. Now I've got that chance. I've always been disappointed with my record because I know I could get goals if I got into the box.'

Hoddle wanted to see him attack more. 'He is a force when he gets into the opponents' box. His goalscoring record isn't fantastic but I'll tell you what, things happen off him as we saw in Moldova, as we saw in the European Championships with the penalty he won [against Holland].'

Ince would not be affected by the added pressure: 'I've done the job about 30 times for Man United, so it doesn't put extra pressure on me that you've got the armband on. And I always feel that even when Alan Shearer is the captain, I'm a kind of captain too because I talk to the players and try to gee up the whole team.'

Hoddle said that the choice of Ince had not been difficult. 'I think it was really a simple decision for me,' said the England coach, who would only confirm that Ince and Stuart Pearce would be in his starting line-up. 'Paul has shown great leadership on the pitch and those qualities are part of his character. He has shown that playing for England since I've been involved as coach and I think that going abroad to play in Italy has also helped his game. He has learned a lot from it. That's added not just to the way he plays, but to Paul as a person as well.'

Hoddle's assessment of his opponents was glowing. 'They have continuity, a full squad and they have had 17 internationals to our five. They have a couple of excellent goalscorers and they've brought in youngsters to blend with the experienced players. They're going to be a hard side to beat.'

The biggest danger might have been the Mexicans' manager Bora Milutinovic. The managerial mercenary has been a horror for both Robson and Taylor. The Serb plotted Mexico's win in 1985 and the humiliation of Taylor's World Cup flops in Boston in 1993. 'He's done a terrific job wherever he's gone. His experience is vast and to be respected,' said Hoddle.

Milutinovic was bemused by the problems England faced. 'In Mexico, the clubs help us so much and there is no problem among the 20 clubs to release players. My problem is that there is not enough competition for places and so our team tends to stay the same.'

Ossie Ardiles warned his old pal Hoddle to beware of Mexico. Former World Cup winner Ardiles, who spent a year managing top Mexican club Guadalajara but is now coaching in Japan, said: 'There are 100 million people waiting to make a saint out of the Mexican who scores the winning goal at Wembley.' Three of the little Argentinian maestro's old Guadalajara charges were in the side. Ardiles warned: 'Glenn won't need me to tell him that Mexico are a very dangerous side and a valid test for any team with World Cup aspirations. In the past, Mexican teams have been liable to flip and lose their concentration, but I can't see this group losing their cool. Glenn will need to be positive because, technically, Mexico are a much improved outfit and they will be happy to keep the ball on the floor and retain possession for long periods. Not only are they very competent collectively, but they have some outstanding individuals as well.'

Hoddle urged the Wembley fans to refrain from booing and jeering at foreign national anthems. Venables had gone public in his appeal to England supporters to show respect for the country's opponents. In the wake of the wholesale booing that met the Italian anthem, Hoddle repeated Venables' plea. 'The players and myself know from experience that booing and whistling actually winds up opposing players and makes them even more determined. It has the opposite effect to the one that, presumably, those who do it really want. During Euro 96, especially, the situation was much better but then before the Italy match things seemed to go backwards. Respecting the national anthem of England's opponents is both the right thing to do and also helpful to our reputation abroad.'

CHAPTER FOURTEEN

Robbie's Big Chance

England v Mexico, Wembley, 29 March 1997

A crowd of over 48,000 turned up at Wembley for the visit of Mexico. Although the result went in Hoddle's favour, it wasn't a stimulating performance by the England team. However, there were some pluses in some individual displays.

Managers love to tell you that a goal changes the complexion of a match and that certainly happened with the 18th minute penalty. Robert Lee, deputizing on the right side of midfield for David Beckham, went on a probing dribble before slotting an intelligent pass into the penalty area for Teddy Sheringham. Sheringham's shot was blocked by the defender, Pavel Pardo, but Paul Ince emerged on his blindside as the grounded Mexican lunged for the ball. Ince tripped over himself as Pardo made no contact, but the penalty was given and Sheringham sent keeper Aldolfo Rios the wrong way from the spot. Suddenly there was a touch of sparkle in England's football as Lee revelled in his new role. The player jettisoned by Venables enjoyed an outstanding first half, enough to convince Hoddle that he deserved to be under consideration for a place in his World Cup squad.

It was not only a chance to experiment with personnel, but also an opportunity for Hoddle to refine his defensive tactics. Normally a disciple of three at the back, he dabbled with a more traditional 'four' against the Mexicans but with Le Saux given the extra responsibility of doubling up as a wing back. Hoddle said: 'Further down the line, if we need to, we can play like that again.' It required a phenomenal amount of work for Le Saux, who had to be at peak fitness to perform in England's new-look back line.

The England coach opted to send on Ian Wright for the injured Sheringham when Stan Collymore might have seemed the more logical choice. But Hoddle stressed that it wasn't because Wright was the next in line, but rather he felt that Wright and Fowler would hit it off as an attacking combination 'despite both being off-the-shoulder players.' Wright played a major role in the second goal after 54 minutes, a blistering far post header from Le Saux's cross forcing the keeper into a flying save which Fowler followed up on to head his first goal for his country.

By then Hoddle had brought on Redknapp for Batty and he later blooded Butt in place of McManaman. Once captain of the Under-21s, Redknapp's progression had been assured since he came on as a second-half substitute against Scotland in Euro 96 and helped turn the game. But then injuries had sent his career into reverse.

The performance of certain individuals clarified a number of doubts in the England coach's mind. Barmby slipped even further down the pecking order and Collymore would now have to set the Premiership alight. Sheringham was given a glowing reference by Hoddle as the pressure grew on the players battling for England's striking places. Even though he played only 36 minutes before he had to go off injured, Sheringham was able to re-establish his credentials as Shearer's No 1 partner. In addition, Wright and Fowler did enough to confirm they would be part of Hoddle's long-term thinking for France.

Hoddle was anxious to re-establish the Shearer–Sheringham partnership in time for the Georgia match. 'I thought about it before the game but I've not had a chance to play them together yet. They would be a good balance, but I don't want to set anything in stone because the best-laid plans can go wrong.'

Hoddle was effusive as he discussed his wealth of strike options. He described Shearer's rivals and possible partners. He said of Sheringham: 'He's a clever player. He lacks pace, but he knows that. He compensates by using his head. He can pull off from the front line and keep possession – and in that he is as good as anyone in the country. At this level it is not all about legs. It's about subtlety. You have to have the right player to do that, and Teddy's very experienced at it. He does it week in, week out at Tottenham.' Asked for comparisons with other leading forwards, he said: 'He is not a firework like Zola but in terms of being clever and creating as well as scoring, there are similarities. Bergkamp is a very similar player, very elusive. Sheringham plays in the same sort of role to Eric Cantona of Manchester United although they have different styles. He's got a great attitude and wants to play in every game.'

Hoddle perhaps saw Ian Wright as a supersub. The England coach said: 'He can be with us right the way through to the World Cup. He can be used from the start or come on as a sub. He still retains that effectiveness, enthusiasm and his movement. You get something different if you use him from the bench. He has those little skills, twists and turns and he was effective with our second goal for Robbie. He's a confident lad, and if he gets a goal under his belt we might even see another side to him as an international player. He's got two seasons at the very top and that's because he's looked after himself. He's as sharp as anyone in the country and has a future with us. I believe it has a lot to do with Arsene Wenger's arrival at Arsenal and the sort of agility work that they do as well as the diets.'

Hoddle also gave his opinion of Fowler: 'The burden of his first goal is no longer there and next time he can play without that pressure, and with a lot more confidence and not apprehension. His overall play has to improve. He has to keep possession when he's up there feeding the line. Defending in the Premiership is a lot different to international football. In his favour, he has the stepping stone of experience of European football with his club.'

Wright believed in Fowler, and talked about the suffocating pressure he had endured himself before ending his own England drought with a crucial goal against Poland. Wright said: 'Although my header didn't go in, I'm so pleased that Robbie scored. In the early stages of my career I was so wound up wanting to score, that when it never happened, I got more and more anxious for the next game. It's very pleasing that Robbie got his one out of the way so that when he plays next time it could be easier for him. He'll have that bit more space where he can maybe have a couple of matches where he doesn't score. Then he'll score again and he won't get that pressure on him with people saying "he doesn't score at this level." Some people may have said this was a meaningless game, but that's definitely not the case.' Wright was overjoyed that he was still part of the set-up. 'Glenn has put a lot of faith in me and I just want to go out there and repay him. He told me he was going to play Teddy from the start and I replied: "Whatever you do is all right with me, I'm glad to be in the squad, and if I do come on then I'll try and make my mark." If it's just two minutes or 30 minutes, I'm not bothered. I just went out there and tried to let people know I've got something to offer at this level. I love it, I enjoy it, to be back involved is a godsend. What helps your confidence is that everybody knows you, you feel involved and it's great because I felt it went well for me. And not even an elbow from one of the Mexicans which caught me right on the temple and knocked me back could detract from it – I was buzzing, I loved it. Glenn has said to me he wants me to keep myself fit and hopefully I can be in and around there. I'll just do whatever job they want me to do, I'll be here as long as they want me.'

Inter Milan told Ince he had to play in their last game of the Italian season and wouldn't be able to join up for the four-nation tournament in France. Ince said: 'I desperately want to play in France but I don't have a release clause in my contract for friendly internationals. It's a difficult situation for me because it's an important tournament for England against three teams who'll be our biggest rivals at the World Cup Finals.' Ince was enjoying his football under Hoddle and had become a more accomplished player for his spell in Italy. 'Before I left Manchester United, I was always nervous about playing the Germans and Italians because everyone always talked about how good they were. But now I've played against these guys every week and it's no longer a problem for me. The main thing I've gained from my time in Italy is the knowledge that I can hold my own against the best in the world, especially for England. I play against all these different countries and I'm not worried any more. Before I might have gone "he's a good player", but now I know they can't be any better than I face every Sunday. I'm a fitter, better player and I hope that confidence helps and inspires other people around me. If it does, I'm pleased about that.'

Ince, who gave a storming performance as captain, added: 'If we'd lost to Mexico, the whole nation would have been down and we'd have been under a lot of pressure for the World Cup tie with Georgia. But now the whole country is on our side again. We've shown a lot of character this week after unfair criticism from people who reckoned this match didn't mean anything. Try telling Robbie Fowler, Robert Lee, Martin Keown and Nicky Butt that this was a meaningless match. We've got 17 or 18 players ruled out by injury, yet we've still put a team together who've done the business and that's given us all a real lift.'

The threat of the England scrapheap inspired Southgate's miracle comeback. He'd given up hope of playing against Mexico when he reported for duty with an ankle injury. But the chance to resurrect his international career after being axed for the Italy game was all the motivation he needed. 'Last season was so brilliant for me and I didn't want this year to be the one when it all dipped away to nothing. I was really disappointed to be left out of the Italy game, but Glenn Hoddle said my form had dropped and that was fair comment. I'd been struggling with injuries, Villa had been going through a bad time and I was playing in midfield. But I was determined to show I could do it again.'

Robert Lee was a success as David Beckham's replacement. The Newcastle man said: 'I've never played wing-back before, but I couldn't see anyone else in training who was going to play down the right so it looked like it was down to me. It's a lot different to what I'm used to and it probably showed a few times. But once I settled down, it was just like playing for Charlton again. It was hard work because you've got to get forward and create things as well as help out in defence. But the toughest part was keeping tuned in all the time. When you're playing in a forward position you can let your mind wander a bit, but I did that a couple of times and their players got in behind me. I didn't think I'd enjoy the job as much as I did. I saw a lot more of the ball than I expected and it worked out well for me in the end.'

The Mexico game was Lee's first England appearance since being axed from Venables' squad on the eve of Euro 96. 'I've proved I can play in a number of positions. I'm not stuck in one role unable to play anywhere else. That's got to help me when Glenn Hoddle and Kenny Dalglish are picking their teams. Euro 96 was a bitter disappointment but I've put it to the back of my mind and never allowed myself to believe it was the end of my England career. I always believed I'd get another chance if I played well enough, but the problem was that with so many young players around I didn't know when that opportunity would come. A lot of people dismissed this game as meaningless but it's given me the chance to show what I can do and now I want to be back here for the Georgia game.'

Among the benefits Hoddle listed were the appearances of Butt and Redknapp. He also paid tribute to 'Gareth's tremendous attitude' in wanting to play after just two days' training out of a possible nine. Pearce was 'terrific' again in his attitude and application. While James had a worrying start, dropping a cross and looking shaky at times, Hoddle felt he had recovered to show 'a lot of nerve, temperament and composure, and he pulled off a good save at the end'. There were players who had staked their claims to places in the World Cup squad. 'People have got to challenge, and the ones in the shirt can't take their foot off the pedal when others are pushing to get in there.' McManaman remained an enigma with a mixed performance. Hoddle observed: 'It would do him the world of good to pop up with a goal at this level. He has tremendous talent. When at the top of his game, he is free flowing and as exciting as anyone in the country.'

Hoddle was already looking ahead to Georgia at Wembley. Priority was the fitness of key players such as Shearer. 'Our best performance was in Georgia when we had time to work on it; every other game has been a headache week together. They have a new coach since we played the game there, but they are still a technical side, their strength is not in defending but it's in midfield. We did a good job over there. I was disappointed that we didn't keep the ball after we were two up and that's down to a lack of experience, but I was still pleased with a lot of the things I saw.'

Hoddle knew it was a long haul to reach the standards he was seeking, notably in defence. His ideal was to discover a sweeper in the Matthias Sammer mould. 'It could take 18 months, even longer, a pre-season and the first ten games, but that's how long it takes to fit in that amount of games, and I haven't really got that time. We don't defend as well as we can do in this country.' Would the future be Dominic Matteo or Rio Ferdinand?

An hour after the Mexico game, Hoddle knew that Italy had opened up a three-point lead at the top of the group with their 3-0 home win over Moldova and that a week later it might be six points. Hoddle said: 'We have to make sure we look after our own results and if we get a break along the way so be it, but that's not set in any of my plans.'

There was a growing confidence in England's ability, and this was reflected in FA chairman Keith Wiseman's programme notes: 'The results between the top sides in our World Cup qualifying group are going to be very important so the defeat against Italy was a setback. Not to play in the World Cup Finals would be unthinkable and I am very confident that we will find a way there, whether as automatic qualifiers or via the play-off route. The expectations are always so high with England and that was particularly evident in the build-up to that Italy game. But the opposition on the night showed that they were an excellent side. Looking at that match as a whole, I felt we were worth a draw, but certainly not any more than that. However, I believe the players are available to Glenn to go and win in Italy if it comes to that.'

England (1) 2 Mexico (0) 0
James, Keown, Southgate, Pierce, Lee, Ince (capt), Batty, Le Saux, Sheringham, McManaman, Fowler.

CHAPTER FIFTEEN

Rio Steps Forward

*Hoddle includes Rio Ferdinand in his
long-term plans, April 1997*

English hopes of avoiding the dreaded World Cup play-offs were given a much-needed boost when Poland held Italy to a goalless draw in Chorzow. So the Italians still led the group by four points but had now played a game more than England. Hoddle was delighted by the Chorzow result. It encouraged him to believe that England would qualify automatically. He said: 'I haven't been able to play anywhere near my strongest team yet, but if we can get that selection out I believe we'll reach the Finals by winning the group. I still have to be guarded because it's dangerous to look too far ahead. We have to make sure that our own house is in order and that we start by beating Georgia. There is no doubt, though, that this result has given us a bit more daylight. I always felt that there were chances that both ourselves and Italy would drop points in this group in games other than when we played each other and that that might decide the group. Italy have dropped their first two now and we have just got to make sure that the same thing does not happen to us.' Hoddle would have preferred a Poland win, but a draw kept Italy within striking distance and Poland at arm's length.

Another detail of Hoddle's masterplan was revealed. He wanted players like Rio Ferdinand to bridge the gap between the Under-21s and the full international side. 'In the past, the gap between club football and international level has been too big. Players make a couple of appearances for the Under-21s and then they are in at the deep end just like I was. It would be much better for them to have two or three years playing for the Under-21s and then the step up isn't so big. The experience of learning tactics and getting used to the international stage is vital.' Hoddle added: 'We have purposely chosen 18- and 19-year-olds to give them three years in the side. When I think back to what happened to me, I had one full season before I was plunged in at international level. The most important thing is the development of our young players to give them the experience they need to make better quality international players for the future. When you look at players like David Beckham, you see what can be achieved. I think we have to emphasize the importance of bridging the gap between club and Under-21 football and the full international side. When you look at the progress David has made over the last 18 months at international level, it shows what can be achieved.'

Rio Ferdinand had rapidly built up a good reputation since his introduction to Premiership football by Harry Redknapp at West Ham. He was proving to be a versatile performer and his specialist position, sweeper, was a role that intrigued Hoddle. The England coach spoke positively about his development: 'We don't have that kind of sweeper in the Premiership, not an English one anyway. Rio is somebody who can play the role. He's not ready yet but he's the type we're looking for.' After his first full training session with England's youngsters, Hoddle was convinced Rio would hold the key to his long-term plans.

A two-month spell on loan with Bournemouth had kick-started the young Hammer's career. He said: 'That spell was excellent for me and stood me in good stead for where I am now. I didn't realize how much of a benefit the experience of playing first-team football regularly and looking at the other side of the coin in the football world would be to me. It's a different world from West Ham. I was suddenly at a club who were fighting for their lives financially and the lads were wondering where their money was going to be coming from. It opened my eyes to a different side of life and I even had to take my kit home every day to wash. But the lads put everything out of their minds when they went on the training ground and on match days and I learned such a lot from my 12 games there. It also gave my confidence a tremendous lift and I came back bubbling to West Ham...The last two or three months have seen so much happen. It all seems to be happening so quickly and I have to keep my feet on the ground. Things have been going really well, and, without sounding big-headed, I was thinking it would only be a matter of time before I got a call-up from the Under-21s. I thought I was doing well enough. Now I hope I can do myself justice against Switzerland and then kick on from there.'

Only in the previous nine months had he been in regular contact with cousin Les. Ferdinand Jnr said: 'I had hardly any dealings with him at all when I was a youngster. It was when we were both at QPR that I got to know him when I was a 13-year-old. We have been closer since Euro 96. We exchanged phone numbers and have talked a few times since – and quite a lot recently. Les has given me a lot of advice on how to conduct myself off the pitch and how to take care of myself – he's been a bit of a father figure towards me. If I can achieve half of what he has managed then I will be well happy. Hopefully we will play in the same England side one day. I would love it to happen – if he is still going when he is about 40!'

Rio committed himself to West Ham for the next five years despite interest from Manchester United, Leeds and Liverpool. He became the highest paid teenager in British football after signing a £5,000 a week contract, netting him £1.25 million by the year 2002, plus further bonus payments for senior England caps. 'West Ham offered me the security of a new contract and I was really happy to repay their faith in me. I know that some people will look and ask "five years?" but I want to stay here for as long as I can. I am not saying I'll be here forever because nothing is certain in football. But for the foreseeable future I want to remain a West Ham player. I've heard all the whispers about other clubs being interested in me, but I don't really take much notice of it. I've still got an awful lot to learn and I want to do it at Upton Park. Alvin Martin once told me he was still learning the trade at 37 so I know how far I've got go. Besides, I'll still only be 23 when this contract expires, so it's not as if I'm signing my entire career away.'

Was it a case of in with the new, out with the old? David Platt's place in the pecking order receded as Hoddle looked to the future. The former England captain criticized Hoddle for not explaining why his international career appeared to be over. The 30-year-old with 62 caps had failed to start under Hoddle. 'I'm disappointed, of course, as anyone would be in the circumstances,' said the Arsenal midfielder. 'I would have expected a phone call from the coach to tell me why I wasn't in the squad but he preferred to call my manager. I haven't spoken to Glenn at all. I hope it isn't the end of my England career, because, like everyone, I still have ambitions in that area.' It was not that he wasn't selected, so much as the perceived cold shoulder, that upset Platt so much. He was aggrieved that Hoddle hadn't even phoned to explain his reasons for dropping him.

The England squad for the World Cup qualifier against Georgia was announced. It was: Seaman (Arsenal), Walker (Spurs), Flowers (Blackburn), Martyn (Leeds), Adams (Arsenal), Keown (Arsenal), Pallister (Man Utd), Pearce (Nottm Forest), Southgate (Aston Villa), G. Neville (Man Utd), Campbell (Spurs), Le Saux (Blackburn), P. Neville (Man Utd), Beckham (Man Utd), Ince (Inter Milan), Batty (Newcastle), Lee (Newcastle), McManaman (Liverpool), Redknapp (Liverpool), Butt (Man Utd), Shearer (Newcastle), Ferdinand (Newcastle), Sheringham (Spurs), Fowler (Liverpool), Wright (Arsenal).

Hoddle had Gazza watched when he returned for Rangers after a long lay-off as a substitute in a 6–0 victory over Raith Rovers, but his lack of an opportunity to play again before the Georgia game had counted against him. It was decided that he had not trained enough or played a sufficient number of games to make the squad.

There were concerns over Adams who had been unable to train for weeks. He was patched up to play by spending hours in the swimming pool and could barely move in the dressing-room after matches. Adams admitted: 'My ankle is still not right and needs a lot of care. I can't move after games. It stiffens up a lot and it's not good, but when you are 30-plus and you've played 550 games, these things take their toll. At the moment I'm doing a lot of swimming and that seems to improve my mobility. But I'm turning into a swimmer, not a footballer, and the lads take the mick because they go off and do their stuff on the training pitch every morning while I go for a nice swim.'

David 'Calamity' James was sent to the back of the goalkeeping queue. Hoddle explained that the Liverpool keeper had sealed his fate with his display in the title decider with Manchester United at Anfield. Arguably to blame for at least one of Pallister's double, James then made an absolute howler to give Cole the killer third and the England coach said the display had cemented a decision probably already made. 'It was a difficult one and one of the reasons I went up to Liverpool on Saturday was to see how David responded. I was hoping that he would show me something he hasn't been showing in the last few weeks, but he knows he didn't have a particularly good game. If he had played really well and justified me keeping him in I might have done but at the moment the way he is playing means he can't get in ahead of any of the other four keepers.' Just three weeks earlier, the 26-year-old had been on top of the world as he made his international debut with a shaky clean sheet against Mexico. But, in a spectacular dive which Roy Evans feared would shatter what remained of his confidence, his Premiership fumbles had pushed him back in the pecking order.

Hoddle ignored Evans' pleas for compassion and ruthlessly axed James from the squad. 'This is a test for him. In many ways taking him out of the pressure might, in the long term, be the right thing for him,' said the England coach. Hoddle had cultivated the image of a caring manager with his treatment of the off-field problems of some of his stars, particularly Gascoigne, Adams and Merson. But there was no mercy for a goalkeeper whose faults had been cruelly exposed. The England coach explained: 'The form of other goalkeepers in the country is ahead of David, similarly to how David's form was ahead of Nigel Martyn at the beginning of the season when I first brought him in. It would be difficult to justify bringing him in ahead of those other people. People have tried to jump to the conclusion that because he played in a friendly, suddenly he was going to be the No 2 goalkeeper. Now that's not what that game was all about. I said it was an opportunity to experiment, to find out things about individuals. Since that game his form has dipped and we've been watching and monitoring that very closely.'

Hoddle waited before breaking the bad news personally to James. 'He was obviously disappointed. I made sure he knows the door isn't shut completely on him. I do rate him as a goalkeeper, I think he's just going through a difficult time and in the long term he will be able to turn it round. He's not become a bad goalkeeper overnight, he's just having a bad patch.'

James, who initially put his poor run down to his addiction to computer games, had not been helped by some dreadful defending in front him, a point acknowledged by Hoddle: 'If you make a mistake as a goalkeeper there's no way back. You can make a mistake in midfield or at the back and the goalkeeper saves you. That's always been the pressurized job and a difficult one. There's many reasons why goalkeepers go through bad patches. You could say the same thing about Tim Flowers, his confidence was knocked when I didn't bring him in right at the beginning. He's had to wait, bide his time, maintain his confidence in himself and he's come on for a very good season. At club level there has to be some responsibility for goalkeepers on their back line. It's ironic that George [Graham] has gone to Leeds, organized his back four and Nigel Martyn has come into very good form. The two go hand in hand, but you don't get that opportunity at international level because you don't get long to work with them.'

James was assured he would return to top form by the man who replaced him in

New tactics, new talent

Paul Scholes has become one of Hoddle's big discoveries on the Road to France, underlying his growing stature with a wonderful goal in the friendly against Cameroon at Wembley.

Left: Liverpool's Steve McManaman has the potential to be a world-beater, but he had a turbulent time during the qualifiers after starring in Euro 96. Hoddle demanded more consistency and goals from him.

Below: Robbie Fowler scores England's second goal against Mexico during the Wembley friendly in March 1997.

Right: Hoddle's mission right from the start was to achieve a relaxed atmosphere on the training ground. Nicky Barmby, Teddy Sheringham, Paul Ince, Les Ferdinand, and Alan Shearer enjoy the joke.

Below right: What's the Gazza hairstyle today? The rest of the England squad appear more interested in observing his exquisite tight control of the ball.

Paul Gascoigne is always going to be a target for the hatchet men ready to stop him at all costs. Here he tangles with South Africa's John Moeti.

Above: The British bulldog spirit personified
in Arsenal skipper Tony Adams. Like Shearer,
his time under Hoddle was dogged by injuries.

Right: A pensive Paul Scholes illustrates
that it's not all fun and laughter as the
players get down to serious work on
the Bisham Abbey training ground.

Left: Oh dear. Gazza up to his
training ground pranks at the
start of Hoddle's reign. Here he
tugs at Nicky Barmby's shorts;
later he was to cause Hoddle's
first embarrassing moment
when he pulled down the shorts
of Paul Ince.

Below: Nicky Butt takes advice from Glenn. Time is precious for Hoddle on the training ground prior to vital games.

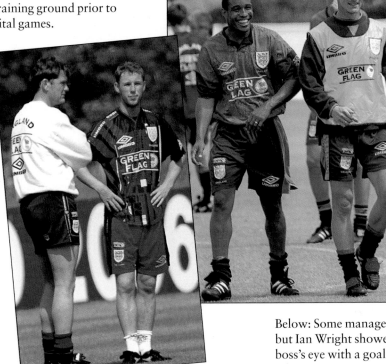

Left: Every effort is made to please the sponsors. Guess who sponsors 'Team England' as Ince and Sheringham are walking advertising boards during an 'open' training session at Bisham Abbey.

Below: Some managers moaned about friendlies, but Ian Wright showed the value of catching the boss's eye with a goal at Old Trafford against South Africa in a rare game away from Wembley.

Above: A World Cup dress rehearsal in Montpellier during England's triumphant Tournoi de France. Here Alan Shearer turns away after scoring the winner against hosts France on 7 June 1997.

Below: Gareth Southgate knows one way to stop Ronaldo, the best player in the world – by tugging at the Brazilian's shirt. Here he perfects the art during The Tournoi de France.

Above: Robbie Fowler on target in the friendly win over Cameroon on 15 November 1997 with Liverpool team-mates Ince and McManaman in the picture.

Left: Hoddle wanted to re-educate Gazza but at the same time didn't want to knock out of him his 'cheeky chappie' ways. There was still room for a laugh and a joke on the training ground, but in moderation.

the England squad. Martyn said: 'James is a good goalkeeper and there will be no problem about him bouncing back. He played hard on his debut and did very well but just as you think things are going great you make a mistake and it preys on your mind. But it happens normally when you think you are on the verge of cracking things. You think it is an easy job, then four go past you and you've had it.'

Hoddle feared for Shearer. Although he was delighted to be able to include the world's most expensive player in the squad, he was unwilling to suggest that the £15 million man was completely over his latest groin operation. Hoddle pointed to the form Shearer had shown ahead of the clash with Italy to explain his caution. Asked about the boost a healthy Shearer would give his side, Hoddle replied: 'Is he fully fit?' That latest operation was Shearer's third in the same area in less than 12 months and Hoddle added: 'Looking from the outside, he seems very close to full fitness but the main thing with Alan's situation is that he doesn't end up in hospital again. It's not so much a case of him being overplayed, but there's the prevention work he needs, to know exactly where the problem is coming from and so he can put it right. That's something his club is aware of and we're obviously aware of when he's with us.' In the event, Shearer would prove his fitness with four goals for Newcastle after his return, and the England captaincy would be his.

Hoddle's 25-man party was missing several of the players he originally chose for the win over Mexico. May, Bowyer and Barmby were axed; Collymore, Le Tissier and Anderton injured. Despite Gascoigne's absence, Hoddle was still reluctant to release Beckham into central midfield. Lee's impressive display on the right against Mexico, coupled with the naming of the two Nevilles, meant that Hoddle had plenty of cover on the right but still he was unpersuaded. 'There's no doubts about him [Beckham] physically, but you have to know when the right time is to play him there.'

CHAPTER SIXTEEN

SAS Reunited

England v Georgia, Wembley, 30 April 1997

The England players could be under no illusions about the importance of the match against Georgia. By beating Poland 3–0 at home, Italy had surged ahead at the top of Group Two and were now seven points ahead of England, who had two games in hand.

Les Ferdinand linked up with England confident the worst was behind him after struggling with injury for most of the season. The then Newcastle striker said: 'It's fair to say I've been having a nightmare, both in terms of injury and in front of goal. So to score against Derby last weekend and get through 90 minutes unscathed was a dream for me. You have no idea how relieved I am. It has put me in a good frame of mind, not only for England but also for Newcastle's run-in.'

Ferdinand was not convinced that he would be selected, however. He added: 'I believe Glenn Hoddle will go for a partnership of Alan and Teddy Sheringham. Because of injury to one or the other, it's the first chance Glenn has to pair them since they did so well together in the European Championship.'

Sheringham had become as valuable to his country as Seaman, Ince, Gazza and Shearer but he did not feel that his place was secure. 'I would never think I'm here to stay as an England player. I didn't even feel like that during Euro 96. One bad game – regardless of it being a friendly or a World Cup match – could mean the end of your international career. That's how I felt before the Mexico game. When there are so many good players around wanting to play for England, you have to perform every time. It was lovely to hear people say I might have made a difference against Italy but Terry Venables said players always seem to improve when they aren't out on the pitch!'

Sheringham added: 'I know that if I don't score goals as well as provide them, I won't be in the team. But when you've got someone alongside you who can score as many as Alan, the expectancy is lifted off you. I always believed I could partner Alan for England and luckily for me, Terry Venables shared that opinion. We've not played together since Glenn took over, but I'll be very disappointed if we don't change that against Georgia.'

Sheringham refused to allow himself to get carried away by the plaudits given to his recent performances; he still hadn't forgotten that for the first two years of his international career his pedigree was constantly questioned. 'It's nice to be appreciated and lovely that people are suddenly comparing me to Zola, Bergkamp and Cantona. But I know it can all change very quickly. One or two bad performances for England and I know it's all back to: "I told you he was too slow, I told you he doesn't score enough goals." And suddenly, before you know it, that's the end of my England career. It was the same situation with Peter Beardsley. For a long time people asked why England relied so much on Gary Lineker for goals. It took them a long time to appreciate Beardsley's contribution. That's why I don't care what people say about me. All that matters is that I'm producing the right stuff for the manager.'

Once again the pressure was on Shearer to get the goals to bring the World Cup Finals closer. But he didn't move a muscle when discussing the implications of his role. 'I love it. I've had demands all my career. And I really enjoy all the pressure and the burdens placed on me. I know people expect goals from me. So do I. But all my career I've lived with one expectation on another. When I first moved to Southampton I was just 15, and the pressure was on to make it. Then when I joined Blackburn I was the most expensive player in England at £3.5 million. After that, I went 12 games without an international goal and the word went around I should be left out of the side. Now I am the most expensive player in the world. And I love that too. The more on my shoulders the more I thrive on it. People always believe I'll score. I don't go into every game believing that myself, but I always hope so. After all, it's my job. And a front player is judged on how many goals he gets.'

Shearer added: 'I always believed my partnership with Teddy would work. It's been said he's not quick enough to play at the highest level. But he has two yards in his head. He's clever and skilful. We link up well. He's the sort of player that if he's in a good position, he would pass the ball to me. If I was in the same situation, I would shoot. However, it's wrong for me to talk about our partnership because there are others the manager might want to use. Les Ferdinand and I are still the leading combination in the Premiership, yet we've missed four-and-a-half months between us through injury and I don't know what the team will be.'

David Beckham could become as valuable for England in the next decade as Gascoigne has been in the nineties. Hoddle explained how he needed to groom Beckham rather than expect too much too quickly. That was why the youngster was playing at right wing-back instead of being given the responsibility of the centre of midfield. Hoddle had earmarked Beckham for a central midfield role but not until the summer tournament, the Tournoi de France, against Italy, Brazil and France – the highest calibre of opponents. 'There will be times when he'll play there and Mexico would have been one of those without doubt had he been fit. So he's missed out there. I feel he's not ready for that role full-time.'

Hoddle didn't believe that Beckham was suffering end-of-season fatigue. The England boss said: 'David had a rest a few weeks ago, and I'm not so sure that it was necessary. Sometimes when you're 21 that isn't the right thing. When you acquire a bit of experience and knowledge about the game it's easy to switch on and off, particularly when you're at the top and know a bit more about football. It's not a problem to do that, you can raise yourself for the games that matter. But you know people will go into form and go out of it again, that's the way it is. It is nothing to do with the amount of games you play. Ten years ago we were playing ten more games a season. I've always found it a fallacy that 21-year-olds can switch back on again. When you've got experience when you've had an injury, you learn how to adjust and get your form back quicker, knowing what you can do and what you can't do, and you know certain things come back but take a little longer.'

The England coach was at pains to play down the accusations that he was at odds with Alex Ferguson over the handling of United's precious fledglings. 'Alex and I have no problems at all. I've probably spoken to him more than any other manager ...'

David Seaman had a lot of sympathy for David James. He remembered the bad times when he thought his own career was in ruins; he'd been through the nightmares now haunting James and Walker. Seaman recalled when he was reviled and ridiculed. 'I've had it. Been through it. And it's hard to take. You know, people taking the mickey in the street. After I was beaten by Nayim in the Cup Winners' Cup Final in Paris backpedalling as the ball went over my head, folk would see me and start walking backwards. You just want to give them what for. But you just can't lose your temper. Then there was the Gazza free-kick for Tottenham against Arsenal at Wembley, and Ronald Koeman's for Holland against England. You go home sometimes in despair. Try to forget about it. Not take your work home with you. Distance yourself from the disappointment. But it's hard. As for being dropped, I wouldn't appreciate that no matter what the circumstances. I've had that too. I went from England's No 2 goalkeeper to No 3. I've been there. Didn't play for my country for something like 18 months I think.'

Tony Adams was carrying a leg injury, the legacy of attempting a comeback too soon after an operation on his ankle ligaments. Rest, of course, is a commodity rarely available to international footballers. It was, however, possible in the summer and Adams would miss England's trip to France. The Arsenal defender was given permission by Hoddle to leave the camp at Burnham Beeches for what he described as a 'gratitude meeting' of Alcoholics Anonymous. Adams, battling his addiction, praised Hoddle for his consideration and compassion. The compulsion to drink was out of his system, but six days without a meeting was a serious threat to his long-term sobriety.

When asked if he could have been a Matthias Sammer had his development not been shackled by George Graham, Tony Adams replied: 'I'm not going to say I'm a better player than Sammer, but I'm a better defender. He'll never be as good a defender as me. I think our defenders are the best in the world. People talk about this system or that system, but players make systems and ours can play in a lot of different ways.'

Sol Campbell had been growing in stature since his England call-up. The Spurs defender revealed his long-term intentions: 'My ambition is to be the best and to win things. I've got two years left on my existing contract at Spurs and we are talking. You can't rush and I want to see what happens. You have to be ambitious. I'm not someone who could do a job just for the money. I wouldn't want to pick up my wages without success. If you get too much money but are not a winner you ask yourself "What's happening here?" Financial security is more important towards the end of your career and you are thinking about the future. But I'm only 22 and I want success. I can't stand still. You keep having to move on to get what you want out of life.'

Graeme Le Saux was concerned that Blackburn Rovers' poor form might jeopardize his England career. 'I'd be devastated if I lost the chance of playing for England because I wasn't achieving the right profile at my club. And the fact that we've been involved in a relegation battle all season hasn't exactly helped the situation.' Le Saux's ambition eventually led him to join Ruud Gullit at Chelsea, his old team.

Paul Ince was determined to revive England's bid for World Cup qualification. 'We simply have to beat Georgia at all costs. With the Italians playing Poland on the same day we simply cannot afford to slip up. We have to hope Italy drop points before we face them in Rome in October. We'll win all right but it won't be as easy as people seem to think. The Georgians will enjoy playing at Wembley more than they do at home where their fans put them under too much pressure. The Italians think it's all over – but they always do. There's a swagger about them since their Wembley win but although it's going to be tough for us I'm still confident we'll qualify.'

They breed them blunt and honest in Yorkshire, so when David Batty smiled at the prospect of hunting down Georgi Kinkladze, the Georgian playmaker knew he was in for a rough ride. You might as well ask the hounds to pity the fox, for Batty takes almost nihilistic pleasure in his work. 'I'd rather win a tackle than score a goal. I've always felt midfield is the most important position on the pitch – win that and more often than not you'll win the game. I've got a poor scoring record, but that's not really bothered me. It's why a lot of players don't like playing in my position. Attacking and goalscoring is the easy part of the game, but I enjoy the other part as much. I've always enjoyed winning the ball. Flair players are always going to get the headlines, because they win games. But I'm quite happy to be in whatever team, doing my job.' Batty added: 'I enjoy playing with Paul Ince, like I do with Robert Lee. There's a lot of trust there. He's an honest lad and he'd probably say the same about me. We're always willing to run for each other, and that counts for a lot in the middle of the park.'

Although there were minor injury worries about Nicky Butt and Les Ferdinand, it was a satisfying contrast with the preparations for the Mexico and Italy games. 'The only time I've had this kind of preparation was before the Georgia game in Tbilisi and that was our best performance,' said Hoddle. 'Even then we were without Alan Shearer. It's the strongest position I've been in   and it's the best one for a coach, that's for sure. In the last two games, I consulted as much with my medical staff as my own coaching staff. This time it's been the other way round.'

On the morning before the game Stuart Pearce was ruled out by a calf injury. Although Hoddle was hopeful, the 35-year-old was forced to accept he would not be involved in what was a must-win game. However, his absence was not absolutely crucial as Le Saux was always first choice and it was still Hoddle's most problem-free build-up to an international so far. 'It's all I could have hoped for really. It's certainly the best get-together we've had in terms of preparation and it's good to be able to get down to some decent work on the training ground with the players I've got in mind for the game. With the other squads I've had we got to this stage, a day before the game, and have still not known the team. For the Italy game I was even getting phonecalls just before I spoke to the press to tell me players were having to pull out.'

Hoddle started the second phase of the qualification build-up knowing that the next two games would fashion England's destiny. 'These games are bigger than Cup Finals as far as I'm concerned. I always thought the group would be tight and the two games with Georgia and Poland would be as crucial as the games with Italy.'

Hoddle was particularly pleased when Gary Neville announced that Alex Ferguson never tried to get him or other United players to deliberately pull out of an international. The older Neville said: 'Alex Ferguson has never stood in the way of me playing for England. People have this myth that we're pulled out of squads because he wants us to rest, but I've been in the England squad 20 times now and only pulled out once, against Mexico last month, because I had stitches in my ankle. The boss has never ever said to me that he's pulling me out of a game. It's been said that he does it for friendlies, but I was in 12 friendlies leading up to Euro 96. When I'm picked for England, we don't even have a conversation about it – when I'm selected, in the squad I just go! He's never said anything about it, other than asking when we're going away. It's no problem whatsoever with us being selected, because he genuinely wants us to play for England. He wants us to play in big games. The experience you pick up playing for England stands you in good stead when you're playing in the big European ties.'

There had been suggestions that Manchester United would want to rest players over the summer but Neville had no thought of asking for time off. 'We're playing Brazil, Italy and France. Of course I want to go. You can't play roulette, can't say I'll miss this tournament or this game, or I'll pull out of that one. It might never happen again. I might never get the chance to play against Brazil again. It's the chance of a lifetime and you can't afford to miss it.'

Georgia's main threat, Georgi Kinkladze, took inspiration from his boyhood hero Diego Maradona. Kinkladze had watched England for the first time on a fuzzy black and white television when Maradona's Argentina beat them in the 'Hand of God' World Cup game in 1986. He was only 11 at the time but will remember forever the dribble and goal which broke English hearts. Kinkladze said: 'Diego is my big hero. I won't use my hand like him but I will try to repeat his masterpiece and take England apart. Even as a kid, I tried to play like him. He inspired me enormously. I played with him for a while at Boca Juniors and for me he's the best in the world. I would love to dribble through the whole of the England defence the way he did. I have never been to Wembley and that would be my dream. I believe we can win and it's a game I want to play well in to show the world about Georgi Kinkladze.'

But Kinkladze had a lot of respect for his opponents. 'We desperately want to beat England but I think that even if we do they are still good enough to go on and win the World Cup. England can be up there with the best in the world – Germany, Italy and Brazil. They have a world-class player in Paul Gascoigne. We're just pleased he's not playing. Alan Shearer, too, is a big, big player. I like Teddy Sheringham, Tony Adams and David Batty who all played well in Georgia. I was so disappointed with our performance at home. They took three easy points off us. But now we have the chance to put the record straight. England are a very good team and it will be difficult for Georgia. I know we will play very well because it's Wembley and the atmosphere will be amazing. It should be a good game.'

Coach David Kipiani refused to write off his team's chances. 'Football is a game in which every team, no matter how small, has a chance. You can never tell beforehand what might happen. We are a small nation but we have some talented young players and we are lifted by the prospect of playing at Wembley, because it is the mother of football. It is every player's dream to play at the stadium.'

Hoddle wanted his England to banish the bad taste left by the Italian job. He said: 'The next two games for sure are ones we have to get a good result from, there's no doubt about that. I felt that determination to put things right in everyone who came together for the Mexico game. If you lose a game and if you're a winner, if you've got pride in yourself, you want to put it right and the quicker the better. There is a positive vein going right through the camp. Everybody wants a place in the side, everybody wants to play and that's how it should be. We're going out to get the right result. If it's a 1–0 win and three points under our belt, then that's what we'll take.'

Hoddle warned that the style of the game would be the reverse of the match in Tbilisi. 'The approach has to be completely different. Tbilisi was an intimidating place, but we played well, quelled the crowd and in the end they enjoyed our play. Now we're at home, we've got a full house behind us and we've got to respond to that.' England had not started well in the World Cup games at Wembley, having to come from behind to beat Poland and never really finding their rhythm against Italy. This was partly because there was now a trend for sides to find it easier to play away from home with the emphasis on counter-attacking. 'That's the way modern-day football has gone,' argued Hoddle. 'Denmark won the European Championship a few years back completely on that basis. There's more and more teams with that style of play. The home game sometimes is tougher, you have plenty of people behind the ball to break down. And if you're away from home and get the early goal it makes your life a lot easier.' Hoddle spent a lot of time with his defenders, trying to convince them of a more flexible style than the flat, zonal ways of the English Premiership. 'It's something we definitely need to get better at. But the work we've put in is bearing fruit. I can't put it right by Wednesday. If we are in the World Cup in France, that's when I need to have everything bedded down.'

Tight security arrangements were in place at Wembley. The Aintree Grand National had been postponed the previous month as a result of a coded bomb warning from the IRA, and other major sporting events were regarded as potential targets for disruption. In the event, there was no trouble off the field, and relatively little on it in terms of sparkle. But the result was all that counted. Turning on the style wasn't the object of the exercise. As Hoddle had explained in the build-up, he would be satisfied with a single-goal victory as the three points were all that mattered.

Shearer's strike as the game ebbed into injury time made the scoreline respectable for England. It also further established Shearer and Sheringham as the undisputed strikeforce. Goals for both against Georgia brought their partnership to thirteen, eight for Shearer and five for Sheringham. A long ball from Le Saux after 42 minutes set up the opener. Shearer controlled the ball on his chest and whipped over a cross which Sheringham, moving swiftly into position, headed past Zoidze. The game wasn't safe until the final seconds when Lee's shot was spilled by Zoidze and the panicking Shediladze played a short back pass to his keeper who picked up the ball, thus giving away an indirect free-kick. As the entire Georgian team lined up on the corner of the six-yard box, Sheringham stood on the ball and rolled it back in one movement for Shearer to crack a shot into the roof of the net, sheer power taking it past the keeper.

Campbell was justifiably nominated man of the match for an eminently praiseworthy performance. His ninth-minute challenge on Arveladze inside his own box was as crucial as the goals. Seaman was a virtual spectator for the entire first half, but had to be alive to an early opening three minutes into the second half. Le Saux was bright and lively surging forward, but was guilty of an elementary slip-up when he mishit a back pass, surrendering possession to Gogrichiani who only had Seaman to beat. But the Arsenal keeper reacted quickly, sprinting off his line and saving with his legs when the Georgian substitute connected first time with his shot.

England responded with one of their more incisive breaks. Although Sheringham slipped as he crossed, Beckham struck a shot that forced a fingertip save. From Beckham's corner, Ince struck a menacing shot that he must have thought was going in, but it hit Adams a foot from the line. Shearer was later just a yard away from connecting with a shot across the face of the goal, while a free-kick from Beckham whistled just wide.

A danger for England was that their sloppy passing would eventually give Georgia a chance for a shock equalizer. That opportunity came in the 77th minute when Tskhadadze cracked a shot from just inside the penalty area that clipped the top of the bar and had coach David Kipiani leaping to his feet.

Two-nil was a flattering scoreline for England after a modest performance, but it was the right result. For many the biggest regret of the night was that it was clear that England still needed the unpredictability of Paul Gascoigne.

But Hoddle was upbeat and positive. Of the striker partnership he said: 'They have a great balance and understanding together. They are opposites in many ways, but it works so well. The first goal we scored was magnificent. If a foreigner had done that, we'd all be purring about it now. It was the sort of goal you see so often on the training ground and you just hope that one day you'll score one like that when it really matters on the pitch. The second goal was a classic case of two quality players on the same wavelength. I'm fortunate that I've got other good combinations I can use, but when we've got those two, Teddy drops off and links us up. They know each other and play for each other and it was great to see the continuity from what they had in the summer. I think that if you pushed them they'd say they do enjoy playing together.'

Hoddle felt Beckham showed increasing signs of coming to terms with the additional demands of the international game. 'I was very pleased with David, especially in the first half. He showed again that he can get crosses in from positions you don't expect, and produce the sort of delivery others only manage from the dead-ball line. If anything, the strikers need to learn how to react a bit more quickly when he gets the ball – maybe our movement was a bit slow. You know that David can cross the ball, can play wide and can go inside. We told him to start out on the right and then pop inside and use the space every now and then. He did that, and did it very well. While he was fresh and the energy was there, he played extremely well.'

A draw in Poland would now probably be enough for England to claim second place behind Italy, but Hoddle was aiming higher. 'We're English, and that means we don't know how to play for a draw. I'm not sure it is a two-horse race, but we're planning to go there and win. It's going to be very tough for Poland after their disappointing result in Italy. I think Italy will have a difficult game in Georgia. They're a talented side and I'm pleased they only had one real shot on target. There's still a lot of football to be played. The important thing is that we've won the two games since the Wembley match against Italy. Winning games breeds confidence.'

He admitted his players were not at their best after being forced to scrap every inch of the way by Georgian spoiling tactics of fearsome fouls and sly overreaction. The French referee booked six players, including Le Saux and Lee. 'It was a physical match and the referee could have booked even more,' Hoddle admitted. 'But we've won a crucial game and I have a great sense of achievement about that. We had to get the three points. We've done that although we should have won by more. I was very pleased with our first-half performance, but we were very disappointing for the 20 minutes after the break. Paul Ince suffered a back injury and we didn't get forward as much as we should have done.'

Teetotaller Campbell left Wembley with a magnum of champagne. The Spurs defender kept the bubbly as a permanent reminder of his man-of-the-match performance in a vital England shut-out. 'I don't drink but I'll certainly be keeping the bottle as a trophy,' said Campbell. 'You don't know when you're going to get another man-of-the-match award.' Hoddle warned: 'I wouldn't like to be marked by Sol, but he's still got to learn to concentrate in the final 20 minutes of the game. He's put in a solid performance and showed he has benefited from the time we've spent with him going through the video of his performance in the Italy game. Now he has to keep it going for the full 90 minutes.' Campbell admitted as much. 'He's right. It's down to tiredness. I've got to be on my toes the whole time at this level. I can't afford to relax for a second. I know I've got to listen and learn. If I don't do that, I'll get nowhere. But I'm happy with my performance. That was the best I've played for England so far. I was blamed for certain things in my previous game against Italy even though I didn't think I did too much wrong that night. But this was a much more solid performance all round and it was encouraging to play my part. You have to give it to them. They kept the ball well in midfield and they were a good side. But we defended really well and we got the win that was needed. We had to concentrate hard when the score was still 1–0 because anything could have happened. We had to get the win because the draw was no good to us, so everybody had to work hard. It was great to get the second goal. Now we have to keep on winning and if we do that it will be a really tight finish at the end of the group. I think it will go down to the last game. We can't slip up.'

He was feeling comfortable, at last, in an England shirt. 'You can't say you're more at home after only three games, and you learn different things from every one. I think that's something you get with games. That's when you're more comfortable with the people around you. It's hard to say much about it after three matches. You'd be better off asking me after 20 games when I've been all over the world and played against different teams.'

Hoddle was again impressed by Robert Lee's performance in yet another unfamiliar role, as a probing inside-forward. The 31-year-old was becoming England's Mr Versatile. 'It was another position but I'll play anywhere really,' said Lee. 'As long as I'm in the team, I'm happy. But I've played in a few now. I've held the midfield, played as the forward man in midfield, on the left and the right, and now inside-left. It worked quite well, especially with Teddy in the side, because with him dropping off it allowed me to get into the box, which is what I like doing.' Lee's interplay with Le Saux was a feature. 'It worked well. Mind you, there were some times when I was too tired. It meant he had to go up and I just filled in for him.'

David Batty showed there was more to his game than the 'destroyer' role. 'To be honest I was glad to see Kinkladze go off because he was starting to play a bit. My job is about breaking things down but sometimes you find yourself in forward positions and I suppose I was that little bit of a link man. I know people give me this 'destroyer' tag but it's never bothered me what people think. I've got 22 caps for England now so I must have a little bit more about me than being merely a tackler. I do get more enjoyment from tackling and playing nice little balls than getting forward and into scoring positions. That doesn't bother me at all. Maybe it should. I could maybe become a better player. But that's me and I think every player has got something missing from their game.'

Batty analysed England's position. 'Without us winning, it would almost have been all over. It's so important that we win our next two matches so it goes down to the wire against Italy. It would be nice for Italy to have a little hiccup along the way but realistically it's not going to happen. From our point of view, it would be a disaster if our hopes of overtaking them have gone before we play them.'

Georgian coach David Kipiani said: 'This was not the best I have seen Shearer and Sheringham play. But in spite of that they did an excellent job. They scored two goals and that was decisive. They are good players and a good partnership. There were some small struggles going on, but the English players are still gentlemen. But after tonight's results Italy have the better chance to win this group. England need us to beat Italy to increase their opportunity.'

The sight of Hoddle darting past the advertising boards to the touchline to scream at his players to pull themselves together in the second half told the true story of his feelings about England's performance. 'The disappointment for me was the 20 minutes after half-time. We didn't go and assert ourselves as much as we should have done. We lost the reins of the game, if I am honest. I was desperate to get the message on that we needed to pass and keep the ball. In the end there were spells when we kept it and that got us back into the rhythm. I've been a player myself, I know you can switch off from certain things, your concentration can go. Those players have got to make decisions for themselves on the ball. You can't do it for them, all you can do as coach is remind them.' Hoddle put the poor spell down to an injury to Ince which he tried to run off until he took a second knock in the same spot and had to retire. 'We slowly got ourselves back in it and kept the ball very well at times. English fans have got to understand that at 1–0, you've got to open people up and be patient. You can never dictate a game for 90 minutes and they weren't getting round the back of us creating chances, you didn't smell a goal coming. At the end of the day we've got the three points and they've had one shot on goal. We had enough efforts on goal. The difference would have been if one of them had gone in earlier, then you see a totally different match. I was pleased with the patience we showed and the finishing when it came.'

Hoddle still wanted to build a team round a playmaker: 'Of course you want a player who can do things, though few players have that talent. We'd all love it to be the beautiful game. But the way the modern game is going even Brazil have had to change their philosophy. The passers are coming from a different area now – just look what Sammer does for Germany. The game is getting so quick, so tight in midfield that it's very difficult to find that sort of player in there. The Germans haven't really got one but they've gone and won the [European] Championship.

If you do have that player, he becomes the jewel in your crown. They weren't available this time, but we've certainly got them. Merson, Le Tissier, Gascoigne, Anderton – they've all been injured or coming back from injury. We have got creative players in this country. Young David Beckham is one who will get better and better as the games come flowing in. We definitely have the players, what we don't get is the continuity of working together.'

Beckham said: 'I've only played five games in the team and you can't put someone who's had just five games into the middle, although I'm quietly confident that I could cope with it if it comes. I'm happy to play anywhere for England. As you know I love playing in the middle but I don't mind it on the right. He [Hoddle] said to come in when I get the chance, but also to keep it stretched out – it was a bit of both really and when I felt I wasn't getting that much of the ball early on out wide I decided to come in a bit more.'

Hoddle's public vote of confidence in Beckham helped. 'It means a lot to me for him to say he thinks I could do it. He's somebody I've always admired and for him to say it gives me even more confidence. I've read that he's compared me to himself when he was young. All I can say is that I'd love to be half the player he was.'

Asked if he was feeling tired, Beckham responded: 'Not at all. All I want to do is play football, simple as that. I've always wanted to do that and it's a dream for me to be with the England team and then to go back to United. There's nothing I'd rather do than play.'

England (1) 2 Georgia (0) 0
Seaman, G Neville, Campbell, Batty, Adams, Le Saux, Beckham, Ince (capt), Shearer, Sheringham, Lee

	P	W	D	L	F	A	Pts
Italy	6	5	1	0	11	1	16
England	5	4	0	1	9	2	12
Poland	4	1	1	2	3	6	4
Georgia	3	0	0	3	0	5	0
Moldova	4	0	0	4	2	11	0

CHAPTER SEVENTEEN

An Historic Date with South Africa

England v South Africa, Old Trafford, 24 May 1997

Glenn Hoddle announced the following 27-man squad for the forthcoming matches against South Africa, Poland, Italy, France and Brazil: Seaman (Arsenal), Flowers (Blackburn), Martyn (Leeds), Adams (Arsenal), Keown (Arsenal), Pallister (Man Utd), Pearce (Nottm Forest), Southgate (Aston Villa), G Neville (Man Utd), Campbell (Spurs), Le Saux (Blackburn), P Neville (Man Utd), Beckham (Man Utd), Ince (Inter Milan), Batty (Newcastle), Lee (Newcastle), McManaman (Liverpool), Redknapp (Liverpool), Butt (Man Utd), Gascoigne (Rangers), Scholes (Man Utd), Merson (Arsenal), Shearer (Newcastle), Ferdinand (Newcastle), Sheringham (Spurs), Fowler (Liverpool), I Wright (Arsenal).

Paul Gascoigne was returning to the England fold. The less than impressive display in beating Georgia had, to an extent, forced Hoddle's hand in the search for midfield creativity. Hoddle wanted Gazza to recreate the bubbling enthusiasm for the game he had shown in his heyday. He wanted the old loveable buffoon on the pitch, passionate about his football, not the obnoxious idiot off it. Hoddle revealed part of a 'private' conversation he had had with the wayward genius. 'I have spoken to the boy and the main thing I said to him, which I think he understood quite easily, is that he's got to get back to loving the game of football again. There's a lot of things on the outside of his life that have clouded that. The injuries he's had and lots of different things in the last couple of years mean he has not been able to prolong his ability. Back in his heyday, when he was really at his best, he was in love with football. You can understand the reasons why perhaps that's gone away. It has to come back. Then it becomes a labour of love again rather than an endured situation.'

Hoddle continued: 'He agreed with most of the things I said to him. There's still some talking to do with Paul and we will do that when he turns up to train with us. It has to be prolonged. It can't be a little honeymoon period, but something over the next few years. This is a very critical period for him. I think he realizes that. He just wants to get back playing for England again, he wants to put his game back together again. I'm reluctant to say it's his last chance, but this period with the squad has just come at the right time. A fit Gazza is very important to me. But he needs to focus on certain things. There will be times when he trips up, falls back down the ladder. But he has got to learn.'

Gazza had been working hard on his fitness and the transformation from fat boy to lean machine delighted Hoddle; he just hoped his sleek figure would be matched by a mental sharpness for the World Cup challenge in Poland. 'His attitude is very good at the moment,' said Hoddle. 'He's obviously given himself the best opportunity by getting himself back fit to stamp his authority on games when he plays. He hasn't exactly lost weight but through a lot of gym work he's now turned it into muscle which is the best thing to do.'

Arsene Wenger believed England were lost without Gazza's inspiration. 'England need Gascoigne desperately right now because when he is fit he can create something special,' said the Arsenal boss. 'I would tell Glenn today to keep him in the squad.'

Gazza's return went down well with the rest of the squad. Even Robert Lee, who was most likely to make way for him was pleased. The Newcastle man said: 'He should always be in the side. There's no argument about his ability. He's different, he's a one-off. If he's on form, fit, in the right frame of mind mentally, he's unstoppable. And he works harder than people give him credit for. He's been unlucky with injuries. But if he's fit then I think he should be playing ... If Glenn Hoddle thinks Paul Gascoigne is a better option in some games than me, then you've got to accept that. Because on his day, Gazza is the best player England have got.'

Gazza's Geordie pal Chris Waddle was vehemently in favour of his England recall. 'The anti-Gazza brigade have had a field day lately, accusing him of being a drunken lout as well as being over the hill. I'm happy to stand as his defence counsel – and I'm confident of a not guilty verdict on both counts. If any heads need examining, they belong to the people who believe Gazza is past his best at international level. Nothing could be further from the truth. He's in his prime and remains the only England player who can turn a match with a single flash of brilliance. I say that with due regard to Alan Shearer and David Beckham. Shearer will always score goals against the best defences, and Beckham is bound to be a major influence for years to come. But Gazza stands alone as the one England player capable of answering the call when a high-stakes stalemate cries out for something different. Every nation with ambitions of being the best needs someone like that. Most have got one. Italy lean on Gianfranco Zola, Brazil draw inspiration from Juninho, and Germany rely on Jurgen Klinsmann's ability to make something out of nothing. England have Gazza – and I wouldn't swap him for any of the matchwinners already mentioned. His 30th birthday is almost upon him, and it's true that he's spent far too much of the past season hobbling around with his leg in plaster. But if he can stay injury-free – and the signs are good after the voluntary overtime that produced a sleek new look this week – he can play a major part in England's next two major Finals. I can definitely see him being player of the tournament in France next summer, and my money's on him still being our chief playmaker in the European Championship two years later. No wonder the other England players love him. He's a massive influence on them with the sheer force of his personality and dedication on the training pitch. Injuries are the bane of his life and have taken a huge chunk out of his latest season in Glasgow. But how anyone can suggest that's a reason for writing him out of England's future is beyond me...I've known Gazza since he was 14, and I won't try and pretend he's an angel. But, equally, I won't accept for a second that he's the villain people make him out to be. He's a larger-than-life extrovert who loves a laugh. He's also a hyperactive bundle of energy who can't sit still for a minute. Sometimes he oversteps the mark, especially when the frustration of being sidelined through injury starts eating away at him and he suddenly finds a cameraman shadowing his every step. But he's not malicious. Far from it. I can say from personal experience that the real Gazza has a heart of gold. He'd give you the shirt off his back – has done, in fact. I was with him on a night out when a couple of lads said how much they liked his tracksuit top. By the end of the night, it was theirs.'

Gazza's return was clouded once again by reports of misbehaviour, and allegations of a drinking binge after playing in a testimonial at Torquay. While the player himself was not talking, Hoddle completely refuted the latest allegations. 'Paul came to me and brought it up because he wanted to speak about it. Some friends of his went out and I can tell you he is a bit annoyed at what's been reported to have happened. As I said, the stories are totally untrue. Fifty per cent of the things written about Paul are just nonsense.'

The squad for the five summer games contained few shocks; the only mild surprise came with the selection of Manchester United's Paul Scholes. The 22-year-old from Salford had been in and out of the United side, making just 19 starts in the season. The versatile Scholes, equally at home up front or in midfield, got the nod ahead of Platt. Hoddle was full of encouragement: 'Paul is one of those players we have been looking at for some time and is in very good form. He's got a great scoring record considering the number of games he's played and he's certainly one for the future. I went to see David [Platt] against Newcastle last week and it didn't work out for him. He's one who was very much in our minds, but in the end Scholes is in very good form and has a very good goalscoring record. But David's got next season. The door is still open for him. If he gets himself back to his very best and is knocking the ball in the back of the net like he did a few years ago, then these doors are still open for David Platt, like they are for Nick Barmby, Darren Anderton and others. But the players in the squad now and involved in these five games have a hell of a chance of staking a long-term claim for the World Cup.'

Injuries to Anderton, Pallister and Walker meant that Andy Cole and John Scales were drafted into the squad. The 21-year-old Norwich striker Darren Eadie was also called up to the senior squad for the first time when injury forced Paul Merson out of the summer equation. For both Cole and Scales, the international call represented a huge boost after two years in the England wilderness. Cole's only previous cap had come was as a substitute in the drab goalless draw with Uruguay at Wembley in March 1995, with Venables making it clear that he did not see him in his future plans. The 30-year-old Scales had made his three previous England appearances in the 1995 Umbro Cup tournament against Japan, Sweden and Brazil, but was subsequently discarded by Venables.

Cole said: 'I had never given up hope on England. The past couple of years have been difficult for me, but you can't give up if you know what you are capable of doing. Everyone knows why they were difficult; the injuries and loss of form. I've been written off so many times that believing in yourself is the only way to get round it. It's going to hurt you if you're proud of yourself, which I am. You can only answer that in the way I did at the end of the season.' Cole admitted: 'I am surprised to be back so soon. The manager has given me a big shot and I'm more than delighted to be here. You lads are all shocked, but no-one's more shocked than me. But I'm sure it proves a few people wrong.'

Hoddle and Ferguson were both impressed with the way he had changed from a mere goal machine to a more subtle player, making chances as well as taking them. 'He's had a tough time but he finished the season very sharp,' said Hoddle. 'I've spoken to Alex and he feels, as I do, that he's a far better all-round player now. He's matured, he's come through a lot of criticism and he's learned a lot from it within himself.'

Steve McManaman and Robbie Fowler were early withdrawls from the squad. Hoddle struggled to contain his fury as he was forced to plan his summer campaign without the Liverpool pair. The Anfield club had told Hoddle that McManaman might need a knee operation and that Fowler must have surgery on his nose. Hoddle accepted that McManaman needed rest for his long-standing knee problem, but was flabbergasted that Fowler would miss out for something as trivial as a nasal operation. Hoddle believed if it was that important he should have had it on 25 April, when he began a domestic suspension, so that he would be available for England. Since Liverpool had not rushed him under the knife, he could not understand why the operation could not wait another fortnight. 'They haven't given me a satisfactory answer,' said Hoddle, fully aware of Evans' well-documented hostility to a crammed international schedule. 'I am disappointed and frustrated, indeed it's the most disappointed I've been as England coach. I picked the squad at 1 pm last Friday week and then at 3 pm received the fax from Liverpool saying they were unavailable. Since then we have been involved in communication with Liverpool to see if we could get them released at least for the Poland game. You can bet I have had some conversations with Roy Evans in the last 48 hours…What's really disappointing is that I didn't know about the situation until after I'd announced the squad. All we've had is a fax from Liverpool explaining the situation although we have now seen the medical reports about them. The main concern from the players' point of view is that it could stop them playing in the World Cup in 12 months. As one door shuts, another door opens for players coming in. They know that. And that's the sad thing for the players ... Andy Cole now has an opportunity that Robbie Fowler could have had.'

Hoddle added: 'I have spoken to both players. It's very difficult for them. They're caught in the middle, between two stools, and they haven't come out and said they want to go with England, they've had to leave it to their club. I respect that. But in the past, certainly as a player myself, there were times when I knew I could have gone in and had an operation but I didn't, I played on because I wanted to play for England. The club have let me down in the sense that after setting my stall out for this trip, two hours afterwards was the first time Liverpool let me know about the situation.' The fax which Hoddle received when he got back to Lancaster Gate was 'very disappointing. I've got a few talents, but one of them isn't mind reading. We should have been told about it earlier and had a chance to discuss it with them. I wouldn't have put them both in the squad.'

It was a double blow for Fowler, who would have played a big role in the French tournament where Hoddle planned for England to practise a counter-attacking style. 'We have the players a little longer than we normally have and that's where Robbie for one would have been very interesting for us to take right the way through.'

Shearer delivered a patriotic approach to playing for England in the wake of Fowler's withdrawl. Would he turn up if Dalglish, his manager, told him not to? 'I'd be very surprised if Kenny said that, after all, how many caps did he get? ... I don't think he would prevent me from playing for my country.'

Nicky Butt felt that Champions' League experience had helped complete his footballing graduation. For the young midfielder, it was just the sort of experience he needed to prove to himself that he could play at the highest level. 'The games we've had this season have taught me more than any other matches I've played,' he said. 'When you're playing against continental players you can't dive in. That's what they want you to do and when you do they'll just flick it past you. Learning to stay on my feet and time my tackles better is a big part of my game now. When you're playing in the European competitions you're up against exceptional players and you want to copy them and try and do the things they're doing yourself. I'm not going to change my game too much and you've got to believe in your own ability, but I've become a better player over the past 12 months. I've matured, taken on more responsibilities and I feel that I can give a lot more to the team now.'

The South African coach, Clive Barker, planned to unleash the 'South African Gazza' on England, 'Doctor' Khumolo. He was the 29-year-old midfield leader who Barker believed could have been ranked alongside Maradona. But in the true tradition of wayward stars, the Doc never found the application to match his abundant skills. Barker said: 'He's the same as your Gazza. He's infectious and a pain in the backside for a coach.' Khumolo shot to fame in South Africa as a young star with leading side Kaiser Chiefs, before moving to Argentina and then

America. 'We know all about the English players. I admire them all, but Gascoigne is special,' said Khumolo. 'He has the skill to take people on and thrill the crowd. Too many footballers are safe and boring. African players all love to be skilful and entertain. I want to do that against Gazza at Old Trafford. That would be a dream. An even bigger dream would be to defeat England for the millions of black South Africans who will be watching the game live back home. We can beat England. Soccer is unpredictable. You get surprises all the time. We have had a good time as a team. We are progressing quickly and we know that we can win.'

Former Manchester United keeper Gary Bailey, capped twice for England and a member of the 1986 World Cup squad, was coming over to cover the game for South African television. He put forward his opinions on England and South Africa: 'I'll bet anyone now that an African country finishes ahead of England at the World Cup in France. Nigeria, for example, are far better than England now. The reality is England do not have enough world-class players to succeed at the highest level. Alan Shearer and Paul Gascoigne, if he proves he can still do it, are the only two who belong in that category. And the irony for Glenn is that he was better at his peak than Gazza is now. He was equally good with both feet.'

Bailey continued: 'Every time a good player comes along, he is made out to be the saviour of English football. That shows just how serious the situation is. Take David Beckham, for example. Too much pressure is being placed on him to assume a leading role. David is nowhere near world class yet. He crosses well and might get you a goal from 30 yards, sure. But he's not going to beat players one on one. He is still learning his trade. In the really top football countries, players like Beckham do that alongside the superstars. They are not expected to be superstars themselves. The same goes for Steve McManaman, who is a long way from being a world-beater yet. There is no spark in England's midfield when Gazza is not playing. Some countries would have thrown him out by now because of his behaviour off the field. That's because they would have other players to step in, but England have to hold their hands up and say "Okay, what Gazza does is unacceptable but let's try and work with him." That's an admission they have no-one else anywhere near the same class in his position. There is simply not enough creative ability in England's midfield. And, though South Africa may well be overawed by Old Trafford, England could learn from some of their individual technique. Italy are certainties for the top qualifying spot in Group 2, and why shouldn't they be? All their defenders are comfortable on the ball and are never beaten for pace. Italy are far better than England. What English players have is guts and tenacity. These are admirable qualities, but you need a lot more. You paint English players to be better than they are. The reality is they are not as good as people think. They have no chance of winning the World Cup on current form and will be rank outsiders if they get to France.'

Hoddle didn't rise to Bailey's bait. He was prepared to 'save' a number of vital players. 'It's an option for Alan [Shearer] and a lot of other players. It's a balancing act, I have to do what I think is right. To throw everyone in would be a wrong thing because the most important game is in Poland and that's only a week away. Paul Gascoigne will play as he needs the game, otherwise I have an open mind.' Shearer has always been booed at Old Trafford as a consequence of turning down a move to United but Hoddle insisted: 'That wouldn't come into my mind. If I don't play him it won't be for that reason.'

Hoddle dropped a huge hint that most of the United players would figure in the game at some stage, if not from the start. 'There are six United players in the frame and a contingent of them will be playing for sure. We have brought this game up to the north, to the best stadium outside of Wembley but we want an England support, we don't the fans just coming because of the United players, we want them getting behind the country.'

Significantly, Hoddle was growing into the job. He said: 'I'm thoroughly enjoying it, but I don't enjoy losing and we have lost one game. But there are many challenges and hurdles to overcome and I feel I am achieving that even though these are early days in my reign. I have fallen into the situation and I've had to learn very quickly. It is not a job for which club management gives you an apprenticeship. When you're at a club you may be able to heavily discipline players if you want. Here I have to go with the flow but the spirit among the boys is exceptional. There are not many big egos flowing around and that gets you team spirit. Everyone is on an even keel, there's no one thinking they're bigger than anyone else. That extra spirit is like taking 12 players onto the pitch. When you're in each other's pocket over a period of time like this it's important that it's running through the camp. We have a good bunch of boys, pretty level-headed lads.' Could he really be talking about Gazza as well?

Despite the constant sniping, Hoddle looked relaxed. 'I'm very content about what's happening to the players in the squad. I'm doing the job in the best way I can and it's up to others to judge me. It depends who's assessing me. I will assess myself and people in the game, notably those who employ me, will assess me. The bottom line is to qualify for World Cups and European Championships and then doing well when we get there.'

Gascoigne was stretchered off in injury time after a performance that was enough to convince Hoddle he was ready for the bigger test of Poland. There were ample bright moments: a couple of glittering touches, a shimmy here, a slide-rule pass there and a wickedly bent free-kick that might have ended up in the top corner. But interspersed were long periods of inactivity. Towards the end of the game he was dispossessed easily in a situation where once he would have simply shrugged his opponent aside with his upper body strength.

South African substitute Linda Buthelezi was guilty of the foul on Gazza. The concern of Gazza's team-mates was clear; Ian Wright gave Buthelezi a fearsome tongue-lashing. 'I wasn't happy with the fellow and I told him so,' said Wright, whose sixth England goal, his first on home soil, won the game after ex-Leeds man Phil Masinga had cancelled out Lee's opener. Buthelezi's claim that he could have caused even more damage only added to Wright's anger. 'That's not nice,' said the Arsenal man. 'What's he saying? That he wanted to hurt him more?'

Opinion was divided on Gascoigne's display. Hoddle said: 'I don't know what other people's opinions might be, but it's only one opinion that counts and that's mine. And my opinion is that Gazza's performance was spot-on.' Hoddle revealed that Gascoigne had performed to precise instructions. 'I said to him that I didn't need a spectacular performance. I didn't want him to go out and think he had to go past three people and score two to get into the Poland game. He did some very good productive things on the pitch, he hit a couple of forty-yarders that were spot-on, he did some very positive things, created in the last third and was sensible. He needed to put in a good performance – and he did.'

Barker suggested that Gazza should abandon his diet and start piling on the pounds. 'A lot of people who pull weight like Gazza has pulled find that they were more comfortable in their original shape. I saw him play a few times before he shed it and I think he's a bit like a boxer pulling weight before a fight. I think he was a better player when he had a bit more weight, he had more strength.' But the Springbok coach believed Hoddle was right to put his faith in him. 'I'm a Gazza fan because he can play, he's a quality player. He's the player I would love to build around if I was in charge of England. He adds a new dimension to their game.'

Hoddle winced at the suggestion that it saved him a selection problem for the Poland game when Gascoigne was carried off. 'Not at all,' he said dismissively. 'That opinion couldn't be further from the truth. If that was the case, I wouldn't have played him in the first place.' Hoddle accepted that expectancy levels were too high. 'Sometimes he turns on a bit of magic and everyone goes over the top, just like against Scotland. Then it was one bit of magic and everyone was doing somersaults over him. I thought against Switzerland he was far better overall, but he got hammered in the press.'

Robert Lee got forward to tremendous effect from the first minute, attacking space and causing problems. His goal, his first for England since his debut against Romania three years earlier, was reward for his foraging and his determination in riding Lucas Radebe's tackle before crashing the ball home after Neville had chested down Sheringham's pass. Lee had now completed a welcome hat-trick of top drawer performances but he was not prepared to take anything for granted. 'I was pleased to get the goal of course, although Phil Neville deserved some credit for getting the ball to me. All you can do is play as well as you can and make it difficult for the manager to leave you out. I'll just go out and play to the best of my ability and hope it's enough. The last three games I've played different roles in all of them and it's good for me to show I can do that. The more you play for England, and the better you do, then your confidence grows and you start to feel a part of the team.'

Ian Wright, given his first start since that Romania game, was a constant handful, and an excellent foil for Sheringham and then Scholes when he came on for his debut. Wright did not care that he had controlled the ball with his arm before scoring. 'It meant a lot to me. I thought I worked hard enough to get something. In the end I got the bit of luck I haven't had in the past. I wouldn't say it didn't touch my arm, and I'm not going to do a Robbie Fowler! I'm going to take the goal because sometimes you make your own luck.'

Wright added: 'I want the manager to know if he's resting Alan or Teddy, or is without them, I can come in and do a good job for England. I've no illusions about things. I know Teddy and Alan are the top men. I want to be in the rearguard behind them, ready to go for it. I scored in Poland last time and if I could get any kind of role out there next week it would be fantastic. If the outcome is also the same that would be fairytale stuff. I'm just looking forward to being part of it.'

Lee gave Wright his support. 'Ian's a great character. A goal for him is tremendous for England. He's shown he can score countless goals at Premiership level and I think he can still do it for England as well. I think true goalscorers always want to score, even if they're not playing well. The fact that we've got somebody like Ian as a standby for Alan or Teddy shows how much talent we've got.'

Sheringham agreed. 'I'm very pleased for Ian. It's difficult at international level to get goals and there's always a lot of criticism. You keep on getting people saying he can't score for England, or I can't, or others and it's great individually for him to get a goal. It's good for us ahead of Poland as well. He got that goal over there last time and it's no bad thing for them to know he's scoring again.'

Wright turned his attention to his return to Katowice, the city where he came off the bench to salvage a draw for Graham Taylor's side in 1993. 'If I get in the squad for Poland then that's great, if I get in the team then that's fantastic, if I get on the bench then that's good. But if not, and I am sat in the stand then I am a fan. Whatever happens I can't lose. The way the season started for me, with Bruce Rioch and Stewart Houston giving me the cold shoulder, I didn't think that I'd end up with 30 goals and get in the England squad. I was worried that because Glenn Hoddle picked so many players initially, I would end up not going to France. It was my aim to train well and just get involved in that.'

Nigel Martyn fully deserved his chance in the keeper's jersey after a four-year wait since his last England cap. Sadly for him though, he had just one real save to make all game and failed to make it. Khumolo's ball slipped away and John Moshoeu was able to produce an acrobatic overhead kick from which Masinga nodded home.

Jamie Redknapp was unlucky enough to break his ankle early in the second half, ruling him out of the entire summer programme and shelving Hoddle's plans to try him at sweeper. Redknapp would probably have been on the bench in Poland but would have been the centre of attention in the French tournament as a sweeper. Hoddle said: 'He was quite surprised when I told him about it but he went away to think about it. The passing side would not have been a problem but it would have been a risk to throw him in as a defender. The shame is now we won't be able to do it and I was going to do it in France. If the old over-age rule was still in existence I would have played him five or six times for the Under-21s in that position. You can't just throw him in there, that's why I planned to do it in one of the games in France. He's someone who, given a little extra time on the ball at this level in that part of the pitch, could possibly do it. Jamie can get his head up and see the sixty-yard pass and the twenty-yarder. The difference is that sort of player has to see the sixty-yarder first. There's no-one playing in that position in the League. I knew there would be a problem defensively and it would be a risk adapting, but if I had a pre-season with him there's not a shadow of doubt that he could adjust. It's the role that Sammer does for his club and country...I wouldn't say we will now throw it out of the window but it's frustrating that Jamie is injured.'

But the move in world football was away from the German system. The Italian giants and clubs like Liverpool and Arsenal were switching from 3–5–2 back to 4–4–2, the style Manchester United always play. But Hoddle insisted: 'The Germans have won European Championships, reached Finals and won the UEFA Cup this season by playing that system. I think it gives other teams that want to play 4–4–2 problems, and I'm quite happy to play it – you outnumber them in midfield and you get width as well.'

The England coach reflected on Paul Scholes' debut. 'He's got a bright future. He showed a lot of maturity, and it was a lovely little flick for the Wright goal.' England had long been accused of blooding players too late in their careers, of ignoring youthful potential, but not Hoddle. 'I go with players who have got talent, whether they are Ian Wright's age or Scholes'. These games are all part of building a future, which is important. And there's a bright future for these United players. They have all got talent. These boys will have great experience at a very early age.'

Martin Keown was pleased with his performance. 'I was playing in the same position as I have for Arsenal all season, and I thoroughly enjoyed it. I'm very confident playing in that role. It's also the case that the longer you're around the England boys the more confident you feel in your surroundings and the more you express yourself. I'd be delighted if he [Hoddle] came to me and said he wanted me to do it. I've had the experience of playing away in competitive games, and I'd be more than happy if the chance came.'

Martyn was hoping that his England future had not slipped through his fingers after his mistake. 'It was a very quiet game for me – quite a difference to what I am normally used to. The ball [for the goal] didn't come on to me as quickly as I expected. I thought I could just scoop it up, but the South African player just stuck out a leg and got to it first. I'm sure the manager is wanting to have a look at everybody. It was my turn this time and Tim Flowers will probably get his turn during the tournament in France. It's about trying different people and giving players as much experience as possible. I'm just keeping my fingers crossed that I'm there as well.'

Clive Barker was not impressed by Hoddle's side. 'They're aggressive, they're strong physically and they know where the goals are. If they had got enough supply up to Sheringham and Wright we would have been in a lot of trouble. But they are too predictable. Even if they had had their full team out they play the same way. I'd like to see a bit more flair, a little more ability to go past people. I don't see that any more. I know the game has changed since the days of Tom Finney and Stanley Matthews, but English players used to be able to glide past opponents. Now they play in front of people too much now. They have the best support in the world, a good league which is exciting and quick, but I don't think English football is all that skilful.'

Mark Fish, the South African defender, felt England were still a few steps short of the top of the world footballing ladder. Fish, picking his words carefully, brought England down to earth a little. 'We've played against bigger teams than England. To me, the likes of Brazil and Germany are bigger than England. They dominate world football in a way England certainly don't. I think they are quite strong but they'll be put in proper perspective this summer when they play Brazil, France and Italy. I watched the game against Italy at Wembley in February and the Italians dominated that game. Brazil are very strong, of course, and the French are very good. It will be interesting to see how well they do against teams like that.' Even so, Fish hoped that England would be in France in 1998. 'It's important for football for England to get to the World Cup. The game originated here and it's important for the tournament.'

England (1) 2 South Africa (1) 1
Martyn, P Neville, Keown, Southgate, Pearce (capt), Le Saux, Redknapp, Lee, Gascoigne, Wright, Sheringham

CHAPTER EIGHTEEN

Up the Pole

Poland v England, Katowice, 31 May 1997

Once the media begin to predict the exit door for a manager, it is usually an early warning sign that the inevitable is on the horizon. The journey to Poland was preceded by one or two comments in the press that Hoddle's position would be threatened if England lost. Defeat would have put England's qualification into serious doubt so the stakes couldn't have been higher. The England coach refuses to read the newspapers before and after England games, but he was aware of the snipers. He reflected: 'The press are always going to start asking questions when a crunch game like Poland comes around. I don't feel any more pressure for this game than I did against Italy, or indeed against Moldova which was my first match in charge. If I was worried about the pressure of managing England I wouldn't have taken the job. You have to be single-minded and almost cocoon yourself away from all the other distractions. The main pressures come from outside. People might think I am putting on a brave face but that is not so. I've got other things in my life, my beliefs, which help me cope.'

Hoddle was only too aware that it would be a tough game. 'Italy found out that they [Poland] are a tough nut to crack over there, and, to be honest, the Poles should have beaten them. They have got to win as well, which is a bonus for us because I think it will be more of an open game than people expect. They are very disciplined in their approach but I don't think they will come at us hell for leather like England would do if we were in the same situation at Wembley.'

Paul Gascoigne had recovered from the kicking he took against South Africa. He was pleased with his performance at Old Trafford although it had failed to convince everybody. He was delighted to have come through a full test for England for the first time since the win in Georgia the previous November. He was a certainty to start, but he opted for a diplomatic approach, of which Shearer would have been proud. 'There are 22 in the squad and I am one of them. If I play in Poland I play, if I don't, then I don't.'

Gazza revealed that he had, surprisingly, been offered the chance to captain England under Terry Venables. Fear of the press raking up every negative in his life had persuaded him to reject the offer. 'All everyone would have said is: "Why is a guy like this being allowed to captain his country?" I had the chance in one game last year but I turned it down. I don't know what I would do if it were offered again. But if I said yes, they would bring up all that happened in the past.' That was the extent of his paranoia at being in soccer's most suffocating goldfish bowl. Gazza continued: 'If I keep getting hammered the way I am, then I'll play as long as I think I'm happy. Then if I think I've had enough, I'll do what's best for me. I can't win. Every game I play now, I get hammered. I thought I'd done all right on Saturday, but I still got a bit of stick for it. Too fat, too thin; not beating five players, should beat five players. It's the same old stories. A lot of footballers do a lot of things outside of football, but he hasn't got a photographer stuck up his arse. He hasn't got 12 photographers hassling his wife or kids. I've got all that.'

Hoddle protected Gazza and encouraged him to a remarkable degree for someone with such a different moral standpoint. 'I'm not under pressure whatsoever from the manager,' said the midfield maestro. 'He just wants me to go out and enjoy my football again, and that's what I want to do.'

Hoddle agonized, for the benefit of the media, and no doubt to keep the Poles guessing, over whether to play Gascoigne from the start or for the last 20 minutes. The players knew Gascoigne was the key to winning on Polish soil for the first time in 31 years. Shearer said: 'If he is playing, I'm sure that will be a bonus for everyone. The only way to tell if he can affect the game is by hoping he plays the kind of game we know Paul Gascoigne can play. Everybody knows what he can achieve, everybody knows what he can do with a football. We know what a fit Paul Gascoigne can do. Let's hope he turns it on if he is selected.'

Shearer elaborated on why, even though he's captain, he doesn't exert any direct influence on players like Gazza. 'Players want to enjoy themselves, have a laugh and a joke – which they do – and not be treated like kids. It would be wrong for me to keep an eye on them, because they're adults and it would be wrong for me go to around finding out what they're up to. Some of us are responsible adults … ' A broad grin cut across Shearer's face as he no doubt thought of Gazza!

Shearer didn't want to miss a single game. He had put up an argument when he was told by Hoddle that he would be rested for the game against South Africa. 'I would have much preferred to have played, and I said that to the manager when he told me that he couldn't have taken a gamble. He told me on the Thursday afternoon, just a couple of hours after I said how much I wanted to play in that game, and I made my feelings clear to him. I was disappointed that I was being rested for the game.'

Tony Adams was out with ankle problems, while there were doubts over Paul Ince who reported back from Italy with a nasty bruise on his knee. An x-ray later revealed no serious damage.

The late addition to the squad, Darren Eadie, was unlucky. His big chance vanished when he strained the tendons in his foot. Like Adams, he was also ruled out of the three-match tournament in France.

With Adams out, Campbell became a key figure. Hoddle saw him as a defensive colossus in the making. 'Sol was caught out in his positioning for the goal against Italy. But he's done very well and has learned very quickly from that. There's no doubt he's grown in stature this season. We've admired a lot of big continental players in the past like Milan's French ace Marcel Desailly – and Sol has that same strength. Whether he can be as good on the ball we'll have to wait and see, but he's much more confident now. In Georgia, where the atmosphere was very intimidating, he was a real plus. The one thing I like about him is that he's not adopted that attitude of "I've made it." In training it's very difficult for players to get past him – and that applies to our best players. That shows to me he's an extremely good defender. He has an air about him that tells people "if you get past me, you've done very well". We've worked on his touch by making him train with the little ball and that takes a lot of mastering. I told him to go away and practise with it and his improvement shows that even at this level players can better their game through practice. He's much more confident on the ball but, first things first, his defending has been excellent.'

Campbell wanted to exorcise the Zola goal. 'I saw Zola peeling off. But he wasn't my man at the time. Casiraghi had made a run behind Gary Neville and I got shifted over. Then the ball dropped behind Stuart and I came across to try and make the tackle, but you learn from those situations.'

Ian Wright never fails to shock. But he surpassed himself when he owned up to regular visits to a therapist for counselling to stop his 'pitch rage'. He explained: 'I am receiving help. I'll probably have it for the rest of my life. I am talking to someone who can sort me out, deal with my anger on the field. I don't want to finish up with people disliking me. Everyone wants to be liked. I have three years left in football and want to finish off without any more controversy. People either love me or hate me. And I am always on the edge of my emotions. But I am fed up with it. Quite honestly, it has started to get me down … It's like being an alcoholic. You cannot accept it yourself and you have to ask yourself why. I don't want people to think I am doing it [the counselling] because I need sympathy. But things have happened to me on and off the pitch. It has made me realize what I am, what I have what I can get, and what I can finish up with. It is very personal.'

Hoddle had twice in his first year in charge been forced to read his version of the riot act to his England stars. The Wembley match with Poland was the first. 'A few strong words is all that is needed for the players to know how I want it done. After the summer they thought they could just put the shirts on. They didn't give Poland the respect they should have done. It could have been the best thing that happened. Since that game they know that they have to do the things I ask them to. If they don't do them, they find themselves out of the team.' There is no set formula to how he delivers his message. 'You can't put in a bottle how you do it, I go with the flow. Sometimes I steam in with a couple of words, sometimes you've got to be cute. There are all ways of motivation. Motivation by throwing teacups around is ridiculous. Just as the best captain is supposed to be the guy who raises his fists and rants and raves. Club management is completely different from this, and I found that out early on in taking the job over. I had a little pop after the Georgia game, but I'm still in control, I don't throw cups around. You have to choose the right moment for the right individual. Some people crumble when they are dug out in front of people. Sometimes you can hit the roof. It has happened after two matches that we actually won. Anger would be the wrong word. Against Georgia, there were a few things I was not happy about in the second half.'

Hoddle was beginning to feel that his message was getting home. 'Slowly this is becoming my England. It felt as though it was Terry's players when I first took over as they had been together for three to four weeks. If it has been stop-start, the transition would have been a lot easier. But that's all yesterday. I have come in and done what I had to do. The satisfaction is working with the cream of the country – when they are all fit. At certain times on the training pitch the standard is higher than I thought it would be. A couple of coaches have come to watch some of our closed sessions. The quality is frightening, but the next step is to reproduce that in a match situation, and it becomes harder and harder because of the levelling off, you can rarely hammer teams these days.'

Gary Neville felt playing for Manchester United was a passport to the England team. 'Rightly or wrongly, you can get into the England team quicker playing for Manchester United than a smaller club. It could happen that we all play for England at one time. We are all 22. Looking that little bit further up the road, we could be in the team together, it will be very close.' Even more remarkable is that four of the United babes came through the same Sunday league side. 'Me, Phil, Nicky Butt and Paul Scholes all played for Boundary Park in Oldham,' said Neville. 'Four of us were in the same Under-16 side and now we are playing for England.' He had no fears of the intimidating tie in Poland. 'We were playing in Cup Finals at 17 and 18 in front of 35,000 people. You don't get that sort of experience at other clubs. We've been brought up that way.' As for England, it had not been such a daunting step. 'I don't think any of the young Manchester United players have gone into the team and looked out of their depth, that comes with the upbringing. We're used to big games, and this one in Poland is as big a game as we're ever going to play. We've played in Turkey against Galatasaray and Fenerbahce. We would want shooting if we come off and say the crowd had affected us.'

Poland's boss Antoni Piechniczek wondered whether Shearer would be as effective without McManaman at his side. The provocative Piechniczek said: 'Poland's task will be made easier by McManaman's absence. Without his service, Shearer is not so good. I would say Shearer loses at least 20 per cent of his capability without the creative threat of McManaman. McManaman is a good sportsman, we saw that at Euro 96.'

Piechniczek promised the Poles would launch an all-out assault. 'For England, either a win or a draw would do nicely. But Poland must win to keep our World Cup chances alive. There is no other choice. We will go for it and we know we can do it The fans will help us. They may only allow 35,000 in the Chorzow stadium these days, but they will make plenty of noise. Traditionally, it is a good venue for us. At Chorzow, anything is possible.'

But Poland were missing their Wembley goalscorer, national hero Marek Citko, with a torn Achilles tendon. Nonetheless, Polish tactical confidence was undiminished. 'It's a blow,' admitted Piechniczek. 'But I have two or three interesting options in mind.' The temperamental Andrezej Juskowiak was one such option. He had refused to play at Wembley but he had now patched things up with Piechniczek, and was Poland's big hope. Skipper Piotr Nowak declared: 'Andrezej was unlucky last year not to play at Wembley. But his presence in this game is crucial for the Polish team. Everyone here knows about the problems he had with the management. There were cross words, but it has all been resolved ... He has the killer instinct a top striker needs. You can always rely on him to finish off what colleagues have started. He has been excellent in the Bundesliga (for Borussia Moenchengladbach), and gets goals against Germany's top defences. The important thing is that all his problems are now in the past.'

Juskowiak said: 'I was devastated to miss the match at Wembley because I was in good form. I'd have had a good chance of scoring against that English defence. I've played four times against English sides and got five goals. Two were for the Under-21 team in a 2–1 win and three were for Borussia in the two [UEFA Cup] matches against Arsenal. I was also in the Polish Under-21 team which won 1–0 at Spurs a few years ago. I think the Polish team did well without me at Wembley but just couldn't finish the job. But we are definitely capable of getting a result in Chorzow. A lot will depend on me in front of goal, but I feel after the injury that I'm getting back to full fitness and I am ready for it.'

Despite Polish optimism, England won the game. Hoddle and his entourage hugged each other in wild delight at making history as the first England team to win a competitive match on Polish soil. Satisfyingly, both of England's goals from the Shearer-Sheringham strike force were conceived on the training ground. Hoddle said: 'We have been working on a lot of functions in training, and one of the exercises is to get the ball in the back of the net within ten seconds of winning it. The seeds have been planted and it was satisfying when it came off.' Even Shearer's penalty miss could not take the gloss off a stirring team performance.

Hoddle issued Gazza instructions to pace himself, but he lasted just 16 minutes before being stretchered off for the second game in a row. Hoddle was visibly concerned: 'This is a worse injury than the last one, this time it's a gash as well as a bruise and it looks worse than the other one. But he bounced back very quickly before, we were surprised how he came back from that calf injury. Now I'm sure this one will settle down by next Wednesday, and by next weekend he might still be around. He's been the victim of two tackles, this one was a 50–50 where the opponent has gone in a little late and caught him high, this was on the borderline compared to that tackle against South Africa. He's been very unlucky. These injuries have not been because he's not been living correctly, it's what I would call armed combat.'

Beckham suffered a slight knee injury but it wouldn't preclude him from taking over in the centre of midfield from Gascoigne in the opening Le Tournoi match against Italy, even though Hoddle still wanted convincing that he was ready for such responsibility.

It might not have been a victory fashioned in Hoddle's image, but it was hard to recall an England team so committed to the cause. Hoddle said: 'It's hard to produce a spectacular 4–0 or 5–0 but, you never know, it might be around the corner. But we are quietly on course, apart from that Italy game, but even then the players felt it was tighter than most people thought. I've had a gut feeling for some time that we would be going to Rome still with a chance of topping the group and now it looks that way.'

He continued: 'I felt Alan Shearer had his best-ever game in an England shirt, he really looked sharp ... Sol Campbell also had a storming match, he's learnt a hell of a lot since the Italy defeat. As a team, we were just so single-minded; there was an inner belief. My message to the players had been positive, and that's how it's been all week.'

The FA hierarchy could be forgiven for their smugness; their decision to appoint the youngest England coach had been vindicated in glorious fashion. As they thought back to the candidates to succeed Venables, they knew they had made the right appointment. Keegan had cracked up at Newcastle, Robson had made a pig's ear of Middlesbrough, Wilkins was sacked by QPR and Francis was living on borrowed time at Spurs.

Hoddle had proved to be a pragmatic boss just as capable of calling up a David Batty as pinning his hopes on Gascoigne or Matt Le Tissier. Quality performances in Le Tournoi against Italy, France and Brazil would only add to the huge surge in confidence that had come in Katowice. No friendly can match a World Cup battle, but beating Italy would be another major lift. Shearer said: 'Italy won the big one at Wembley, but victory on Wednesday will hammer out a message to them. We are only one point behind them now and they still have to go to Georgia. It was always our belief we could finish top of the group and nothing has changed. Our win over Poland means we have a great chance of qualifying as the best runners-up. But that's not enough. We want top spot.'

Poland (0) 0 England (1) 2
Seaman, G. Neville, Campbell, Ince, Southgate, Le Saux, Beckham, Gascoigne, Shearer (capt), Sheringham, Lee

	P	W	D	L	F	A	Pts
Italy	6	5	1	0	11	1	16
England	6	5	0	1	11	2	15
Poland	5	1	1	3	3	8	4
Georgia	3	0	0	3	0	5	0
Moldova	4	0	0	4	2	11	0

CHAPTER NINETEEN

Tournoi Triumph

Le Tournoi de France, 4–10 June 1997

Le Tournoi de France was a dry run for the World Cup Finals the following summer in more ways than one. Glenn Hoddle wanted a limit on the amount of beer his players consumed and insisted that they would be confined to base for the nine days they were away. He said: 'This is not a Fred Karno's trip. I believe I would lose the respect of the players if I allowed them to go nightclubbing and out on their own. Any relaxation time will be controlled and in the team hotel. There will not be situations where the players are out and about. We are here for business reasons, to learn and win matches.' No-one would be allowed to leave the party's HQ without Hoddle's permission. 'There will be lessons learned in the next nine days that are going to be so important to us in 12 months' time if we get to the World Cup. To win the World Cup, you have to make sacrifices. There is not one big-head in the squad off the pitch – somebody like that could cause all sorts of problems. We must be professional and apply ourselves. This tournament can take us further down the line. If we win all three matches, we can set the country alight.'

There was one allowance made to the squad, however. They were given the all-clear to negotiate transfer deals during the tour. That interested Paul Ince, who planned to seek Hoddle's advice as to whether he should stay in Italy or return to England. Robert Lee also wanted to clarify his club future. He was baffled by constant speculation about him leaving Newcastle and wanted to establish if he was still wanted at the club. For Teddy Sheringham, the transfer business was underway even before he reached Luton airport. The then Spurs forward was distracted from his England duties in the morning by a telephone call from his chairman, Alan Sugar. The brief chat ended with Sheringham threatening to hand in a written transfer request.

Hoddle provided the striker with a glowing reference. 'Teddy is the sort of player every club is looking for. There will be a lot of English clubs interested as well as clubs abroad, with him doing so well at international level. He is at an age where he realizes everything is important. Even doing stretching exercises, he is totally focused. He is a true pro. He even wins the table tennis and the golf tournaments. I've always rated Teddy. When I came back from Monaco, I was training with Chelsea and their manager Bobby Campbell told me to look at a player at Newcastle. They were playing Millwall and I came back and told him: "The player I saw was on the other side – Sheringham." He was five or six passes above anybody else – and that was seven years ago.'

Hoddle felt that the Tournoi de France was a chance to experiment. He said: 'I'd like to see us playing with a sweeper next summer and it would be nice if it worked. It might only be needed in one or two games and that was why I wanted to try Jamie [Redknapp], because he can see the sixty-yard passes that somebody like Paul Ince can't see so often. Now Gareth [Southgate] will be encouraged to do it. Against Mexico there were five or six times when he could have played Graeme Le Saux in, but didn't. We've been working on that with him. This tournament is about being further down the line if and when we qualify for the World Cup. There are going to be things thrown at us in the World Cup that we are not prepared for yet and the players need to be educated.'

The England manager was plotting the blueprint for the next 12 months. With Beckham on the inside, Phil Neville was likely to be given a run on the right against Italy. Hoddle said: 'Phil has certainly got the defensive ability. What we need to see is whether he can be as effective in the last third of the field. One thing he has up his sleeve is that he can play either flank, which is an added bonus.'

David Beckham was upset by comments that his social life, especially his time spent dating Posh Spice Victoria Adams, was affecting his game. 'It's very unfair to suggest that,' Beckham retorted. 'I take my football very seriously, and I wouldn't do anything to damage that situation. I certainly don't need a rest.'

Spurs winger Andy Sinton missed out on an England recall after a four-year absence – because no-one could find him as Hoddle sought a last-minute replacement for the injured Nicky Butt. Lee Clark was called up instead. On the same day that Clark quit Newcastle for Sunderland he walked into the England squad. The England coach said: 'Lee has immense possibilities. I was very impressed when I saw him playing in the Under-21s a couple of seasons ago. There have been various reasons why he hasn't played so much for Newcastle but he certainly hasn't become a poor player – the talent is still there and he will flourish over the next few seasons.'

The England squad assembled at the Hotel du Golf International at La Baule to watch the tournament's opener, France against Brazil in Lyon. They were on their feet as Roberto Carlos scored a sensational goal with a bending free-kick. He began his run near the halfway line and his shot bent like a banana round the French wall. Goalkeeper Fabien Barthez watched in disbelief as the ball nestled inside his left-hand post. His 34.6-yard bender, hit with the outside of his left foot, touched a speed of 85.2 mph as it swerved round the French wall and into the net. Hoddle said: 'There were some oohs and aahs in the room when that went in. I don't think I have ever seen a ball bent as much. I doubt we will see a better free-kick.'

Despite all the excitement over the free-kick, Ronaldo and Romario failed to live up to their extravagant reputations and a 1-1 draw was a fair result.

Nonetheless Brazil remained favourites to win the tournament. 'Brazil are the best team in the world,' said Hoddle. 'We all admire them and we all have to work to catch up with them.'

Rather than allow an England victory to gnaw at his squad's morale for four months, Italy's Cesare Maldini was planning to field a full strength team, apart from his injured son, against Hoddle's men. Maldini pointed out that: 'It might be a friendly tournament, but where we come from, if the team doesn't get results, it's always the end of the world.' Hoddle responded: 'If Italy want to put out a full-strength team, that is up to them. To win and get off to a flyer in this tournament would be smashing, but we have got to look at things that are going to help us if we get to the World Cup next year. We have got to take the chains off for this one.'

Paul Ince suspected that the result mattered more to the Italians than the English. 'They would have been choking on their spaghetti [after England's win in Poland]. It's not going to be easy for them now, and they realize that.'

When the game came, Hoddle's team finally destroyed the myth of Italian supremacy over England. Goals from Wright and Scholes would live in the memory as England beat the Italians for the first time in 20 years. England had never before made Italy look quite so vulnerable in defence or so lacking inspiration in midfield. It all seemed too good to be true as Beckham, transformed into England's playmaker, came of age. His first experience of centre stage in England's midfield was an enormous success. Despite the occasion, Beckham played without any semblance of nerves or inhibition. 'I went into this game not the slightest bit nervous and it's been like that all season,' he said. 'Paul Ince helped me and gave me some ideas on how to play against the Italians. When I stood there before the start and looked at their players against us, I felt they were the same as us, no different, and I went out to enjoy myself and, after just 20 minutes of this game, I felt "We've got 'em". We proved to a lot of people we are as capable as the Italians, we played some great football. We surprised a lot of people by the way we played in the first half with one-touch football, we made people sit up and take notice and obviously this is going to give us a lot of confidence.'

At first, Hoddle's experiments had looked in urgent need of refining as Sheringham dropped too deep, occupying Beckham's space and congesting the midfield. But once England had sorted themselves out, and stood firm against a couple of early Italian chances, they produced high quality football. With Shearer on the bench, the England coach gave Wright a chance to prove he could score against world-class defenders. In the 25th minute, he did so. Scholes picked him out with a peach of a long ball, and Wright timed his burst to perfection to leave Ciro Ferrara and captain Alessandro Costacurta looking as flat-footed and square as an old-fashioned England back-line. Wright repaid the compliment to Scholes in the 43rd minute, unselfishly squaring a pass that the young Manchester United wonder thumped past Angelo Peruzzi from ten yards with amazing assurance.

Italy's cause was not helped by the early loss of Chelsea's dynamic midfield player Roberto Di Matteo. After just nine minutes, a clever Di Matteo chip was met with a glancing header by Zola, but the chance went well wide. Then after 12 minutes, Zola's defence-splitting pass went straight into Di Matteo's stride inside the box, and when he cut inside Keown, he must have thought he would score – until he felt the force of a Pearce tackle. Di Matteo hobbled around for five more minutes before he was replaced.

Flowers punched out a vicious long-range effort from Dino Baggio just before the interval and as the game progressed he dealt competently with a number of problems, including another long-range shot from Pierluigi Casiraghi. Blackburn's No 1 also made a crucial tackle on the Italian centre-forward.

A measure of the ease of this England victory was that Hoddle was able to give Cole a run-out, the substitute nearly scoring with his very first touch. He latched on to a bad back-pass, and from an acute angle forced a good save from Peruzzi. With 12 minutes to go Hoddle threw on Gazza, who was desperate to get back into England action after injury had forced him to miss the glory in Katowice. He made his mark, but only in the referee's book, for a foolish, late challenge on Diego Fuser.

L'Equipe described England as 'chic' after beating Italy. Maldini was now the man seeking retribution after suffering his first defeat as Italian coach. He told Hoddle and England: 'We'll see you in Rome.' For a pleasant change it was Hoddle's turn to laud it over the mighty Italians. He said: 'I was very impressed with the three Manchester United lads, and Paul Scholes has proved a point. He looked at home as soon as he joined the international squad, and this competition has given us a chance to play him and see what he can do and he has not disappointed. It was our opportunity to use him in a system that suited him and the greatest quality he has got is that he's a true goalscorer. It was a hell of a full debut performance. We changed the system, playing Wright up front on his own with Scholes and Sheringham in midfield. It suits Scholes because it gives him the freedom to do what he's good at – scoring goals.'

Scholes commented: 'It is just marvellous to play with such good players. All I know about the goal is that Ian Wright squared the ball to me and I just hit it. It was the greatest feeling of my life and must be the best goal I have ever scored. The manager told me in the morning that I was playing and for me to go out and enjoy myself. That's what I did. I'm fortunate that I do not suffer with nerves. I haven't had much opportunity yet with United and it's fantastic for me to be in the England team at this stage of my career.' Scholes refused to swap his shirt with any Italian. He had done the same against South Africa. He explained: 'Keeping my white shirt means more to me than anything. I'll never give any of them away.'

Hoddle had plenty to please him but he also had a great deal to sort out. He warned Beckham that not even his brilliant display in centre stage of England's midfield would have saved him from being hauled off in disgrace for back-chatting to the referee. Beckham was booked in the first half and Hoddle was worried that his running feud with the referee would lead to a second yellow and dismissal. Hoddle said: 'Young David needs to understand that when he's been booked, whether he agrees with it or not, he can't afford to stand there arguing. At half-time I said to him "the way you're playing don't make me take you off, because in a minute you're going to be sent off". The reaction to his booking could have got him a second yellow card, but he learned and didn't continue it in the second half.'

Beckham wasn't alone. Scholes, Gascoigne and stand-in captain Ince were also booked. Hoddle added: 'The three boys got booked unnecessarily. It was unprofessional, but this was the only blemish in a performance against Italy that was again outstanding. But at least they've learnt their lessons now and not next summer.'

After the win against Italy the England manager was more convinced than ever of the value of the competition. He said: 'I always said that in this tournament we would see which players had the right temperament, which can handle situations and which can't. We've found that out against South Africa, in the Poland game, and now here. The competition for places is tremendous. People with shirts on their backs still have to keep them, but they are in the driving seats. People like Robert Lee – over the last four games he has been great for me and taken his opportunities. Ian Wright's been brilliant to have around the place, his enthusiasm is so infectious – playing for England means everything to him. In the two games he has shown me what he can do with two goals and you can't ask for anything more from a striker. Certainly he is one who has put himself right up there.'

Pearce was accused by Cesare Maldini of elbowing Zola. But he showed no sign of remorse and had a one-word riposte for the Italians: 'Shame!'

Hoddle explained that he had left out Shearer because he wanted to fog Italian perceptions ahead of the World Cup showdown in October. He then hinted that he would continue to use Shearer sparingly in non-competitive games leading up to the World Cup Finals to protect the Newcastle striker. He said: 'Alan will play against France but there could be games when I might not use him. I accept Alan wasn't best pleased with my decision, but if you have got a jewel in the crown sometimes you have to protect it. When you look into a player's eyes you can see that he needs a rest. I see in Shearer's eyes that he wants to play but those eyes might also be tired. I want players to be angry and frustrated when they are left out. It's the reaction I'm looking for.'

Following England's first win in Poland for 31 years and their first over Italy for 20 years, they were seeking their first away win over France for 48 years. English optimism was at new heights on the eve of the match against France in the potentially hostile environment of the Stade Mosson, Montpellier. Hoddle's side was on the verge of putting together a run of six successive wins on foreign soil, a feat last achieved under Bobby Robson in the mid-eighties. Not since October 1993, against Holland in Rotterdam, had England lost abroad; not since a month later, against San Marino, had they conceded an away goal. The statistics were enhanced by the fact that the vast majority of Venables' games were played at Wembley, but it was still an impressive record.

Scholes, England's newest discovery, would miss the chance to build on his sensational international introduction. A tightening hamstring forced him out of training and Hoddle had to rethink his plans. Hoddle had planned to look at Scholes in tandem with the returning England skipper, a possible long-term partnership if and when age catches up with Sheringham. 'I wanted to see if he could reproduce that performance, to find out a bit more about his temperament when the pressure is on. Once you set a standard, it's harder to maintain. If he could do that then I think to myself that long term, yes, we do have a player on our hands here. If he doesn't, it's not a disaster. He is still very young and I want to see how things shape up. But I won't put pressure on the boy if he's not 100 per cent fit.' Gazza was brought back for his 50th cap, while Ince was rested.

Shearer's 11th goal in as many internationals, plundered five minutes from time, gave Hoddle six wins on the trot. After all the intricate passing against the Italians, this was a grafting performance rather than a compelling one, but nonetheless commendable for that. In a country where they had not won for 48 years, England had to contend not only with technically accomplished opponents but also a dodgy Moroccan referee.

Dugarry had a storming match as the focal point of the French attack. But Shearer was better. One of those curling, teasing crosses which are Le Saux's trademark was met with a howitzer of a header, athletically saved by Barthez. England had a great chance when Beckham played the ball up to Shearer in the inside-left channel and as the captain squared it across the six-yard box it seemed Wright must score, but his shot hit the goalkeeper's shoulder. France went close from a Djorkaeff free-kick which Seaman had covered until Dugarry, standing behind England's defensive wall, gave it a backheel. But Gary Neville cleared. Seaman then produced a world-class save when left-back Pierre Laigle fastened on to a misplaced clearance and let fly with a bristling twenty-yarder. The match was decided, however, when Sheringham, on for Wright, delivered a cross from the right which Barthez spilled for Shearer to prod in the easiest of all his international goals.

The referee seemed to be in a world of his own; instead of booking Patrick Vieira for a challenge which threatened to cut Beckham in half, the Moroccan eccentric turned a blind eye to the assault. Worse still, he showed Beckham the yellow card for hobbling to the touchline, and spurning the obligatory stretcher. It was a petty decision which deprived England of their best midfield player for the Brazil game.

The Beckham booking came after just 13 minutes and prompted Hoddle to rush down to the bench from the stands to try and calm the youngster down. Hoddle said: 'I was comfortable, looking from upstairs, but that forced me on to the bench; we had to calm him down. We're still trying to find out whether it was for dissent or for not trying to get on the stretcher, but the players and the physio are adamant that he didn't say anything to him. It was a ridiculous situation for a young lad.' Beckham himself was distraught. 'I didn't hear the ref tell me to get on the stretcher. I got treatment off the pitch and when I wanted to come back on, he showed me the yellow card. I'm gutted.'

Beckham's performance was praised again by Hoddle, who felt that his partnership with Gazza in the centre of midfield had worked well. Gazza might not have put in an eye-catching performance but he worked hard enough to satisfy the England coach. 'If you tracked his runs, it would probably add up to seven miles when most players run between five-and-a-half to six miles in a game. He tried extremely hard. Some people have been trying to say "that's him finished". Or, if he'd had a fantastic game, "what are you doing, thinking about throwing him out?" It's not just about Paul Gascoigne, it's about the England team over the next 12 months. It's about taking stock and getting ready for Moldova, getting our qualifying head back on. Then, the minute we qualify, we can switch to how we're going to go from there.'

Ince again demonstrated why he's so important to Hoddle's team. He was not in the starting line-up because the coach wanted to ensure he avoided a second booking which would have made him ineligible for the game against Brazil. But with Batty picking up an injury, Hoddle sent on Ince for the entire second half with the instructions: 'Don't get cautioned.'

Clean sheets inevitably mean safe goalkeeping and sound defending. Seaman made a top-class flying tip-over from Laigle, and in front of him the combination of Southgate, Campbell and Gary Neville looked formidable. Campbell was growing in stature although Hoddle admitted: 'For the first ten to twelve minutes he was not at the races. Defensively he made a couple of fouls and Dugarry got round the back of him a couple of times. We had to send out a few messages. He started iffy but then, wallop, he was back to his best. It's a good sign that a youngster doesn't crumble and was capable of turning an individual performance around. He was as strong as anyone after 90 minutes. He's still a young lad with a lot to learn, but the good thing is that he's going to get better.'

The 3–3 draw between Brazil and Italy meant that England had won the Tournoi de France before even playing the world champions. It was the team's first piece of silverware but Hoddle vowed to finish the tournament in style with a performance to savour against Brazil.

Hoddle felt that England would not be frightened by the challenge of Ronaldo and company. 'Sometimes people give Brazil too much respect, they think they come from another planet. But we shall look at ourselves for this one – we have inner belief. I hope we have still got that belief when the World Cup comes around. If this tournament had been a disaster it wouldn't have mattered, because it would have meant we have been learning things. We're not in this game proving things to people, they will make their judgments, come what may. But this is a prestigious tournament and we have proved to ourselves, just to ourselves, that we are a good side and we have enjoyed it.'

England's final game of the tournament would mean an opportunity to compare Ronaldo and Shearer. Shearer said: 'Some people might think I'm better than Ronaldo, some might think he's better than me ... When you play the best it is an opportunity to gear yourself up to see how far you have come. There is no doubt that Ronaldo is very streetwise. He is strong, very pacy, with a good first touch and has the ability to beat four opponents from the halfway line and score a spectacular goal.'

An attacking partner, with special qualities, is important to bring the best out of both Shearer and Ronaldo. The Newcastle striker observed: 'Romario's a little more deceptive than Ronaldo with his little flicks and little darting runs, but they link up well as a partnership. Romario's been around a long time and he's good for Ronaldo.' In comparison, Shearer has been tried with a series of potential partners. 'When I started, I was up front with Gary Lineker and that helped me a lot. Everyone is different and a lot can depend on different systems, different opponents. Les Ferdinand and myself have not been given a lot of time at Newcastle to develop our partnership because of injuries, but we still scored plenty of goals. Teddy [Sheringham] and myself have come together for the international team and we have been reasonably successful so far.'

Campbell, although only 22 years of age, was looking forward to the challenge. The emerging pillar of the England defence said: 'Everyone wants to see Ronaldo but I want to find out how good I am. This game for me is not about Ronaldo and Brazil. It is about discovering new things about me. I change mentally for international football. Your mind has to be perfect. When I go out there I am saying to myself, "Yes, you can do this, you can stop him scoring."' If Campbell still had a flaw in his game, it was lapses of concentration. 'I realize that I will have to be focused for the entire 90 minutes against Brazil. I try to start preparing myself mentally the night before a match. It takes time to get it right. You can't just snap your fingers and say "Yes, I'm an international player". It will be a while before I'm completely comfortable. But you want to find out how good you are, and you can only do that by testing yourself against the best.'

Hoddle was relishing pitting his coaching wits and his players' talents against the nation he considered the masters of the world game. 'They are the best in the world and they will provide us with another type of test. When we saw them against Italy they were still playing in spells, like they did 30 years ago, and that's very difficult to do. The first half they found it hard to get off the hook against the Italians' man-for-man marking, but it was difficult even for the Italians to make it work for 90 minutes, as we saw in the second half. I think we have the capability of giving any team in the world problems. Now we have to see if we can defend against them and then go for their Achilles heel, which is our strength.'

It was Ronaldo and Romario who most concerned Hoddle in his tactical preparations. 'They're exceptionally talented, and if you allow the pair of them too much space they will kill you. But we don't expect to concede goals. We expect to win. If the whole team is on song, we now feel that we can beat anyone.'

Hoddle saw Shearer as the man to punish suspect Brazilian defending, but he added: 'They have the ball longer than anyone else, they can keep it for as much as 75 per cent of the game, so we have to hit them on the break. Brazil only enjoy the game when they are on the ball, they have a reluctance to defend. Even their defenders want to caress the ball. They have changed their mentality over the years, bringing in players like Dunga, but they still have this Achilles heel, whether it's crosses into the box, set plays or something else. You are never out of the game against them, equally you are never safe as the Italians found out. Our defenders will have to be vigilant, on their toes. It's a game you're hoping your goalkeeper will have a solid game, maybe even a bit of luck, and perform to his best.'

Hoddle had warned his team not to treat the world champions as if they had come from another planet, but, unfortunately, as far as the gap between England and Brazil was concerned, they were another galaxy away. The game represented a steep learning curve for Hoddle's men.

Even though it ended in defeat, the game couldn't obscure some of the class and resilience shown against Italy and France. In what was always going to be a fascinating contrast of styles, the magical, mesmeric, marvellous skills of the Brazilians always threatened the England defence. It was the veteran striker Romario who eventually secured the important breakthrough. Collecting a Leonardo pass in the 61st minute, he slid his precise angled ground shot wide of David Seaman and in off the far post.

There were no goals for Shearer or Ronaldo but they did come face to face, in a most unexpected way. The fireworks began, not in front of goal as everyone anticipated, but when the two No 9s challenged for the ball a couple of minutes before the break on the halfway line. Ronaldo had come deep in a bid to evade the tight-marking English defence and Shearer was chasing back in his typical non-stop style. When Shearer tackled Ronaldo with full force, the Brazilian lashed out and Colombian referee Toro Rendon raised a yellow card in front of both of them.

The importance of not conceding possession against the Brazilians was underlined from the very start when Seaman badly sliced a clearance into touch. It was seven minutes before England regained possession! However, it was not all one-way traffic as England did have a good chance when Gazza's clever backheel sent Ince racing forward. His twenty-five yarder was turned round the post by Taffarel. Apart from that there were precious few opportunities, except free-kicks from Shearer and Gazza.

So Shearer lifted the trophy for England after the game, in spite of the defeat by Brazil. Hoddle said: 'We have no reason to fear anyone. I don't think that we are all that far away from the best. The teams involved in this tournament are the teams who will be going through to the semi-final area of the World Cup next summer. We put in great performances and we're learning as a team. Against Italy we passed the ball extremely well, but against Brazil we didn't have the skills in the second half to cause them problems. The key thing has been the experience of playing at tournament level and the way we played against Italy is the way we should be playing all the time. The squad have been a credit to themselves. The spirit has been good.' Hoddle gave Gazza a vote of confidence after his 'trial'. Asked whether he still felt Gazza was a big-match winner, he said: 'He can still do that. It is something he has always had and at 30 years of age he is maturing. He still has good vision, quick feet and he's creative. He has a stature within teams as good creative players can do. Most important, he needs three or four months at the start of next season injury-free when he can gradually build back to his best. I was pleased with Paul against Brazil, and there were times I felt he was back to his best and there is a chance that he can be.'

As Hoddle gave his end of term report, Ince, Campbell, Scholes, Southgate and Phil Neville were named as the other major successes of the tour. But the England coach added that the absentees, Ferdinand, Fowler, McManaman, Le Tissier, Anderton, Merson and Adams would all be pushing for places in the competitive final sprint to the line to make the World Cup squad.

Hoddle felt the tournament had been a great success. England had regained its self-respect and instilled within itself an inner belief. He said: 'Off the back of a marvellous result in Poland we've been amongst four teams here that all will have a chance in the World Cup of going close. We've come up against world-class opposition and come out of it with respect. There is still a gap to be bridged against Brazil but there is a lot of energy taken out of you when you're playing them as they are still the best in the world.'

Le Tournoi de France

Italy (0) 0 England (2) 2
Flowers, Pearce, Ince (capt), Southgate, Le Saux, Beckham, Sheringham, P. Neville, Keown, Scholes, Wright

France (0) 0 England (0) 1
Seaman, G. Neville, Southgate, Le Saux, Beckham, Gascoigne, Shearer (capt), Campbell, P. Neville, Batty, Wright

Brazil (0) 1 England (0) 0
Seaman, Ince, Southgate, Le Saux, Gascoigne, Shearer (capt), Sheringham, Campbell, P. Neville, Keown, Scholes

Final Table

	P	W	D	L	F	A	Pts
England	3	2	0	1	3	1	6
Brazil	3	1	2	0	5	4	5
France	3	0	2	1	3	4	2
Italy	3	0	2	1	5	7	2

CHAPTER TWENTY

All Change

The new English football season, August 1997

The influx of more than 150 foreign players to the Premiership was having a profound effect. On the opening weekend of the 1997/98 season, of the 264 players who appeared in the Premiership, Hoddle could immediately discount 111 of them because they were not eligible for England. Of the 153 remaining, at least 40 are well past their peak or still too raw. It left, roughly, only ten candidates for each position. While that may seem untold riches to Wales or Northern Ireland, it marked a severe cutback for England. Hoddle acknowledged that it was a worrying situation: 'It has been a problem that was around the corner with the Bosman ruling, and now it's happening. It's not too alarming yet because I have a good crop of youngsters like those from Manchester United and like Rio Ferdinand, and I believe the best English talent will always come to the top. The problem is when players are brought in from other countries who are no better than some of our young players, because they are more experienced and do not cost so much. The Zolas and the Bergkamps bring a great deal to our game but it is the average foreigners who are the concern.' Hoddle warned: 'There will be a problem for the long-term future of the game. Until people stop pushing £6–£7 million back in their faces, then everybody will go abroad and find a free transfer player from places like Zaragoza. I always believe that cream will rise to the top, and there will be no real problem for our talent, but there might come a stage when every team in England has eight to nine foreign players. They are the rules and they can't be changed. David Beckham, Nicky Butt, and Paul Scholes have come through and they are up there as good as anyone in Europe at the same age. But the long-term future, well, unless the overall situation changes, it will become a problem, there will be a blockage eventually. Division One will get stronger and stronger and full of English players.' Hoddle was an advocate of the change proposed for the 1998/99 season whereby players will be permitted to move to another English club at the end of their contracts without a fee, as happens now post-Bosman with transfers from one country to another, so that domestic talent is able to compete equally.

How best to keep English football on track was again an issue when Howard Wilkinson presented the FA with his challenging 12-point plan to raise the standard of quality in the English game and catch up with the rest of the world. He outlined a national strategy that would put the future of England's international ambitions at both club and country level firmly in the hands of the professionals, rather than schoolmasters and enthusiastic amateur administrators. Two days after Chelsea and Middlesbrough had fielded 16 non-English players in the FA Cup Final, England's first national technical director said: 'Foreigners are rubbing their hands with glee at the fact that we don't make the most of what we have. They are very happy that we have overcrowded fixture lists and a lack of qualified coaches. In this country, as far as football is concerned, we certainly have the quantity but now we need the quality because we are underachieving compared to countries like Norway, Holland and France. In terms of per head of population we are certainly not in the top three. Football is at the height of popularity here but we are still lagging behind so many others in so many aspects of quality. This report is all about producing improved English players for England teams and my fervent hope is that the FA take it seriously and do not just let it go the rounds. I realize it has got to go before the usual committees and will take some time, but it is an action plan and I want it to be acted upon. This is the first time ever there has been a proposal for a national strategy and in my view we will never have a better opportunity to make it work.'

Hoddle had another idea for improvement, but it received short shrift from the Premier League. His plan to shift the Premier League programme to a Sunday in order to have midweek overnight debriefings with his players was kicked out by the club chairmen. Ken Bates was one of the many chairmen who had no sympathy for Hoddle's plea. He said: 'As for putting matches back for Sunday, what about the extra police charges, the reduced traffic accommodation, corporate hospitality going out the window and don't forget the FA pay bugger all for taking our players.' Bates went on to reveal his true loyalties: 'A healthy international team is no good to me. We find the players, we teach them and we pay for them. And we hand them over to an organization run by amateurs. The England team keeps a lot of people in work, it helps solve the unemployment problem in England! Just look at the number of people in the FA's PR department. My beef is simple. We pay our players' wages and we should have a bigger say. The role of the FA has changed. They used to be above money in the past. But those Corinthian amateur traditions have been taken over by television, endorsements and commercialism. The South African friendly was fixed up because it made the FA half a million quid.'

Hoddle responded by accusing some clubs of undermining his bid to qualify for the World Cup Finals. In a thinly-veiled attack he said: 'I've never stopped an international player going to an international get-together because I've played for my country. Unfortunately, some people haven't played international football.' He also pointed out that Brazil's national side were on tour despite the consequence of their domestic club season continuing without their top internationals. 'If that was happening in England, people would be up in arms about it. But Brazil are serious about winning the World Cup again,' said Hoddle.

While the game held its breath over the arrival of so many overseas names, there was still the usual explosion of big domestic transfers, many involving Hoddle's squad. Sheringham signed for Manchester United for £3.5 million, Ferdinand replaced him at Spurs for £6 million. Merson left Highbury for Middlesbrough for £5 million, while Pearce walked out on relegated Forest for Newcastle, Collymore switched from Liverpool to Aston Villa and Le Saux returned to Chelsea from Blackburn for £5 million.

Liverpool ended their six-month chase for Ince when he signed a four-year contract worth £25,000 a week. His brief was to whip Liverpool's talented but underachieving stars into ruthless title winners. Ince said: 'I am well aware of the reputations of people like Graeme Souness and Steve McMahon and what they did for this club. But like them, I like to think I'm more than just a ball winner. I don't think Roy Evans has bought me simply to win the ball and give it to other players. I feel there is a lot more to my game than that. I'm aware people are saying I could be the final piece in the jigsaw here but the pressure doesn't worry me. That's what I am here for. It's the challenge to help Liverpool win the championship after a seven-year gap.'

Merson, who had won 15 international caps, hoped to stay in the squad and did not see why being a first division player should count against him if he was playing well enough..'Of course it's possible to be picked – Steve Bull did, Steve Stone will if he plays well and then there's Gazza – he's in Scotland and he still gets picked for England. If you can do it playing against Dunfermline, you can certainly do it playing for Middlesbrough. If you play well and you're consistent, you'll get noticed. We get as much coverage here as a lot of Premier League sides, so there are no worries about being out of the spotlight. But my job is to be in the Middlesbrough team and get promotion. Anything else is a bonus.'

Pearce had signed a contract with Newcastle worth more than £2m over three years. He said: 'I haven't come to Newcastle to see out my time. I'm hungry for success, I want to win things and be in the first team. It was a magnificent move for me but moves are only as good as you make them.' 'Psycho' was desperate to continue his England career a little longer. 'Playing for England means so much to me and I'd love to be able to make it to the World Cup Finals next summer. To stand any chance of doing that, I feel I need to be playing my club football at the highest possible level. Anyone with aspirations to be one of our best players must perform at Premiership level all the time.'

Top of Les Ferdinand's priorities after his move to Spurs was to ensure he was in Hoddle's squad. Ferdinand said: 'It was disappointing not to be part of the set-up in France. But the hernia operation was something that needed doing. But I still feel very much part of the England set-up because Glenn Hoddle has shown he is willing to pick sides to suit particular matches. Some new faces have come in and done well. But it's now up to me to start the new season well and start banging in the goals.'

Collymore hoped to revive his England aspirations by moving to Villa. Brian Little's £7 million club record signing denied he had failed to do himself justice at Anfield where he and Fowler had plundered 102 goals between them in two seasons. Collymore said: 'People say I left Liverpool without making the fullest impact, but in the first season myself and Robbie Fowler were the top partnership goal-wise in the Premier League. Then last season only Alan Shearer and Les Ferdinand of Newcastle scored more goals, so I don't think my time at Liverpool was that bad. Now I'm hoping that playing alongside Dwight Yorke will yield as many goals as Stan Collymore–Robbie Fowler did together. I'm also hoping we can go on to be as big a threat as I'd like to think myself and Robbie were over the two seasons we were together.'

Chelsea had snatched Le Saux from under the noses of Arsenal. They paid £5 million for the Blackburn left-back, who had stormed out of Stamford Bridge for £690,000 four years ago. Chelsea managing director Colin Hutchinson said: 'We admit making a mistake selling Graeme. It's taken four-and-a-half years and £5m to rectify that error.' Le Saux was so desperate to quit Stamford Bridge in 1993 that he said he would have 'parachuted out of a snake's backside' to get away. But he insisted: 'Circumstances change. I have ambitions and I feel that Chelsea can fulfil them.'

One thing never changes – the injury problems. Matt Le Tissier broke his right arm on Southampton's pre-season tour, falling awkwardly during Saints' 1–1 draw with German club SVP Ansbach. Of even greater concern to England was Alan Shearer, who fractured his fibula and ruptured ankle ligaments at Goodison in the pre-season Umbro tournament against Chelsea. The initial diagnosis was that he would be out for several months.

John Gorman arrived home from holiday to be confronted with the news about Shearer. He commented: 'Alan is a crucial player and what has happened is terrible news for us. Glenn is aware of what has happened, and like the rest of us he is devastated to hear about it.' Gorman spoke to Shearer in his private hospital room by phone and said: 'Alan was his typical, positive, usual self. He told me that he knows he's just got to get on with it, but that whatever it takes, he'll get on with it as soon as possible. That's the sort of guy he is.' A year after being ordered to surrender the Newcastle No 9 shirt to Shearer, Ferdinand was now ready to replace the crocked superstar in the England side. 'It's unfortunate for Alan, but if I get a good start to the season I'll be banging on the door to replace him for England.'

Shearer's horrendous long-term injury dominated Hoddle's thoughts but he refused to be downhearted. He said: 'It is a blow. We've got one of the best strikers in the world out. But the positive side is that it hasn't happened just five days before we meet up for a game, there is plenty of opportunity to look at other people. It is ironic that the last time we played against Italy in Le Tournoi, Alan didn't play. We won the game convincingly. That proves to people in the squad, to myself and my staff that there are other options in there, it proves the strength we've got in the squad. But there's no two ways about it, when it comes to a crunch game like that you would definitely want Alan Shearer as captain and first name down on the team sheet. Our chances are obviously going to be less by taking that player out of your side. You would be a fool if you thought any different.'

Hoddle boldly declared that, without Shearer, he viewed Sheringham as the key to his World Cup hopes. After watching Sheringham in the Charity Shield against Chelsea, Hoddle had no doubts he would fill Eric Cantona's boots. He said: 'You would have thought Teddy Sheringham had played in that team for six or seven years. I do believe it's given them an added bonus for the Champions' League. Eric Cantona, for all the great things he's done for Manchester United, wasn't playing international football. Teddy's been playing in the European Championships, he's been playing extremely well in our qualifying games for the World Cup. To a certain degree he's stepping down the ladder to play in the Champions' League rather than Eric who wasn't playing international football for the last two or three years. It will be an added bonus which I think the United fans will see over the coming months.'

There appeared to be more bad news for Hoddle when Robbie Fowler was stretchered off during Liverpool's 3-1 defeat of a Norway XI in a pre-season friendly. Roy Evans said: 'We heard a crack and thought it was serious, maybe even a cruciate ligament.' However, the diagnosis proved less concerning and the Liverpool striker was ezpected to be out for no more than a couple of weeks.'

Steve Stone was hoping to come back into the reckoning after long-term injury problems. Hoddle turned up to see Stone help Forest to a 4–1 victory over Norwich but the unlucky player was soon out again – this time with hernia trouble and had to abandon any hope of an early recall to the international scene. His chances of making the World Cup Finals looked slimmer than ever. Stone said: 'It's a terrible disappointment to be ruled out like this. I've obviously done something to upset the football gods. After working right through the summer so I could be fit for the big kick-off, everything seemed fine. Then all of a sudden I found myself suffering from excruciating pain. I couldn't even think about kicking a ball. I've bounced back before, though, and I will bounce back again. You can bet on it.' Forest boss Dave Bassett declared: 'There is no braver player than Steve in the entire country. He beat three broken legs as a teenager, then battled to overcome a very serious injury last season. I never expected him to be available so quickly, so the games we have got out of him can be counted as a bonus. Steve looked as good as ever, and everyone at the City Ground can't wait until he is wearing Forest's shirt again.'

Chris Sutton was on the verge of full international recognition after a couple of B team performances and 13 appearances for the Under-21s. But frustrating injuries since his £5 million move to Ewood Park three years ago had put his England career in cold storage. Sutton's new coach, Roy Hodgson said: 'I am sure he will come to Glenn's attention. I know he follows the players very closely. If Chris can do well for Blackburn, then other things could follow. So far he must take the credit for everything he has done. He's worked hard and got his head down. And he's determined to stay free from injury this season.'

Meanwhile the squad for the game against Moldova was announced: Seaman (Arsenal), Walker (Spurs), Martyn (Leeds), G Neville (Man Utd), Southgate (Aston Villa), Pallister (Man Utd), R Ferdinand (West Ham), Campbell (Spurs), Le Saux (Chelsea), P Neville (Man Utd), Batty (Newcastle), Butt (Man Utd), Beckham (Man Utd), Gascoigne (Rangers), Scholes (Man Utd), Lee (Newcastle), Ripley (Blackburn), Sheringham (Man Utd), L Ferdinand (Spurs), I Wright (Arsenal), Collymore (Aston Villa), Heskey (Leicester).

The big news was that 18-year-old Rio Ferdinand had been called up because of a spate of injuries. Hoddle accepted that Ferdinand was not yet the finished article but believed he deserved an opportunity. 'Rio has put in some quality performances and with his form so good we have a chance to look at him while others are injured. He is accomplished on the ball and is a wonderful player with a great future. Maybe he needs to defend a little better and there are other aspects of his game he could improve on. But the potential is there.'

Harry Redknapp rated him so highly that he threatened to quit West Ham if the Upton Park board tried to cash in on their teenage prodigy. He insisted: 'We are not a feeder club for the Manchester Uniteds and Liverpools. If we were to sell Rio to United in six months' or a year's time we shouldn't be in the Premier League. We would be deceiving our fans, and I wouldn't want to stay in those circumstances.'

Rio joined the untried Emile Heskey as Hoddle summoned another teenage star in the absence of Shearer. Heskey reflected on his meteoric rise from YTS football to the international stage; only 16 months earlier he had been with the YTS apprentices at Filbert Street. He revealed: 'When Martin O'Neill called me over to say I was in the England squad, I thought it was a wind-up. It took several moments for the news to sink in – because this is the highlight of my career so far. Every player dreams of representing his country, and while I don't expect to get on to the pitch for this game, I'm certainly no different. It's quite unbelievable. I never thought I would make the senior squad so soon. The last couple of years have been quite miraculous for me, what with promotion, winning the Coca-Cola Cup and getting into the England Under-21 team. I haven't a clue what the procedure will be for joining up with the full England party. I hope they send me a letter with full instructions, and even then, it will need somebody to point me in the right direction.'

O'Neill revealed: 'The big joke among the Leicester players is that Emile could definitely go all the way to the top – provided he develops a bit more strength and a turn of speed. That's their way of saying that Emile already possesses both those qualities in abundance, plus everything else that is required to help him become one of the best strikers in Britain.'

He had scored 12 goals in his first Premiership season, and been linked with Liverpool and Celtic. He said: 'I have to think that I stand a good chance of making the breakthrough to the England team. This will be a big season for me and there will be added attention because last season went so well. I am going to find myself under pressure to play well all the time – but it's pressure I can handle.'

Liverpool's Steve McManaman, who had angered Hoddle by having knee surgery instead of playing for England in the summer, was left out. Hoddle recalled winger Stuart Ripley, whose one previous appearance for England had come four years earlier, instead. McManaman's absence was put down to indifferent form and because his failure to make the French tournament had given others their chance. His absence was seen as a warning that not even a player of his extravagant ability is an automatic choice.

Hoddle also recalled Stan Collymore because 'he gives us something a bit different. I'm pleased in what I've seen of him. He's done enough to show me he's got a hell of a gift, even though Villa have not picked up a win and confidence there is low.'

Hoddle said that he had decided to stick with Ian Wright despite the Arsenal man being under threat of disciplinary action for angrily questioning the referee's ability to keep time in a 3–3 draw at Leicester. He did not feel 'that there was too much case to answer'. Hoddle maintained there was no link with his decision to keep faith with Gascoigne, Merson and Adams after their personal problems. 'It's not a question of forgiving. There is no comparison between this and Paul Gascoigne or Paul Merson. If Ian Wright had run on the pitch and smacked somebody in the mouth, or smacked the referee, he wouldn't have been in this squad. But I think we're going over the top. I've got to make a decision over what I think. The situation isn't going to be dealt with in a few days, or by the time we play Moldova. Selecting him wasn't a difficult decision at all. Ian Wright still has a case to answer although a lot of people seem to have given the answer already.' Had Wright received the 12-match ban suggested, Hoddle would have faced a major crisis for the critical tie in Italy.

CHAPTER TWENTY-ONE

Match for a Princess

England v Moldova, Wembley, 10 September 1997

After the tragic death of Diana, Princess of Wales in a road accident on 31 August, Hoddle and the FA had an opportunity to help ensure that the positive, good works of the Princess lived on. They were approached by Christian Aid to organize a football match for the victims of landmines in Bosnia. Christian Aid had previously contacted the FA before Diana's death with the proposal and it had received a warm reception. After the tragedy in Paris, the charity again got in touch with David Davies, asking to press ahead with the game as a 'tribute' to the Princess's work.

Hoddle wanted something positive to emerge from the tragedy. He hoped that it would bring a change in the media treatment of celebrities. The England coach observed: 'A line has to be drawn. People who are in the public eye deserve more respect. Perhaps those doing these sort of things [hounding celebrities] should ask themselves how they would feel if it were happening to them. How would their own children feel about it, how would their mother or father feel about it? That is their only chance of understanding what they are doing and seeing it through a different set of eyes. Respecting other people's privacy is important. They [the *paparazzi*] stepped over the mark with Princess Diana. If something good were to come from the tragedy, it would be another positive to have come from her life.'

Paul Gascoigne, in an interview with *Match of the Day* magazine, compared his suffering at the hands of the press to that of the Princess of Wales. He said: 'I was not obviously hounded as much as her, but I have been chased and I have done exactly the same things. It is a wicked feeling. And they [the press] have turned round and said "yeah, we'll leave Princes William and Harry alone". They'll do that until the situation dies down and then they'll start hounding them again.' His own advice on how to deal with the problem was equally forthright. 'What I would like to do, my ambition, is to get about ten to twenty pals, buy them a camera each and tell them to go and hound the editor, his kids and family, 24 hours a day, morning and night, for at least a month. Shove the cameras in the kids' faces, in his wife's face, follow them to restaurants, sit outside his house, knock on his door, bang on his window, and shout abusive things all day. I would love to do that, that would be my dream come true – then a hat-trick in the World Cup Final.' He added: 'I do not have any respect for any journalist, none whatsoever. I've always been like that. They build you up to knock you down, especially the tabloids. Now with what has happened to Lady Diana, it is water off a duck's back. I hate them, I absolutely hate them. I really detest them.'

Although the tragedy had cast a large shadow over the nation, the World Cup qualifier against Moldova still had to be played. Rio Ferdinand blew his chance by having too much to drink when celebrating his call-up. An imposed 12-month drink-driving ban prompted a disciplinary clampdown by Hoddle. Although the 18-year-old was axed from the squad, the blow was softened as he was allowed to train with the England team in the build-up to the Moldova tie. Rio said: 'I am just so sorry because I have been very naive and I am being forced to pay a heavy price. It is a harsh lesson for me to learn, especially as I was so close to my first England cap. I made a mistake for which I am dreadfully sorry. I cannot apologize enough. This will show a test of my character. I have to prove to people who have stood by me that I can bounce back.' Rio insisted he had drunk two halves of lager before switching to what he thought were soft drinks, but were, in fact, alcopops. Hammers managing director Peter Storrie said: 'Rio thinks the drinks could have been changed without his knowledge. He is full of remorse.'

It seemed that you could play for England if you beat up your wife as long as you took counselling, that you could play for England if you took drugs as long as you admitted it, that you could play with a gambling addiction as long as you admitted it, but not if you had committed the comparatively minor offence of drink-driving. But there was a big difference in the cases of Gascoigne, Merson, Adams and young Rio. He made the big mistake of hiding his crimes from Hoddle, the FA and his club, and his timing was bad as he appeared in court the day before England were due to assemble. Hoddle had no choice but to take firm action. He knows that Rio is a player of immense talent, but he also understands that developing the right temperament is crucial to international success.

Hoddle was quizzed as to why he had hit Rio hard but shown mercy to stars like Gazza. He responded: 'Was he taken to court? Was there an assault charge against Paul Gascoigne? I know Paul admitted it, but if it had gone into the courts, it would have been out of my situation. For Paul to overcome his problem it wasn't going to help by chucking him out, he wanted to try to change. I have to deal with facts, and at the weekend Rio was called up into the squad he was done for drink-driving. When I found out the situation and that he was due in court on Tuesday when we were meeting up later in the day, I felt I didn't have any option but to do what I have done. But I wanted him here training as well so he can see what goes on and see what he's missing out on. I think the lesson will get home to him that way. I am not saying that he won't play for England in the future. He hasn't robbed a bank, he hasn't killed anybody, he hasn't shot anyone, he hasn't mugged a granny, but between Harry Redknapp and myself we will see how he reacts to what's happened. I don't want to crucify him and we have had a good long chat. He's very disappointed with what's he's done and feels he's let himself, his club and his family down.'

Merson backed Hoddle's decision. 'There's no point in saying it was only a minor incident. That minor mistake could have killed someone. I didn't grasp it at first and he probably hasn't grasped it yet, but he's a big-name player now. He's not Rio Ferdinand playing in the reserves, he's as well-known a centre-half as anyone around now. That's the other part of it. Probably six months ago it would never have been in the news, and that's what he will learn. This will make him a better person. You have got to feel for the lad, particularly as he would probably have played in the match. It's up to the manager what to do, but you can be sure that Rio won't go out and do something like this again. He's learned his lesson. At least he's only 18. It's not as if he's 28 and waiting to make his debut. It's a shame what has happened, but it will make him a better all-round player for it.'

Rio was the sacrificial lamb that Hoddle hoped would keep all his other young England starlets out of trouble. 'Normally you have to experience it yourself to learn from your mistakes. But our youngsters can learn from Rio's mistake. It's a signal to anyone at that age who has ambitions of playing for England in the future. If players are playing for England, they know there is an expectation there – on and off the pitch.'

The injured Adams, along with the suspended Ince, were at Bisham Abbey for tactical briefings. Hoddle asked Adams to talk to Ferdinand about drink-related problems. 'It has got to be good for the boy to speak to someone like Tony, who's been through it all and can explain the implications. It's a chance to nip it in the bud. We'll see how he [Rio] reacts.'

Emile Heskey, who had become teetotal after getting so drunk in the dressing room and on the coach that he missed the Coca-Cola Cup-winning banquet, spoke of the excitement of training alongside Ian Wright for the first time. 'He's a great bloke, and to train and be with him is a dream come true for me. I've admired him for a long time, from when he first came into the side at Crystal Palace, scoring goals from all sorts of different angles. Then when he moved to Arsenal his first game was at Leicester. I was in the youth team then, but just to watch him was brilliant. Ian's been an inspiration to me, I think he is for everybody really, a role model. It's a mixture of all the things he brings to the game, his attitude and the way he plays. He plays with so much fire.'

Stuart Ripley had produced a devastating comeback to his career at Blackburn; his exciting wing play was a major factor in the club's early-season form and he was now back in the England squad. He said: 'I think I can go past anyone. I don't see a better one-sided winger in the country than me. But I know that whenever changes are made in a squad, it's always the winger who gets dropped first.' Hoddle said: 'He's back to his best. And is as good as anyone I've seen this season. He will give us width, get crosses in, and just might suit a couple of situations I'm looking at.'

Stuart Pearce was out because of hamstring trouble. Tim Flowers was also missing after a summer groin operation. Teddy Sheringham was ruled out by broken ribs, a blow which possibly robbed him of the England captaincy. Hoddle said: 'Everyone talks about the so-called SAS but we've now lost both of them, and that's a big concern, it's a big blow.'

Hoddle likened Paul Scholes, Sheringham's replacement, to some of football's greats. He said; 'I've not seen his mould of player with that physique – he's a little bit like Alan Ball. I suppose he has the same style as Zola although the end product is not the same, insomuch as he doesn't have the same elegance. But he has everything going for him and I could see that from his first training session at Mottram Hall when he joined up with us. He has got better and better and the amazing thing is that, on the training ground, the boy's at home. He's a very talented player, mature for his age and his goal against Italy was fantastic. The pass he hit for Wright was like a Platini ball.' Hoddle added: 'Teddy is a long way down the line in terms of experience but Scholes, like the Nevilles and Nicky Butt, has done so much so early – won championships and played in a great side. Playing with better players has given him that maturity. He's not someone who has hit the headlines as such. I would have brought him in earlier but he'd been in and out of the United side…Paul has the ability to play off the front players, he's very astute on the ball, good vision and finishing. He's also a solid little player, who can put his foot in and level-headed.'

Gary Pallister pointed to five good reasons why he should be selected again: the five clean sheets Manchester United had kept in their unbeaten start to the season. The big defender suggested a reason for this success – one that fitted in with Hoddle's preferred style of play: 'Maybe the reason we've not conceded a goal so far at United is that the boss always keeps us on our toes. We are not properly covered in the middle of the defence so we have to make certain we play well. Otherwise we all know what will happen. Big names have gone out of the door before at Old Trafford, and Alex Ferguson is not afraid to change things.' Pallister added: 'It angers me when it's claimed I am always injured. All I can say is that I'm happy with the way I feel. It's not a problem for me. I'm careful with my back. I take care of it. And travelling has never been an issue. All the talk of me having a special bed in the team coach is nonsense. So I'm happy to be in the squad. If the chance comes to get into the side, I've got to take it. The better I do for United, the more it will increase my opportunity to get back and stay in the England side again.' Of course, it was not long after Pallister had complained about his reputation that his back trouble started playing him up again!

Les Ferdinand feared he was running out of time to secure his England future. Even a hatful against Moldova wouldn't ensure his place. 'It seems like I've been waiting for a long while to establish myself and I'm running out of time. But I don't go worrying myself about it, all I can do is – if and when I get my chance – do my best, like I've done in the past. Football holds no guarantees. The competition for places up front now is the fiercest it's ever been. You just look at the strikers we've got here and what's to come back in, and that keeps you on your toes all the time. Because you know you can't come late, have a bad game and then expect to be in the next squad. And also with this manager he'll pick the side to suit the opposition, to suit the game. We know if Alan Shearer is fit he's going to be the main striker. But I don't think it would really matter if I or anyone scored in my next game, it wouldn't guarantee you playing in the one after that. If the boss sees fit to change he'll do so, but I don't get upset because you know what this manager's thoughts are. I've always got a smile on my face. It's a squad game and the whole idea of a squad is coming more into British football.'

David Beckham was more concerned by off-the-pitch problems. His blood boils at the constant attention over his relationship with Posh Spice, Victoria Adams, and he is sick of being branded a heartless brat when he is splashed across the front pages of the tabloids after supposedly bad mouthing young autograph hunters. He insisted: 'No, I haven't changed. Not at all. No. But when people say I've changed, well, it's things like that that upsets me. It upsets me more than anything. People say I am a confident person, but when people say I've changed and got big-headed ... I'm not like that.' Pursuit by photographers has become part of his life, so much so that Beckham has been forced to become a semi-recluse. 'I think it does get a little bit tedious, I'm sure everybody who gets cameras pointed at them all the time feels like that. But it is part and parcel of being in the limelight that they want to catch you out doing things. When I go out now I try to be low key. I don't want to be on the front pages coming out of a club or restaurant. But you've got to go out and enjoy yourself. I can't understand why people want to take pictures of you coming out of restaurants.' But with Posh Spice on his arm, the footballer and the pop star made an attractive couple for the showbiz pages.

Hoddle wanted to see an antidote for a nation grieving and mourning Princess Diana. Although it would be only four days after the funeral, Hoddle ideally wanted a bumper Wembley crowd to remember Diana, and then celebrate a handsome victory that would put the country firmly en route to the Finals. Hoddle explained: 'The nation is in mourning and although it is only a football match, we shall be searching to lift the nation, and that makes the game even bigger for us. The game is going to be very difficult for everyone after what happened at the weekend. It is going to be a very, very emotional time. When we get a group of 75,000 people inside Wembley and the nation is playing then three points will only be secondary. We shall all be reminded it is only a game of football, but it would be lovely to turn it on to lift the country. Diana was a very professional lady and we have to try to be professional as well.' Moldova would normally mean a half-empty Wembley, but the combination of a vital World Cup tie and the prospect of another opportunity to pay homage to Diana ensured a capacity crowd.

It would be a delicate balancing act to ensure laughter and a light-hearted approach on the training field, knowing the country was mourning. Ian Wright said: 'It's been preying on my mind all week. Although there has been a good buzz about the England training camp, and I've enjoyed meeting up with some of the boys for the first time since the summer in France, nothing has felt normal. You try and go about your work in a businesslike fashion, but in a quiet moment the first thing that pops into your head is Princess Diana. It makes you well up and feel a bit sombre inside ... so how can anyone feeling like that go out and play for their country in a World Cup tie? I'm a big fan of the Royal Family and it's hard to take in that someone who was only three years older than me has been cut down so suddenly. Usually I'm full of energy and I hope I never turn into a couch potato, but I'll never forget last Sunday, spending the whole day flicking from channel to channel and trying to take it in that Princess Diana was really gone.'

Robert Lee summed it up when he said: 'The whole country is grieving and I don't think anything could take away the hurt the country is feeling. But we have got a chance to try and lift people, even if it's only a tiny bit. If we can go out there, put on a good show, get a good result, then it might lift them and we could have some smiling faces back again. But I know it's not been at all easy and we haven't managed either to escape what's been going on. Most of us have just been sitting in our rooms really, most of the afternoon. It's on the television all the time and the players still talk about it. So you can't get away from it, whether you're with England or not. It's a tragedy, it's like one of your family dying. I don't think people realize how hard it's hit them, and it's definitely affected a lot of people who maybe didn't think it would hurt them so much.'

Hoddle wanted to balance the need of the nation to continue their dignified mourning and the necessity to return to 'work' and win a World Cup tie. But he was in favour of Elton John's new version of 'Candle in the Wind' being played. He said: 'A lot of people know of the record, but there will be 75,000 people in the stadium and this will go a long way to selling the record. Whether it is the right thing to do – we shall get stick whatever happens. We want an uplifting atmosphere, then we have to put on a performance and win the match, whether it is 1–0 or 7–0, that is the bottom line. The icing on the cake is that we really perform well and get people off their seats, then the nation can come together for another reason.'

Whatever the public might believe, Hoddle knew it wouldn't be a foregone conclusion against Moldova. 'It would always have been tricky whether I'd have had my main side out or not. It will not be a walk-over game, they drew 1–1 with Italy and although they lost 3–0 in Italy, it was no disgrace as they didn't get hammered by seven or eight. We have to focus our minds on winning the game and I have to pick the right team... We've got to be professional and make sure we switch on and don't slip up. It's a big occasion, the nation are looking to us and it would be lovely to score an early goal and to put on a show because then we would lift the nation.'

David Seaman had been one of the many to travel to Kensington Palace and Harrods to lay flowers and pay his personal respects to Diana. Seaman, who would be captaining the side, helped strike the right mood between reverence and professionalism. He said: 'The worst time will be leading up to the kick-off but after that it will hopefully be back to Euro 96 style. Once the National Anthem has been played it's work for us. You don't want to use it as an excuse because you can't. We've got a serious job to do. But we will show our respects before that, as the whole stadium will, with the whole country watching. It's only right.'

Seaman would be only the sixth goalkeeper to captain England after William Moon, George Raikes, Frank Swift, Ray Clemence and Peter Shilton. He was at least experienced in the role, having captained Arsenal and his old club QPR. The big bluff Yorkshireman with the ready smile and throaty chuckle was a popular choice. His penalty-saving exploits in Euro 96 had made him a national hero and his performances then had led many to label him the finest keeper in Europe, if not the world.

Hoddle warned his players that the one-minute silence would be the most testing time of the night. 'It will be easier once the game starts, but I think the hardest thing is going to be the minute's silence. There is no way round that. We will have one, and rightly so. But it's going to be the hardest time. All we've been talking about, all week, will find its focal point in that minute's silence. As players we have to be professional. We will give a thought for what we're doing, but suddenly we then have to switch off from that, to go into professional mode again. The Princess would want nothing but that.'

The Moldovans would also pay their respects by joining England in wearing black ribbons sewn into their shirts. Their coach, Ion Caras, was well aware of the emotion of the occasion. 'The whole world regretted and bereaved the loss of Diana. We express our shock and sense of loss and grief for Diana.'

Hoddle urged the fans to grieve with the nation and then help 'take the roof off' as they cheered the country to victory. He had a football match to win and he called on the sell-out crowd to honour Diana and then roar out their passionate support. 'I'm hoping the match will give the crowd the opportunity to give themselves and the team a lift. There aren't that many times when the nation is together. It came together in mourning and now it can be again for a football match, for a different reason. I'm just not sure how the supporters will react. I'm hoping we'll get an early goal, because then I will know exactly what the scenario might be. There's normally a big reaction at the end of a silence. Let's hope they take the roof off as a show of respect. That would be the best thing possible.'

Hoddle wanted his players to help change the national mood. 'If we start well, especially after what the whole nation has gone through, we can lift them. Once the whistle goes we've got a job to do, and so have the fans. They can play an important part. They're coming to enjoy the game, be entertained and get behind the team, and hopefully help us get a good win under our belt to go to Rome next month. We will be focused and professional enough to do the job.'

'Discipline' was the key note of one of the most difficult dressing-room addresses of Hoddle's career. No Englishman could afford to disgrace himself on such an occasion when the eyes of the world would be on Wembley. Beckham, in particular, was reminded of his responsibilities. Hoddle toyed with the idea of leaving him out because a second yellow card would have ruled him out of the match in Italy. Hoddle explained the argument: 'It's a delicate one. As a coach you never want to look ahead to the next game but unfortunately I have been forced into that position. I have got to get the balance right between picking the right team to win this match with the possibility of protecting all four [players on yellow cards], or putting them all in and taking a chance. I've got to keep an eye on injuries. I wish I had a crystal ball. I could have three midfield players injured come Rome and then you wish you had protected that situation. It's the first time I've had to think about that and it's something you could do without. At this stage of the qualifying games a lot of the coaches are going to be in the same boat. Any of the players left out, if I give them the honest reasons, it won't affect them and I'm sure David will be the same. Those players who do play on a yellow card must understand they mustn't get booked for something stupid, like back-chatting the referee or not getting back ten yards. If it's a mistimed tackle or something like that, that's life, you've just got to deal with that. The players that play will have to be a little constrained on the day.' Hoddle decided to gamble on Beckham but, as soon as the game was won, he would be substituted.

Hoddle went for an attacking line-up with Scholes playing behind Ferdinand and Wright but cautioned that the game might not be the romp many predicted. 'I've heard that one before,' he said. 'The first 15 minutes over there in my first game they put us under a bit of pressure. They certainly did the same to Italy, they were 1–1 up to the 72nd minute.'

The Moldovan coach, Ion Caras was less confident. He said: 'We are facing one of the strongest teams in world soccer. This is one of the strongest – if not the strongest – groups in the qualifying round. It is a tremendous opportunity to learn and gain experience.' Caras felt the greatest achievement his country could hope for was to score a goal. 'With the exception of David Seaman – who I hope will not threaten our goal – every England player is a danger to us. Everyone is capable of doing us damage. If we score, it will be a great achievement. Even if we lose and lose heavily, it will not be an embarrassment or the end of the world for us. If we play well and get beaten, it will still be a great occasion. To play at Wembley is the pinnacle of any footballer's career, and this will be a momentous day in our nation's brief history.' Caras called his team the 'novices' of world football, having been formed as a nation only six years earlier. In contrast, he saw England as being at the other end of the spectrum. He said: 'For me, England have been the best team in Group Two. Even when they played Italy and Gianfranco Zola won it for the Italians, England were the better team and dominated most of the game. It was an undeserved win for the visitors. I saw England play in the Tournoi de France and was very impressed. England are on the ascendancy and are now one of the top superpowers in world soccer. We were aware from the beginning that we were drawn against some of the strongest teams and so far we haven't managed to get a single point from our games. To us, as a new footballing nation, it is a tremendous opportunity to learn and gain experience. It is a tournament of experience to us, for gaining wisdom for use in the future.'

Wembley was transformed into the stadium of lights as candles, lighters and torches were held aloft as Elton John's revised version of 'Candle in the Wind' drifted across the ground. The one-minute silence in memory of Diana was one of the most haunting times in English soccer history. After the impeccably observed tribute, there was a enormous cheer and some fans started singing 'Football's Coming Home'.

It took 28 minutes before Paul Scholes' breakthrough but Wright scored after 57 seconds of the second half, making the game safe. Scholes' diving header was superb and Wright's finish was powerful but the night belonged to Paul Gascoigne. He produced a superb, disciplined performance, capping it with his tenth goal for his country ten minutes from time. He was back to his dazzling best of Italia 90, and didn't he know it. His goal came when he ran deep into Moldovan territory, showing all his former strength before powering a flick pass which Wright returned for him to produce a calculated finish. Wright then grabbed his second of the night, an opportunist poacher's goal cunningly taking advantage of a limping opponent playing him onside. His finish was precise as he curled the ball round the keeper.

Scholes' diving header from Beckham's cross on his World Cup and Wembley debut was a salutary reminder to the absent McManaman of the value of turning up at Le Tournoi. Scholes' Man Utd teammate Beckham was removed from the fray to avoid a yellow card and was replaced by Ripley who lasted just six minutes of his comeback before pulling his right hamstring.

The nation could be proud of Hoddle's team. With the Italians embarrassingly held to a goalless draw in Georgia England went top of Group Two. 'Are you watching, Italy?' and 'We are top of the league' resounded around the stadium on a night that began in a sombre and grieving mood. By the end the smile was back on the face of English football ... if not back on the nation as a whole.

A jubilant Hoddle saluted Wright and Gascoigne and looked forward. 'We've never taken our eyes off the fact we could still win the group – now it's all in our own hands. I think a lot of people would have thought we would have to go to Italy needing to win to go through, but that's not the case now [because Italy had only managed to draw with Georgia], even though I believe we are perfectly capable of winning out there. It's still going to be a tough game though, a massive match, a real titanic battle. It's going to be a pressurized situation and that pressure will be building up on the Italians. Sometimes that can work for you and against you, and if it builds up it could be their downfall. I was delighted with Gascoigne, that was one of his best games for us for a very long time. Now if he can stay injury free for, say, four to five weeks, then his fitness levels are going to get even better. On the ball he was back to his best and after that performance he can go from strength to strength. I was very pleased also with Wright. Ian scored two goals, showed a lot of good movement and energy ... Ian has waited a long time to score at Wembley and really celebrated it and that's a good philosophy to have. I thought the crowd were fantastic, the minute's silence was impeccable before the start, and I've never heard it observed with so much respect and feeling. I asked the fans to take the roof off and they did, and they set the tone for the rest of the match and they were magnificent, really uplifting.'

Gazza dedicated his stunning performance to the memory of Princess Diana. He had answered all his critics with his best England performance for years. 'It was an emotional night for all of us and Diana was always in my thoughts. But I've really enjoyed myself tonight. It's been one of my best games for England. We've played to our potential and showed just what we're capable of. Now we're going to Rome top of the group and only needing a draw. But we can't afford to sit back. We won't want to take any risks of slipping up. We've got a big job to do and we're looking for all three points.'

Beckham believes that Gascoigne motivates and lifts all those around him when he's in that sort of form – himself included. 'To play alongside the quality guys we've got out there is good – but to play with Gazza as he did is great for us all. To see him do so well in an important game like that is tremendous. And it is an inspiration to everyone playing around him when you see him doing things like that. Of course he likes a joke but when he gets out on the pitch, there is a serious side to him. He talks to me during the game and helps me and says things like "just keep going" – not much really. There was a lot of emotion around this game and obviously the spotlight was on him and how was he going to do but he played brilliantly. He's been out of the papers all summer and I think he's been able to concentrate more on getting on with his life. I guess I've helped him a bit there, haven't I? But he's a great player and he will do it whether he's in the papers or not.'

'It was a really special night for everyone and it's worked out just lovely,' beamed Ian Wright. 'My wife always says to me to score one for her and another for our boy Stacey. Well, I've done that tonight. I'm just so pleased to get two goals at Wembley. The boss told me to link up and you'll get the chances from Gazza, Becks and David Batty. That's what happened. We had to go out there and do a job and we did it well. We dug in and once Paul Scholes got that first goal we were on a roll. Now we're going to Rome to win. We're not going to go for a draw. We want to beat them after what they did to us at Wembley.' Wright scores goals for fun and doesn't give a damn about his detractors. That's the single-minded philosophy that has propelled him back into England's front line at almost 34 and the brink of an amazing World Cup Finals debut appearance.

Gascoigne was warned to stay off the booze to return to greatness in time to play the key role in Rome. The combination of discipline and understanding shown by Hoddle has rescued him from the brink of international oblivion. Hoddle has done it his way, dispelling his critics' view that he was too soft, too inexperienced and too lightweight for the job. He has handled Gazza better than anyone else and in far more trying circumstances. He could be excused trumpeting his success with Gascoigne but he was reluctant to take any praise. 'You can only help them,' he pointed out. 'There's a small amount of credit, not just to myself but Johnny Gorman and all my staff. There's a couple of people who have really helped him on the outside of things as well, which we won't go into because that's private. But at the end of the day you can only lead a horse to water. The player has to learn and look at things for himself, and I think Paul has done that.'

The game had begun in a peculiar atmosphere. Wright described his feelings as the teams prepared to leave the dressing room for the pitch. 'You hear a buzzer and you start going out. All you could hear was the players' studs. Then we could hear 'Candle in the Wind', it was like it was just forcing itself up the tunnel. Everybody stopped and listened. Usually when there are records on before a game, you can't hear them because the fans are making noise. This time, it was like being in a cathedral. When there are nearly 75,000 people and you can hear every word of a song, it's amazing. And the sound of the studs just got me. It was as if everybody suddenly realized what the music was and stopped moving. The studs were the only sound, then they stopped. We went out and heard the crowd cheer and I moved on to a different emotional level altogether. I was thinking, "Yeah, come on". The National Anthem came and you get back into that sombre emotion again. Then the crowd roared and I felt, "Right, I'm off again, let's go". There was the minute's silence and you are back down again. In that 15 minutes or so, you went through four different levels of emotion. When I knew we had to do the minute's silence, I kept gearing myself because I knew it would upset me. After me and my wife listened to Elton John during the funeral and then heard Earl Spencer's speech, I was still going through emotion. So when I heard 'Candle in the Wind' the next thing on my mind was Earl Spencer's speech. As we got to the silence, that was the first thing that forced itself into my mind. I kept looking at the referee to see how long we had got left, because I felt like I was welling up a bit. I didn't want to look at anybody else, I just tried to concentrate on the ref. There was a generator humming which you wouldn't normally hear. I didn't want to look at anyone else, like Gazza. We know he can cry and if he had started, it would have just triggered everything off. If I saw Gazza or anybody crying, then I would have cried. Just before the end of the silence, I was back and I was composed. I was just thinking about what he said and I was thinking, "Yeah, nice one". Once the ref blew the whistle, I was relieved because I didn't want to cry. I didn't want people to see tears and think, if I maybe didn't have a good game, "Oh, it affected him".

Back to the football. Italy were racked with self-doubt following their 0–0 draw in Georgia. 'Psychologically the edge has swung round to us now,' said Hoddle. 'We don't need to go there to win to qualify any more. I've always thought we could go there and win, but it takes the edge away because a draw will do us in the end. The pressure is just a little bit more on them now than on us. The Georgia result was a nice surprise. I didn't expect it. I thought Italy would go there and win. All in all it just shows what a good result ours was when we went out there and won 2–0.'

Not only had Italy dropped two vital points by only drawing with Georgia, they had also lost Roberto Di Matteo for the game against England as he picked up a second yellow card. There was also something of a crisis of confidence as the Italian media went to town. 'Maldini, what have you done?' blared the headline in Rome's daily *Corriere dello Sport*. 'The most practical, realistic and simple coach in our soccer was in the clouds for a day,' roared an editorial on the front page of *Gazzetta dello Sport*.

However, Zola came back fighting, and predicted that Italy would shatter England's World Cup dream. He warned that England would face a different Italian side. Zola said: 'Italy never makes mistakes on the big occasions. The destiny of the Italian team is to perform miracles and we are resigned to that reality. At Wembley we managed a miracle and we will have to repeat that feat in Rome. We can do it. We suffered in the first half against the Georgians and we admit they put us in difficulty. But in the second half it was one-way stuff and we dominated. I have always said that September is a difficult month for Italians and this team deserves faith from others because it has always responded well at difficult times. And in October, when we play England, we will be in much better physical condition. English morale will be up in the stars but we can count on home advantage. I am telling everyone to be optimistic – even those who are upset at the moment.'

One player who already felt his chances had gone was Chris Sutton. 'I think the best chance I have of going to Italy on 11 October is if I take the family on holiday. If England lose three or four strikers, then maybe I will have a chance. I said when the last squad was announced that if I couldn't get in then, perhaps I never would. But I want to play for my country. It's not for me to say I deserve a chance. That's up to Glenn Hoddle. But I'll be terribly disappointed if I don't get that opportunity.'

England (1) 4 Moldova (0) 0
Seaman (capt), G Neville, Southgate, Campbell, Beckham, Scholes, Batty, Gascoigne, P. Neville, Ferdinand, Wright

	P	W	D	L	F	A	Pts
England	7	6	0	1	15	2	18
Italy	7	5	2	0	11	1	17
Poland	6	2	1	3	7	9	7
Georgia	6	1	1	4	3	9	4
Moldova	6	0	0	6	2	17	0

CHAPTER TWENTY-TWO

Build-up to Rome

*England plan for the final showdown
against Italy, September 1997*

Gary Neville spoke for his fellow players when referring to England's most important match for many years, the final World Cup Group Two showdown with Italy in Rome. He said: 'You won't play in any bigger matches this year. If we don't qualify for the World Cup, then it's going to be an absolute disaster. I am confident, though, that we can go to Rome and get a good result.'

The police planned tough security measures: two security cordons around the Olympic Stadium, close searches, confiscation of anything that could be used as a missile – chains, heavy belt buckles, cigarette lighters, handfuls of coins and even keys. Detective Inspector Peter Chapman, head of the UK's National Criminal Intelligence Service Football Unit, warned: 'Whether it's your favourite cigarette lighter or a pocketful of loose change, you will not be allowed into the ground with it. We want fans to enjoy the game and we don't want them to have to part with anything of sentimental value. My advice is leave anything you don't need behind. Wear belts with small buckles, carry boxes of matches and not cigarette lighters, and change your money into notes.'

British police warned that up to 700 known hooligans – including 60–70 'hard-core' troublemakers – were expected to make the trip. The head of the British government's soccer task force, David Mellor, said: 'We mustn't allow the fact that there are some poisonous yobs who pollute our game to stop us speaking out for decent treatment for the overwhelming majority. Some people will behave badly but the art of policing is to differentiate between people who behave badly and those who do not. We made it clear we have no truck with these people. We wish they would go and lock themselves away for the weekend, they bring disgrace and shame on our country. We know that there are some scum who follow England, but the overwhelming majority are decent citizens.' Mellor reiterated his criticism of plans by Italian police to confiscate coins and other personal property that could be considered dangerous objects. 'I don't think asking respectable people to take coins out of their pockets does anything to stop hooliganism at football matches.'

The threat of violence at the game was put aside as Hoddle announced his squad. Hoddle's decision to axe Steve McManaman for the Moldova game had rekindled his appetite. Hoddle had carefully monitored his reaction to being dropped. 'Leaving him out has perhaps made him reflect a bit and I've seen an urgency that perhaps wasn't there in the beginning. He's worked hard to get back into the squad. I made a decision on what I felt was right at the time and I think it has worked out well. Steve has taken it in the right way. I wanted to see a positive response and I have. He is a talented player. When he's playing at his very, very best, he's up there among the best. He started the season slowly for whatever reasons, but he's picking up now and it's probably a good time to bring him back into the squad.' His team-mate Fowler also returned, despite not being back to full fitness.

Adams, Ince and Sheringham were among the list of 24 names that Hoddle was praying would still be fit when they got to Italy. Gascoigne and Seaman were also key men of vast experience and pedigree back on Hoddle's list of 'indispensables'. Wright, never really in contention in the early part of the campaign, was so fired up that he cushioned the loss of Shearer. Hoddle even had Andy Hichcliffe back, and Southgate had returned to form.

Hinchcliffe's return was timely as Ripley was ruled out by his hamstring injury. The Everton player had been a surprise debutant in Hoddle's first game in Moldova and had put in solid wing-back performances there and against Georgia and Poland before damaging cruciate knee ligaments. Hoddle said: 'There's quite a shortage of left-sided players in the country, let alone the squad. Andy's worked extremely hard for eight or nine months to battle back. He's almost there. It's been a bit stop-start but with Stuart [Pearce] not quite making it, it gives us a nice balance. The lad did excellent for us in the three games that he played so I'm very pleased to have him back in the squad. He's got a quality left peg.'

Hinchcliffe vowed to repay Hoddle for his faith. 'This is a real bonus and something I was not expecting. I just hope I can do well enough to say thanks to Glenn.' Hinchcliffe added 'Glenn has kept in touch with me throughout the time I have been out injured. He's rung about once a month and John Gorman has been on the phone a lot. It's been nice to know that they have not forgotten me, were interested in my progress and still felt I was in their plans.'

Adams, England's most experienced defender with 47 caps, was back to his best in the centre of Arsenal's defence. The 31-year-old would play alongside Campbell, who had filled the centre-back position with such distinction in the Tournoi de France. Arsene Wenger endorsed the selection of Adams. He said: 'When Tony came back from his injury a few weeks ago, I wondered if he could play so many games or if he would still be at risk with an old ankle problem. Yet he seems to have improved in fitness from game to game. I am confident he will do a good job for England and my feeling is I want England very much to go through. It is my football country now and also my Arsenal players are in the national squad.'

Hoddle's reputation would hinge on his final team selection, his decision to play Le Tissier at Wembley forgotten if he got it right in Rome. It was, as Hoddle

The Road to France

Right: Into the unknown for Hoddle in England's first World Cup qualifier, in Kishinev on 1 September 1996. But little seems to faze the newly appointed England captain Alan Shearer as he challenges the keeper Romanenco.

Right: The next mission abroad was in the equally hostile Georgia on 9 November 1996, but again England emerged with a clean sheet and a victory, Teddy Sheringham scoring the first goal.

Left: Alan Shearer comes to England's rescue with the first goal against Poland at Wembley. Hoddle was far from pleased with this performance even though England won 2–1.

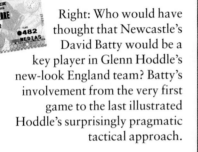

Right: Who would have thought that Newcastle's David Batty would be a key player in Glenn Hoddle's new-look England team? Batty's involvement from the very first game to the last illustrated Hoddle's surprisingly pragmatic tactical approach.

Left: England 0 Italy 1, Wembley, February 1997. Zola whips his shot past Walker before Campbell can make the challenge. Sol owned up to his error in England conceding the goal; more senior players did not.

Right: Chelsea's soon-to-be 1997 Footballer of the Year points to Costacurta in acknowledgement of the long-range pass over the head of Stuart Pearce that led to his Wembley goal.

Left: The game that will haunt Ian Walker for the rest of his life. As understudy to the injured David Seaman for the vital tie with Italy at Wembley, Walker's dream was shattered by Zola's winner.

Right: Down and out. Matt Le Tissier never recovered from the night England lost to Italy at Wembley when he shouldered the brunt of the blame along with the man who picked him.

Above: There was ample pain as well as glory on the Road to France. Stuart Ripley's big chance ended in abject misery, wheeled off in the World Cup tie with Moldova.

Above: Can anyone enjoy scoring goals for England more than Ian Wright? Unlikely. After taunts of 'you'll never score for England' over the years, he finally proved his international pedigree.

Above: A candle in the wind for Diana as the Wembley fans pay a special tribute before the game against Moldova on 10 September. There were tears as Elton John's song echoed around Wembley.

Right: A small but nonetheless touching floral tribute outside Wembley before the start of the game, now referred to as 'The Diana Match'.

Left: Busy, full of energy, and capable of scoring from deep positions – Paul Scholes is invaluable to England. Here the Manchester United player is about to be challenged by Moldova captain Alexandr Curtean at Wembley.

Above: The defining moment for Gascoigne. A cracking Wembley goal in a convincing 4–0 victory over Moldova on the night Italy drew in Georgia … it was all building up nicely for the showdown in Rome.

Right: An emotionally charged Wembley occasion comes to an end with Hoddle congratulating goalscorer Ian Wright. The black ribbons were a mark of respect for Princess Diana.

Left: Ian Wright's fine strike from Gascoigne's pass in the Wembley win over Moldova.

Right: Paul Gascoigne said that captain Paul Ince had looked like a pint of Guinness! This was the scene of Hoddle's greatest triumph on the Road to France. England will never forget their draw with Italy in Rome on 10 October 1997.

Below: Joy unconfined on the bench as the final whistle goes in Rome … and England are through to their first World Cup Finals' appearance for eight years.

United for Manchester and England – Teddy Sheringham and David Beckham celebrate qualification.

put it, the 'Cup Final of Cup Finals'. Despite the temptation to play it safe, Hoddle stressed: 'We're in a positive frame of mind and we are not approaching the game to get a draw, that would be a mistake.'

Hoddle had always insisted he did not read the papers – by picking Stan Collymore he seemed to underline that! Even by his own admission, Collymore was not living up to his £7 million reputation after moving to Villa from Liverpool. Ten games had brought only one goal, his partnership with Dwight Yorke was not working and there was plenty of adverse publicity. Collymore admitted the stick from the fans was getting to him, leaving him 'hurt' at being 'slaughtered' by the Holte End faithful. Yet Hoddle kept faith with him, explaining that he felt that deep below that troubled surface remained a superstar waiting to get out. 'I'd agree that Stan's not pulling up any trees in the way he and Brian Little would have liked,' said Hoddle. 'But I can see things in Stan that, if we can get him back to his very best, might suit us in international football. Sometimes you have to put that international head on, go for things that you're looking for as the England coach, rather than on the basis of what he's showing for his club at this moment. At the beginning of the season when I saw him, Stan was doing some very good things, and you know what a couple of goals could do for him. What I want to see is for Stan to be the player he was at Nottingham Forest, at his very best. I still think that's within his scope and if he can do that we've got an international footballer.'

Hoddle gave a less than coded warning to Sutton to keep his criticism quiet if he wanted to stay in his thoughts. The striker had publicly wondered what he had to do to get on the right side of Hoddle – the answer appeared to be to stop moaning and carry on playing well. 'If Chris wants to talk to me, I'm at the end of the phone,' said Hoddle, with scarcely-hidden annoyance. 'There are certain things we're looking for, certain moulds of players, and there's a possibility that Chris could be drafted in if certain people get injured. He's done nothing wrong and has had an excellent start to the season. But other players are pretty close to getting in as well.'

Manchester United had an opportunity to put a big dent in Italian confidence with their Champions' League match against Juventus. 'It would be great if United could get the result,' said Hoddle, who included seven Old Trafford stars in his 24-man squad. 'They've got to be confident because they played extremely well, particularly in the second half, last year. If they can get the result then there will be a psychological carry-on. A few firm tackles wouldn't be a bad idea either!'

The result was a good one as the English champions finally laid the bogey of Juventus in a heartstopping 3–2 victory. Beckham was brilliant along with his fellow England stars in demolishing Juve with goals from Sheringham, Scholes and Giggs. Beckham said: 'It's one of the great Manchester United performances that I have played in. It does give England a psychological boost before going to Italy next week.'

Attilio Lombardo could not believe how United had swept aside his former

Juventus colleagues. 'In some ways it means everything psychologically regarding the Italy–England game,' he said. 'In other ways it means nothing. United's team had several foreigners. Even their great goal was scored by a Welshman, Ryan Giggs. Does this truly represent an English side? I don't think so, although Teddy Sheringham and Paul Scholes took their chances well…England might think it is a dry run, but this was a club game. Nothing more, nothing less. Italy–England is important to both nations. There is hope it will be a beautiful game. I doubt it. Italy will score two quick goals and then close the door.'

Hoddle challenged his players to follow Manchester United's lead. 'United have done their bit and now it's our turn. We have learned a lot from this result, particularly mentally. I have always maintained that England are every bit as good as the biggest foreign teams, both at club and international level. United have proved that and now the players will all believe we can go to Rome and get the result we need.'

Paul Merson was a late call-up as a replacement for the injured Rob Lee, and although he wouldn't kick a ball against the Italians he still had a vital mission, his presence in the camp providing Adams with on-the-spot 'therapy'. Together in Rome they could provide 'counselling' for each other, saving the FA an enormous amount in telephone calls! However, Hoddle made it clear that Merson had been selected not as a 'mind minder' for Adams, but purely on footballing credentials. But he stressed: 'If the pair need a bit of time together, they can have it. Certainly in the early stages, when we played in Georgia, it was a problem area, but he has become a lot stronger in that area, as has Paul.'

There was an unexpected face at Bisham Abbey on the first morning of training. Liverpool's teenage sensation Michael Owen joined up with the squad at their Buckinghamshire training headquarters.

The 18-year-old striker had made a massive impression on the England coach since his arrival on the Premiership scene in the final fortnight of the 1996/97 season. He had continued to impress, initially filling in for Robbie Fowler and then keeping German striker Karl-Heinz Riedle out of the Liverpool team. His reward was the chance to get a little taster of the international scene.

Hoddle and his staff rammed home one simple message throughout the build-up to this crunch tie: 'You are good enough to do it.' Hoddle explained: 'I've always been focused, a guy that's had total belief in my own ability. As a coach now I have to get that through to my players.' Hoddle went on: 'We need to go down that tunnel in Rome with every single player 100 per cent in his mind and in his heart that we can do the job. If they've really got that belief and that inner steel, then we can do it. We're going over to Italy a day earlier than we would probably have done. We have a nice training camp over there, tucked away from anyone and the pressure that builds up subconsciously when you stay in this country. You can do without that. Perhaps we won't even let them have a paper when we're over there. I've never let outside things affect me. You have to cocoon yourself away where you're just wrapped up in your team.' But Hoddle emphasized that the greatest strain was on Italy. 'I like to reverse the roles and if you say this was at Wembley and we needed to win, that says it all. That is when the pressure and expectations would really be on. We haven't quite got that, but going to Rome is an absolute difficult task to get the result we need. But we will have the inner belief amongst us to go out and do the job.'

The England coach felt that this was the great test. 'This was always going to be the crunch game. It's got to be the biggest challenge I've had as a manager. I wish the game was tomorrow. I can't wait for it to come, especially as we haven't got any injury problems to deal with. I'm in a positive frame of mind, I know what team I want to play and I just hope I get the chance to play it. It's one of those games where you are desperate to play, you want to play more than any other game. It's going to be a fantastic occasion. As a player or a coach it's one you relish and look forward to and I can sense that in the players today.'

Gary Neville was still flying after the Champions' League destruction of Juventus. 'When Italy came to Wembley in February, we were probably in awe of them. But we're not any more. I don't think they're anything special. Look at Brazil, with a forward line of Ronaldo, Romario, Leonardo and Denilson, then look at Italy's forward line of Zola and Casiraghi and it's just not the same. It's definitely helped us playing against these guys every week in the Premiership. We build them up, but when you play them a couple of times you realize they're no better than us. They're very strong physically and mentally. But they're only human. They're not supermen. And I think the whole England team now feel the same way. For Zola we've got Wright, for Casiraghi there's Teddy Sheringham, Ince for Di Matteo, Beckham for Albertini. We match them man for man in every department. And in some we're better than them.'

Gianluca Vialli knows how Roman crowds can turn faster than the tide on the River Tiber. Chelsea's Italian stallion gave Glenn Hoddle a boost just 48 hours before D-Day in the Olympic Stadium by warning that the hostile Italian crowd could be to England's advantage. Vialli also identified Sol Campbell, Ian Wright and Paul Gascoigne as Hoddle's three lions likeliest to leave Italy in mourning after a mauling the night before. In an astonishingly frank assessment, Vialli said: 'If things go very, very wrong for Maldini, the crowd can be the 12th player for England. The Italians are apprehensive, not just because they are playing England but because they have to go out and win the game. The pressure is going to be intense because they dare not make a mistake. Manchester United's win against Juventus last week was very important because it has given the English confidence about playing Italy without an inferiority complex. That result was so important for England psychologically. If you always seem to lose against a nation, or teams from that nation, you can develop a complex about it. In the past, Italy have always had the ability to win the big games against England in World Cup qualifiers, but now I'm not so sure. In the past, I was always certain that we were ahead of the English, but now their level is virtually the same. It has been an important step for the Premiership to bring in managers and players from abroad and England have consequently improved a lot under Glenn Hoddle. On Saturday night, Italy have got to play an attacking game, and Campbell is going to be a key player in shutting out Casiraghi, Inzaghi and Zola. He is improving tactically and technically, he is growing stronger and tougher, he will have learned from the game at Wembley and I believe he is going to be a great player for Tottenham and England in the future. England will have to be very aware defensively, but that's where Campbell can be so important. The danger for Italy is that England can afford to sit very deep and play on the counter, and that's where Wright is the right man to give Italy real trouble. He is such a good player – he never seems to miss the target when he is given the right service. He is going to be a big worry for the Italian defenders.'

Gascoigne's return to the Olympic Stadium, where he had played two seasons for Lazio, was another source of concern for Vialli. 'He will feel it is something special to play in his former stadium and in front of so many people who used to cheer for him. Gascoigne knows it is a big match and I guess he is going to feel big pressure. But he has turned 30 now, and he should know how to handle the occasion. We all know he can be an important player for England and, deep down, he may feel it's his last chance of playing in the World Cup Finals. There is always the danger that he might get too worked up, too excitable, but he should have enough experience now to read the game and to be perfectly tuned in. I have a feeling he's going to play very well.'

Rome was to see a new Gascoigne. Gone the clown on crutches who suffered such public torture during his time with Lazio. For Gascoigne, the trip back to the Olympic Stadium represented his greatest challenge. He was beset with off-the-field problems with the threat of a writ from a photographer he clashed with during his time with Lazio and reports that the authorities wanted to speak to him about tax evasion but he needed to concentrate on his football.

When it comes to the moment of magic that can win a game, Hoddle remains a champion of Gazza as an equal of Zola, ironically both players he tried to buy for Chelsea. 'We had a good chat on Sunday when he arrived. The way he approached the Moldova game was different. I've not seen him do that before, in his preparation and the week's build-up he was a lot more focused and quieter. Then he went out and performed like that. He's learned a lot from that. Even his reaction after he scored, the interview he gave when he came off – it wasn't the normal Gazza. I think it's the Gazza that's needed at this moment in his career. That's going to stand him in good stead for this game. I don't think he will get carried away by all the hype. He knows now it's going to be a team effort if we're going to get the result.'

The signs were good. When Hoddle cut short the opening training session because the players were over-enthusiastic, Gascoigne was not the ringleader but one urging restraint. 'Paul's understanding now that he can add something to his game this way. He has the ability. He was a great runner with the ball, he still is at times, but the balance now is for one- or two-touch football which he plays excellently. That in many ways will make him an even better player for different reasons. I've seen him doing that more and more in training in the past 12 months. What changed him? I think the injuries have changed him. You have to adjust. The chats we've had over a period of time have also sunk in. People were saying I had to make a decision on him for the Georgia game away – it was never the case. With Paul, he needed some time for the things to sink in. Gradually he's understanding that at 29 or 30, for a footballer another set of curtains opens up and Paul is learning things about himself and as a footballer ... I'm a firm believer that if you look after your body and your mind you can play until you're 35 or 36. Baresi played in the World Cup Final at 36. You have to adjust your game and Paul is beginning to do that. This is the longest period of time he's had for many a year without a major injury. Nearly every time he's come with England he's always recovering from an injury, he's not quite 100 per cent fit. Moldova was the first time he was relatively fit. Now he's had more games under his belt.'

Ince has first-hand experience of the Italian mentality and feared that Gazza would be targeted. 'I played in Italy for two years and I know the way the Italians think. If they want to stop people like Gazza they will do so. When I arrived in Italy, our coach Ottavio Bianchi told me "if you don't get the ball, make sure you get the player". It's not that they put their foot in maliciously, it's how they block an opponent, little kicks that the Italians are good at. If they are winning 1–0 and Gazza is on the ball they'd rather stop him in our half than theirs.'

Ince still recalls the pain he and the rest of the England side felt in Rotterdam in 1993 when referee Karl Jozef Assenmacher, Ronald Koeman and Dennis Bergkamp conspired to end English dreams of a World Cup place in the United States. Ince believed that the fear of missing out on a place in the greatest show on earth would play a massive part. 'Saturday is similar to Rotterdam, but the difference is that for me and some of the other players, this is our last chance of playing in the World Cup. It was a big disappointment when we lost in Holland, but at the back of my mind I was able to tell myself that I had another chance, that I hoped I'd be in the same situation four years on. Now that's where we are today, and it makes it that much more important. If we don't make it this time, I'll feel that I'm never going to play in the Finals. The World Cup is the pinnacle of anybody's career and I can't think of how much it would hurt to miss out. It's not just me either. There's people like Ian Wright, Teddy Sheringham and Tony Adams as well. It would be a massive shame if all of us missed out on that.'

The Liverpool captain was adamant that he was entering his own last chance saloon, and added: 'We've just got to go out and do the business. We had the chance last year against Germany in Euro 96 and didn't do it, had the chance before that in Holland and missed out then. This is another chance, for many of us the last chance. But this time we're stronger and a lot better equipped. We want to go and win.'

Graeme Le Saux warned his World Cup team-mates about the smiling assassin. The Chelsea defender had seen the ruthlessness and sheer profession-alism of Zola at close quarters. 'I've really got to know Franco in the past six weeks since I joined Chelsea and we've been having some interesting conversations. He told me that he wouldn't speak to me for two weeks before the game ... and a week before would start kicking me! We've been having a few laughs about this game and he's been walking around the training ground with a John le Carre novel and an Anglo–Italian phrasebook recently. Maybe he's trying to get inside the English mentality. More likely, he just needs the books to stand on! We all know what Franco is capable of, and we have got to respect his fantastic ability as a player.'

As the Italian players gathered for training on the same day as England, the potential absence of veteran defender Ciro Ferrara was their most troubling problem. Alessandro Nesta was destined to be his replacement but the switch would mean a drop in talent and experience. Midfield also presented problems, with Roberto Di Matteo suspended and Antonio Conte injured. AC Milan's Demetrio Albertini, usually the motor at midfield, had been sub-par all season, but it was unlikely that Maldini would drop him from the starting eleven. For England, Les Ferdinand was forced out with a recurrence of his stomach strain, while Robert Lee was 'devastated' to miss out also through injury.

Cesare Maldini warned his players about going hell for leather at England. Counselling his men against committing themselves too soon into attack, he said: 'We will not make the mistake of throwing ourselves scatter-brained into attack,' he said. 'We have to play with judgement and intelligence, playing in a certain way but being ready to change if the first way is not working. The truth is that if we attack in a chaotic way, we will be open to the counter-attacks from England.'

Maldini then dismissively suggested Hoddle's side were easy to read and lacked the tactical nous to change their own game plan. 'The English are not like the Spanish, the Germans, or ourselves,' he said. 'They can only play to a certain way. We know what that is, and that they will always play the game with 100 per cent effort. That is their mentality – they play with their hearts.'

For all Maldini's words, the jitters were beginning to affect the Italian camp and the coach admitted Manchester United's win over Juve had been a psychological blow. 'That game counts to a certain point,' he conceded. 'It was a game played in an excited atmosphere and the crowd played their part. But we must look to our fans to do that in the Olympic Stadium. I remember the magical nights they created for us in Italia 90, and we want the same on Saturday.'

Maldini tried to be positive about his side's chances, although, perhaps tellingly – and unlike Hoddle's undimmed confidence and belief – he was prepared to countenance the prospect of Italy not winning. 'Italy doesn't hide and we always go out to win, but we have to be aware of our opponents,' he said. 'There can be bad luck, however, and your efforts are not always translated in the result.' Maldini added: 'The history of English soccer shows that English teams have a certain idea about playing games, even away games. I mean they come to win them, they come out to play, not to look for a draw.' Maldini believed that Italy might have a slight psychological advantage, not just from playing Saturday's game at home, but also from beating England 1–0 in their first group meeting. 'No matter what you say, that was a nice stroke,' he said. 'Not many sides go to Wembley and win a World Cup qualifier.' The Italian coach was unconcerned by England's revenge in the friendly tournament in France. 'We weren't in the right condition either mentally or physically, for that game. England came into that match after a period together in preparation for their World Cup game against Poland, while we played them on a Wednesday when most of my players had been playing in Italian league games just three days before.' Maldini conceded, however, that England might have improved since last February. 'I said after England beat us in France that they had played more carefully, more cannily than before.'

While Hoddle stressed that this was a game for experience, he also made the point that you don't need grey hairs to be a veteran. Beckham agreed: 'Personally I feel very experienced, experienced enough to play in any game. At Manchester United the pressure is always high enough, but I go into most games hoping to play well and win. I've played in teams that have won a lot of trophies, great teams, and it's nice to be associated with such teams as Manchester United and England who like to play great football.'

Beckham would face the world's greatest left-back, Paolo Maldini, for the second time. He said: 'It's great to play against someone like him and it can only be good for my career. All opponents have different qualities and Maldini is great going forward as well as defending. He might be a great player but I don't fear anyone. I'm not scared about facing the Italians, we play against a lot of them in the Premier League now anyway. Alex Ferguson brings us up to win right the way through the youth ranks and we're not worried about anything, we certainly cannot fear the Italians. We're not fearing them at all, we're looking forward to facing them. There is an air of confidence around the place, we're really hyped up for it, I'm a confident person and in the England training camp there's a good atmosphere.'

Paul Gascoigne would be cheered on by his four Italian fan clubs in Rome. The Italians still love him for his exploits with Lazio, even though they were cut short by injury. Gazza refused to talk about his first return to Rome for nearly two years but his close confidante and advisor Mel Stein told me: 'He still receives bundles of fan mail from Italy, the fans out there still follow his fame and fortune. Gazza knows just how popular he still is out there and so many fans have told him they will be cheering him on although of course they want Italy to win. They all accept how unlucky he was through injuries and what a difficult situation it was for him out there.' Stein also explained the reason behind Gazza's rehabilitation. He told me: 'For a whole year he's been out of trouble because he has realized that football is his livelihood and he has become very, very focused. It's as simple as that.'

CHAPTER TWENTY-THREE

'Here We Go…'

Italy v England, Rome, 11 October 1997

There was an air of anticipation as England's players boarded the 15.30 charter at Luton airport. On their arrival in Rome after a near three-hour journey, they were whisked away to their hotel, the upmarket La Borghesian on Via Della Capanna Murata. During the build-up to the Italy match, Hoddle instructed the FA's Head of Media Affairs, David Davies, to contact all newspaper sports editors, requesting that they steer away from team insights and strategy secrets. But with no co-operation forthcoming, Hoddle was left with the usual tactic of giving as little away as possible, and even deliberately misleading the press.

Hoddle's elaborate attempts to keep all team news strictly confidential seemed to be sabotaged by Roy Hodgson who was seconded as part of the 'management team' for this one-off tie. Hoddle made a point of refusing to divulge any specifics when he announced an injury problem with Gareth Southgate but his interpreter, Hodgson, rose from his seat next to Hoddle and pointed to his right thigh just above the knee! Just a moment before Hoddle had refused to give any details of the injury. Was it a blunder or, just another smokescreen? In reality, Hoddle was more than happy for everyone to think Southgate was a serious doubt because he wanted to throw the Italians off the scent of his line-up.

There was also subterfuge over David Beckham. When I asked the England doctor, John Crane, at Luton Airport, he told me that the player was on routine medication and that there was no real problem. But Hoddle eagerly perpetuated speculation that Beckham might not make it to try and confuse the Italians even more. He readily told the gathered media: 'Beckham has a heavy cold and I'll have to keep an eye on that. I wouldn't say it's got any worse, but I wouldn't say it's got any better, he's just got some sort of heavy cold on his chest. We've still got some work on him, but we do have another couple of days to shift what's on his chest but sometimes these things take a lot of time. Because it is such a big game it will be left open, a decision will be made between the player, myself and the medical team.' Hoddle said more significantly: 'We can all play with a cold, and with three substitutes there are plenty of options for changing it. It is now a squad situation.'

Tony Adams had discovered a more subtle form of motivation than his old head-banging style. The day before his 31st birthday, the Arsenal man revealed:

'Me banging on toilet doors never won a football game. My scoring a goal or good defending is what wins games.' So he wouldn't be hyping anybody up – he would be calming them down. 'We will all be motivated for this one, so it will be a case of calming some of the younger boys down. You can go over the top in terms of enthusiasm and running around like headless chickens.' Adams continued: 'We've always had determination, we've always given 100 per cent. Now we need a bit of knowledge, a bit of calming down, a bit of focusing on the right way to do things. That would be my only advice. The players have enough talent, there is a fantastic amount of it in this squad, but I see my role as passing on a little bit of experience. We've always known we've had talent and heart but sometimes we've lacked knowledge. For too often, English players have been stereotyped in the way they've performed, but there's been a big switch at international level because we've now examined the way we play.'

He reflected: 'In the past I've been jumping up and down with anxiety before a game like this. Now I'm relaxed about the way I feel. I will have the normal kind of anxieties before a football match, but I can control them because I am aware of what they are. I'm out there to be judged. But I judge myself more than you will judge me and that judgement will be based on whether we qualify.'

Adams agreed that it was some senior players' last chance of appearing in the World Cup Finals. 'I'm running out of time now, so it all intensifies for me. I realize it probably is my last chance, as Paul Ince said it was his last chance. I know what it's all about. The qualities that made me a success in my professional life are the good points I work on for my private life now. Whatever I managed to focus on in the past 17 years, I can use now. I can still put that into my football game. Sometimes I don't succeed, but I try. Yes, I have an addiction now. For some time I've had an addiction which makes me get up on Monday mornings and try to improve myself on the football pitch. I just handle it differently these days. It's still a wonderful game and that's why I have done it for so long. If I didn't love my profession I'd get out. I've realized what a great profession I'm in and I don't think I take it for granted – in the past, maybe I got lost. But I realize I'm a lucky guy given a wonderful opportunity and the reality is I'm still here. I might have been looking for work – that could have been my reality.'

Hoddle wrote to Adams when he was in prison. The two go back a long way as they were team-mates during the European Championships of 1988. 'He needed a bit of encouragement. Even though he wasn't ready to listen to it at the time, he is now,' said Hoddle. 'He has had to go through an awful lot before the penny drops. But he has changed his ways, he is a changed person. He has grown up as a person. He has had to endure an awful lot to come through it all and it has also made him a better player because he appreciates his football more than before. I would have loved to have had Tony more often in my team than I've had. He has experience of his own game and he can also help others, and he will need that against Italy.'

David Seaman exuded his usual calm. He commented: 'We just have to focus that much more. I know what is building up, I know that if I don't concede a goal, that is it – England qualify. Hopefully, I will keep a clean sheet, but it's all about the result, whether it's 0–0 or 4–4.' Although Seaman was as laid back as ever he admitted that he was worried at not seeing the ball clearly in the glare of the Olympic Stadium's unfamiliar floodlights during the training session.

Teddy Sheringham was as pragmatic as ever. 'Hopefully, I'll be playing,' he said laconically, 'so, I'll be a target of some kind. I am looking forward to it.' He then gave his views on Italian defenders: 'They are very clever in their manner. Perhaps it won't be a straight-out kick like the English, but they will have their first 'tackle' in some way. Football is always physical, but in different ways at different levels. Against Italy, it won't be like Wimbledon pumping the ball up in the air and then battling for that. If you watch from the corners, Italian defenders don't let you move at all. They actually start with the hands round you. How it's not a foul, I'll never know. But they seem to get away with it and so you have to adapt to that. You have to manoeuvre away from that and find your own space by losing your man.'

There would be no frills, no Le Tissier experiments, no risks. Hoddle had been bold in the past, but now the priority was getting his defence right. Adams, Campbell and Southgate would form a secure three-man central defence with two full-backs ensuring the Italians had limited options in attack.

Hoddle divulged that Paul Ince, not Adams, would be captain. 'The reason I've gone for Paul is because he's made for this game. He has come back from Italy with a lot of respect after playing extremely well in Serie A. The Italians respect him as a player and our own players respect him. He has skippered the team before and I have every confidence in Paul leading the team for this match. He's at the hub of the team – the area of the field that will be central to controlling the game. If we are going to win the game, midfield will be the vital area.'

Hoddle took Adams to one side to explain and was delighted by the reaction. 'We had a short conversation to explain the situation and he was 100 per cent fine. He hasn't been long back from injury and I told him that if he had ten games under his belt and he was flying there was a good possibility that he would have been skipper. But if he is out there, I want him concentrating totally on doing the job in hand.'

Hoddle, as deliberately devious as ever, was not even prepared to concede that Adams would make the starting line-up. 'If Tony plays, it would have been difficult for him with the added responsibility when he's been out for such a long period. Some of the games have been a test – but others have not. His last game was a 5–0 win against Barnsley, and that was not a big test. Character? No problem. In fact, he's a lot calmer off the pitch and he still shows signs of being as good a captain of Arsenal as he ever was. If the game was another three weeks away, there's every likelihood he would have led the team out – but the game is tomorrow. I suppose if I'd given it to Tony, I would have been asked why I had not given Paul Ince the captaincy.'

Hoddle equally gave every indication that Adams would play, just falling short of actually naming him. 'If I feel Tony is right mentally and physically Tony will play.' Confused. Well, you had to be well briefed to follow the plot.

Ince was predictably delighted. 'I am always very proud to captain my country, but never as chuffed as I will be tomorrow night. Leading the team out in Italy, where I had two terrific years, will be such a big thrill. To win the match would mean everything to me. Usually I like coming out last, behind the rest of the team, but this will be very different. Glenn spoke to me on Thursday evening and told me of his decision. It was the most thrilling moment of my life.'

Hoddle's choice was backed by Hodgson, who had managed Ince for 18 months at Inter Milan. 'Paul's perfectly equipped to rise to the job he's been given and I feel it was a very intelligent choice by Glenn,' said Hodgson. 'I know Paul, and I know he'll be extremely motivated for the task. He will be very proud to lead his country out and it could not mean more to anybody. Glenn's obviously given the matter a lot of thought and I can only congratulate him on his choice of skipper.'

The Italian press were keen to interview Gascoigne, but the England star was being kept under lock and key by Hoddle. One correspondent accused the England coach of operating a 'Soviet regime'! 'We can't keep everyone happy,' said Hoddle. 'We never made any commitment as far as Paul was concerned.'

Paolo Maldini saluted his opposing captain. 'Ince is a leader, whether he has an armband on or not. It comes naturally to him. He is a great player who puts his heart into everything he does, and we know it will be hard with him as England leader.'

Hoddle put forward his thoughts on his main striker for the game, Ian Wright. He said: 'We proved that in the tournament when we left out Alan against Italy and Ian Wright gave us an extra bit of pace and movement, probably more than Les or Alan. Ian Wright can get round the back of defenders with his pace, and that is a dying art but something we will need. In many ways Ian Wright has made that his way of playing, particularly away from home.' Hoddle demanded a disciplined display as for most of the game he would be a lone striker. 'I want his hold-up play to be spot-on. Sometimes it is, sometimes it's not. But if it is, he will give us a base up there which will be an added bonus. To be at his best he has to feel very, very relaxed, but there have been times when he's played for England and he's been uptight. Perhaps when he's uptight, not on the same wavelength as the coach, there can be problems with him and I know that can be a fact because it wasn't so long ago that I was playing myself. Ian Wright is an infectious character, he puts a hell of a lot into his training and in many ways that's a good example. He's looked forward to this game for a long time in his mind, he's been hoping to start and put in a good performance.'

Hoddle believed England had to score. 'We've been working exactly on that. If we can get our noses ahead, it will be a pressure pot for them. The intimidation thrown at us in the early stages will be thrown back at them. We have to make movement to open them up and make it happen on the night, but it's up to the players because you go to sit on the bench and they go on the pitch. We have to show the mental qualities we did in Georgia and Poland, and the atmosphere around the camp is so relaxed, you wouldn't believe it's such a big game coming up.'

It was by no means a classic Italy team, but under Cesare Maldini they had not conceded a goal in five World Cup qualifying matches. The word from within the Italian camp was that they feared a partnership of Sheringham and Wright and were unsure of their own front pairing. They were also unsure of the defence and had not decided whether to go with a back four or three.

In theory, England could have qualified before they took the field if Scotland had performed one of their infamous slip-ups against Latvia. Hoddle laughed as he said: 'If Scotland trip up, we will come out at half-time with our party hats on!'

Two hours before the kick-off, the giant screens at either end of the Olympic Stadium showed a selection of great Italian goals – Luigi Riva, Paolo Rossi with a stooping header in his hat-trick against Brazil in the 1982 World Cup, etc. Predictably, the footage of Zola's strike against England got the biggest cheer. The England squad sauntered on to the pitch to sample the atmosphere, some with their tracksuit tops tied around their waist. For a couple of minutes, they watched familiar images such as the events of the 1966 World Cup Final. No-one could mistake the figure of Bobby Moore as he limbered up in a rather more gentle way than players warm up these days.

Sir Bobby Charlton had predicted a goalless stalemate. In order to fulfil his prophecy, Hoddle outwitted Maldini as England became the first nation to stop the formidable sequence of 15 straight World Cup wins in Rome. Hoddle started it with one of the shortest and sharpest pre-match team talks. All the hard work, the preparation, the ground work had been laid down on the training pitch and in the team hotels. But before his players left the privacy of the dressing room, he made this address. Hoddle recalled: 'I said: "I can see you, you, you and you getting too excited." I went on: "I'm throwing the challenge down to you before the game even starts to deal with it. We will win this game. We will get this result if we keep eleven players on the pitch."' Hoddle explained: 'All the work had been done by that stage. I was just concerned to keep up the mental strength. We had to go down the tunnel with that inner belief and when I looked at the players in the dressing room before the game, I knew we had that. When I looked at the players' eyes, I knew.'

Hoddle talked briefly about the Italians playing three up front and how to combat that; everything else had been covered in the build-up. Hoddle's game plan came off in every category. 'Kidology' used to be a weapon of England's opponents but now Hoddle won the mind games. Beckham was supposedly wheezing with influenza to the extent he couldn't breathe at the end of Friday's training session and had to be helped off by the doctor clutching his chest. Southgate supposedly had no chance because of a thigh injury. Yet both played a full and powerful part in the triumph. Hoddle gave the game away over the true extent of Beckham's ailment, when he said: 'He had a cold, yes, we played it up a little bit, but he had a cold.' But it was the Italians who caught cold and Maldini, to his credit, paid tribute to the way the England team had negated the menace of Zola. 'England are a very good team, especially in the middle where their players had personalities. We suffered a lot and battled very well. I have no reason to reproach anyone. I think our team did everything possible to win. Zola played too wide, wider than we intended, but I don't blame him for that. To England's credit he was forced to go wide.' Zola was substituted after 62 minutes for Del Piero – to a great cheer from the England fans.

Hoddle was delighted when Maldini changed his strategy. He said: 'I was surprised Italy changed their system to 4–4–2, which suited the way we were playing. We were pleased to see four across the middle with Zola wide on the left, and when he was pushed inside, that gave us more space for Beckham. Everything we attempted came off, apart from getting a goal. It was a very professional, very controlled performance. My main concern just before the game, what I said to the players before we came out was to concentrate on our temperament, it was most important to keep eleven players on the field at all times and it's all credit to players like Beckham, Ince and Le Saux.'

'That wasn't the England which used to just boot the ball upfield. They've improved a lot even in the time since we played them at Wembley,' said Paolo Maldini, who hobbled out of a bruising encounter with a badly twisted ankle.

Dutch referee Mario van der Ende booked six Italians and sent off Angelo Di Livio for a vicious tackle on Campbell. The idiotic suggestion that he would be biased because he loved anything Italian was disproved with a courageous performance. 'Absolutely magnificent,' was Hoddle's assessment. 'I'm sure the Italians wouldn't agree! Even if we hadn't qualified, I'd be saying the same thing; it was the finest refereeing performance I've seen for many years and I shook his hand afterwards and told him so.' In such a hostile atmosphere few referees would have shown such bravery.

Paolo Maldini limped out after his attempts to foul England's skipper backfired; he was carried off after bouncing off his intended target and twisting his ankle. 'The ref was really good because there was a lot of stuff going on out there,' Ince added. 'I thought he'd given a penalty when Del Piero went over in the box, but he showed he wasn't going to be pressured into home decisions and that gave us encouragement to make our tackles.' That was a view shared by Wright, who said: 'Some of the stuff they were up to was quite intimidating, but we weren't going to let them bully us. We beat them at their own game and did a real Italian job on them.'

The game's most tense moments came at the death, when no sooner had Wright struck an upright than play switched to the other end where the Italians came close to a goal four minutes and 29 seconds into injury time, Christian Vieri heading inches wide from Del Piero's cross. Hoddle had always said he would know the moment his players walked out of the tunnel whether they were focused enough to win and he said: 'I had that feeling ... until that header! It's amazing how a game can take you through so many emotions, we hit the post, Teddy nearly scored from the rebound and that was the first time they opened us up. I really thought it was in the back of our net. David Seaman said afterwards: "It was always going wide, gaffer." I wish I'd known that at the time.'

Hoddle and his coaching entourage were deliriously happy at the way England had qualified at the top of a tough group. 'It was a proud moment when the whistle went,' reflected Hoddle. 'It was a proud moment when I joined the players in the dressing room. We have lifted the country and anyone who enjoys their football, it shows you what football can do to unite them and we have given them fantastic enjoyment in how we have qualified, with mature performances ... I'm extremely proud. Not only for qualifying for the World Cup after an eight-year wait but I'm also proud for the nation. We deserved to win and as a perfectionist I'm a bit disappointed. The Italians deserved seven out of ten for their performance. We were eight out of ten and that's why we got the result we needed.'

In the pandemonium at the final whistle Wright led the extravagant celebrations. His temperament had held impeccably under provocation ranging from blatant to brutal and he was coming home a national hero. He was not basking in the personal glory of a priceless goal but in a display of selfless running and absorption of crude tackles. He proved he could take a battering without responding in kind. But the everlasting imagery would be of Paul Ince and his head swathed in bandages, his shirt red with his own blood – Terry Butcher personified. The inspirational skipper battled on despite six stitches in a gaping head wound. The only threat to his complete dominance of the battle zone came from kit manager Martin Grogan. Ince said: 'I had to go all the way down to the dressing room for the stitches but when we got there the door was locked. It's a hell of a long way from the pitch as it is but we were stuck in the corridor for at least five minutes before we could get the door open. Glenn Roeder was going mad and I was shouting and screaming at all these geezers in Italian but the physio, Gary Lewin, had to go all the way back to the dug-out to get the key from Martin Grogan.'

Ince, one of the most focused and self-assured players in the business, admitted that even he was affected by the huge occasion. 'I've never been so nervous before a game as I was tonight. I cared so much about this game that I felt physically sick. I spoke to Dave Seaman and he said he felt sick too. He even said that at one stage he felt he was going to have to go to the toilet and physically be ill, it was that bad. I could feel my stomach going. But I just kept on telling myself: "It will be all right, it will be all right." And it turned out that way as well. I didn't want to come back to Italy as the captain of a losing side, so to do the business here has got to rate alongside anything I've achieved in my career. I've won League Championships and played in FA Cup Finals, but this night is right up there with them. The feeling at the final whistle was just unbelievable. I just wanted to grab hold of everyone, hug them and start singing. Wrighty came through to me and he was in tears and that made me feel like crying as well. The last ten minutes were pretty panicky because we gave them silly free-kicks and put ourselves under pressure and it's such a great relief that I'm finally going to the World Cup. But there was no champagne flowing in the dressing room because I think what we've achieved is only just beginning to sink in. After Euro 96 we all felt we could really go on to achieve something. If we hadn't got a result tonight we'd have achieved nothing. We owed the Italians this one because it really hurt to lose to them at Wembley. We felt before the game that we were the better side and we've gone out and proved that.'

Ince was convinced that England would continue to progress under Hoddle. 'A lot of people said Terry Venables should have stayed on as manager, but Glenn has taken us to a new dimension. We've played four World Cup qualifiers away from home without conceding a goal. That shows just how well Glenn has prepared us. He told us before that game that we had to have absolute belief in ourselves, and if everyone did that, he was convinced we'd go out and get a result. We're getting to be a very good team. And we're going to be even better. We've got four or five friendlies before the Finals next year and there's time to improve even further.'

Terry Butcher was part of the media corps. I spoke to him as he strolled into the conference room for the post-match interviews. He knew exactly how Ince felt as the torrents of blood began staining his England shirt. Eight years ago Butcher's face and white shirt had been painted red after a head wound in a World Cup qualifier in Sweden. The central defender had refused to leave that Stockholm pitch after being bandaged up and headed balls away all night as Bobby Robson's team claimed a vital point. 'There wouldn't have been any thought in Paul's mind about staying off,' said Butcher, who winced as he saw Demetrio Albertini's elbow crack into Ince's head. 'It's a difficult place to get any protection on the wound, but when you're the captain of your country, in a World Cup qualifier, you just don't want to come off. If he'd been forced off, that's a different matter, but no Englishman in their right mind would want to come off in that situation. A continental-type player might only need that as an excuse in a game like that but when you pull on that shirt it's in our make-up to shrug it aside and get on with your job.' Butcher smiled at being told Ince had ended up with six stitches. 'He's almost there. I had nine! But I knew what he was going through. When it happened in Sweden it was clumsiness on my part. You haven't got much flesh there, and the blood vessels are near the surface – it's going to bleed a lot. If anything, though, it makes you more determined. You can't really see what's happened – although you can feel it. It doesn't hurt. You know there's something not right – you can hardly miss that – but it doesn't stop you running, tackling and heading. You don't feel it that much. It's just an inconvenience.'

Revenge was deliciously sweet, and Gascoigne made sure his Italian critics knew all about it. He avenged the put-down he received when he was shown the door by Lazio. He crowed: 'The club's President Cragnotti said the next time I'll be in Italy, I'll be on holiday. Wasn't it a nice holiday?' It was a sobering thought for Italian football as Gazza gleefully explained how England had outwitted, outplayed and outfought the Italians. 'We played the Italians at their own game. Diving, cheating and wasting time, if they had scored a goal they'd have done all that. So, wasn't it just lovely to keep the ball away and let them chase it. It was great seeing them running after the ball, they were desperate.'

Gazza was at the hub of some truly beautiful possession football, usually the exclusive prerogative of the Italians. Hoddle's team negated their trickery, not just on the ball, but also the slippery tactics for which they are famed. Gazza said: 'They know it all, pulling shirts, diving, feigning injury, and we really had to concentrate as well as play our game. It was hard. Some of our lads stayed down when they were not hurt. The crowd threw bottles and coins on the pitch at me and that was good as well, it wasted even more time.' An England team successfully sneakier than the Italians! It wasn't a pretty match, but you'll never find a more tense, nail-biting experience. You felt proud to be an Englishman – provided you turned away from those notorious scenes of violence off the pitch, if that were possible.

Gazza epitomized that spirit. Normally he needs cajoling to face the media, even a hand-picked sector, but this time he was only too eager to accommodate the senior football writers. When he walked into a small room in the bowels of the Olympic Stadium to be greeted by less than a dozen journalists, he hardly needed to be asked a question, he could hardly stop talking. 'I can walk out of here with my chest out, I can be proud. It's been a long time since Italia 90, almost eight years with no World Cup, sad football times. Then we had a good European Championships, we qualified for the World Cup and now let's have a great World Cup. As a team performance it was absolutely brilliant, and if I make it to the World Cup I can't ask for anything more. My career has been great, I've never had any regrets about it.' Without drawing breath he then proceeded to discuss all of his regrets! 'There are regrets about the stupid things I've done, the bad times, the ligaments, the kneecaps. But the good times are right now. I left Italy in 1990 in tears, but I was proud to come back with Lazio and injuries let me down, and again I left on a sad note. Now I'm leaving Italy with a smile on my face.'

Hoddle paid tribute to Gazza's controlled, more calculated, intelligent approach: 'Particularly in the first half, he was magnificent. They couldn't get near him. He had the respect of the Italians. OK, he's not got that explosive burst, and even now his fitness levels could be higher, and I took him off at the right time as fatigue levels were setting in. He still lacks high-power games.'

Despite Gazza's fears that the Old Trafford kids would usurp his place, Hoddle will leave a place open for Gazza. However, if for some reason he doesn't make it, Gazza's great wish is for his fellow eccentric, Ian Wright, to be there at the ripe old age of 34. Wright is a kindred spirit. Gazza said: 'I hope Ian Wright plays in the World Cup. He has come into the game late and broken records, but I'll never forget when I spoke to him after he was left out of the Euro 96 squad, he was so sad and gutted. But he picked himself up and broke records, that man deserves it, he ran and ran for the team, it was a thankless task, but no-one could have done it better. There were a few tears from him at the end. I'll be a year older at the next

World Cup and I'm going to have to work harder, but if I don't get to the World Cup, I want Ian Wright to go.'

Gazza and Wright shed tears of joy while hugging each other at the final whistle. Wright could not hide his elation. 'It was one of the most exciting nights of my life. We're going to France and after our performance in Rome, we're the team everyone will fear. So why shouldn't we have a great chance of winning it?' Gazza was full of belief. 'We can win it. If I didn't think we could go to France and succeed, I wouldn't even bother making the trip. It would be a waste of time. But we can go all the way and I believe we can because of all these young lads who will be a year older and a year wiser.'

Gazza intended to prove that he remains good enough to play on the biggest stage of all and beat off the opposition of the Manchester United wonder kids. 'When I was first in the England team, there were experienced players like Terry Butcher, Bryan Robson, John Barnes, Chris Waddle, Trevor Steven and Peter Beardsley, they brought me on, you could always learn from them. Now, over the next year, year-and-a-half, they can learn from me – perhaps not off the pitch, but certainly on it. Next year I'll be a year older and I'll wish I could turn back the clock by the time the World Cup comes along because I've got to keep all these little gits off my back. It's going to be a great tournament, but there will be a fight for places.' Gazza reached the heights in Italia 90. He saw signs during Le Tournoi of how close England are coming to taking the Brazilians' world crown. 'It was great stuff out there in France last summer. We could see how the Brazilians can play, how they can keep the ball, and we've got to bring that into our game as well. We've got to punish teams as we did against Holland in the European Championships and against Moldova in the World Cup, even though with Moldova it was a great performance.' Gazza knows, deep within himself, that despite Hoddle's caring assertion that he can play into his late thirties, he's only going to be in his prime for the next two years.

Ian Wright said: 'It's not every week we get to put one over on Italy, and I was gutted that my shot hit the post when I had the chance to win it deep into injury time. The boss was brilliant about it, told me I had played my part in a real team effort and that I made an important contribution in other ways apart from putting the ball in the net. That's what I like about the England set-up: it doesn't matter how much of a superstar you are at your club – we are all just part of a team once there are three lions on your shirt.' Wright was very keen to make the trip to France 98. 'The longer your career goes on, the more you want to play against the biggest teams on the biggest stage, and in the past I had wondered whether the chance to play in the World Cup Finals would slip away from me. I wasn't that far away in 1990, when Bobby Robson picked me for the B-team which included Tony Adams, David Batty and Gazza. Graham Taylor said he would have picked me for the 1994 Finals in the States – but, of course, we didn't manage to qualify. And when the qualifying draw for this tournament was made, all the talk was about who would finish second behind Italy in our group. I'm told that, when our name came out of the hat with the Italians, everyone in the arena went "Phooaarr". Now we've beaten them to qualifying, I'll bet there's a few people across Europe going "Phooaarr" at our achievement. When it was all over on Saturday night, I can't describe the feelings of elation and relief of a job well done. It was one of the greatest moments of my life and certainly my proudest moment in football. The vocal support from our fans inside the stadium was magnificent and I threw my shirt to them at the end because we did it for them and everyone back home. In the dressing room afterwards, all the boys were hyper, hugging each other and savouring the moment. The buzz was fantastic – I was so psyched up to do well that it's hard to express our satisfaction in words. On the plane home, everyone was still on cloud nine. I've been on some long trips abroad before when the long journey home has been a real drag, but this one was special. When we collected our bags at the airport, it was a tremendous feeling to think that, next time we meet up, we'll be safely in the World Cup Finals – and who knows how far we can go from there?'

England now feel equipped to take on the best in the world, based on the dominance of the defence. Seaman said: 'We can get better. We had a great Euro 96 and we have carried that on. You can be proud to be English. I heard someone say afterwards that it is our turn now and I agree with that. There is a positive and confident atmosphere among the players. You saw that in the way we played against Italy. It was a hell of a decision to go with three at the back in a match like that but it worked. And it worked well. We have won the group and that is a magnificent achievement. We are in the Finals and there is no need for us to fear playing anybody.'

For Le Saux, the result was something of a milestone for English football. 'We showed we were able to handle pressure. As Tony Adams said afterwards, the atmosphere against Italy was the most intense we have ever faced. And we handled it brilliantly as a team. We are getting confidence and belief and that showed in how we created the best chances in the match.'

Southgate said: 'The noise was so great, we couldn't even hear the National Anthem. But I found the atmosphere inspirational and there was a surge of confidence throughout the team. We were unafraid, even on such a big night, to play football from out of defence. There was a time when other nations thought all we offered were standard English attributes of speed and power. We wouldn't have been mentioned in the same breath as the Italians or Spaniards. That has changed as we have become more sophisticated in the way we play.' Forever doomed to be identified as the man who missed that penalty against Germany at Wembley in the semi-finals of Euro 96, a lesser man might have shrunk from the challenge to reclaim his place.

Typically, Hoddle was almost instantly thinking ahead to France. 'The hard work starts now. We've come through a tough group, winning three away games and drawing in Rome when we deserved to win.' As he spoke to a handful of journalists in the bowels of the stadium, the chants of 'England, England' were still echoing in the background. He said: 'Let's hope there is more to achieve, that we can put our 'wedding suit' on when we win the tournament. For the moment it is a proud night for me personally and for the nation, it is eight years since we qualified for the World Cup. In many ways it's more satisfying to reach the World Cup Finals as a manager than a player because I have to look after every single angle. Now we've qualified, the hard work starts because we are setting ourselves standards and we want to do well when we get there. We are growing as a squad and that's because we've done so well away from home off the back of playing at Wembley throughout Euro 96. We are not the finished article to take on the likes of Brazil and Germany although during the summer tournament we made progress. But that would have been a waste of time if we hadn't qualified.'

Now Hoddle set his sights on winning the World Cup. He said 'We've got no more chance than anybody else and no less chance. The important thing is that we are there and have avoided the play-offs. Something is growing in the squad, we have an inner belief.' Success brings glory and prestige, defeat brings ridicule and the sack. Even in his proudest moment, as he reflected on England's triumph, he said: 'You either get a massive pat on the back, or a massive knife in the back. You know that from the very first moment the coach is on a hiding to nothing. You can be the greatest one minute and then make a bad substitution and lose 1–0 ... '

In the aftermath of the game, the coach containing the England team was held up in one of the underpasses leading away from the stadium. The FA's head of security, Adrian Titcombe, explained that an FA cameraman had been detained in the stadium because of the security measures, so the coach had to wait for him to be let out with members of the England Travel Club ... at a very late 1 am!

Italian police chief, Stadium Commander Filippo Piritore blamed the English for the trouble inside the stadium. 'I don't want to criticize the English authorities or anyone else. But I would merely point out that we were told to expect 10,000 England fans and I have calculated there must have been 15,500 of them in different parts of the stadium. In future, if we know how many are coming, it would be better to give them an entire end of the stadium. We know the England Football Association has a Travel Club with tight restrictions on membership to stop troublemakers from joining. But it is not an ideal situation to have supporters in different groups all over the place. We suspended ticket sales here in Italy two weeks ago and we will have to see how they obtained their tickets.'

The tense atmosphere in the stadium was heightened by constant skirmishes between England fans and police in full riot gear. Baton-wielding police pushed some 200 English supporters away from a bank of Italian fans after the two groups started hurling plastic chair seats and water bottles at each other. There were 30 arrests and ten injured. Piritore defended the brutal tactics of his police force after they waded into England fans with truncheons. 'My officers did not use exaggerated force. They used what force was necessary to contain the situation, having been provoked by England fans in that area of the stadium. Three of my officers were injured and I think that tells its own story.'

Hoddle was not prepared to condemn the English football supporters. 'In the past, people have jumped on the bandwagon too quickly. Do we know what happened? It's often the case that English supporters suffer intimidation from rival fans.' He declined to make any assessment while he was concentrating totally on England's magnificent performance on the pitch. Hoddle, however, observed that there was nothing that occurred on the field that would have provoked a violent reaction off it. There was no flashpoint, no violence to the degree that would have sparked a reaction among the fans.

There was abundant coverage of the violent excesses of English fans in the Italian media. The *Corriere Della Sera* wrote: 'The hooligans spread terror even in the centre of Rome. Bars destroyed, passers-by attacked. A heavy final reckoning. Thirty injured, the most seriously a policeman with cranial trauma. Forty arrests, 100 detained.' Italy seemed unable to accept responsibility for anything that happened in Rome – either on or off the pitch. *La Repubblica* said: 'Hooligans go mad. A draw on the pitch and guerrilla warfare in the stands.' *Il Messaggero* had the headline: 'Hooligan fury, Rome trembles'. There didn't seem to be a line about the Italian police's heavy-handed tactics, and all the blame was firmly placed at the visitors' door.

Hoddle and the FA must have a trouble-free World Cup and need to establish a code of control if England are to have any chance of hosting the World Cup in 2006. David Davies stressed: 'An awful lot of countries have this problem of one sort or another. We had extensive consultations with FIFA, the Italian Football Federation and the police and now we will have a debriefing about events in the first half. It goes without saying that safety and security are of the highest importance as far as we are concerned.' Hoddle was present when Poland played Germany as part of his World Cup fact-finding mission and he was appalled at the amount of violence among the fans. Not surprisingly, the incident hardly merited a mention. In contrast, events in Rome attracted worldwide attention.

Hoddle said: 'I think a lot of it was provoked, to be honest, but until we look into it it is difficult to say what went on. I have spoken to friends of mine this morning who were out there and they said it was terrible. From what they have told me some of the fans were provoked by police. Some of the supporters didn't do anything and were treated a bit harshly.' The FA announced they would draw up an urgent report into ticketing and security measures taken at the game.

Days later it emerged that Rio Ferdinand, West Ham team-mate Frank Lampard, Liverpool pair Danny Murphy and Jamie Carragher, and Wimbledon's Ben Thatcher, had stepped out of line and upset the management team after the Under-21 side had pulled off a great win over Italy. All of them were banned from watching the senior match and were sent packing to the airport in disgrace. The problem began when some of the players were allowed to go shopping on the morning of the main event, provided they returned in time to check out of their hotel ready for the journey to Rome from their hotel in Rieti. Peter Taylor received a telephone call from a local bar owner complaining that some English players were becoming rowdy. He was understandably angry that the players had not returned to the hotel as they were instructed and that they were drinking in a bar just a few hours before England's big game. He had little option but to punish them, but there was no damage or drink-related problems. It was the second time in little more than a month that Rio had been in trouble with England.

Sol Campbell was also not as happy as might have been expected. He was banned from the opening World Cup tie after picking up a yellow card for a foul on Inzaghi. However, there was hope for him as the FA would launch a campaign, backed by other nations, for a World Cup yellow card amnesty.

Twenty-four hours later the tales of woe and disenchantment came flooding over from Italy. Zola was involved in an extraordinary public row with his coach, risking his international future. Although he accepted his share of responsibility, Zola hardly took the heat off the coach by suggesting he should not have played if Maldini only wanted to play him out of position. He started diplomatically enough, when he said: 'I'll take my share of responsibility for the result.' Then came the 'but', and it was a huge one. 'But Maldini asked me if I could play behind the two strikers to make up for losing Roberto Di Matteo. I was honest with Maldini when we talked of the possibility of me playing on the left of midfield instead of as a striker. I said the game was too important and we could run into difficulties. I have played on the left with Chelsea but as a third striker, not like this. In this role, it is better to have someone else. I even told him to leave me out if he didn't think I was in form. It was too important to win. I accepted his instructions in the end, but pointed out that to give my best I had to play up front. The game started and the English took control of midfield so I had to come back and provide extra manpower alongside Demetrio Albertini and Dino Baggio. So I ended up running around like a madman behind David Batty. I wasted a lot of precious energy in this way. Let's be honest, I was no longer fish or meat – I was neither one thing nor the other. I didn't know what to do any more. Under these circumstances, it would have been better for another player to be out there, not me.'

Maldini responded that he had decided several weeks ago to shuffle his side for the England match, pulling Zola back from the front line to just behind the strikers. 'I'd already decided to play with two-and-a half forwards ... Zola was happy to play in that position and told me he'd sometimes played there for Chelsea.' Amid the Roman ruins, Maldini said: 'We suffered a lot, because we found ourselves up against a great team, but I have nothing to say to my players. They fought really well, even if we encountered some difficulties in the first half, especially in midfield, where we could have done better. We created few scoring chances because they shut down the spaces very well, but England were not dangerous either. However, I repeat, I don't have to reproach anyone for anything. They were all really good. I tried to make all the changes possible. Unfortunately, my son, Paolo, was injured, but the team continued to attack. We couldn't do more than that. I started with Inzaghi to keep the team on the attack and give more support to Vieri. That was not enough, either. We are talking about difficult games, which can be won on certain incidents. Unfortunately for us, it did not go well. We did everything possible, not only this time but in the preceding games. We won at Wembley, the English drew with us here. The truth is that, in six games, we got three wins and three draws, yet we have not qualified and this is an injustice that leaves a bad taste in the mouth. In midfield, we suffered because we missed Di Matteo, who was suspended. Unfortunately, I have to repeat that in this area we have many difficulties, because in Italy there are so many foreigners in the most important teams playing those roles. And in a year, or a year-and-a-half, the problems will be still greater.' He added: 'There are too many foreigners in Italy and it's very negative because it deprives our young players of places. In England it's different, because there are fewer foreign players and they're of a higher quality. Isn't it a fact that Gianfranco Zola was named player of the year in England and Paolo Di Canio Player of the Year in Scotland?'

Paolo Maldini said: 'Now, we are psychologically destroyed. And I am also physically destroyed. I badly twisted my ankle. It's giving me tremendous pain and I hope it won't cause me to miss too many matches. Unfortunately, we failed in our first mission. Fortunately, we still have a lifebelt. Unluckily, we paid for our psychological uneasiness, which became more obvious as the minutes passed. Our state of mind was completely different from theirs – and this had considerable weight.'

Del Piero admitted that he had tried to con the ref into a penalty by diving as Adams challenged. The Dutch referee had booked him for play-acting. Del Piero confessed: 'The referee saw it correctly, and it was a con-trick on my part. I was convinced that the English defender would make contact with me, but he didn't. I got up quickly to apologize to the referee. It had been an instinctive act by me, and I hadn't wanted to deceive the ref. But he already had his yellow card out and he booked me – and, I'm afraid to say, he was quite right. It was a bizarre moment, though. I would have bet any amount of money on the defender making contact.' Costacurta observed: 'The referee certainly did not like us. But the draw with England, one of the strongest teams in the world, could suit us. We go on to the play-offs. I wouldn't bet on our not qualifying.' Del Piero readily admitted England were the better side. 'It was an unusual game for us, but Glenn Hoddle's side played it to perfection. They all sat back in their half waiting for us, and then hit us on the break. We seldom found a decent opportunity to attack them. A draw was good for them and they played accordingly. So much possession, but it seemed they only had a couple of shots. When you think how things went and that we took four out of six points from this team, the bitterness becomes almost intolerable.'

Cesare Maldini heaped praise on England. 'They've become a great side. They've got a great physical presence in midfield, technically accomplished players like David Beckham and Teddy Sheringham and a defence made up of towers. It's a great combination.'

The Italian coach went on to criticize FIFA's World Cup qualifying system as unfair because it favoured weaker countries ahead of the more powerful European nations. 'FIFA's qualification system is open to criticism because a European country – undoubtedly a strong one – will be excluded to make way for Jamaica, for example.'

Italy were drawn against Russia in the play-offs, and Ince believed Italy would qualify, but he was equally convinced they would not win France 98 if they continued to rely so heavily on Zola. 'Zola is a great player, make no mistake – but he can't do it every game and it is unfair to expect it. The Italians rely on him to produce the goods all the time and that's a serious problem at international level. All week it was Zola this and Zola that in England and Italy. Maybe the pressure got to him. I still think Italy will qualify but they all need to take greater responsibility.'

There were no such problems for Hoddle's team who, even without Shearer, produced a brilliant display. Ince was convinced the impressive depth among the England ranks would be a critical factor behind their challenge next summer. 'The reason why we're doing so well is that every player in the team knows there is another who could come in and do the job just as well. There is Nicky Butt for me, Paul Scholes and Robbie Fowler for Wrighty and Teddy Sheringham – and that's excluding Shearer and Les Ferdinand. It's the same all over the park. You have to be at your peak to stay in the side. It is why England have regained respect around the world.'

Graham Kelly added his bouquet to the laurels of tributes heaped on Hoddle. 'Glenn's done a great job. I've been impressed by the quiet confidence he's always shown. He's certainly come through the first test. He's carried on from what Terry Venables did in his spell in charge. Terry brought the young players through and Glenn's gone on and increased the self-belief they have. I feel he's done an excellent job in building on what Terry started, and he's done that by working hard and doing all the right things.'

Chelsea skipper Dennis Wise got his own back on the Stamford Bridge Italian mob. Di Matteo, Zola and Vialli had been quick to rub salt in England's wounds back in February after Italy's 1–0 victory at Wembley by turning up for Chelsea training wearing Italian team shirts but Wise didn't miss a chance for revenge. 'When the Italian guys arrived at training we were standing there wearing our England shirts with "England–France 98" on the front and "Italy?" on the back. We weren't going to let Saturday pass without getting our own back. They've just about got used to our sense of humour and took it all right.' Wise hoped Italy would beat Russia to make the Finals. 'It's probably the toughest draw they could get but I tip them to win it. After all, the World Cup would not be the same without them.' Wise was determined to be there as well. 'It's a big motivating factor that we have qualified. I still think I have more to offer as an international.'

Success in the World Cup would bring fabulous rewards. England's stars are on £300,000-plus a man to win the World Cup. 'Team England' bank an immediate £500,000 for reaching the Finals with bonuses for reaching the quarter-finals, semis and then Final in France. Each player in the squad receives a cut worked out on a complex calculation depending on appearances in the squad and the team. Success in France would generate at least £1 million from existing sponsorship deals in bonuses and a further £2.5 million from licensing and image right contracts. FA marketing officials calculate that World Cup success would generate a 20 per cent rise in a football market already worth £600 million a year. The £1,500 match fee is an irrelevance. The players had already received in excess of £50,000 per man from the contracts with Green Flag, Carlsberg, Mars, Coca-Cola and Ariel. Negotiations with the five main sponsors would begin as soon as qualification was guaranteed, with a players' committee of Shearer, Seaman, Adams and Pearce. The marketing team have been astonished by the level of interest and commercial offers; the World Cup Finals would dwarf any previous commercial deals.

On their return from Italy, England were in the news ... for good and bad reasons. Hoddle was beseiged at his family home in Ascot. Asked about the behaviour of the English fans in Rome, he said: 'I think a lot of it was provoked, to be honest ... I have spoken to friends of mine who were out there, and they said it was terrible, with some of the fans provoked by the Italian police. Some of the supporters didn't do anything and were treated a bit harshly.'

Italy 0 England 0
Seaman, Campbell, Le Saux, Ince (capt), Adams, Southgate, Beckham, Gascoigne, Wright, Sheringham, Batty

	P	W	D	L	F	A	Pts
England	8	6	1	1	15	2	19
Italy	8	5	3	0	11	1	18
Poland	8	3	1	4	10	12	10
Georgia	8	3	1	4	7	9	10
Moldova	8	0	0	8	2	21	0

CHAPTER TWENTY-FOUR

Welcome Home the Glory Boys

England v Cameroon, Wembley, 15 November, 1997

Hoddle knew there was only one way to celebrate the achievement in Rome – by taking the pizza! The England coach said: 'We wanted to sit the lads down and say "well done" to them. So we took them to an Italian restaurant. It was rubbing it in – but you've got to, haven't you? We just went out as a group, everybody together, with a few glasses of wine. It gave us the chance to realize what we'd achieved. We could easily have stayed in our hotel and celebrated there, but it wouldn't have been quite the same. This was an opportunity to get everyone together and to enjoy ourselves.'

The light-hearted night out was an essential part of squad bonding but, sadly, there was some bad news as well. Just two days after the glory of Rome, there was a heartbreaking announcement from Lancaster Gate: the Hoddle marriage was over. It came as a great surprise as the couple had always seemed well-matched and the marriage had long been regarded as one of the strongest in football. It emerged that while Glenn was helping with the problems of players such as Gazza, Adams, Merson and Wright, he was having domestic trouble of his own. Such a revelation served to indicate not only his selfless nature, but also his determination to take England into the World Cup Finals.

Hoddle went to stay at the home of faith healer Eileen Drewery. Eileen, a 56-year-old grandmother, has known him since he was a teenager. Her healing powers cured Hoddle of a series of injuries during his footballing career. Eileen once said: 'I have an affinity with Glenn. I feel he is like my child and felt that from the word go. Glenn told me his grandma on his mother's side was a great believer in faith healing, but he had always been sceptical until he met me. If Glenn got hurt while on tour, I told him to sit down by himself and picture my face. That may sound conceited but I know I am only an instrument. I have no special gifts. I am only being used.'

John Gorman is well aware of the extraordinary faith Glenn places in Eileen. While still a player Gorman had two operations on his torn knee and was advised to quit football by a Harley Street specialist. But, at Hoddle's insistence, Gorman had three healing sessions with Eileen. He made such a good recovery that he was able to return to play at senior level.

In the eight months between qualifying for a World Cup and the actual Finals,

teams can change in composition quite radically. Injuries, the vagaries of form
and the emergence of new talent can force change on what seemed a settled team
or squad. In their first match of the 1982 tournament against France, for
example, England showed five changes from the team who had contested the last
qualifying match, against Hungary, the previous winter. Four years later, there
were three changes and in 1990, the last time England qualified, two.

The long-term injured hoped to be back in time for France. Darren Anderton
said: 'I've spoken to Glenn a few times while I have been trying to get myself fit
and he's given me a lot of encouragement. England's qualification for the World
Cup has given me something to aim for.' Jamie Redknapp hoped to play alongside
one of his Liverpool team-mates. He said: 'I'd love to play alongside Paul Ince.
He's a great player – there's no doubt about that. I think we are different sorts of
players but maybe we could complement each other. I hope we will!' Could a
Redknapp–Ince partnership blossom for Liverpool and England?

The friendly against Cameroon would bring back memories of Gazza's
greatest days in Italia 90. He recalled: 'It was a great time, a great spirit and I feel
we are getting that now. We had it with Terry Venables and it's even more with
Glenn Hoddle.'

In the absence of the injured Les Ferdinand and Stan Collymore, Andy Cole
and Chris Sutton were called up. Cole had been depressed after wasting so many
chances at Old Trafford that his future as a United striker was in question. His
response: a glut of goals. But there was still a doubt over his ability as an
international-class striker. 'I would throw that back,' responded Hoddle. 'That
was said about Ian Wright. I don't know, and that's why he's been brought into
the squad, but if I didn't believe he could do it, I wouldn't have him in the squad.
Whether he can achieve at this level, we shall all see. His major strength is in and
around the penalty box, he can get off the back of defenders, off their shoulder.
He's been working extremely hard off the ball as well as on it just lately, and now
he has the chance of pushing people who are already in the squad. He is not quite
at his very best, but he's getting there. Maybe a couple of years ago there might
have been doubts whether he really wanted it, but now he has proved he has an
inner belief, an inner grit.'

Sutton celebrated his first England call, vowing that it wouldn't be his last. He
had waited so long for recognition that he was cautious about his long-term
future. 'There are lots of good strikers about and some of them are injured,' he
said. 'Hopefully I can grab the opportunity when I'm down there and do well. I
hope it's not a flash in the pan. I want to be in this time and the next time and the
one after that. I'm just pleased to get the chance. I've been fairly consistent this
season but I've got to keep that going.' Hoddle was impressed by his efforts in
training. He commented: 'He shouldn't feel he's got anything to prove to me. He
was close to the squad for the Italy game but I needed experience. Having him in
the squad this time keeps everyone else on their toes because his attitude is right
and he's already shown what he can do this season.'

Of more long-term significance was the call-up for Rio Ferdinand. Sweeper is the position dearest to Hoddle's heart, a strategy the England coach would love to take to the Finals as part of his armoury. Ferdinand was a real prospect to fill that role, but while Hoddle would love to see him assume the mantle, he feared that it would not be until after France. 'I'm not sure there's enough time to see if he can do it,' said the England coach. 'If I had, say, fourteen games until the World Cup, then I could experiment for the first six and know by then if Rio or anybody else was the right man. Ideally I'd like to play that way, but you can't do it if you don't have the right individuals. You can work on the training ground as much as you want, but it's not the same as playing in front of 75,000 at Wembley, in a vital away game or in the World Cup. It's a difficult one for me. We've played with three at the back and what we've worked on is when to play zonally and when to play with a sweeper. I'd love to have a defender who could step out from the back with the ball so we could go to the World Cup Finals with a player like Germany's Matthias Sammer. But I'm not sure if we have the time or the individuals.'

Hoddle pointed to the precious few world-class stars who have performed the role to perfection. 'Ruud Gullit could do it, so could Krol and Koeman. Koeman would hurt you by stepping forward and striking a sixty-yard pass and nullifying eight or nine players. Bobby Moore would do it in a different way, not with long passes but by becoming an extra man in midfield. You can learn from yesteryear as well as from the current players like Sammer. The risk is that you can get caught with your pants down and concede goals. Most important, the player has to know when the time is right when to best spring the trap, when to use it and when it can hurt opponents in that area. Beckenbauer was a massive example of how that can be done. If I'm going to make that decision to use Rio, then I would recommend him to watch videos of Beckenbauer.'

Young Rio vowed to stay out of trouble after his recall on his 19th birthday. 'Obviously, I have dirtied my slate, but hopefully I have learnt from that. If I make the same mistakes again, then I've got to be a stupid boy. You've got to rein yourself in sometimes and make sacrifices. It was so painful to miss out against Moldova. It was a hard blow to take, it hurt my pride. My parents and friends helped me a lot. Being part of the England squad is the best feeling ever.'

Joe Kinnear, meanwhile, accused Hoddle of prejudice against Wimbledon. Eight of his players had represented their countries in the World Cup but Kinnear was still waiting for an England coach to be brave enough to pick one of his men. He said: 'They've been scared of picking anyone in our colours. They prefer names of Liverpool, Chelsea, Newcastle or Arsenal on their team sheets. I've been here seven years and not once has an England manager been brave enough to pick one of my players. Yet everyone makes me manager of the year and then buys my players. Every player who has left here for those clubs has gone on to play for England. Make what you will of that.'

Newcastle's Steve Watson received the call after Hoddle was forced to plan without Pallister, who withdrew after suffering a recurrence of his back problem.

Watson's adaptability had been something of a stumbling block for his career. When he was in charge at St James' Park, Kevin Keegan, a big admirer of the player, had used Watson as centre-forward, centre-half, winger, full-back and orthodox midfield player. Watson realized that he was falling between too many stalls, and decided to specialize. He had now established himself as Newcastle's first-choice in the right-sided defensive role, although he had operated as one of three central defenders as well.

Alex Ferguson wanted to withdraw Sheringham from the squad because of a knee injury, but Hoddle insisted that the player still reported to the Buckinghamshire base. An exasperated Ferguson said: 'Instead of being there today he could be getting treatment with us back at Old Trafford. He can get some treatment with England, but it's not the same in a hotel, because we've got all the equipment.'

Hoddle played down the confusion over Sheringham. 'My relationship is excellent with all Premiership managers. Some people are trying to drive a wedge between myself and managers. I spoke with Alex Ferguson after the match at Arsenal and he said that Teddy needed some rest but that he had left the ground. He said he would leave me to track him down, and we had his mobile number so it was no problem. Teddy will get first-class treatment while he is here and by Wednesday he could be back at his club.'

Gary Neville joined the list of crocks when he pulled out with a hamstring injury. He joined Sheringham, Pallister and Adams in dropping out. In the absence of Adams and Shearer, the captain's armband would once again be worn by Ince.

Hoddle wanted to go into the World Cup with an unbeaten sequence but Cameroon would provide a test. 'We wanted a nation like Cameroon because after six games with Moldova, Poland and Georgia – they all played in a similar type of way. Now the Cameroons will be completely different. And it is important to learn, particularly if young players come in, and even the experienced players can learn to cope with a different mentality.'

Hoddle planned to use the games to fine-tune his personnel and strategy, catering for every eventuality in France. 'There will not be drastic changes, more continuity. It would be nice to have the same 11 or 12 all fit to play in every one of the six remaining games to go into the tournament with. In Brazil's last 24 games, in 21 of them the same eleven have started.' But he also warned: 'Any of the players think they are turning up for friendly matches, I will tell them these are very important games, possibly as important as the qualifying games. Places are up for grabs and they should go for it.'

With less than eight months to go to the start of France 98, Hoddle was already contemplating the moment he would have to tell more than a dozen hopefuls that there was no place for them. 'I've only got room for 22 players, and there are more than 22 quality players in this country. Realistically we're looking at around 35 or 36 players, and they should all feel the door isn't shut. That means a lot of pruning by next June – and breaking a few hearts. But if it's got to be done, it's got to be done. It's a lovely headache to have, and the challenge to the players is to give me the biggest headache they can.'

Hoddle commented on some of the players he thought might challenge for a place in the final 22. He said, 'I've gone out personally to make sure Darren [Anderton] is fit and that shows you what I think of the lad. Le Tissier and Redknapp are coming back from injuries and Matt is another one I'm looking at. Stuart Pearce is also knocking on the door, an experienced player who has done well in the past. Michael Owen? Who knows what might come up in the next few months, someone always comes from nowhere before a World Cup.'

Southgate was aware of a number of quality young defenders pushing for places. He said: 'Everyone is keen to make a good impression and force their way into the squad. We know we can all improve, and there's no sitting back and saying we're there now and simply relax. It's about working hard from now on. I think he [Hoddle] will want to look at other players. It's only right, but I am sure he won't want to make too many changes. It depends what situation he finds himself in with injuries. I would imagine he will look at the first few games between now and the World Cup as an opportunity to look at new people and he might also take a look at our tactics. He might change the formation. If this affects me I just get on with it. You always want to play for your country – no question of that.'

Andy Hinchcliffe was back in contention after a long lay-off caused by serious damage to his kneecap ligaments. But now he was back, and believed he was all the better for the rest. 'I feel that I've come back stronger mentally,' said Hinchcliffe. 'That was an important part. I think it's made me a better player – because it has to. Physically I worked very hard, but I looked at my game too and told myself I had to work at this and this and this. It's taking stock of everything and I knew I had to come back under-weight and fairly strong.'

Competition among the forwards was the most intense within the squad. Robbie Fowler was just one striker who believed that he was ready for the demands of international football. Despite an impressive tally of 124 goals in his first 200 games for Liverpool, he had made only two starts for his country. He said: 'I know people have said they don't think I'm ready for England, but I have felt for a long time I can do it on the international stage. The trouble is that I haven't had a real chance yet. I've got six caps but I've only started two of those games and scored one goal. In football terms, playing at international level is far more difficult than for your club. The standard is almost frightening. As a forward, you have got to think quicker and move quicker. Everything happens quicker. But I know I'm ready for it. I've got a good scoring record and I've plenty of experience at club level. Now I need to make that extra step up and gain experience at the highest level.' Hoddle commented: 'Robbie's got a talent – the major talent of finding the back of the net. If you're going to win the World Cup, you need that, somebody who will get you five or six goals in the Finals, like Paolo Rossi in 1982 or Maradona in 1986.'

Fowler might have been even more encouraged by Hoddle's warning to Wright. He said: 'What Ian and the rest have to understand is that there are only a few players who are cast-iron certainties to go to France if they're injury-free … Ian knows he isn't one of them. He's got a lot of work to do and has to rediscover his form to get in the squad. He has to tone down his appearances off the pitch. Credit to him, he's realised he's doing too much peripheral stuff. The Arsenal all-time goalscoring record was a bit of a barrier for him. Now he's broken that, maybe he needs to imagine there's another record to break.' But Fowler knew that Wright would do everything in his power to satisfy Hoddle that he was in the right physical and mental state to score goals in France.

While several of Europe's soccer powers were still scrapping for a World Cup berth, England's players were waging individual campaigns to earn their places in France. 'I think we're all worrying about it,' said defender Phil Neville. 'We qualified in Rome and it's now that the work really begins. I think there's only a few that have a cast-iron spot and the rest of us have just got to fight for it.' Neville considered Seaman, Shearer, Gascoigne and Ince as the certainties. 'Gazza has always been one of my heroes and you think there's no way he's going to be left out.' There was never a moment when he did not worry about his own chances. 'I'm thinking about it. I know that every time that I go out on the training field, if I perform well, it's another step closer to France. It's always at the back of your mind.'

Robert Lee was taking nothing for granted. He said: 'I thought I'd made it in Euro 96, I won't be falling into that trap again. I played in the last home game before the tournament, against Hungary. And I was due to play against China as well in late May, but had to pull out with a slight calf injury, but still thought I'd be in the squad. I was then called into Terry's Hong Kong hotel room and he told me face to face I wasn't – it's probably the biggest disappointment of my career.' Lee then failed to be selected for Hoddle's first two matches. 'Whenever you are left out of a squad, you think your chance might have gone. But all you can do is keep playing as well as you can and it helps being at a big club like Newcastle. Because you win more games than you lose, and then if you play well you get noticed. Everybody wants to play in a World Cup, and probably the older players believe it could be their last chance of going there. And then there's always someone who comes into the squad whom nobody expects – so there's probably 40-odd players trying to be in the final 22.'

Fowler was handed the chance to play alongside Scholes against Cameroon, forgiven at last for the nose job that had put the England coach's nose out of joint in the summer. Hoddle put him on the spot: 'We know that Robbie can score at Premiership level and in Europe, but the jump to international level is a massive one and we need to find out if he can make it. He's had six caps now, started twice, and got off the mark against Mexico last season. I've only got six games before the summer, and I've got to look at others as well. If a player gets the opportunity, he's got to take it – and it might be that being rested works as a positive, if I think we're missing something without somebody.'

Although Hoddle was waiting to see if Fowler could make the step up he had every confidence in his partner for the game, Paul Scholes. He said: 'I rate the lad highly, and he's only going to get better and better. He can play in midfield, or more advanced, or as one of the inside-forwards off the main striker, and you know that if he gets two chances he'll stick one of them away. That's a superb talent to have. Paul has been one of the big bonuses I've had in the job. He's come in, taken everything in his stride and been very level-headed.'

Jean Manga, Cameroon's coach wasn't sure that his current squad had the potential to make the impact of the 1990 outfit knocked out of the World Cup quarter-finals in Italy by a Gary Lineker-inspired England. He said: 'We have a strong defence and some good individuals at the front, but we need a little more time. We have to play three or four more games against European opposition to discover just what we can do.'

The game was won by goals from Scholes and Fowler. Scholes, the day before his 23rd birthday, caught the eye with a clever chip over the keeper after a glorious dribble from Gascoigne. Gazza had lost the ball a couple of times, but a typical tackle by Ince retrieved possession for him as he set off on a run reminiscent of the midfield maestro at his peak. Hoddle described it as a 'magic little goal, even though we had a bit of luck.'

The coach had devised a different role for Gascoigne which had 'worked a treat'. Hoddle explained: 'Robbie was alone up front with Scholes and Macca withdrawn and Gazza deeper, which gave him plenty of possession. I told him I wanted him to dictate the play and he did, and I only took him off because I didn't want a repeat of what happened against South Africa when he was injured with a late tackle. I just wanted to protect him.'

While Shearer's understudy was still in dispute, Scholes cemented his position as Sheringham's most serious threat. Hoddle said: 'I'm delighted with the boy. I brought him in to see how he would cope. Some players don't fulfill their potential, but he is fulfilling his. He takes everything on board, has the right temperament, he has a very bright future. He could be the jewel in the crown.'

Scholes, however, was not so impressed by his performance. He said: 'I got a bit sloppy towards the end of the half. And I was giving it away a bit more than I should have done, and the goal made things better for me. You have to feel confident when you go out there, there's no point in staying in your shell. I think you have got to express yourself as much as you can – and I believe the more I play at this level, the more confident I'll become. A lot has happened to me very quickly and first and foremost I just want to be involved in the squad. A year ago I was hardly playing for United and now I've started a few games for England and it's going well for me. You have just got to take it in your stride, play as well as you can every time you go out and remember you are only as good as your last game.'

The second goal came when Ince found Beckham on the right and then continued his run into the box, before ducking under the cross for Fowler to score with a stooping header in injury-time at the end of the first half. Fowler commented: 'The second goal for England will obviously give me confidence for what lies ahead. But I know there's still a lot of work to be done before I can even start dreaming of France and the World Cup Finals next summer. You only have to look at the quality of strikers in this country to know that you can take absolutely nothing for granted. Every international is like a Cup Final. You just have to be 110 per cent committed every time you cross that line. Every time I play for England I think it does add a bit of pressure because everyone expects me to score goals. And I think it's a bit harsh because I do it at Liverpool everyone expects me to do it for England and it is a lot harder. But I've got seven caps now, started three games and scored two goals, and that's not bad at any age. I'm 22, still learning the game and hopefully I'll get another few chances before the actual squad is announced.'

Hoddle refused to criticize McManaman's performance. 'I was pleased with him, he produced the movement we asked him to make with Scholes and Macca playing just behind Robbie Fowler. In the second half there were some good productive things and he made himself some great positions finding more space and time. He has a lot of energy, a lot of talent, he can be electrifying. Going into a tournament you need players of different attributes and he is unique in this country, there isn't a player like him, apart from Ryan Giggs, and he's Welsh.'

Perhaps the most significant moment of the match came when Rio Ferdinand went on for his debut. He appeared unexpectedly early when Southgate was stretchered off after just twenty minutes. Hoddle said of his performance: 'It's difficult enough coming off the bench at the best of times, but for your debut and for a lad still finding his feet in the Premiership, he acquitted himself well.' Rio had only expected to get about 20 minutes at the most. The youngster reflected: 'It was a proud day for me. I didn't know if or when I was going to have an opportunity to get on but with Gareth's injury happening like it did I never had time to be nervous. I felt that I did alright but it helped having quality players like Sol Campbell, who has to be one of the best centre-halves in England, around me. If I had been feeling nervous then those sort of people help you settle into the swing of things. It was the sort of thing I dreamed of when I was a youngster and I felt so proud when I strode onto that pitch. I also felt proud for my club because it's the first time for a long time that someone from Upton Park has worn the three lions.' Campbell was full of praise: 'Rio did marvellously well, he's a confident lad and showed that by his performance. Everyone is relaxed and focused in this squad and he is no different. He's a young lad, one who has got great potential and obviously is a contender next year for the 22. Nerves? Did you see any from him?'

After the game Hoddle reflected on his personal progress. 'We're on course. In my 14 games we've had two defeats against the world champions and the runners-up, both by 1–0. But more than any records, what is pleasing the players and the staff and everyone involved is that we are really optimistic that we can go into the World Cup and do well.'

The question now being posed was not so much whether England could beat the rest, but who among the rest could beat England? Hoddle picked his favourites. He said: 'The leading countries have never been closer, everybody is condensed, there's so little to choose between the top six and that's why there are more games going to penalties. Obviously, you see Brazil apart as the most offensive side but, whether they can sustain the defensive part of their game over seven matches in the tournament is another matter. Then there's the Germans, Dutch, and Spain have talented players and I believe will be a force, and if Italy can get themselves back I still think they will be a threat. African nations are coming through and we really still don't comprehend how good they can be, but one day they will come close to winning the World Cup. Cameroon will be tough, Nigeria will be a threat, and there are others emerging all the time. Don't discount Romania because I always think they have a chance. To run away with their qualifying group as they did tells you they are a good side. Romania and Bulgaria have more World Cup experience than us and have very talented squads, particularly the way the Romanians qualified. I've always liked their players and on their day they can be as good as Brazil or anybody but they have to change their levels of consistency. There are a lot of good sides out there. Brazil are the favourites and a lot of teams can come close and we are very much in that bracket.'

Paul Ince felt that England had become a force to be reckoned with. He said: 'Two years ago I'd have said we had no chance of winning the World Cup, but this side has come on significantly and we're closing in on the likes of Brazil and Germany. Fortunately we have a few games before we go to France to work on things and improve further. Glenn certainly deserves a lot of credit for what we have achieved so far. When Terry Venables went, people wondered if we could find the right person to replace him and when Glenn was selected, people questioned his appointment. But he's taken this team to a new dimension. He plans well, motivates players and tactically he's ahead of the game. Yet we can't afford to get carried away. The hard work is still ahead of us.

Hoddle waited patiently to start his first World Cup as manager. 'I'm not going to get too excited yet. We've still got seven months until the tournament starts. For the World Cup Finals, we will be away for seven weeks, and working out how to cope with that is one of the most important aspects of my job. I've been in that situation as a player in the World Cup and European Championships and I know things can go wrong because of the boredom, or because the players are in each other's pockets. How we deal with that is very important to me. If it was a borderline case between taking two players, you might go with the one who would be good to have around the camp. Players could be missing their families, and that's something we'll have to look at as well.'

England (2) 2 Cameroon (0) 0
Martyn, Campbell, P. Neville, Ince (capt), Southgate, Hinchcliffe, Beckham, Gascoigne, Fowler, Scholes, McManaman

CHAPTER TWENTY-FIVE

Who's Who in France 98

The World Cup Finals Draw, Marseille,
4 December 1997

The big debate, as the Draw for the 1998 World Cup Finals groups approached, surrounded the seedings. It came as a surprise when FIFA warned that England's chances were 50–50 or less to gain one of the precious eight seeded places. Without that protection, England would be in danger of being drawn with either Brazil, Germany, France, Spain – or even Italy! Despite only qualifying via the play-offs against Russia, the Italians were guaranteed a seeding, even though they were at their lowest ever position in the world rankings at 16. Six other nations were guaranteed to be seeded: Germany, Spain, Argentina, Holland, France and Brazil. That left England scrambling with Romania and Bulgaria for the final place. Hoddle and the FA lobbied for the current FIFA official world rankings to have a major influence. Hoddle conceded: 'I'm sure Italy would have been peeved if they had not been seeded and I appreciate that FIFA need to take into account past records in the World Cup. But they should also consider that past records belong to different management and different sets of players and the current teams shouldn't be affected by what happened in the past. The seeding procedure should be reshaped. If you are going to have a world ranking system, it should count for something and not just tickle your ears if you're No 1 or No 2. It has to have some credence.'

But in the end the decision went against England as Romania claimed the last of the eight seedings. No-one was left in any doubt about the cause of England's second rating. FIFA General Secretary Sepp Blatter said: 'We took into consideration 60 per cent from the last three World Cups and here England were naturally penalized for not being in the World Cup in 1994 and that tournament carried a multiplier of three. In the rankings it is correct that England have sixth place. This means the performances of the current national team reflects that ranking, but that counted for only 40 per cent of the final calculation. For the next World Cup, the principle calculation will be decided at the first meeting of the Organizing Committee of FIFA World Cup 2002.'

Former England manager Graham Taylor refused to shoulder the blame. 'I'm used to getting blamed for many things, but it is not my fault this time,' he said. 'If people think England have been left out of the seedings because of what happened in 1994, they should look at the rules.' Taylor claimed the glut of friendly games under Terry Venables before Euro 96, when England were hosts, had also counted against them. 'It's not just about non-qualification for World Cup 94. You have to take into account friendly games since then because every international match counts and if you play friendly games at home, you don't get as many points.'

But the condemnation for England's failure to be seeded was universal. Even from the Germans! Liverpool striker Karl-Heinz Riedle said: 'England are one of the most famous teams in the world and in my view they should always be seeded. OK, they didn't qualify for the last World Cup, but that was four years ago and they have done very well since then. I am very surprised that Romania have been seeded as one of the top eight teams and not England.' Lawrie McMenemy, Graham Taylor's World Cup assistant when England failed to qualify in 1994, added: 'On current form, England should be seeded. What is the point of having current world rankings if you don't use them? I think Glenn Hoddle will be disappointed with FIFA's decision, but equally I don't think any team in the Finals will relish the prospect of playing England.'

But there was some good news when an amnesty on yellow cards was agreed. It meant that Sol Campbell would be eligible for England's opener. Hoddle said: 'It is a logical decision and correct. Virtually every coach in the world said the same thing – that we have to start on an even keel. It is only right because players made massive efforts to get us here and it would not be right if they were punished for it. I'm delighted for Sol and for us.'

Hoddle refused to be downcast about the seedings. His message was, bring on Brazil or Germany … England are ready for anyone. He said: 'There are six or seven countries who can win the World Cup, including us. Eventually we will have to meet and beat the best, Brazil, Germany, Italy or whoever. Wherever and whenever we get them, we will be ready for the job.'

Before the groups were decided, Hoddle analysed the pros and cons of drawing Brazil. 'I won't lose any sleep if we are pitched in with Brazil. If we beat them or lose to them we still have two other games and don't have to play them again until the Final. It will be an advantage if Brazil are in our group. What we don't really want is Brazil, Croatia, Nigeria. We don't want a Group of Death situation. We virtually had that to a degree in qualifying. Yes, we came through it and we're hoping for an easier ride this time. But this is the World Cup Finals and quality is increasing and matches are getting harder.'

Hoddle ended up avoiding all the big guns, England's group consisting of the weakest seed, Romania, plus Tunisia and Colombia. With just two balls left in the draw, Colombia or Iran, things might have been even better. But Hoddle was hardly going to quibble. He admitted: 'It's not a bad draw. They are all tough games. We've struck the middle ground; it could have been a lot harder – for example, when you look at Spain's group with Nigeria and Bulgaria, that's the toughest. Then again there are a lot of easier groups … far easier.'

England open up with an early afternoon clash in Marseille against Tunisia on 15 June. Then come the Romanians seven days later in Toulouse, before facing Tino Asprilla's Colombians on 26 June in Lens – a negotiable passage to the second round. Hoddle said: 'When you look at our group we are well capable of qualifying, but first we have to do our homework on Tunisia. Tunisia is our first game so we must focus in on them because we don't know as much about them as the other teams. As it's the first game we have to concentrate, I've seen them on television but not in real life.'

Shearer looked ahead to the possibility of facing his then Newcastle team-mate Faustino Asprilla. 'It should be fun possibly coming up against Tino – it's just about impossible knowing what he's going to do.' On the other hand, Asprilla felt his Newcastle strike partner's goals might prove decisive. 'Alan is a magnificent player and will prove it to the rest of the world in France. He will score plenty of goals and cause a lot of problems for even the best defences. Apart from his eye for goal and lethal finishing, he is so difficult to mark. It's impossible to keep him quiet for 90 minutes. People in Colombia know all about that and respect Alan enormously. They watch Premiership football on television and realize it's going to be very difficult stopping England advancing from the group. Alan gives England such a strong base. He is so important to them and is one of the main reasons why I believe they will do well. I'm not afraid of anyone in the England team. But they have several players who demand the utmost respect. Alan Shearer stands out among those – he has the most important role to play in the England side. I rate England as favourites to win the group. In fact, I believe it's possible for them to go all the way and win the World Cup. It's a nice group for them. They must be feeling very confident. I know the England boys at Newcastle are, because we have been joking with each other all morning. They kept telling me that Colombia have got no chance, so I just told them that they would be heading back home after a week. It was only a bit of banter, though. They will be there longer than that and could even go on to win it.'

Asprilla spoke of the sadness he still felt about his Colombian team-mate Andres Escobar's fatal shooting after the 1994 World Cup in America. 'All the Colombia players want to put a special effort in next summer as a tribute. We lost to Romania and the United States in the last World Cup and did not do ourselves justice. That was bad enough, but Andres' death put it all in perspective and left us all terribly shocked. We have plenty of players who are capable of making an impact. Who are the dangermen? Tino, Tino and Tino ... No, I'm only joking. We have a talented squad and are looking forward to the challenge of facing England. England are the obvious favourites in the group and we must give them lots of respect.'

Romania are the in-form team with the best qualifying record of nine wins and one draw. Known as the 'Colonel', Anghel Iordanescu is one of the most technically accomplished coaches on the international scene. Now with Galatasaray, Georghe Hagi is past his glittering best but even at the age of 32 can conjure a touch of magic and with over 100 caps will be one of the most experienced performers. The Premiership knows all about Petrescu, Dumitrescu and Popescu. Iordanescu said: 'Anyone who thinks England is the best team could be mistaken – Colombia could also surprise us. It's not an easy group, maybe it's even one of the hardest along with Spain's. But I'm quite happy that my team, which is very experienced these days, has what it takes to get through.' Petrescu said: 'We've been very unlucky in the draw. Not many teams wanted to play England but, for me, Colombia are just as dangerous for us in the group. We beat them 3–1 in the Finals in America four years ago, but they played very well then and now we've got them in the first game again. They will want revenge. Maybe it is best to play the toughest team first because you can see then how strong you are, but England have got Tunisia first and I'll be very surprised if they haven't already got full points before they meet us. I'm still a bit surprised we were seeded instead of England, although I know it was because of our World Cup qualifying record. The first game in the Finals is always so important. It is often very tense but somebody who can start with a good win is really well placed. It will be tough for us, but we can still do well. We always qualify but don't often get much further than the first stage and we are determined to change things.'

Colombia will be best remembered for their visit to Wembley in September 1995, where keeper Higuita's scorpion kick brought a touch of humour. He is no longer first choice but they still have the aging Valderrama. Armed with over 100 caps, the 36-year-old is in semi-retirement with Tampa Bay in the States. Antony de Avila has a touch of Zola in his style, but again he's well into his thirties and plays for MetroStar in the States. But Asprilla, with 17 goals in the qualifiers, is the striker coach Hernan Dario Gomez will be looking to for inspiration. The coach said: 'Romania and England are two teams with great character, they'll be difficult opponents. Tunisia play a focused, physical game. But we know Romania well after they beat us 3–1 at the 1994 World Cup in the USA. England showed a lot of quality and were impressive technically during Euro 96.'

Tunisian coach Henry Kasperczyk was a member of the Poland side that ended Sir Alf Ramsey's England reign at Wembley in 1973. 'I've put England out of the World Cup once. Why shouldn't I help do it again? The so-called smaller teams are going to cause surprises, and we could be one of them. It is difficult to say who will qualify from this group as they are all good. Romania have looked even stronger since the last World Cup and their unbeaten record in the qualifiers says it all. However, we are not frightened by anyone and have nothing to lose.'

Chris Waddle believed England would be in for a sharp shock if they regarded Tunisia as mere whipping boys. He said: 'It will be absolutely sweltering, red hot, because the game is scheduled for the afternoon. I remember making my debut for Marseille. It was July, but the game kicked off at 8.30 pm and the temperature was still well into the seventies. On a June afternoon it will be absolutely baking. That will suit the Tunisians – the hotter the better for them. It will obviously take its toll on the England players. Glenn and his players face a severe test.'

But David Beckham spoke confidently of England's chances. 'We have so many potential stars, it's frightening,' he said. 'Alan Shearer will hopefully be fit. There's Paul Ince, Teddy Sheringham, Sol Campbell and David Seaman. Every player in that squad has the potential to become a national hero. But I think Paul Gascoigne can illuminate the whole thing. Look at the way he played during Euro 96, he thrives on all that, he's in his element. His enthusiasm is infectious and you need people like that around you. One of the great strengths of this squad is we have players for all occasions. Ones who can keep us composed, others who can pick us up and players like Gazza who can have a laugh and a joke to calm us down. A lot of players need that before games because you can get very tense.'

As for the draw, Beckham said: 'You cannot afford to underestimate anyone. Even the so-called small nations are capable of holding their own to a certain extent. And at World Cups, they always cause the major upsets. It's largely unimportant who you draw, the important issue is the results. I think we've been drawn in an interesting group. Romania have been very impressive in the qualifiers and they have a good record against England. Colombia are unpredictable and Tunisia, while regarded as the group underdogs, will still be a hard test and a team nobody wants to lose too.'

Beckham felt that England would be going into the tournament on such a high that an early battle with any of the pre-tournament favourites would only have reinforced their quest for glory. 'If we had drawn, say, Brazil, France or Italy, we could have got them out of the way. The chances are if we did well, they would either go out of the competition or we wouldn't meet again until the later stages. If you're going to win the World Cup you have to meet the best teams, so leaving it late is just putting off the inevitable. The tournament favourites are predictable anyway – the obvious ones like Brazil, Italy, Germany, Spain and France. But you should count England amongst them. I think we have proved beyond a shadow of a doubt that we are capable of living with the best in the world. We have nothing to fear going into this tournament. We qualified as group winners and last summer in the Le Tournoi we proved to people that we wouldn't be intimidated by the big occasion.'

Hoddle won't be short of intelligence. 'A lot of scouting and collecting of information has been done already. We've got dossiers and reports on all the qualified teams. Now we can get three files out and three sets of tapes out. We can even channel in on who we might meet in the second stage. The first job to home in on is Tunisia – we've got to get off to a good start. I don't believe in flooding players with information. But the coach must be 100 per cent definite on how the other team plays, what shape they are on the field. Nowadays that can be the difference between winning and losing.'

Hoddle looked forward to the prospect of one of his players illuminating the world stage. He commented: 'The World Cup is a great opportunity for players to make their name and we have players capable of achieving that. Look at players at Manchester United like Scholes and Beckham, they have earned respect and now it needs to be driven through all the way. It's a realistic respect, not a false one. One thing the World Cup always does is throw up new names. Players come through from nowhere. Do you remember who scored the goal of the tournament in the USA? It was some bloke from Saudi Arabia. You can't remember his name, and I can't remember his name either. That's my point. People come from nowhere. Players like Schillaci and what about Roger Milla? Not too much was known about them before the World Cup. It's a great stage, a place to make your name and become world superstars. These players and other young lads have developed nicely. But the pressure will not be on them when they arrive here. Shearer, Gascoigne and Seaman are our big names. The world will know they are coming, and that takes the pressure off people like Scholes and our other young lads. But the youngsters haven't seen failure, they don't know fear and they won't be coming here saying "we cocked it up last time, we've got to put that right". Of course, inexperience causes problems and we have to remember that we do have a squad without real World Cup experience. We need the mixture if we're going to win it.'

Shearer felt all the big guns were concerned about facing England. 'After what we have achieved in the last two or three years, everybody will be saying to themselves that they really don't fancy having to play us. We know we've got one hell of a chance. There will be eight or nine sides who will be thinking they can be successful – and we're one of them. We really believe we've got a chance of doing something special. With what we've done to get there, our confidence is sky-high. We'll need a bit of luck, of course, but so will anybody else. I don't think we're that bothered at not being a top seed – if we're going to win the thing, we've got to beat teams.'

To finish top scorer, Shearer would have to outscore Argentina's Gabriel Batistuta, Brazilian pair Ronaldo and Romario, and Holland's Dennis Bergkamp. He said: 'This is the big one. Scoring in the European Championship is one thing, but pitting your wits against the best in the world is what I want to do most. I have been lucky to have played against them and know how good they are. It will be interesting to see how Ronaldo copes with all the attention and publicity that will surround him and Brazil. Batistuta always scores when it matters. His consistency in the tough Italian League is tremendous. Bergkamp is a slightly different type of striker in the withdrawn role he prefers. He has caused the Premiership a lot of problems and I am sure he will be asking questions in the World Cup ... I remember Rossi scoring all those goals for Italy in 1982. When I was growing up, it was Gary Lineker and Toto Schillaci. People still talk about them. It would be great for me if in years to come they talked about Alan Shearer.'

But as the World Cup drew ever nearer, Shearer was beginning to feel the heat generated by other players after his place in the team, notably Michael Owen, the young Liverpool star. His club team-mate Paul Ince gave him a vote of confidence. He said: 'I think Michael has every chance of going to the World Cup. Age does not come into it and Michael is a very good prospect. A lot can happen in the next six months. Players can get injured or lose form and there is a whole bunch of strikers competing for a place in the squad. As long as Michael keeps his feet on the ground – and I'm sure he will – he has every chance for France if the goals keep coming. The most important thing is that he keeps doing the business for Liverpool and that applies to all of us.'

Owen was equally sure that he could make a contribution for England. He said: 'I am confident of my ability and I think I could do a job in France. Glenn Hoddle has said that he will give a few people their chance, and if he is thinking of taking me to the World Cup Finals, I hope he will give me that chance before the summer. I'm hopeful of playing and showing what I can do.'

Hoddle and the development of the England team impressed Pele. The greatest player the world has seen said: 'One of the surprises for me is the development of the English team. I have seen several of their games in the last few years, I saw several games before and now I have been surprised by some of the changes, maybe the new coach has given a new style. I've seen England's three games in Le Tournoi and maybe the coach has tried to change a little bit more and not play a rushing game. Yes, more patience, a little more control in the game. I remember the game against Portugal, it was a good game and England drew 1–1. In the second half, England ran like crazy. But now the coach has given a little more confidence to the players. Maybe over the last two years a lot of foreign players who have come into the English game have helped to achieve that.'

As for the outcome, Pele seemed to be edging towards a Brazil–France Final. He laughed when he said: 'I always think of Brazil in the Final, no doubt. But don't forget France, they have good players and a good team and have a chance to be in the Final.' Pele selected five European teams, of which he believes three will make the semi-finals – France, Italy, Germany, Spain and England. 'The four semi-finalists will be three from Europe, and Brazil. This is the best level of European teams I've seen in the last three World Cups, no doubt. I haven't seen the same strong sides in South America. Brazil have good players, but they have a problem with their teamwork. Coach Zagallo has to work hard to get the team to combine, you can't win the World Cup with only stars. Argentina have a good young team but Peru, Chile and Paraguay are not in good shape.'

Hoddle planned to take his players to La Manga in southern Spain directly after the FA Cup Final for a relaxation and training break. The players would be able to return home before travelling to their base in La Baule on the Atlantic Coast, where they were based during the successful Le Tournoi. Hoddle planned to make his players sweat by taking them to Morocco for three games late in May to acclimatize for the heat as part of his meticulous build-up.

Hoddle only wants one thing this summer. The World Cup coming home.

New Kid on the Block

Michael Owen sets a new record, England v Chile,
Wembley, 11 February 1998

Roy Evans was asked to assess young Michael Owen's World Cup chances. 'As an England fan, I would want him in the squad for France.' The Liverpool boss told Hoddle that Anfield's young striker was ready to beat the legendary Duncan Edwards' record of the youngest player to appear for England this century. Edwards was 18 years and 183 days old when he played against Scotland in April 1955 – Owen was just 58 days after his 18th birthday.

Owen's brilliant winner and all-round display at St James' Park against Newcastle strengthened his claims to complete a remarkable hat-trick of caps at Under-18, Under-21 and senior level in the space of six months. With Shearer just back from injury, Ferdinand still laid up, Collymore out of sorts and Wright and Fowler enduring lean spells, Owen was soaring up the England pecking order.

Evans was adamant the precocious kid from Chester can handle it on and off the pitch. 'If I was Glenn Hoddle, Michael is someone I would be looking at very seriously. And I don't think it's any secret that Glenn is doing just that. Whether he thinks it is the right time, only Glenn can say, with his experience of being an international manager. But taking off my own managerial hat, and talking purely as an England fan, I would take him with me to France. There's no doubt Michael has arrived – and he's done it with his feet on the floor. He's still the same lad. Nothing fazes him, he's determined and single-minded. And physically and mentally I think he's up to it. He's done fantastic at such an early age but he's got the capability to improve. We feel there's more to come from him.' Evans bought the vastly experienced German international striker Karl-Heinz Riedle to partner Fowler, fully expecting young Owen to push the two senior men – but not to keep one of them out of the team! Riedle, a European Cup Winner with Borussia Dortmund only the previous May, was having to be content with a place on the subs bench such was Owen's startling progress. Liverpool's early fears that their young teenage prodigy would suffer burnout from too many games, largely disappeared. Evans has no intention of holding him back on the international front. 'From what we had seen from Michael at the end of last season and in pre-season matches, we knew he was ready and was going to challenge for one of the striking positions. We were forced to play him from the off because of Robbie's injury, but to be fair the lad has taken his chance brilliantly and made it difficult to leave him out. We still need to be aware of his age – he's only just 18 – and the amount of games he's playing, but he seems to be getting away with it just fine. He's been looking tired towards the end of the last couple of games, but then he has dug deep and finished as strong as anybody. I've no qualms about him being called up for England. He's a young man who thrives on the ambition of playing for his country. He doesn't want to be held back, and I wouldn't stop him. It just needs a bit of commonsense. We have a very good relationship with Glenn Hoddle. If Michael was called up and I felt he didn't need too much training, I would say to Glenn: "Fine, have him, but make sure you don't kill him". That should be the relationship between a club manager and the international coach.'

Owen was showing remarkable maturity. 'The pressure doesn't worry me because I have high hopes for myself which, hopefully, will lead to me being involved with the full England squad for the World Cup Finals.'

Referring to his dismissal when playing for the England Under-21s, Owen said: 'It was a stupid thing to do, even though I don't think I deserved to be sent off. It was just down to frustration and I blew up in a split-second reaction. Any player can get frustrated if they're dragged back and kicked every time they get the ball and the referee lets the defender get away with it. I know a lot of people expect a lot from me and I hope I can live up to those expectations. You see what happens to other players who start off with a bang in their career only to fade away. But I'm not worried about myself. I'm confident enough to say that won't ever happen to me as long as I work hard to maintain my form and keep on scoring goals. Right now, the Liverpool team is the most important thing, but I want to do well for myself, for my own ambition and to prove to the manager and the fans that I am the man for the job. It's a big leap being with youth team players one day and the next day training with world class players. But I'm part of the first-team squad now. I've adjusted and the players don't think of me any differently to anyone else in the squad. Some defenders are quite physical and I've taken a lot of punishment, but you just have to put up with it. That's the way some people defend and you have to live with that. The only answer is to stand up for yourself and answer them by sticking the ball into the back of the net. I don't see it as a big problem really. You've got to remember, I am playing against grown men who've been in the game a long time and they know different ways to handle players they see as a threat.

'It's great to hear people link me with the full England squad. I'd love to go to France in the summer. But all I can do is carry on playing well in any game I play – and then hope I'm handed the chance!'

Owen had already rewritten scoring records in youth and junior football as the greatest scorer in the history of the England Schoolboy side, and his strike rate in Liverpool's minor sides shattered the records set by Fowler just a few years ago. 'To compare me with Robbie is impossible at the moment. I would put Robbie up there with someone like Alan Shearer. He's as good a finisher as there is. I'm still learning the game and people like Robbie and Karl-Heinz Riedle offer me advice which I'm quick to listen to. They have proved themselves at the top over a period of time, while I'm just starting out.'

Bryan Robson played down the chances of Owen forcing his way into the World Cup squad. 'I think he's going to have to play really good football to break in because there are a lot of top strikers about. There could be injuries and he could catch Glenn Hoddle's eye, but he still has something prove. He's got a great future, I haven't seen anyone better at his age, including Robbie Fowler. But he's still got to go on and handle the pressure. In the first year kids can come in full of enthusiasm and do really well. But when they know they're in there week after week, year after year, it's a different kind of mental pressure keeping your performances high. Robbie's done that, but Michael is only in his first year.'

Hoddle was conscious of the clamour for Owen to be promoted. 'He is very exciting. I know that he, like Rio Ferdinand, will be a hell of a player in five years' time. But I have four months. I have to decide whether they could do, in a World Cup, what they are doing in the Premiership. Those boys are no problem for 2002. But can one score goals and the other defend in a World Cup this summer? Sometimes you get four or five injuries and the situation lands in your lap. The decision is made for you. Or you might say, the boy is good enough anyway and I'll go with him. It also depends what your needs are. Take strikers. Do we go for subtle movement or do we want a bit of a battering ram? It all depends on how you are going to play. So the composition of my World Cup squad is very complex.'

Owen made his debut for Liverpool in May 1997 when he came on as a 57th minute substitute against Wimbledon in the penultimate game of the season. Seventeen minutes later he scored his first league goal. He has got the right temperament and what he is doing, week in and week out, for Liverpool suggests he can get into the final World Cup 22,' said Hoddle. 'Sometimes youngsters can be in awe of more experienced internationals, but he never looked out of place even on his first day training with England. He displayed a lot of maturity. There is a time to show them [top players] no respect, and that's in the 90 minutes of a football match. Sometimes, you can be in awe of your opponents and your performance suffers, but Michael can do it.

'He suggests that he might get into the final 22. But we have four or five months to find out . So, can he do what he is doing in the Premiership against the best defenders in the world? It's a different league, and he has not had that much experience in Europe ... there is a gap there, another hurdle he has to get over.'

It was at 'work experience' at Bisham Abbey where Hoddle formulated the opinion that Owen had the temperament to go with his talent – even at such a tender age. 'From the first day he came in to train with the senior squad he didn't look out of place. Sometimes younger players can be in awe of older ones so they don't perform – but not in Michael's case. He's only 18, but age isn't a hurdle, ability is. That comes first, followed by temperament. He has potential and has consistently shown the temperament, while off the pitch he's been perfect.'

Owen said: 'I am delighted to have been called up for the England squad. It is no secret that my ambitions have always been to play for Liverpool and England. At this stage of my career it is vital for me to stay fit, keep learning and keep my feet firmly on the floor.'

Evans had 'sensible dialogue' with Hoddle this season to make sure Owen does not 'burnout'. Owen's enthusiasm is such that it is very difficult to hold him back. Evans added: 'Michael is a very special case. You always worry about him playing too many games but, if Glenn thinks it's the right time, Michael won't argue with that because he's not a guy you can hold back. If he sees his chance of stepping up a grade he will take it with both hands. On several occasions this season, I've started the week thinking it's about time I gave the lad a rest but, to be fair to him, he has very rarely looked jaded so we have stayed with him. Obviously in training, if we feel we need to give him a break, we pull him out of one or two sessions, but that doesn't please him too much either.'

Owen's double in the 3-2 home defeat by Southampton took his tally to 14 for the season and the honour of being Liverpool's leading marksman, one ahead of Robbie Fowler. Dennis Bergkamp said: 'It is amazing when you consider Liverpool have two such good young strikers. Fowler has scored a stack of goals for them. I think Michael could be in line for a long and exciting international future. I do believe he has a good chance of going to the World Cup and would not let England down if he got there. He is very, very quick, knows how to finish and does not seem at all affected by nerves, and they are qualities any striker would want.'

Alan Shearer knew the youngster was ready, endorsed by Newcastle's three defeats against an Owen-inspired Liverpool in the space of 23 days. 'Michael's a very special talent and he's had a tremendous start to his career – I just hope he doesn't get too much pressure put on him. From what I've seen, he looks as though he can handle it and what he's done so far has been unbelievable. I got a decent look at him in the three games against us and it was clear his pace is a huge asset to him. but what I've noticed is that he doesn't appear to be fazed by anything or anybody. If the manager gives him his chance I know he wouldn't let anybody down.'

Owen has already demonstrated his ability to take everything in his stride, helped by the closeness of his family – his father, former Everton player Terry and his solid roots in North Wales. 'I think I'm ready. I don't see myself as a young lad coming into the game, just as one of the lads at Liverpool, and that's how the rest of them see me too. And playing for England won't bother me. I'll relish the opportunity. I'm confident in my ability to do well, and I certainly don't think age comes into it – as the manager said, if you're good enough, you're old enough.'

'Michael plays with his head up,' explained Hoddle. 'Anybody who does that will score and create, and Michael does. Age doesn't come into it. He's here because of his talent. We've groomed him over the last couple of get-togethers and he feels at home already. He's got the right temperament and he's shown no signs that he can't handle it. I'm putting no pressure on the boy. He is in good form, he's been called up by his country but if he doesn't make the World Cup squad he's got another ten years of going to World Cups and European Championships. I don't want to put that burden on him now. I just want him to go out and express himself as he has done since he started playing football.

'There's no problems with his ability or his decision-making on the pitch. He's a unique player. He's something you don't see, a striker who really attacks people with the ball, very direct and as quick with the ball at his feet as without it. If you've got somebody who can do that in the last third of the pitch, and he's proved he can in the Premiership, it's a huge asset. He'll be a star of the future, it doesn't take a genius to work that out. What we need to find out in a short period of time now is if he's ready for the World Cup.'

For Owen, it was the challenge he could hardly wait for. 'Driving in to training every morning, I think about what I'm doing for Liverpool and hopefully what I could do with England. It doesn't worry me at all, it doesn't scare me. I'm very excited, and my family are as thrilled as I am. As far as I'm concerned, I have the challenge of proving I'm good enough for the World Cup. I've got nothing to lose.'

Record breaking has been Owen's hallmark, just like Jimmy Greaves – from Hawarden High to that Deeside School team, breaking Ian Rush's season-best 72 by a clear 20 goals, and playing in a side three years ahead of schedule to break Gary Speed's appearance record; followed by scoring debuts at every England level, Under-15s up to Under-21s, and that off-the-bench goal at Wimbledon in his Liverpool debut last season.

Four years ago, Brazil's squad for USA 94 included a young, 17-year-old striker, who did not get a kick. Ronaldo is now known throughout the world, and while Hoddle tried to play down comparisons, he was not entirely successful. 'They've got a different physique, but they both have the same directness of running at people. Ronaldo has a lot more experience at international level. Perhaps the Brazilian players who didn't go in 1994 resented him, and if Michael goes it would be because of his form, for football reasons. I'm not putting pressure on him. He'll go if I feel it's right. I don't expect that he should go, he's only 18. But he's blossomed and emerged very quickly. He should be saying "I want that challenge; I can cope with it". He's got that confidence and ability.'

The Owen family made their last-minute preparations for their trip to Wembley. Michael's father, Terry, said they would make the journey from their home in Hawarden, near Chester, to see Michael make soccer history. Owen snubbed the 'Spice Boy' tag, preferring to live with his parents in their detached home on a suburban housing estate and relaxing with a quiet game of golf. Terry, himself a former professional footballer, who played for Everton and Chester, is now extremely proud of his son's success. Michael, a former Deeside Primary School's player, now receives up to 300 letters from football enthusiasts from across the world each week – all asking for the autograph of soccer's fastest rising star. Michael's modesty, said his father, means that he is more than happy to sign autographs and is genuinely pleased to meet his growing army of fans.

The last time England played Chile, one of the lowest attendances in Wembley history, a mere 15,000, was recorded, but the national stadium was close to capacity for the forthcoming friendly match, with Hoddle explaining: 'The nation has caught World Cup fever.' Owen's history-making appearance debut had transformed a low-key World Cup warm-up into the must-see event of the season to date. Hoddle had no last-minute doubts that Owen has what it takes to become a world star in the future, but he doesn't want the country to expect instant miracles. 'I'm determined to take all the pressure off him. If he doesn't make this World Cup, he's got plenty more, so the lad's not under that pressure. I'm just not having that – the World Cup must be a bonus. People might be expecting too much, but he's only 18 years of age, has played one Under-21 game and a handful of Under-18 games. It's impossible to bring him in and play a part without those expectations coming with him. That's the way it has to be. But let's not put the standard so high for an 18-year-old playing his first game.'

Owen convinced Hoddle with his attitude in just two days training at Bisham Abbey. 'He's looked the part on and off the pitch, doesn't suffer from nerves, and he's a credit to himself, his club and his family. It wouldn't be fair to have put him in [against Chile] unless I felt he could cope with it all. It might not be fair anyway, with all the hype that's around it, but he knows what I feel. He's not going to get the blame if we get a bad result and if he puts one over the bar, no-one's going to say he hasn't got the right temperament.'

Winning the World Cup is a job for men, not boys. But it wasn't the young debutant who let Hoddle down against the Chileans at Wembley. The Boy Wonder shone like the star we know he can be, only for England's more-experienced campaigners to fall short. Here was a chance for a multitude of players to stake their World Cup claims as Hoddle despatched only three of the most likely to make his World Cup starting line up against Tunisia in Marseilles. On the night the nation was willing young Owen to complete his remarkable record of scoring at every level for his country, he failed to get the support from his team-mates.

Eventually Hoddle had to bring off Sheringham and the combative Batty in favour of Shearer and Ince, but whatever the permutations Owen was starved of more than a couple of genuine chances. Yet, Owen's electrifying pace was as much a menace to Chile as the trickery of Marcelo Salas was to England's sloppy defence. The Chilean captain's double-strike, a brilliant piece of finishing for the first and a well-taken penalty for the second, created a piece of history for the South Americans – it was their first-ever victory over England.

Owen's nomination as Man of the Match was justified considering the circumstances surrounding his debut, the inevitable hype and expectancy. He had emerged from the tunnel eighth in line, his tiny figure dwarfed from behind by the powerfully built Sol Campbell. By the end it was Owen who could stand tall. The clean-cut kid, his eyes always fixed ahead in total concentration, the square chin and short back and sides, Owen was a throwback to the Tom Finney era. Fittingly,

Sir Tom was the guest of honour and presented to the teams on the night. Owen's baptism as an England international ensured that he would become England's first footballing teenage millionaire.

Hoddle was delighted for the kid. 'It was the best international debut by an 18-year-old I have seen. It certainly hasn't hindered his chances of going to the World Cup.' Hoddle admitted: 'We've been brought down to earth, Chile deserved their win. You're never happy to be beaten, but it's not a disaster. I was never going to lose in the long term. You can't lose when you're experimenting. It just shows that this World Cup is not going to be a stroll. We can obviously put out a more experienced side. But I felt that right from the first whistle, we just weren't on our toes. The two new lads up front [Owen and Dion Dublin] did very well on their debuts. Very well indeed.'

Owen said: 'It wasn't a good team performance, but I feel I did all right. I could have been a lot better, but I could also have been a lot worse. I'm quite pleased. I had one early chance which came to me quite quickly. I hit it with the outside of my foot, but maybe I should have given it some power instead of trying to place the ball. The South Americans showed that they are very good on the ball and can cause big problems, and that's what they did to us tonight. The fact that I was creating a new record didn't affect me during the game. In the build-up I was told early by Glenn Hoddle that I would be playing and it was a great feeling.'

Shearer approved of Owen's debut. 'There were no nerves beforehand. There wasn't anything. The way he went about things, you'd think he'd been around for a long, long time. He wasn't frightened at all. I think he proved to everyone that he won't be fazed by anything. Michael was one of the positive things to come out of the game. Let's put it this way – he hasn't done his World Cup chances any harm, has he? He has certainly given Glenn Hoddle something to think about.'

Owen won't be at all worried that he's lost his enviable record of scoring on his England debut at every level. Shearer, of course, did hit the net when he made his full debut against France in 1992. He has spotted in Owen the same strength of purpose, drive for success and, don't forget, sheer talent so patently recognisable in himself. 'I did things my own way and it hasn't done me any harm. Michael did his own thing at times and he did the right thing. He's got everything going for him. The boss keeps saying, if you're good enough you're old enough. His pace was frightening at times. He's caused problems with it all season in the Premiership and he caused problems against Chile. But there are other aspects to his game. He did very well getting round the back of defenders.'

World Cup winner Nobby Stiles backed Owen to follow in the footsteps of Geoff Hurst and Martin Peters by making a dramatic late surge into the final squad. He felt defeat may well work to England's advantage – in the same way as a 3-2 home defeat by Austria during the preparations for the 1966 tournament galvanised Sir Alf Ramsey's side. He said: 'The real bonus from the match was Michael Owen – he was great. He showed sharpness, pace and control but the biggest thing was that he didn't freeze. It's nerve-wracking enough to make your

England debut, never mind when you're still 18, but he showed great confidence. The main thing now is that he doesn't let it all go to his head and that he keeps his feet firmly on the ground. But I know Michael, he's a smashing lad, and I don't think that will be a problem for him. Martin Peters and Geoff Hurst came late into the England set-up for the 1966 World Cup and Michael can do the same now.'

Roy Evans reckoned Owen had boosted his World Cup hopes with his sparkling debut. Owen was keeping his thoughts to himself after training at Melwood but Evans said: 'I was very pleased by the way Michael played and I think he was too. He did himself a lot of credit. He won't have done his chances any harm – definitely not.'

Evans told Owen that if he is to play in France he needed to keep playing well for Liverpool. 'There is a fair while to go between now and France. He's got to keep playing consistently well for us, which he has done, and if he gets one or two chances with the England squad he has to do well there. The main thing from our point of view is that we make sure he does his stuff here because that's what gets him so far down the line. This is where he earns his living and he's got to make sure he keeps doing it week in and week out to keep his name in the international frame.' Evans was not surprised by how well Owen did on his debut. 'Nothing surprises me about Michael. He's a sensible lad and we have given him some assistance on that side, but overall he takes it well, he speaks sensibly, and keeps his feet on the ground. At every level you improve and learn and hopefully Michael will have learned from last night and will keep on improving his game.'

APPENDIX

The Road to France

Moldova (0) 0, England (2) 3
Kishinev, 1 September 1996

Moldova: Romanenco; Secu, Nani, Testimitanu, Gaidamasiuc, Epureanu, Curteanu, Belous (Sischin, 58), Clescenco, Mitereu (Rebeja, 61), Popovici.
England: Seaman; G. Neville, Pearce, Ince, Pallister, Southgate, Beckham, Hinchcliffe, Gascoigne (Batty, 80), Shearer, Barmby (Le Tissier, 80). *Scorers:* Barmby (24), Gascoigne (25), Shearer (61).

England (2) 2, Poland (1) 1
Wembley, 9 October 1996

England: Seaman; G. Neville, Pearce, Ince, Southgate (Pallister, 51), Beckham, Gascoigne, McManaman, Hinchcliffe, Ferdinand, Shearer. *Scorers:* Shearer (24, 38).
Poland: Wozniak; Wojtala, Zielinski, Joswiak, Hajto, Michalski, Waldoch, Baluszynski, Nowak, Warzycha (Saganowski, 75), Citko. *Scorer:* Citko (7).

Georgia (0) 0, England (2) 2
Tbilisi, 9 November 1996

Georgia: Ziodze; Lobjanidze, Tskhadadze, Shelia, Gogichaishvili, Nemsadze, Jamarauli, Kinkladze, Kobiashvili (Ghudushauri, 67), Arveladze (Gogrichiani, 52), Ketsbaia.
England: Seaman; Southgate, Adams, Campbell, Hinchcliffe, Beckham, Ince, Gascoigne, Batty, Sheringham, Ferdinand (Wright, 81). *Scorers:* Sheringham (15), Ferdinand (37).

England (0) 0, Italy (1) 1
Wembley, 12 February 1997

England: Walker; G. Neville, Campbell, Pearce, Beckham, Ince, Batty (Wright, 87), Le Saux, McManaman (Merson, 76), Le Tissier (Ferdinand, 60), Shearer.
Italy: Peruzzi; Ferrera, Costacurta, Cannavaro, Di Livio, Di Matteo, Albertini, D. Baggio, Maldini, Zola (Fuser, 90), Casiraghi (Ravanelli, 76). *Scorer:* Zola (18).

England (1) 2, Georgia (0) 0
Wembley, 30 April 1997

England: Seaman; G. Neville, Adams (Southgate, 87), Campbell, Beckham, Ince (Redknapp, 77), Batty, Le Saux, Lee, Sheringham, Shearer. *Scorers:* Sheringham (43), Shearer (90).
Georgia: Zoidze; Tskhadadze, Chikhradze, Sheqiladze, Shelia, Machaviariani (Gogrichiani, 32) (A. Arveladze, 76), Jamarauli, Nemsadze, Ketsbaia, Kinkladze (Gakhokidze, 61), S. Arveladze.

Poland (0) 0, England (1) 2
Katowice, 31 May 1997

Poland: Wozniak; Joswiak, Zielinski, Kaluzny, Ledwon, Bukalski (Swierczewski, 45) Waldock, Nowak (Kucharski, 57), Majak, Dembinski, Juskowiak (Adamczyk, 51).
England: Seaman; G. Neville, Campbell, Southgate, Beckham (P. Neville, 89), Le Saux, Ince, Gascoigne (Batty, 17), Lee, Sheringham, Shearer. *Scorers:* Shearer (6), Sheringham (90).

England (1) 4, Moldova (0) 0
Wembley, 10 September 1997

England: Seaman; G. Neville, Southgate, Campbell, Beckham (Ripley, 67) (Butt, 76), Scholes, Batty, Gascoigne, P. Neville, Ferdinand (Collymore, 82), Wright. *Scorers:* Scholes (28), Wright (46, 90), Gascoigne (80).
Moldova: Roumanenco; Stroenco, Fistican, Tistimitstanu, Spin, Shiskin (Popovich, 61), Curteanu, Culibaba (Suharev, 57), Rebetadj, Miterev, Rogaciov.

Italy (0) 0, England (0) 0
Rome, 11 October 1997

Italy: Peruzzi; Nesta, Maldini (Benarrivo, 31), Albertini, Cannavaro, Costacurta, Di Livio, Baggio, Vieri, Zola (Del Piero, 65), Inzaghi (Chiesa, 46).
England: Seaman, Campbell, Le Saux, Ince, Adams, Southgate, Beckham, Gascoigne (Butt, 88), Wright, Sheringham, Batty.

FINAL GROUP 2 TABLE

	P	W	D	L	F	A	Pts
England*	8	6	1	1	15	2	19
Italy	8	5	3	0	11	1	18
Poland	8	3	1	4	10	12	10
Georgia	8	3	1	4	7	9	10
Moldova	8	0	0	8	2	21	0

*England qualify for finals

Scorers for England:

Shearer	5 goals
Sheringham	3
Gascoigne	2
Wright	2
Barmby	1
Ferdinand	1
Scholes	1

Index